FICTIONS
OF DIGNITY

EMBODYING
HUMAN RIGHTS
IN WORLD LITERATURE

ELIZABETH S. ANKER

CORNELL UNIVERSITY PRESS
Ithaca and London

This book has been published with the aid of a grant from
the Hull Memorial Fund of Cornell University.

First published 2012 by Cornell University Press

Printed in the United States of America

Library of Congress Cataloging-in-Publication Data

Anker, Elizabeth S. (Elizabeth Susan), 1973–
    Fictions of dignity : embodying human rights in world
literature / Elizabeth S. Anker.
        p. cm.
    Includes bibliographical references and index.
    ISBN 978-0-8014-5136-2 (cloth : alk. paper)
1. Human rights in literature.   2. Social justice in
literature.   3. Postcolonialism in literature.   4. Literature,
Modern—20th century—History and criticism.   I. Title.

    PN56.H79A55 2013
    809'.933581—dc23
                                    2012015418

Cornell University Press strives to use environmentally
responsible suppliers and materials to the fullest extent
possible in the publishing of its books. Such materials
include vegetable-based, low-VOC inks and acid-free
papers that are recycled, totally chlorine-free, or partly
composed of nonwood fibers. For further information,
visit our website at www.cornellpress.cornell.edu.

Cloth printing   10 9 8 7 6 5 4 3 2 1

❧ CONTENTS

❧ Acknowledgments

Like many, the story of this book follows a circuitous intellectual odyssey that, however, both begins and ends with the influence of my parents, who bear foremost responsibility for cultivating the intellectual curiosities and commitments that it has tried to bring to fruition.

The opportunity to work with Martha Nussbaum at the law school at the University of Chicago was central to my scholarly development. In many ways, my independent studies on law and literature as a third-year law student remain foundational to the core philosophical questions that have motivated this book.

I can hardly conceive of a more intellectually stimulating or vibrant environment than the one I encountered as a graduate student in the English department at the University of Virginia. I remain especially grateful to my primary advisors—Rita Felski, Michael Levenson, and Peter Brooks—for providing multiple kinds of encouragement and inspiration. An especially warm thanks to Rita for her continued support and friendship over the years. Her astute and thorough feedback on my essay "*Elizabeth Costello,* Embodiment, and the Limits of Rights," published in *New Literary History* 42.1 (2011), helped to guide this book into its present form. I'd additionally like to acknowledge the many other faculty then at Virginia, as well as my former peers whose guidance and friendship have nourished me. I worry that I'll inadvertently exclude many, but my deep thanks to Steve Arata, Elizabeth Fowler, Eleanor Kaufman, Jahan Ramazani, Caroline Rody, Jennifer Wicke, and the late Greg Colomb, as well as to my friends Michael Lewis, Justin Neuman, Eric Song, and Joanne Vander Woude. Omaar Hena deserves a separate statement of appreciation for the camaraderie he has offered and credit for being the first to urge me to frame my ideas in terms of human rights.

My two years as an assistant professor at Wake Forest University were immeasurably rewarding. The English department at Wake Forest not only provided dear colleagues but also supervised the most profound transformations in this project. I am especially appreciative of, among others, Jeff Holdridge, Scott Klein, Jessica Richard, and Olga Valbuena. Herman Rappaport has been more influential than he may be aware, as it was Herman who first suggested that I look to Merleau-Ponty for an optic through which to theorize embodiment. And an especially heartfelt thank you to Dean Franco, who facilitated innumerable kinds of intellectual dialogue and exchange. Not only were those conversations crucial to this book's evolution but Dean, perhaps more than anyone, also modeled to me how to comport myself as a fully engaged teacher and scholar at a key stage in my own career.

The English department at Cornell has offered an ideal home in which to compose the majority of and ultimately complete this book. Indeed, the community at Cornell has often felt closer to family than mere colleagues, allowing me to integrate my professional and personal lives in profoundly satisfying ways. If space allowed, I would enumerate almost every faculty member in my department. But I feel especially indebted to the thoughtful support and intellectual engagement of Neil Saccamano, Dan Schwarz, Satya Mohanty, and Tim Murray. Shirley Samuels has been an invaluable mentor and friend, shepherding me through highs and lows alike. I am also extremely grateful for my friendships with Bernie Meyler, Simone Pinet, Samantha Zacher, and Lyrae Van Clief-Stefanon, which are some of the things I cherish most about Ithaca. And I would be remiss if I did not attempt to acknowledge at least some of the many others who have made Ithaca more than a stopping place. Thanks to Kevin Attell, Mary Pat Brady, Laura Brown, Cynthia Chase, Eric Cheyfitz, Margo Crawford, Jonathan Culler, Grant Farred, Ellis Hanson, Rayna Kalas, Jenny Mann, Natalie Melas, Masha Raskolnikov, Nick Salvato, Lily Sheehan, Matt Smith, and Dag Woubshet.

Beyond those within my different home departments, I'd also like to thank the many other people who have engaged this project at different stages. First, thanks to my co-fellows at the Cornell Society for the Humanities during the 2010–11 academic year: Jennifer Bajorek; Bruno Bosteels; Kay Dickenson; James McHugh; Adam T. Smith; and Joshua Clover, who is owed an especially warm statement of gratitude. While I fear that I omit the names of too many, thank you to Homi Bhabha, Cynthia Bowman, Pheng Cheah, Simon During, Karen Engle, Peter Fitzpatrick, Peter Gilgen, Elizabeth Swanson Goldberg, David Golumbia, Paul Kahn, Dominick LaCapra, Bruce Robbins, Camille Robcis, Lisi Schoenbach, Alexandra Schultheis, Chantal Thomas, and Patricia Yaeger for contributing to the project over the years in various ways. In addition, Anna Kornbluh and Renee Newman Knake are dearly valued friends with whom I can share not only scholarship and ideas but also other confidences. I've also been privileged over the years to be able to rely on highly adept research assistants; much appreciation to Rose Casey, Stephanie DeGooyer, Emily Moore Young, and Krupa Shandilya.

This book has also benefited enormously from the various conferences, workshops, and symposia at which I have presented material based on its content. Thank you to hosts at Cornell University, the Cornell Law School, the National Humanities Center, Penn State University, the University of Missouri, the University of Virginia, Wake Forest University, and Yale University, as well as to audiences at the annual meetings of the American Comparative Literature Association, the Modern Language Association; the Association for the Study of Law, Culture, and the Humanities; and the International Society for the Study of Narrative Literature. Conversations with other National Humanities Center Summer Institute Fellows in New Haven and Berlin, with participants in the Cornell Mellon Interdisciplinary Writing Group on "human rights and cosmopolitanism," and with members of the Cornell Mellon Humanities Seminar on "the human" were also extremely beneficial. In addition, a Faculty Fellowship at the Society for the Humanities provided irreplaceable support when I was in the final phase of finishing the manuscript.

By no means last or least, I can't imagine a more involved or helpful editor than I discovered in Peter J. Potter. Many, many thanks to Peter for multiple kinds of careful guidance, criticism, and advice as this project has traveled the route to publication. In addition, I'd like to thank Joseph Slaughter and two other anonymous readers for Cornell University Press for their indispensable feedback and many rigorous and perceptive comments. A version of chapter 5 appeared as "Human Rights, Social Justice, and J. M. Coetzee's *Disgrace*," in *Modern Fiction Studies* 54.2 (2008), and I'd like to thank that anonymous reader for his or her comments. This manuscript also benefited enormously from the help of Candace Akins, Romaine Perin, and rest of the production staff at Cornell University Press.

Finally, let me return to thank my family—my parents, Roy and Ellen; David and his wife, Milay; Christina; and my dog, Jefferson (yes, thanking a dog is fully within the spirit of this book's intellectual project)—for their sustenance and affirmation. Needless to say, this book would not have been conceived or undertaken or completed without them. Apart from being ever-ready proofreaders even at the last of last minutes, my parents created in me both an abiding sensitivity to matters of social justice and an unflinching belief in the redemptive capacities of literature. This book has, above all, attempted to fuse as well as to pay tribute to those twinned passions.

Introduction
Constructs by Which We Live

> Affronts to the innocence of our children or to the dignity of our persons are attacks not upon our essential being but upon constructs—constructs by which we live, but constructs nevertheless.... The infringements are real; what is infringed, however, is not our essence but a foundational fiction to which we more or less wholeheartedly subscribe, a fiction that may well be indispensable for a just society, namely, that human beings have a dignity that sets them apart from animals....
>
> The fiction of dignity helps to define humanity and the status of humanity helps to define human rights. There is thus a real sense in which an affront to our dignity strikes at our rights. Yet when, outraged at such affront, we stand on our rights and demand redress, we would do well to remember how insubstantial the dignity is on which those rights are based.
>
> —J. M. Coetzee

It is hard to imagine a viable approach to social justice today that does not rely on the language of human rights. The proliferation of the many norms and ideals associated with human rights no doubt represents a hallmark achievement in international law, at the same time as it exemplifies the salutary repercussions of globalization. The late twentieth and early twenty-first centuries have, in turn, come to be widely touted as the era of human rights—a sentiment that captures both the growing preponderance of rights talk and the immense promise that it invariably carries. This internationalization of human rights has led Michael Ignatieff to deem human rights "the lingua franca of global moral thought" and Elie Wiesel to call them a "world-wide secular religion."[1] The global culture of human rights has, among countless advances, worked to combat the oppression of women, to consolidate international opposition to torture, genocide, and severe rights infringements, to minimize conditions of economic disenfranchisement, and to encourage sociopolitical rapprochement in the aftermath of rights abuses.

1

Yet it is also fair to say that these accomplishments have come with corresponding costs. In particular, critics have decried the many exclusions and impediments that prevent human rights from attaining universal reach. From a legal perspective, these exclusions and impediments are sometimes dismissed as unavoidable, a necessary by-product of the very structure of the nation-state and the circumscribed frontiers of citizenship.[2] For others, however, the failures of human rights have been attributed to everything from the challenge of their practical enforcement on the ground to what critics at times identify as their predominantly Enlightenment-based philosophical heritage.[3] In fact, it has become a near truism to say that human rights have "only paradoxes to offer," and these paradoxes often appear even more fraught when approached from a postcolonial perspective.[4]

Such long-standing and intractable debates provide an important backdrop to this book's inquiries, both contextualizing and prompting many of my analyses. In the pages that follow, however, I focus specifically on two of the many paradoxes that especially bedevil what I describe as "liberal" articulations of human rights. The first of these paradoxes emerges from the contradictory status of the body within dominant definitions of human rights. As I will show, liberal human rights discourses and norms exhibit a profound ambivalence toward embodiment. Not only are they underwritten by the dual fictions of human dignity and bodily integrity, but they yield a highly truncated, decorporealized vision of the subject—one that paradoxically negates core dimensions of embodied experience. Over the course of the book, I will look to literature to gain access to as well as incarnate those facets of selfhood that liberal human rights discourses obscure.

The second paradox I examine in this book extends from a problem inherent in the very language of human rights. In the present geopolitical climate, the discourse of human rights has grown distant from the early hopes that forged it, becoming an obstructionist idiom that increasingly fulfills the opportunistic ends of selfish actors. This semantic colonization directly pollutes and compromises the social and political meanings of human rights, forfeiting their bearings on social justice. While this problem of language is far from unique to human rights, I explore the contemporary rhetoric of human rights to open up far-reaching questions about aesthetics and politics—enabling us to ask, above all, how certain modes of aesthetic expression can play a meaningful role in salvaging, as well as recalibrating, our existing social and political imaginaries.

Ultimately, I defend literature's crucial role in adjudicating both of these intertwined paradoxes of human rights, a claim I pursue through analysis of four widely read postcolonial novels: Salman Rushdie's *Midnight's Children* (1981), Nawal El Saadawi's *Woman at Point Zero* (1973), J. M. Coetzee's

Disgrace (1999), and Arundhati Roy's *The God of Small Things* (1997). Each of these narratives is concerned with both real-world and philosophical dilemmas facing human rights, and each variously censures liberalism's practiced vocabularies for eclipsing key facets of selfhood—foremost of which inhere within embodiment and the body's faculties of perception. By investigating how these writers aesthetically reclaim and reanimate registers of corporeal engagement, I develop this book's framework for deciphering the diverse traffic between narrative literature and human rights. Such an "embodied politics of reading"—a heuristic that is self-consciously indebted to Maurice Merleau-Ponty's phenomenology—will thus guide my overarching effort to conduct an imaginative repositioning of human rights, along with the strangely bloodless human currently tethered to their liberal norms. Moreover, precisely such focused debates about human rights will compel a rethinking of the prevailing theoretical orientations within postcolonial studies, gesturing past that field's available interpretive horizons to consider what kinds of questions they, too, have excluded and foreclosed.

The Compass of Liberalism and the Dignified Social Body

While the body might on the surface appear fundamental to human rights discourses, liberal articulations of human rights in fact evince a deep ambivalence toward embodiment. Here, Coetzee's reflections on human rights are a useful point of entry. In the epigraph above, Coetzee first takes note of how the construct of "dignity" consolidates most definitions of human rights.[5] Indeed, the concept of dignity has been central to formulations of human rights since the end of World War II and is widely invoked as essential to both the broad ethos and intellectual coherence of human rights norms, representing something of a constant reconciling the manifold ideals subsumed within their logic. For instance, dignity assumes key rhetorical force within the 1948 Universal Declaration of Human Rights (UDHR), the Preamble of which opens with the statement "Whereas recognition of the inherent dignity and of the equal and inalienable rights of all members of the human family is the foundation of freedom, justice and peace in the world."[6] While a symbolic document, the UDHR lends precedence to dignity, almost casting it as interchangeable with, if not prior to, the notion of rights. To related ends, some theorists cite this emphasis on dignity as what fully renders human rights universal, in effect positing that it finds counterparts in virtually all cultures.[7]

Yet Coetzee also alerts us to the exclusions that this "foundational fiction" of human dignity smuggles in, particularly how an alleged lack of dignity has warranted the mistreatment of and denial of rights protections to animals. This premium on dignity has, in addition, sanctioned multiform hierarchies, inequalities, and discriminations within the human community—an irony I explore in greater depth in later chapters. As liberalism scripts the human, the dignified individual in possession of rights is imagined to inhabit an always already fully integrated and inviolable body: a body that is whole, autonomous, and self-enclosed. This premise turns corporeal integrity into something of a baseline condition that precedes the ascription of dignity and rights to an individual. At the same time, it posits a dangerously puri-fied subject, one purged of the body's assumedly anarchic appetencies: its needs and desires, its vulnerability and decay. And when the body cannot be thus ignored, the liberal tradition generally treats it as an entity that must be repressed, quarantined, or otherwise mastered by reason. Chapter 1 considers at length how this animus toward embodiment plays out within the philo-sophical assumptions that subtend human rights, including received delinea-tions of the democratic public sphere, the secularism thesis, and established models for theorizing the literature-human rights nexus. This reluctance about corporeal being has further contributed to a symbolic economy in which the liberal body politic is imagined as comparatively impermeable, nuclear, and cleansed of alien or subversive elements. Yet, paradoxically, the dual conceits of human dignity and bodily integrity simultaneously require for their legibility the threat of bodies being violated, broken, and defiled, entailing that human rights discourses and norms are ironically vindicated by inverse images of corporeal unmaking and abuse. In short, liberalism's deep-seated wariness toward the body has produced a conception of individual selfhood and collective life alike that is as disappointingly idle and uncon-vincing as it is abstract and idealized.

One way to diagnose this anxiety is to say that liberal human rights norms display a classically Cartesian bias against embodiment, a latent dualism that privileges mind and intellect over embodied, affective ways of knowing. By extension, we might further conclude that human rights descend from a spe-cific trajectory of post-Enlightenment thought often tied to Kantian moral law.[8] That genealogy, however, risks endowing human rights norms with an overly Eurocentric inheritance, overlooking circumstances wherein local, or indigenized, human rights vernaculars operate without reference to such a limited philosophical blueprint. In other words, accounts of human rights that dwell exclusively on their Enlightenment-based lineage inadvertently buy into the very model of globalization that postcolonial studies has labored to dismantle, discounting how human rights discourses and standards are actively reworked when adapted within regional legal and political cultures. That said, such a framing does gauge important reservations about human

rights, and this book in many ways revisits such a characterization and critique. Core liabilities that beset the culture of human rights do emerge when
we refract their claims to truth through the prism of a predominantly (if
not singularly) European heredity and its lingering traces within political
thought. Asking about the imperial residues that taint present-day articulations of human rights, then, is not to erect another center-periphery binary
or to presume a unilateral circuit of globalization's influence and exchange
or to relegate non-Western cultures to a secondary or provincial position
relative to what gets deceptively termed "Enlightenment." On the contrary,
using such a broad compass to examine human rights is necessary to understand the complicated and contested energies of the liberal tradition.

As may be clear from the preceding discussion, I rely on the term *liberal*
rather than *Enlightenment based,* given that *liberal* is less overtly periodizing
while further implying the distinct economic order associated with late or
global capitalism. In deploying the label *liberalism,* I therefore intend it as a
placeholder through which to correlate broad ideological currents that, for
better and for worse, regulate basic expectations about political existence.
Human rights discourses are accompanied by a spectrum of ideas about
"freedom," "conscience," "reason," "deliberative speech," "self-possession,"
"autonomy," "self-determination," and the legal "person," which together
conspire with beliefs about the democratic public sphere, secularity, the rule
of law, systems of finance capital, and historical progress. I should note that
this construal of human rights responds in large part to the complaints staged
within my literary examples about the itinerary of both individual subject formation and collective life prescribed by such "liberal articulations of human
rights." My textual archive, in other words, requires this particular plotting of
the ideological-cultural-institutional terrain that at once harbors, promulgates,
and is itself signposted by the proliferating meanings of human rights. Nevertheless, this matrix of values that fortifies dominant understandings of human
rights is neither static nor homogenous; rather, those values are as shifting and
protean as the political institutions and practices that shape and anchor them.
That being said, in this book I aim to register why we might be suspicious
of what I call the "liberal cartographies of selfhood" that are simultaneously
naturalized by and themselves lend explanatory authority to human rights.[9]

The Proliferating Languages of Human Rights

One of the key aims of this book is to consider how literature can help
negotiate the progressively diffuse and turbulent discourses of human rights.
On the one hand, the languages of human rights provide crucial ideological
support for law, governance, the neoliberal economic order, and the many

engines of globalization, as those forces together accelerate and jeopardize human rights norms and their many migrations. Appeals to human rights define and enable subject positions, along with their legal correlates; they verify some worldviews while discrediting others; they install regimes of knowledge and truth; and they naturalize certain, particularly Eurocentric, genealogies of the nation-state. As many theorists thus maintain, both their languages and practice have become inexorably "contaminated," or complicit with the neoimperial technologies that outfit them.[10] Whether in light of the rise of muscular humanitarianism, the commercialization of the human rights franchise, or ever more dexterous manipulations of rights rhetoric, the discourses of human rights do deserve legitimate, vigilant skepticism.

Yet on the other hand, the vocabulary of human rights remains a potent force with enormous opportunity for transformation and resistance. As Seyla Benhabib has noted, the sociopolitical meanings of human rights are not unitary, constant, or coherent. Rather, their languages mutate as they travel over history, geography, and context to become incorporated into varied legal cultures, thus mirroring the vast heterogeneity of our ever more interconnected world.[11] Within such a model of their circulation, human rights discourses and norms are disbursed through reciprocal, interactive processes that reflect both the unevenness of globalization and its collaborative, dialogic relays of enunciation and exchange.

This dynamic malleability that imbues human rights with fertile potentiality, however, also renders those discourses exceptionally prone to misuse. Human rights have come to mean virtually anything to anyone, marking injuries large and small and justifying causes noble and inglorious, leading critics to deride human rights as little more than nebulously floating signifiers that increasingly fall victim to "rights inflation."[12] Indeed, the vocabulary of human rights seems to possess an innate penchant for hyperbole, or an inborn impulse to self-escalate in the face of political pressure. Such slipperiness can lead to absolutism and defensiveness that, ironically, silences competing, historically marginalized claims.[13] It is of urgent necessity to therefore question why human rights are invoked with disturbing regularity to endorse the socially antagonistic entitlements and pursuits of the monadic individual. In this book, I ask: What happens when appeals to human rights gratify whatever self-serving designs are convenient to a given speaker? What transpires when their emancipatory hopes are overshadowed by deceptive, exploitative uses? Has the language of human rights devolved into a primarily reactionary, alarmist idiom, invoked strategically, even cynically, stripped of sensitivity to the complexities of situational and historical context? Can a legal and political lexicon become so thoroughly polluted as to forfeit its promise? Have we in fact reached "the end of human rights," as Costas Douzinas forecasts, or might critique somehow provide a tonic for restoring their discourses in the midst of an ailing future?

This dilemma further demands that we analyze the discourses of human rights as a culture—or, as Charles Taylor might put it, as a collection of "human rights imaginaries."[14] A cultural study of this sort must begin by acknowledging that the languages of human rights have grown unmoored from their formal legal statements as well as their philosophical origins to take on scattered and abundant lives of their own, preventing their arrest either by theoretical analysis or within the machinery of law.[15] The assiduous, energetic, mobile discourses of human rights will invariably exceed and defy whatever positive content they might be vested with, in their very pandemonium flouting the aspirations of law and philosophy alike. This is also to say that human rights talk works *both* to shore up the exclusions that have historically compromised their universalizing ambitions *and* to challenge those limits. A central feature of human rights discourse is to be itself "doubled," or to be captive to centripetal forces while yet ceaselessly regenerative and dispersing. These dual gravitations require us to become what Patricia J. Williams once referred to as "multilingual in the semantics of evaluating rights."[16] While Williams sought to recuperate American rights talk after coming under assault within the Critical Legal Studies movement, the predicament of *human* rights discourse within a *global* context is in comparatively urgent need of such a metric.[17]

Toward an Embodied Politics of Reading

It is far from original to claim that the language of human rights is intimately, if not organically, tied to literature, in particular narration, although theorists have proposed strikingly divergent rubrics for theorizing that relationship. Trauma studies has provided one such analytic. When deciphered through the lens of trauma studies, human rights violations, in their defiance of speech and other forms of symbolization, are explained as exacting a psychic injury, whereas acts of narration initiate recovery from that state to put the fractured self back together again.[18] From a different vantage, the link between literature and human rights has long been traced to the very evolution of the novel as a genre, a connection that usually figures humanitarianism as grounded in sympathetic feeling or sentiment.[19] More recently, theorists have delineated the narrative–human rights nexus via the notion of "ethics," although that term can denote varied theoretical commitments and schools of interpretation. For some, ethics betokens the practical, material, and other constraints that can either facilitate or impede the empathetic recognition of human rights abuses, thus explaining why human rights advocacy can selectively fail—and in ways that echo fairly predictable categories of socio-political disenfranchisement.[20] Yet for others, the term signals the agenda of deconstructive ethics. In this vein, it heralds the demand of radical Other-ness for forgiveness, hospitality, and sociopolitical inclusion, and many such accounts of social justice likewise embrace literature as singularly poised to induce such awareness. By no means last, the term *ethics* has also been employed to indicate the particular "ethics of subject formation" mandated by human rights norms. Certain literary genres are here understood to per-form a critical role in naturalizing those norms—or, as Joseph Slaughter puts it, in working to "complete" the abstract doctrines of international law and render human rights norms equally operative within the realm of culture.[21]

In *Fictions of Dignity* I self-consciously depart from these established for-mulas for theorizing the assorted commerce between literature and human rights. By doing so, I aim to compensate for certain of their methodological shortfalls and omissions—especially the tendency to reproduce the anxiety about embodiment that haunts liberal human rights discourses and norms. As I will show, many of these received frameworks for delineating the affinities between literature and human rights subscribe to the same pauperized, unidi-mensional, and strangely lifeless vision of the human that not only underwrites liberal articulations of human rights but also authorizes the democratic public sphere's many exclusions. By privileging reasoned intellection, such interpre-tive models implicitly endorse what we might call a "semiotic ideology" that further ratifies a misleading portrait of the autonomous, self-possessing subject. It is both in opposition to and as a remedy for that neglect that I craft this book's particular metric for evaluating the fertile sites of interchange between literature and our available sociocultural imaginings of human rights. In this way, I intend to recuperate precisely those layered attributes of affective, embodied experience that have erroneously been submerged in liberal theo-ries of selfhood and in many definitions of the literature–human rights nexus.

To elucidate this "embodied politics of reading" I draw on the phenom-enology of Maurice Merleau-Ponty. While Merleau-Ponty's corpus emerged prior to the so-called linguistic or cultural turn, he was highly concerned with the many liaisons between language and power, or the propensity of dis-course for duplicity, corruption, and decay—as especially occurs within the theater of politics.[22] Yet Merleau-Ponty also affirmed the generative elasticity of language, and he studied how distinctly embodied habits of perception can foment semantic replenishment and renewal. Merleau-Ponty's phenomenol-ogy of embodied perception thus clarifies why the two paradoxes of human rights that absorb this book must be knotted together; for Merleau-Ponty, linguistic refurbishment necessarily harnesses the body's many faculties of engagement. It is in this respect that his thought provides an optic for scrutinizing the status of human rights as a proliferating discourse, while also showing why theoretical attention to embodiment might redress liberalism's ambivalence about corporeal being.

As such, Merleau-Ponty's philosophy furthers another important goal of this book—to reimagine our predominantly liberal understandings of human rights. According to Merleau-Ponty, art and aesthetics are unrivaled in their capacity to actuate and, indeed, simulate embodied perception, both rupturing stale, habituated discourse and reinvigorating language with newly resonant meaning. It is precisely by contemplating aesthetics, then, that we can begin to theorize the lived realities of embodiment and thereby repair the body's quarantine and erasure within much liberal political theory. Merleau-Ponty's nondualist ontology refuses to prioritize mind over body, instead elaborating a nuanced account of the body's valuable contributions to both selfhood and collective existence. If liberal human rights norms have ironically evacuated the human of the body's energies, then an embodied politics of reading might reincarnate that subject with a vital porosity and (in Merleau-Ponty's lexicon) "fleshiness." Moreover, insofar as liberal portraits of the human marshal a distinct symbolic economy of embodiment, phenomenology might instead imaginatively delink that condition from its conventional stigma. In sum, I will argue that Merleau-Ponty offers much to a theory of social justice that takes embodiment as its starting point, mitigating that condition's historical depreciation and denial while along the way furnishing a rich, timely, and innovative schematic for charting the many solidarities between literature and human rights.

I realize, of course, that advancing a phenomenology of embodied aesthetic experience is not without risks. For one, such a bearing not only deciphers human rights with primary reference to a European intellectual tradition (assuming that liberalism should be construed thus) but also recruits yet another Western European thinker to unfold its reservations about human rights. Similarly, the particular novels that I examine might elicit objections from some critics, drawn as they are from within the Western literary tradition and securely canonized by postcolonial studies. Suffice it to say that although I am levying an internal critique of human rights (even while doing so with reference to the global South), I believe that my central argument has the potential to yield significant profit for theorizing indigenous epistemologies and supplementing liberal constructions of human rights accordingly, even while such aims are not within my main project.

My focus on embodiment may appear to entail related pitfalls. Indeed, Coetzee's semi-autobiographical *Summertime* (2010) directly comments on the casualties of reading postcoloniality through the lens of embodiment. While on the one hand Coetzee's characters surmise that "disembodied" existence is antithetical to being "human," on the other they question whether a "philosophy of the body" is not only "politically unhelpful" but ultimately filters Africa through a "haze" of "old-fashioned Romantic primitivism."[23] Here, Coetzee cautions that embodiment in and of itself may be too facile an analytic, the hazards of which become especially pronounced if postcoloniality is conflated with corporeal being. Such a projection of a nondualist, assumedly more holistic perspective onto indigenous cultures comes perilously close to committing a series of classically imperialist moves—whether relegating postcolonial peoples to the body's chaotic, irrational drives or mystifying their ostensibly more spiritually attuned rhythms of existence. As such, neither phenomenology nor the prism of embodiment can be adopted wholesale or uncritically, lest we further return to a naive yearning for the transcendental, dehistoricized subject. Only through a carefully historicized phenomenology might we resuscitate certain of Merleau-Ponty's insights without nullifying the evolutions in theory since his work.

Both the posture and the stakes of this approach will become evident within the literary case studies that make up the second part of the book. As we will see, Salman Rushdie, J. M. Coetzee, Nawal El Saadawi, and Arundhati Roy all insist that human rights and their discourses be painstakingly contextualized with reference to the specificities of history, geography, and other accidents of circumstance. For instance, Coetzee's *Disgrace* directs the reader to the uniquely charged valences assumed by the idiom of human rights in the aftermath of the South African postapartheid reconciliation process. Differently, El Saadawi's *Woman at Point Zero* was written and first published at a moment before the languages of women's rights became internationally hegemonic, and its narrative equally experiments with alternate vocabularies of women's autonomy and liberation. Yet while each text pointedly interrogates human rights discourses and norms, they all simultaneously exhibit caution toward the various alternatives they propose. For instance, both *Disgrace* and Roy's *The God of Small Things* celebrate art as a type of antidote to liberal rights logic; however, at the same time they portray the self-enclosed space of the artwork as by no means exempt from its own routine cruelties and foreclosures. Likewise, although each text converges in differing ways on an ontology of embodiment, those appeals, too, are self-reflexively fraught. For example, Rushdie's *Midnight's Children* invokes the metaphorics of the liberal social body only to reinforce embodiment's customarily negative associations. More generally, each novel casts the body's arguably ethical sensitivities as by no means a prophylactic against its destructive energies. This is all to say that, while I pursue both phenomenology and an embodied politics of reading as a theoretical program for transcending many of the contradictions that currently trouble liberal statements of human rights, those dual hermeneutics must themselves be approached with healthy and sustained suspicion.

Beyond the Horizons of the Postcolonial

In recent years, the field of postcolonial studies has witnessed earnest self-appraisal, inspiring some to sound its death knell and others to actively rethink its central paradigms.[24] The very label *postcolonial* has, of course, long met with contention, whether for being an overly homogenizing lens, for misleadingly casting imperial oppression as a bygone phenomenon, or for erroneously downplaying the forms of disenfranchisement experienced by regions of the global South that were not formally colonies. At the same time, literary criticism is slowly replacing the term with the arguably depoliticizing *contemporary world literature* or *post-1945 Anglophone writing*. Perhaps most severe of the impasses confronting the field, however, are those attributable to the imprints of theory. Here, *Fictions of Dignity* joins increasingly widespread objections to the diminishing returns of postcolonial studies' reigning methodological allegiances. Indeed, the field is currently mired in something of a theoretical stalemate, for many its poststructuralist commitments in particular having run their course.

For some time, disagreements over globalization have been a lightning rod for wider schisms within the field, acting as proxies for more thoroughgoing disputes over theory. Not surprisingly, parallel fault lines can be detected within many recent conversations about human rights; if anything, the magnitude of the methodological vacuum facing postcolonial studies becomes especially apparent within such analyses. I'd like to suggest that these debates about human rights signal even more troubling theoretical blockages with reverberations far beyond the somewhat confined purview of postcolonial studies. In other words, assessments of human rights can magnify deeper limits afflicting theory's favored approaches to social justice, catalyzing the need for an escape from those frameworks along with the inquiries they have predisposed. As such, my textual archive is composed of novels that postcolonial criticism has typically glossed to verify its received interpretive horizons, and my close readings aim to enact that limits of those methodologies, demonstrating one avenue for traveling beyond them.

On the one hand, certain strands of postcolonial theory have been animated by highly celebratory accounts of globalization that privilege the motifs of hybridity, migrancy, crossing, and diaspora over realities of cultural confinement and stasis.[25] Partner to this emphasis on mobility is a romance with cosmopolitanism and related antipathy to local structures of belonging, which get dismissed as inherently inhibiting and regressive.[26] Many theorists have plotted the internationalization of human rights in such enthusiastic terms, applauding them as the progeny of a truly global melting pot of cultures and worldviews.[27] Indeed, Derridean conceptions of a "democracy to come" also betray such a logic, wherein the failures of human rights are annulled and redeemed within a messianic future. Yet these triumphant narratives of human rights often elide the unevenness and other shortfalls of globalization, downplaying the deep histories of imperial oppression that continue to fuel its imbalances. Moreover, deconstructive theorizations of human rights have tended to oppose justice and ethics to the institutions and judgments of the law. Within this formation, justice and ethics emerge only under circumstances that are, in Derrida's terms, "exceptional and extraordinary, in the face of the impossible."[28] This insistence on exemplarity, however, ends up writing off actual, proximate, and commonplace scenes of decision making wherein "impossible," unannounced alterity is not at issue. This dichotomy between justice and ethics versus the rule-bound domain of law derives in large part from the deconstructive patterning of justice and ethics on semiotics and textuality—or, in other words, on *différance*.[29] That said, while both justice and linguistic meaning may indeed be riddled with parallel deferrals and foreclosures, it's necessary to ask whether that focus on textuality reinscribes the very sort of dualism that an embodied politics of reading reacts against.[30] Such a question becomes especially pressing in light of the extent to which a deconstructive hermeneutic has regulated postcolonial literary analysis, leading critics to prefer texts that can be seen to dramatize the plea of radical Otherness for inclusion or recognition.[31] Indeed, this concentration on alterity has at times produced a fetishization of that condition and a sublime fascination with victimization that inadvertently covers over rather than encourages critical scrutiny of the material disparities that generate such failures of justice as well as law in the first place.

On the other hand, different veins of postcolonial theory have fostered highly pessimistic accounts of globalization, reducing it to the machinery of either global capital or neoliberal governmentality. Within such frameworks, human rights become little more than conscripts of those forces, with little residual potential for empowerment or resistance. Not only are human rights thus seen to instate what Inderpal Grewal calls "powerful technologies of knowledge production" that converge within "an ethical regime that put into play a whole range of instrumentalizations of governance" but they also legitimize structures of international policing, which in practice are overwhelmingly targeted at the postcolonial world.[32] Such a vision of the geopolitical landscape often weds human rights advocacy to development policy in a partnership that merely transacts new cycles of indentured servitude to Northern credit—cycles that incite fears of dependence that become internally exorcised within the postcolonial state rather than directed outward at globalization's encroaching tides.[33] It goes without saying that even the best-intentioned human rights advocacy is invariably compromised by such circuits; however, a unitary focus on the complicities that sully their norms and practice becomes itself blinkered, given that it discounts the enormous good also achieved in their name. Foucauldian and Marxist analytics, in turn, often obscure both vital dimensions of selfhood and ontologies of belonging that cannot be thus explained. Moreover, this bias has unsurprisingly created noteworthy deficits within literary scholarship, contributing to a preoccupation with how structure and form operate as cognates to ideology and corresponding neglect of alternate facets and registers of aesthetic engagement.[34]

In short, the dominant horizons of postcolonial theory have begun to appear increasingly circumscribed and constraining, producing an explanatory poverty that becomes especially glaring with reference to debates about human rights. As means of passage beyond this crossroads, some critics have evoked the time-tested languages of humanism and the Enlightenment— languages that postcolonial studies has historically sought to subvert. Such a paean to humanism can be found in Edward Said's late lectures, published as *Humanism and Democratic Criticism* (2004). Within these talks, Said rebukes Derrida and Foucault for what he calls a "cynicism" manifesting itself in reading practices that culminate in little more than "fruitless standing aside."[35] In place of such apathy, Said champions "the non-humanist humanist," or the scholar who has absorbed the critical posture of theory yet retains an active devotion to improving humanity's lot. This homage to humanism is far from isolated or unusual. For instance, Simon Gikandi bemoans the poststructuralist bent of globalization studies in comparative terms, namely, by suggesting the purchase of "the very language of Enlightenment that postcolonial theory was supposed to deconstruct."[36] Yet, we must ask, have the humanist orientations of the field been the most enduring and influential, as K. A. Appiah argues?[37] Or do these appeals mark a retraction and reversal of currents that Appiah at least categorizes as postmodern? But if Said's humanism correctly forecasts the need to relinquish certain insights of poststructuralism, are there other theoretical standpoints from which to embark on such a project?

As should be clear by now, this book is motivated by a fatigue with poststructuralism that echoes many of the concerns voiced by Said and Gikandi. In drawing on phenomenology, however, I propose a very different route to surmount those obstacles. My critiques of the liberal logic of human rights are equally meant to query the reliance on secularism, liberal models of democracy, and "participatory citizenship" that inflects Said's late thinking.[38] Likewise, whereas Said defines humanism as "text-and-language-bound" and advocates a "return to philology,"[39] I instead seek a departure from primarily language-based patterns of analysis. It is from this vantage, then, that phenomenology enables a rethinking of the legacy of what is often termed the *linguistic turn*—or the preoccupation with language, textuality, and culture that infuses not only the posthumanist humanism of Said but also much of Continental philosophy.[40] This theoretical exit additionally puts strict constructivist theses of subjectivity under pressure, even if by way of what Judith Butler frames as the onus "to imagine the human beyond its conventional limits."[41]

In sum, *Fictions of Dignity* participates within a far wider theoretical transition toward an emphasis on "things," affect, embodiment, and what has recently been called the "new materialisms."[42] Along with the proponents of this shift working within postcolonial studies (such as Achille Mbembe and Sara Ahmed),[43] an "anthropological" or "experiential" turn is happening within fields as diverse as anthropology (Talal Asad, Charles Hirschkind, Saba Mahmood), political theory (William Connolly, Jane Bennett, Diana Coole), cognitive science (George Lakoff and Mark Johnson), and literary criticism broadly speaking (Bill Brown, Lauren Berlant).[44] My own intellectual odyssey has thus emerged as merely one permutation of a broader (re)conversion to the merits of a historicized phenomenology.

In *Fictions of Dignity,* however, I set out to account for the specifically aesthetic and literary character of particular modes of affect and experience that are overridingly embodied in their texture. As such, a theory of how and why we read lies at the heart of this book's venture. While such an embodied politics of reading accordingly charts one path of egress from the current juncture within postcolonial studies, it also proposes a distinct frame for connecting aesthetics with politics. Such a hermeneutic, then, self-consciously foregrounds the exorbitant stakes of the sheer act of reading, defending literature's intimate bearing on social justice and human rights. Indeed, it is not accidental that Coetzee's reflections on "dignity" and "human rights" in the epigraph to this introduction are taken from a collection that meditates on censorship and the fate of literary production in such a climate. At one point in the same essay, Coetzee despairs of how the censor cannot fathom that "magical powers" might inhere within mere "representations," thus missing something vital about literary creation. And with such reflections in mind, it is precisely within the spirit of this book to contemplate a spectrum of different kinds of "magical" transformation and inspiration that ensue from literature and its many "powers."

✣ CHAPTER ONE

Bodily Integrity and Its Exclusions

> For why is the postwar social body so bloodless, so emptied of desire, so abstract?
>
> —Carolyn J. Dean, *The Frail Social Body*

Theorists have long invoked the notion of paradox to explain human rights, and many of the most entrenched of these paradoxes ensue from the exclusionary anatomy of human rights discourses and norms. While inherent in the basic philosophical architecture of human rights, exclusions arise on each of the intersecting levels of law, political practice, and discourse. It goes without saying that, as a legal-philosophical construct, human rights carry significant normative force, their standards and rhetoric implicitly defining the parameters of the human. And although human rights enshrine certain qualities as constitutive of humanity, they simultaneously ostracize others—along with those lives seen to exemplify them—from the purview of full personhood. Human rights discourses and norms, as such, have denied sociopolitical membership to countless populations over history, largely along the predictable lines of race, gender, sexual orientation, class, disability, and species. No doubt many of these stigmatized categories disproportionately mark formerly colonized and now postcolonial lives, a reality only exacerbated as the commerce between human rights enforcement and programs of development covers over the global South's coerced consent to its own exploitation. Whether because of the racialized undercurrents of human rights talk, the dynamics of humanitarian policing, or patterns of economic disenfranchisement, the postcolonial world bears the brunt of many contemporary human rights paradoxes.

Theorists have long attributed these structures of exclusion to the basic institution of citizenship. As Hannah Arendt famously noted in the aftermath of World War II, the denial of rights to a given population almost automatically incurs their "expulsion from humanity altogether."[1] Indeed, refugees and stateless persons still today are widely deprived of viable channels through which to effectuate their human rights. Yet the contemporary geopolitical landscape has entailed that the inequitable disbursement of human rights protections increasingly mirrors the imbalances of globalization—which is to say that the growing economic stratification of the world renders the human rights of peoples of certain nations virtually nonexistent. The global South here again inordinately endures those disparities, which both create conditions of social and political atrophy and incite hostilities that frequently turn militant and predatory.[2]

Many different factors contributing to the foreclosures of human rights are, as such, epidemic and unavoidable. Yet in this book I am especially interested in how those failures of human rights can be explained in terms of the profound ambivalence toward embodiment that pervades liberal human rights discourses and norms. This ambivalence broadly informs liberal articulations of human rights, along with their underlying assumptions about human flourishing. In general, liberal topographies of the human acquire legibility by obscuring both the enabling and constraining aspects of corporeal existence, as embodiment is imagined to be eclipsed entirely, vanquished through reason, or normalized through calculations of symmetry and likeness. This anxiety about the body finds its central expression in the dual myths of human dignity and bodily integrity. While those twinned ideals act as important baselines that lend force to many invaluable human rights protections, as enabling fictions they nevertheless marshal a highly abstract, disembodied, and anemic vision of human selfhood. In effect, the liberal subject entitled to rights is understood to possess an always already inviolable body, one fully integrated and thereby dignified through reasoned self-determination. This idealized human body, moreover, finds an important corollary in the construct of the unified, nuclear, impermeable body politic. However, both the myth of the integrity of the natural human body and the symbolic economy of the national body politic are paradoxically consolidated by the specter of abused, broken, and profaned bodies, which in popular human rights discourses are often complexly raced and gendered.

This chapter concludes by examining one popular instantiation of human rights discourse—a genre I call the "human rights bestseller"—in order to track and probe such tensions. In doing so, I explore how liberalism's aversion toward the body historically and presently masks and condones concrete discrimination against raced, gendered, and otherwise disadvantaged populations. Those discriminations find official sanction within politics and law—which is to say that liberalism's reluctance about embodiment lurks silently though prominently behind many of the missed opportunities of human rights. Let me now proceed to reckon with the various manifestations and repercussions of this animus toward embodiment, paying particular attention to the ways it comes to be reproduced within theoretical models for plotting the traffic between narrative literature and human rights.

Liberalism and the Ambivalences of Embodiment

The body has long inspired anxiety within the liberal philosophical tradition. In post-Enlightenment metaphysical thought, embodiment is generally conflated with those aspects of the self that must be mastered or abjured. This reluctance about bodily existence is deep seated, persistent, and controlling. While Elizabeth Grosz traces such an aversion to Plato, theorists have ascribed a related antipathy toward embodiment to Immanuel Kant.[3] By elevating pure practical reason over sensory perception, Kant is seen to erect a binary between thoughts and feelings that casts embodiment as an automatic affront to moral judgment. Yet perhaps most influential has been Rene Descartes's privileging of the intellect, which both naturalizes the priority of reason and presumes the body's inferiority. In part resulting from the intellectual legacy of Cartesian dualism, corporeality has come to be negatively associated with everything unreliable, transitory, and base—namely, the emotions (rather than the intellect and will), the private (versus the public), nature (rather than civilization), exteriority (as opposed to interiority), the animal (versus the human), and so forth. Overall, such bias has installed within moral and political thought a continuum of oppositions that remain foundational to liberal frameworks for evaluating social justice.

Most immediately, such assumptions about mind-body dualism permeate the law.[4] The rule of law itself gains legitimacy through the conceit that it offers a crucial route to abstract equality, although I will show how that conceit itself erases the disparities inherent to embodiment. For instance, Miguel Tamen argues that the construct of legal personhood historically evolved to render "the juridical ... a sphere of bodies symbolical" rather than actual, which for Tamen in particular grounds and lends coherence to rights-bearing subjectivity.[5] Indeed, Tamen's claim that "the notion of a self-evident physical body is thus inadequate to describe the notion of a rights-holder" captures much about the exclusions that jeopardize human rights.[6] A related Cartesianism inflects the law's evidentiary requirements and other protocols governing legal procedure. In this respect, Moira Gatens argues that the legal standard mens rea reinforces such a wariness about embodiment; for Gatens, the expectation that perpetrators' mental knowledge must be determined prior to establishing their guilt implicitly favors the intellect over alternate faculties of perception.[7] To such ends, while much trauma scholarship, as I will discuss, betrays its own investment in the integrated liberal subject, studies of the affective texture of trauma have sought to expose the limits of juridical forms of testimony, complaining that they censor experiences that are not reason based.[8] Whereas traumatic memory is understood to defy closure, coherence, and rational containment, the law mandates teleological, intelligible, and objective truth, which leads it to silence and distort certain subject positions and experiential realities.[9] The affective fabric of trauma thus exposes the falsity of the law's facade of abstract neutrality, revealing how that pretense not only provides an alibi for society's many prejudices but also promulgates a constricted, unidimensional portrait of the subject. In sum, we can grasp how and why the legal emphasis on empirically verifiable truth can depreciate corporeal aspects of selfhood. Such evidentiary thresholds of authority are, no doubt, meritorious given that they safeguard "innocence until proven guilty"; nevertheless, as staples of legal procedure they also illustrate the pervasiveness of a particular species of mind-body dualism.

The broad imprint of dualism on liberal theories of the subject also manifests itself within the tendency within liberal thought to configure human progress in terms of the successful subordination of the body to the reasoning will. Such logic conspicuously emerges in the dual premiums on freedom and autonomy. Here, Nikolas Rose has explored how, in the nineteenth-century aftermath of the French and American declarations of rights, liberal values became "inextricably linked to a norm of civility," rendering "modern individuals...not merely 'free to choose' but *obliged to be free,* to understand and enact their lives in terms of choice."[10] This onus to self-determine effectively licenses the intellect's trump over the body's capricious, ungovernable demands, which are seen to compete with and risk impinging on reason's free exercise. On one level, rational choice thus becomes the avenue through which the individual surmounts their bodily captivity, transcending a state of sheer animality. Accordingly, dualistic thought provides a central equation that consigns embodiment to mere animal being, a connection that equally furnishes a key philosophical warrant for the denial of rights protections to animals. Human progress, as such, is charted as gradual independence from material want, a trajectory that again relegates embodiment to a condition of relative bondage, poverty, and privation; whereas on another level, the liberatory self-overcoming actuated by reasoned intellection is seen to integrate the self into a cohesive, internally reconciled whole, a process that likewise subdues and conciliates the body's ostensibly anarchic, uncontrollable energies. While bodily integrity thereby becomes a predicate to human dignity, in order to be attributed with dignity the liberal subject must actively possess a highly particular kind of body—one that can abide by that mandate to be inviolable, autonomous, and self-enclosed.[11] Within such a framework, then, clearly not all bodies are worthy of protection; rather, only bodies that have been successfully subjugated through the conquest of reason deserve rights-bearing subjectivity and its entitlements. And while this concentration on the body within liberal accounts of subject formation might seem to testify to its importance, the overarching ideals of dignity and corporeal integrity in fact marshal a highly specific vision of embodiment that ultimately confirms the intellect's superiority.

Much as freedom becomes compulsory, theorists allege that liberal formulations of the "individual" sow human rights with exceptions. For instance, Joan Scott argues that the legal-philosophical construct of the individual serves antithetical purposes. On the one hand, the individual represents an abstraction that encodes the goal of equality, rendering it formally antecedent to the universal applicability of human rights. However, this myth that people exist in symmetrical positions before the law depends on the profoundly *un*equally disbursed ability to self-abstract from and thus surmount one's idiosyncratic circumstances. As such, the juridical fiction of the individual paradoxically elides as well as sanctions the countless variations that ubiquitously compose human experience—variations that translate into material injuries and injustices.[12] Yet on the other hand, for Scott this notion of the individual at once betokens the onus to individuate, or to autonomously self-fashion. That mandate, in contrast, venerates personal distinction and uniqueness—ideals that place the subject at potential odds with the collective, and by extension with the expectation of formal equality. As Scott explains, "Individuality require[s] the very difference that the idea of the prototypical individual was meant to deny," capturing from one vantage why human rights norms might appear to supply incommensurable dictates.[13] Indeed, my literary analyses that follow will wrestle with precisely such tensions.

Such an account of the liberal individual has also provided a model for explaining statehood and the texture of nationalism, contributing to a larger metaphorics of the liberal social body. Transposing the natural body onto the institution of the state in order to posit the nation's health, fortitude, and insularity has a long history that can be traced to the Middle Ages, wherein the king's sovereignty was associated with the reasoning mind that unifies the unruly social body.[14] Yet in the era of democracy and rights, this metaphor of the state as body politic has assumed more explicit parallels with distinctly liberal subjectivity. While for the individual reason's dominion is seen to integrate the chaotic self, democratic process is believed to unite a national population into a balanced, self-authorizing whole. The self-determination of the liberal individual is thus mirrored in the constitution of the body politic, wherein the subject's autonomous development becomes an analogue for the mechanisms that incorporate the nation-state, especially through democratic legal and political institutions. In both cases, political process is seen to discipline and quell the insurrectionary impulses of both the natural and liberal social bodies. As we will see, this figural correlation recurs throughout postcolonial literature, for instance, as chapter 3 examines with respect to *Midnight's Children*. In Salman Rushdie's novel, his protagonist Saleem Sinai's feint of autobiographical self-inscription into a coherent, reasoned subject allegorically mirrors the consolidation of the disparate Indian populace into a democratic whole. Whereas Saleem must steal his own physical body (and narrative) against cracks through the imposition of rational purpose, those efforts parallel how civic reason is understood to harmonize internal discord and overcome political-ideological fissures that otherwise risk rupturing the unified body politic of the state.

As may be clear, however, such imagery of the state as body politic depends on an idealized vision of a particular kind of body—one that is undivided, impermeable, and successfully assimilated. The corollary of the body politic metaphor, then, is that defiled, decaying, or broken bodies become the insignia of atrophy, failure, and the breakdown of orderly, egalitarian legal and political process. Indeed, Saleem's body is imagined to explode at the end of *Midnight's Children* precisely to reify Indira Gandhi's suspension and infringement of the rights codified in the Indian Constitution during the 1975–77 State of Emergency. To cite one other literary example, Bapsi Sidhwa's *Cracking India* (originally published as *Ice Candy Man* in England in 1988) similarly employs the figure of the violated, desecrated human body to analogically vivify the wounds exacted to the subcontinent during partition. Within Sidhwa's narrative, the ravages of partition are inflicted on the body of a young female nanny through her rape and forced prostitution. While that device registers the actual fate of vast numbers of women, it nonetheless genders the nation and land in counterproductive and paternalistic ways. As we can see, the body politic metaphor is by no means value free; rather, it frequently promotes a particular conception of embodiment that not only polices certain corporeal energies but ultimately reinforces the notion of the liberal subject as abstract, integrated, and otherwise idealized. Insofar as national resilience and prosperity are aligned with corporeal purity and wholeness, discipline and suppression become warranted as means to equally save and subdue the threat of the nation/body that is porous, violable, and fragmenting. As such, this symbolism that imagines statehood in terms of embodiment does significantly more than perpetuate the aversion toward the body that is broadly endemic to liberal political thought. To the contrary, the specter of the ailing body penetrated by subversive or alien contaminants can offer symbolic license for programs of national expurgation and containment, xenophobic and otherwise. Within this metaphorics of the liberal social body, the prosperous, functioning state is accordingly figured as cleansed of discord, dissensus, and other hazards to its welfare, contributing to a political imaginary that can find ready recruitment to apologize for predatory nationalisms.

This deep-seated and persistent notion that the body's appetites are fated to endanger the individual's moral faculties (as well as, metaphorically, the livelihood of the state) has consequently provided a core philosophical justification for oppressing scores of populations over history. In one sense, the dual myths of the integrated individual body and the unified body politic conspire to authorize the exclusion and domination of those peoples deemed insubordinate, foreign, or otherwise infectious. The perception that a given group is hostage to embodiment, and hence less rational or developed, has legalized a wide range of discriminatory practices, whether resulting in full-fledged persecution or more subtle expulsions from political life. In the relatively distant past, the science of eugenics capitalized on such a view that moral, intellectual, and other depravities directly correlate with abnormal or deficient physical traits. While eugenics today is commonly taken to indicate scientific racism, Lennard Davis has shown that the eugenics movement in fact stigmatized a range of bodily and other disabilities for their alleged menace to the civic order, with the effect of condoning the policing and curtailment of those conditions.[15] Notably, mere indigence was pathologized as one such condition of confinement to the body and its physical wants that was believed to erode a person's moral sensibilities. Although the eugenics movement is admittedly an extreme case, the supposed symmetry between bodily deficiency and moral decrepitude continues to haunt much liberal political thought. Relatedly, structures of sociopolitical oppression have long been supported by the characterization of a given population as enslaved to the body, whether due to profligacy, disease, or lack. In this vein, feminist theorists have widely observed how a central ruse of patriarchy is to consign women to the body and its supposedly wayward demands, thereby authorizing their subservience. A similar though somewhat more complicated pretext has sustained racial domination; indeed, a neoimperial rhetoric of savagery and barbarism continues to relegate peoples of the South to a condition of bodily excess, irrational superstition, and resultant moral blight. By no means last, the belief that animal life is pure carnal being without self-consciousness, reason, or a soul has allowed animals' instrumental use and dietary consumption. Indeed, it has been well documented how people overcome their aversion to cruelty through psychological mechanisms of dehumanization, or the imaginative reduction of human lives to mere embodiment or animality. This is all to say that the embarrassing history of eugenics is in fact quite familiar, disclosing a more thoroughgoing linkage between contempt for the body and Western modernity's ubiquitous but routine exclusions.

At the same time as bodies prone to either deficiency or excess have inspired legal and political regimes of disenfranchisement, an individual's immanent, subjective relationship to their embodiment can, practically speaking, elicit concrete injustices. It is a truism that harms to the body, along with whatever hereditary incapacities afflict the individual, can frustrate the exercise of that person's human rights, in addition to other steps in what is often scripted as liberal individualist subject formation. From this vantage, it is not surprising that theorists of disability have produced some of the most trenchant critiques of rights logic.[16] As is argued, speech, reason, belief, and other more intellectual components of personhood are not independent from but rather both harnessed to and enabled by bodily experience. In turn, a person's potential to authenticate the liberal dictates of freedom and autonomy is constitutively predetermined by the relative limitations of—as well as opportunities afforded by—that person's embodiment. Yet liberal theories of selfhood disavow this basic fact when they presume rational choice to occur in a type of vacuum, or with the mind sequestered from the body's needs. That expectation sanctions material outcomes; in other words, the liberal feint that self-abstraction through reason will procure both equality before law and individual autonomy metes out penalties and rewards, all the while imposing them on lived, actual bodies. While this bias against embodiment thereby distributes concrete exclusions, it also yields more amorphous, less clearly quantifiable ramifications. Indeed, the liberal privileging of mind and anxiety about embodiment can work to minimize forms of suffering that are a ubiquitous reality of all lived experience. All people eventually confront the flesh's wasting and frailty as it falls victim to illness, dying, and death, in addition to whatever transitory and mundane injuries beset the body. While human rights abuses offer poignant reminders of such radical unfreedom, it often seems that the body's sheer vulnerability is what induces its at times aggressive regulation and censorship. Perhaps because the flesh is fully guaranteed to disrupt the utopian ambitions of human rights is the body's plight so religiously disavowed.

A similarly decorporealized account of the subject also supports standard formulations of the democratic public sphere. Within liberal political thought, public decision making is typically understood to incur validity when a consortium of rational actors enlist reason to surmount their subjective prejudices and loyalties, paramount of which are seen to extend from the arbitrary whims of affect and embodiment. Such an ideal of disinterested, egalitarian dialogue underpins Jürgen Habermas's discourse ethics, wherein reasoned speech is lauded as what both coheres a public and secures consensus. Within such an analytic, deliberative exchange both endows collective decision making with validity and allows individual interlocutors to successfully jettison their idiosyncratic, biased, changeable fidelities and differences. However, such theories of political engagement discount not only the private and domestic but also those components of personhood that cannot be sanitized by the alleged neutrality of reason—the central of which, again, emanate from embodiment. By lauding objective, dispassionate speech as the only reliable and equitable mode of political participation, liberal measures for evaluating democratic legitimacy construe the body as inherently subrational, antiegalitarian, and untrustworthy—in sum, as an automatic affront to democratic process. This contrivance that self-abstraction through reason is what certifies political practice thus erases vital, productive dimensions of corporeal experience and engagement, denying the ethical merit of those affective and embodied faculties. As a consequence, Habermasian constructions of the public sphere ironically envision it as convened by remarkably abstract, disembodied, unreal actors—with the net result that political life gets deciphered in terms that are at once overly optimistic and anemic.

Another point of entry into these foreclosures is to say that liberal theories of politics obscure the ways that real lives are beholden to the radical disparities stemming from embodiment. Such neglect further emerges within established definitions of secularism. The view that the democratic public sphere is inherently secular relies on what William Connolly calls a "twofold strategy of containment" that "quarantines" corporeal modalities of involvement for their alleged threat to reasoned tolerance.[17] Yet, as Michael Warner argues, such theories of public decision making valorize "utopian self-abstraction" only to submerge distinctly embodied habits of cognition. While the ideal of neutrality provides the illusion that secular publics are constituted by impartial actors, for Warner "a residue of unrecuperated particularity" haunts that facade.[18] Although "personal abstraction" is treated as a predicate to formal equality, it in fact disguises "a major source of domination, for the ability to abstract oneself in public discussion has always been an unequally available resource."[19] In this way, too, we can observe how conventional formulations of the public sphere both exacerbate and conceal the many sociopolitical exclusions that derive from the discrepant realities of embodiment, inadvertently authorizing rather than reversing those sites of injury. Such an implicit depreciation of embodiment also evaluates public life through a constricted, falsifying prism; secularism's dualistic prioritization of discourse and reason discredits many factors and motives that, in actuality, sway people's choices and orient them toward socially valuable action. As a result, the secularism thesis not only overlooks how real people negotiate complex, multisituational, and affectively charged decisions but also fails to calibrate how embodied modes of participation can cultivate ethically attuned social and political engagement. As both Warner and Connolly imply, a theory of justice that instead accounted for the body's faculties of cognition might supply a more nuanced, faithful rendition of political existence that could help mitigate the many harms justified by liberalism's truncated portrait of the human.

In addition, these omissions work to negate what Connolly calls the layered densities of human suffering. Critics complain that liberal theories of politics, beyond being weak and unconvincing, occasion a blanket condemnation of pain.[20] While this aversion no doubt valuably interdicts many harmful sources of oppression, the question remains whether liberal thought is not overly quick to label every manifestation of suffering corrosive, debilitating, and pernicious—and therefore something to be flattened, controlled, and ideally triumphed over by reason. By cleansing human subjectivity of the body's signature, liberal articulations of the human write off the possibility that certain types of pain might engender both individual meaning and a culture's common ethos and fabric of belonging. For many, precisely such a denial renders human rights norms antonymic to social formations that organize their collective identities around rituals of suffering—bodily and otherwise—and their communicative function.[21] Once again, while many pain-centered practices deserve legitimate opprobrium, that does not obviate debates about whether liberal definitions of politics reductively cast those practices as backward and regressive. In many ways, the body's encounters with pleasure and pain cannot be tidily compartmentalized to fulfill the goal of progressively diminishing suffering while enhancing pleasure. Indeed, as Nawal El Saadawi's *Woman at Point Zero* will later compel us to consider, those energies are more accurately imbricated in a murky intermixture of tension and synthesis. In turn, we can only ask whether this nullification of the body's overdetermined, protean, and life-affirming capacities forfeits liberalism's ability to explain and thereby redress broader patterns of suffering—which is to say that an antipathy toward the messy facets of embodiment also directly squanders some of the transformative potential of human rights.

When unable simply to elide corporeal being, liberal articulations of the human typically posit bodily integrity and uniform likeness as the status quo.[22] As Warner suggests, the body imagined by liberalism is white, male, straight, fully healthy, and free of disabilities. Rights-bearing selfhood, as such, is effectively contingent on the individual's possession of a body with optimal conditions for both survival and sociopolitical recognition, yet that expectation that bodies exist in conditions of parity is far from value free. It is a matter of fact that some bodies are unusually afflicted and burdened, whereas others are exceptionally capacitated and benefit from those advantages enormously. Beyond the extreme cases that history presents us, Catherine MacKinnon's analysis of what she terms the "equality principle" offers further insight into the latent biases smuggled in through the law's conceit of neutral impartiality and resultant effacement of bodily disparity. While MacKinnon examines the touchstone of equality within the United States' Fourteenth Amendment and antidiscrimination law, she traces that principle back to Aristotle, treating it as foundational to the rule of law itself. For MacKinnon, it is axiomatic within legal reasoning that people with similar predicaments deserve similar treatment. As such, claimants must prove their likeness to or equality with prior claimants and circumstances before an entitlement to a social good becomes legally cognizable. Conversely, if commonality cannot be established because of some previously incurred handicap or debility, then a given appeal falls on its face, since the equality principle permits unlike results when structural dissimilarities can be cited to condone those verdicts. While on the surface a "leveling" means to "formal equality," the law's pretext of equality in fact transforms pre-existing and empirically verifiable differences into routine, legally permitted patterns of unfairness. If already established incongruities can be deemed material and innate—in other words, inscribed on the body—not only will the equality standard fail to abate them but it will sanction disproportionate outcomes. The juridical precept of formal equality thus both camouflages injuries that derive from socially naturalized bodily variations and prevents their correction, absolving law from the onus to reverse rather than merely conserve its precedents. As MacKinnon shows in *Women's Lives, Men's Laws,* the casualties of this prescription become especially pronounced when they have an impact on women's bodies. As she bemoans of sex-based antidiscrimination law, "Sex equality becomes something of an oxymoron, a contradiction in terms" (50). In sum, MacKinnon's analysis, too, suggests how greater attention to embodiment might remedy not only the law's broad shortcomings but also the missed opportunities of human rights.

Embodiment and the Exclusions of Human Rights

This ambivalence toward embodiment that plagues liberal theories of self-hood and political practice equally animates dominant human rights discourses and norms. Needless to say, respect for human rights is overwhelmingly motivated by the desire to prevent as well as correct injuries to the body. In a sense, the human body is the entity that their standards most vigorously protect, leading some to conclude that the primary goal of human rights as a construct is the reduction of wasteful pain.[23] However, and paradoxically, the generalized anxiety about embodiment that, I have argued, is endemic to liberal articulations of the human comes into especially high relief within human rights discourses and norms. Although human rights on the surface safeguard the body's inviolability, that end is consecrated not because of the body's independent merit but rather because suffering is seen to usurp reason and interrupt liberal individualist subject formation. Human rights standards, in other words, extol corporeal self-possession not as an end in and of itself but as indispensable to autonomous self-fashioning—much as bodily integrity is cast a necessary though far from sufficient predicate to human dignity. As such, many liberal formulations of human rights ultimately verify the priority of the intellect, privileging its authority over the body that is, for all other appearances, their focus. Dominant human rights discourses echo the broad presumption within liberal political thought that reason and the will must discipline and thereby integrate the porous, anarchic body, mastering its appetites and demands, before a subject can be conferred with autonomy and independence. This is also to say that human rights discourses can be seen to defend the sanctity of the body so resolutely precisely to pacify corporeal being, or to insulate the intellect and preserve its sovereignty over the body. In sum, within the dualistic framework that guides liberal definitions of human rights and their corresponding cartographies of selfhood, the body is generally either idealized through the invention of its integrity, reduced to calculations of identity and likeness, or treated as a mere nuisance.

Even theoretical approaches that we might expect to depart from such liberal mappings of the subject in large part confirm this presumptive aversion toward the body. For instance, an animus toward embodiment inflects much postcolonial theory, with its poststructuralist commitments, emphasis on textuality and language, and constructivist accounts of the subject. My literary case studies that follow accordingly aim to mine the limits of postcolonial studies' prevailing theoretical frameworks as they have influenced the field's treatments of human rights. But for now, Hannah Arendt's thought is highly revealing in the extent to which it displays its own reluctance about corporeal being, even while Arendt decries troubling exceptions to the universality of human rights. Indeed, it is not accidental that Arendt's reflections—which represent one of the most widely cited statements offering insight into the exclusionary nature of human rights—betray the very aversion toward embodiment that, I have suggested, has long impaired liberalism. Many of Arendt's philosophical descendents have not surprisingly inherited this apprehension, raising the question of whether biopolitical thought is not ironically infected to its core by precisely such a dualistic antipathy toward the body. Arendt famously diagnoses the "plight" of stateless populations as being "not that they are not equal before the law, but that no law exists for them; not that they are oppressed but that nobody wants even to oppress them."[24] Most immediately, Arendt attributes the aporias of human rights to the institutions of citizenship and the nation-state and, in doing so, confronts the reality that, to be practically enforceable, human rights require the backing of a juridical authority and system of law. Above all, Arendt thereby registers why stateless populations deprived of a nation's support will lack a viable channel through which to effectuate their human rights, thus identifying structurally unavoidable circumstances that are guaranteed to interrupt rights' universal purview.

However, Arendt's lament is overlaid with disregard for the very populations whose predicament she ostensibly mourns. For Arendt, the circumscribed margins of citizenship are ultimately disturbing not so much because they compromise the universal reach of human rights but rather because they refuse stateless populations the opportunity for political existence, at least as Arendt defines it. Arendt therefore is not troubled solely by the multiplication of human rights violations in the twentieth century, as is often assumed, but rather by how the expulsion of vast demographics from political life and rights-bearing subjectivity consigns those peoples to "the abstract nakedness of being human and nothing but human."[25] As Arendt states the problem: "The greatest danger arising from the existence of people forced to live outside the common world is that they are thrown back, in the midst of civilization, on their natural givenness, on their mere differentiation" (302). While there is little question that Arendt despairs of the many rights abuses produced by this outcome, the real tragedy of statelessness for her lies not in those injustices but in how the "abstract nakedness" of such displaced peoples "threaten[s] our political life" (302). These conclusions clearly demonstrate the degree to which Arendt is a classically liberal thinker, as is further evident in her segregation of the "dark background of mere givenness," or the realm of nature and the private, from the achievements of politics, public life, and culture (301). Yet the important point here is that Arendt founds her definition of politics on its opposition to spheres of being that, in her view, disallow the individual the capacity for action and agentive change. And, for this reason, she claims that civilization has "a distinct tendency to destroy" those competing domains that she sequesters from political life, in part because they jeopardize social relations of "equality" (301). However, while she bemoans such an inevitability, her regret is tempered by the belief that those chronic foreclosures are directly constitutive and enabling of the political itself.

It is within this dualistic orientation of her thought that an implicit hostility toward the sheer condition of embodiment emerges. As Arendt explains, the "merely given" is "relegated to private life in civilized society," being "a permanent threat to the public sphere" (301). Arendt, however, naturalizes this antagonism by locating it at the fore of her conception of politics, both apologizing for it and resigning herself to the impossibility of its reversal. Accordingly, we can observe a conspicuous contempt for what Arendt dismisses as thought and speech doomed to passive irrelevance because of its ban from public life. Such a misfortune of "existence without leaving any trace" is one that Arendt further associates with being "thrown back into a peculiar state of nature" and its "wild elements" (300, 302). Yet, as I have shown, precisely such disdain for those chaotic, anarchic, ungovernable realms of experience—realms conventionally associated with nature and the body—has authored global modernity's most pervasive exclusions. Arendt's subtle scorn for the mere "nakedness" of being human consequently represents more than a blind spot within her philosophy. Quite the contrary, this dualistic animus toward embodiment suffuses her theoretical apparatus as a whole; indeed, there is a way in which she excuses those very habits of thought that have licensed the most profound crimes against humanity. It is deeply ironic, then, that one of the most widely cited accounts of the failures of human rights perpetuates the core logic that has justified some of the most egregious human rights abuses of the twentieth century.[26]

Since this book's foremost métier is literature, let me now turn to investigate how a parallel ambivalence toward embodiment informs many approaches to theorizing the nexus between narrative literature and human rights. Much scholarship that explores that affinity indirectly verifies the central work that the twinned constructs of human dignity and bodily integrity serve in acquiring legibility for human rights norms—yet without interrogating either those constructs or the exclusions that they shore up. Most immediately, the very rise of the novel has been widely connected to the historical emergence of humanitarian and reform movements, a link theorized as particularly apparent in eighteenth-century sentimental literature. As scholars explain, sentimental literature sought to give imaginative expression to the view common within eighteenth-century moral philosophy that moral life extends from sympathetic feeling, a view encapsulated in David Hume's famous celebration of sympathy for being "the chief source of moral distinction."[27] As an evaluative frame, however, sympathy is usually understood in terms of its capacity to elicit the perception of commonality or symmetry; it is thus achieved when the object of sympathy can exhibit sufficient proximity and likeness to the reader-observer. As such, it has long been criticized as a potentially conservative response just as likely to ratify the subject position of the person bestowing charity as to challenge their relative privilege— meaning that it will obscure and condone conditions of hardship or suffering with which the observer cannot identify. To such ends, some caution about the unpredictable, even capricious nature of sympathy as an affective impetus. For instance, Susan Sontag warns how photographic portraits of atrocity can escape a photographer's intentions to fulfill "the whims and loyalties of the diverse communities" that appropriate them, revealing sympathy to be a potentially "impertinent—if not an inappropriate—response."[28] As a consequence, debates about sympathy have often surrounded whether it requires mediation by reason before it can be validated as a legitimate or trustworthy factor within political decision making.[29]

The problems with hermeneutics that foreground sympathy in order to establish literature's bearing on human rights become apparent in *Inventing Human Rights* (2007), by the French historian Lynn Hunt. Hunt also connects the historical emergence of the novel to the culture of human rights and explicitly defines empathy by way of liberal notions of "interiority," "autonomy," and "the self-enclosed individual." Her formulation of sympathy thus ends up prioritizing reasoned intellection in terms that, I have argued, are counterpart to a denigration of embodiment. At once, Hunt maintains that the operations of sympathy furnish a direct avenue to social "equality," thereby also buying into the liberal premium on equivalence that MacKinnon criticizes for eliding corporeal and other predetermined disparities (41, 32). All in all, Hunt's construal of sympathy displays a predictably liberal anxiety about the body's exposure to exteriority (versus the interiority of the intellect) and vulnerability (meaning those elements that render the subject less than fully self-contained), both of which she assumes to automatically detract from rationally self-determining personhood. Hunt's theory of sympathetic reading accordingly endorses the dualistic biases that we have seen to underwrite the liberal democratic public sphere's historical exclusions, and needless to say such an explanatory model reduces narrative literature to an overridingly conservative force that foremost entrenches and

confirms liberal norms. Even though for Hunt human rights incur persua-
siveness through the workings of a species of emotion, her idea of affect is
strikingly unidimensional, stripped of other protean, variegated energies that
are equally affect based in their origins.

Explanations of the relationship between traumatic memory and narrative have often relied on an analytic with a striking resemblance to Hunt's.
Critics indebted to trauma studies commonly celebrate narrative for playing
a crucial role in enabling both individuals and communities to recover from
human rights violations. In doing so, such scholarship understands human
rights abuses to fracture a victim's subjectivity; whereas by submitting trauma
to narrative organization, the sufferer exerts epistemological control over
those otherwise destabilizing events. Trauma is accordingly defined as inherently resistant to symbolization, in large part because of the unfathomable
character of extreme pain, violence, and cruelty. As a result, the narrative
rendition of traumatic experience will tend to defy realistic, mimetic, teleological, truth-oriented genres of storytelling—although those are precisely
the modes of narration required by the law's evidentiary-based procedures.
By highlighting such dilemmas, trauma theory has both lent key insight
into the horrific afterlives of human rights abuses and launched important
critiques of legal reasoning. That said, much trauma theory can be seen to
usher in problematically negative associations of embodiment with debasement. In attempt to capture the extreme nature of trauma, trauma studies figures corporeal suffering as something that automatically jeopardizes rational
subjectivity, narrative, speech, and by extension, full personhood. Moreover,
such scholarship implicitly deciphers trauma in terms of how it ruptures the
preformed, rationally constituted subject, entailing that, as a heuristic, trauma
can reinforce the artificial and idealized image of the integrated, impermeable body possessed by the liberal subject entitled to rights.[30]

The liberal signposts that guide such a topology of trauma are visible, for
instance, in Elaine Scarry's influential work on torture. In studying the impact
of physical pain, Scarry argues that it "actively destroys" language to become
"unsharable," enclosing the sufferer in a condition of "doubt" that is effectively "world-destroying."[31] "The body in pain" thus lays siege to both the
rational self-overcoming dictated by Kantian moral law and the certitude of
empirical truth, and the magnitude of corporeal pain is for Scarry measured
in direct proportion to the degree it inhibits reason, or consigns a victim to "a
state anterior to language."[32] This conflation of physical pain with privation
and radical destitution has led theorists to critique Scarry for overlooking the
social meanings that suffering can accrue.[33] More crucially, Scarry's logic also
certifies the exclusionary and dualistic version of the presumptively rational

human that is central to many liberal theories of selfhood and rights. Within her analysis, the foremost reason corporeal suffering is cause for distress is that it limits the victim's experiential universe to the body alone—imprisoning perception within the senses, cutting off the outside world, short-circuiting the foremost indicia of the human (namely, speech and reason), and ultimately shattering subjectivity. Thereby reinstating liberalism's customary animus toward embodiment, Scarry leaves open the question of whether corporeal pain that failed to impinge on rational subjectivity would be quite so alarming. In keeping with much trauma scholarship, Scarry's description of pain begins with an individual who, prior to his or her victimization, has successfully vindicated the liberal mandate to self-master via reason and the intellect; in other words, Scarry's diagnostic depends on a unified will that has disciplined the body, which trauma subsequently overwhelms to fragment that formerly integrated subject. Although she is largely interested in the representational motifs that designate physical pain, she nonetheless presupposes a liberal trajectory of subject formation that relegates the body to a condition of relative captivity. Her seminal account of torture and pain thus ironically marshals a strikingly purified conception of the human that, in the end, upholds the stigmatizing reduction of embodiment to dehumanization that taints many liberal articulations of human rights.

A comparative prioritization of speech animates other academic work on human rights less explicitly derived from trauma studies as a paradigm.[34] Much as freedom of expression is commonly touted as paramount of the values that rights enshrine, speech is widely consecrated as the nucleus of the human. Speech rights are, in turn, viewed as threshold rights that offer prophylaxis against a spate of ancillary rights infringements, whereas censorship is condemned as almost inevitably parasitic on other liberties. While not to diminish the essential importance of those freedoms, this precedence demonstrates how even the most essential safeguards of human rights can be read to harbor innate exclusions. If the capacity for speech acts as a barometer for a being's relative humanity, then it regulates the more comprehensive equipment of citizenship, providing a key warrant for deeming some lives and not others worthy of inclusion. Rational speech consequently risks becoming a benchmark that can deny merit to certain contributions to politic dialogue, much as Arendt excluded certain modes of existence from the domain of properly political life. While we might philosophically explain this as a natural symptom of the dualistic architecture of rights, the doubled status of speech nonetheless illustrates how even the most sacrosanct of rights protections do not come without costs.

Other recent scholarship concerned less with human rights violations than with the ideals they prescribe similarly mobilizes such a liberal cartography of the subject, from which the body is notably absent. In *Human Rights, Inc.* (2007), Joseph Slaughter charts how the global circulation of the Bildungsroman—a genre that for Slaughter emerged in tandem with human rights—has generated an "ethics of subject formation" that "completes" the abstract doctrines of international law, making human rights norms equally operative within the realm of culture. Within Slaughter's analysis, human rights are legal technologies of subjectification that preside over what he calls "human personality development," a process of "emancipation" that parallels other kinds of political modernization (9). Like other theorists, Slaughter contends with the exclusions that human rights have historically ushered in, which Slaughter, on one level, attributes to the Bildungsroman's tendency to "make[] legible the inequities of an egalitarian imaginary," or to secure sociopolitical consent to the fact that rights are in practice selectively disbursed (39). But on another level, for Slaughter these foreclosures inhere within and are authorized by the juridical construct of the "person," thus honing in on the same legal-philosophical term of art that Miguel Tamen and other theorists scrutinize.[35]

Further building on Slaughter's analysis, we can observe how the faculties of embodiment come to be occluded within the "abstract, universal human" that formalizes the legal category of the person (58–59, 61):

> It is not the name of individual, irreducible difference but of sameness, the collection of common modalities of the human being's extension into the civil and social order. "Personality" is a technical term that means the quality of being equal before the law. . . . It is the basis of the law's symmetrical disposition to each human being. Thus, "person" is the legal vehicle of human dignity. (17–18)

In effect, Slaughter latches onto a key basis for the exclusionary anatomy of human rights, which, as for MacKinnon, resides within the law's facade of formal equality. This ruse of equality, as Slaughter indirectly suggests, elides circumstances of "irreducible difference"—which is to say that the "person" recognized by human rights law and endowed with dignity is one cleansed of the body's multiform energies. The law's neutral impartiality thereby both covers over sociopolitical disparities and apologizes for their resultant injustices. As such, Slaughter's rubric inadvertently indexes why the legal "person" tethered to human rights is, as I have argued, truncated and anemic, or divested of those corporeal dimensions of selfhood that cannot be regimented through reasoned self-abstraction. While Slaughter does not aim to weigh in on the substance of what the twin alibis of equality and legal personhood censure and erase, we can nonetheless ask whether this neglect is partner to his conclusion that the Bildungsroman is fated to be no more than "reformist." As within other literary analyses invested in a Foucauldian hermeneutic, Slaughter ultimately favors ideology critique over attention to alternate formal and stylistic properties of literature, leading him to put forth a rather one-sided description of aesthetic experience. That said, Slaughter's analysis productively illumines how and why the fantasy of egalitarianism that buttresses liberal human rights discourses requires a corresponding myth of the decorporealized, disinterested, and remarkably fleshless subject for its intellectual coherence.

As we have seen, many theoretical investigations of human rights diminish, if not gainsay entirely, the role of embodiment in both liberal individualist subject formation and human experience in general. They consequently perpetuate the broad tendency within liberal political thought to sidestep and thereby discount the many paradoxes and enigmas of embodiment. As I have maintained, these liberal mappings of the subject tend to submerge the phenomenology of corporeal suffering through a collection of interrelated fictions: of symmetry and likeness, of self-transcendence, and of bodily self-possession and wholeness. Whether the body finds itself sequestered, idealized, or outright ignored, liberalism has largely failed to register the manifold and dense energies that compose corporeal experience, denying how they together actuate human selfhood, facilitate judgment and decision making, enliven collective life, and purvey multifaceted kinds of meaning.

On the one hand, I have accordingly sought to register how the illusion of the disembodied, abstract actor, typically localized within either the legal notion of the "person" or the philosophical construct of the individual, sustains many liberal human rights discourses and norms. Yet on the other hand, the descriptive authority of human rights as a discourse is simultaneously fortified by narratives and other imaginings of bodily violation, excess, decay, and unmaking. As the remainder of this chapter will discuss, the dual prescriptions of human dignity and bodily integrity are ironically made legible and socially persuasive by the specter of bodies that are not successfully unified or self-enclosed through reasoned self-determination but instead are invaded, broken, sullied, and disintegrating—in other words, bodies reduced to being no more than bodies, and to abject, often bloodied ones, at that. Human rights discourses and norms are, as such, consolidated by a symbolic economy of bodies both pure and contaminated, and that ambivalent social imaginary of embodiment mobilizes a complicated erotics that is yoked at once to the categories of race and gender. As a result, the importance of corporeal self-possession as a standard paradoxically comes to be certified and rendered plausible by incessant reminders of the potentially tragic repercussions of its own effacement.

We have already glimpsed how this layered metaphorics of embodiment regulates the expectations about embodiment that are brought to bear on not only individual bodies but also the civil body politic. In *The Frail Social Body* (2000), Carolyn J. Dean offers one account of how those dual imaginative registers overlay and mutually reinforce one another. Dean examines how anxieties about national decline in interwar France were offset by the fiction of the "ideally dignified, impermeable body" (1). For Dean, this invariably "masculine" as well as "self-enclosed" "liberal social body" is vital to the ideological coherence of both the precept of equality before law and human rights as a broad legal–philosophical ethos (3, 13). Here again, we confront why and how the ruse of formal equality erases sites of difference, as those variations paradigmatically derive from embodiment. However, counterpart to this mythology of the idealized body is what Dean calls the "metaphorical degradation and violability of the integral body" (19). Such imaginings of defiled bodies, according to Dean, become especially necessary to bolster the national self-image when it is under siege or when the state's boundaries are perceived to be overly porous. Dean examines how, within 1930s France, pornography and homosexuality in particular were seen to emblematize such forsaken human dignity and, in that tense political and economic climate, helped to immunize the national body politic against fears of its own vulnerability. At the same time as she shows how these inverse narratives of bodily pollution and profanation paradoxically confirmed the liberal premium on autonomous, self-determining personhood, Dean underscores the explicitly sexualized tenor of those figurative threats to the liberal social body. As Dean maintains, sexual desire above all must be purged in order to render both the body politic and the liberal individual equal, disinterested, and abstract—suggesting that norms concerning sexuality can offer privileged sites for investigating the social meanings of human rights, along with the juridical mechanisms that exclude certain lives from full rights and personhood (14).

As the final section of this chapter will consider, our contemporary expectations about human rights are solidified and rendered meaningful through precisely such eroticized narratives of bodily breakdown, invasion, and defilement. Dean's conclusions about the liberal social body of postwar France thus apply with prescient insight to explain the frequently pornographic violence enacted on the distant postcolonial body within popular narratives and portrayals of human rights. Yet while the peril of sexual degeneracy may confer legibility on human rights norms, the liberal social body that such a scourge consolidates is, today, also distinctly European American. Within the present-day symbolic economy of the body politic, race and gender often function as mutually imbricated contaminants that menace the antiseptic picture of embodiment implicit to liberal theories of the human. Within such an imaginative landscape, the postcolonial body prone to sexual excess and perversion serves as a placeholder onto which those appetites and disorders that the liberal social body must exorcise from its own self-understanding are projected, rendering postcolonial atrophy and dereliction a predictable foil to the West's fragile identity. And much as those threats palliate fears of waning national sovereignty that have only intensified post-9/11, they simultaneously legalize the structures of domestic and international policing that forestall such knowledge. As such, it is no accident that much human rights discourse today takes disproportionate aim at redeeming the postcolonial world, even while it capitalizes on classic tropologies of the rhetoric of empire that confine postcoloniality to a fatal deficit of human rights. Ironically, then, the postcolonial world comes to be fictionalized as rampant with the very assaults on human rights that simultaneously jeopardize and naturalize the vision of the idealized body sustaining human rights as a social and political imaginary.

Redeeming the Postcolonial: The Rhetoric of Empire and the Human Rights Bestseller

The remainder of this chapter looks to one especially revealing popular archive in order to track these recurring rhetorical devices and explanatory motifs. A genre with both fictional and journalistic instantiations, the "human rights bestseller" will enable me to chart how contemporary narratives of human rights marshal many well-rehearsed conventions of imperialist discourse, along with paternalistic conjectures about the need of the "Third World" for salvation through recourse to the very values that those conventions smuggle in.[36] These apologias for humanitarian intervention are replete with exoticizing, infantilizing, and other demeaning stereotypes, even as they deploy the aesthetic codes of sentimental literature to cultivate sympathy for postcolonial despair. While they thus require that we revisit historically antecedent manifestations of imperialistic discourse, these narratives in addition perform relatively new work in cementing the descriptive authority of the languages of human rights, along with the liberal topographies of selfhood that they imply. While frequently marketed for women's book clubs, these texts increasingly circulate beyond that circumscribed readership. Accordingly, we might think about the popular genre as assembling what Michael Warner calls "a public." For Warner, a public exists independently of any given political or social institution, instead being congregated "by virtue of being addressed" vis-à-vis a "concatenation" of cultural forms that require at least minimal participation from their audiences.[37] The proliferation of the human rights bestseller, as such, organizes a readership based on its investment in shared values, political commitments, and yearnings. And while that genre on its surface depicts postcolonial reality, it more accurately registers crises within the liberal body politic to which its northern readership belongs, indexing the contemporary structures of sociopolitical exclusion that underwrite that idealized self-image.

Many human rights bestsellers levy a theological idiom laden with conspicuously Judeo-Christian overtones, construing human rights activism as a contemporary *mission civilisatrice* wherein the Western crusader acts as "savior" to the postcolonial victim. Humanitarian interventionism and aid alike are thereby cloaked within the facade of manifest destiny, and conversion to human rights norms likewise carries the force of a divinely authorized command. This dynamic entails that the bestseller frequently follows the spiritual development of its European American, or otherwise Westernized, protagonists, plotting a predictably liberal (while religiously inflected) itinerary of self-overcoming through the acquisition of moral agency. For example, Greg Mortenson's *Three Cups of Tea* (2006) documents Mortenson's evolution from a "climbing bum" into a tireless champion of the Third World, casting humanitarianism as a vector for his more comprehensive deliverance.[38] Mortenson nearly dies descending the summit of K2 before being rescued by the inhabitants of an isolated mountain village in northern Pakistan, and he vows to repay their hospitality by building a school for the local children. This pursuit eventually finds itself enlarged to include a sea of such facilities across Pakistan and later Afghanistan, although that project is ironically levied to corroborate the secular orientation of human rights norms. A similar trajectory propels Deborah Rodriguez's *Kabul Beauty School* (2007), which recounts its author's expedition to bestow Western-style beauty salons on Afghanistan as a vehicle for proselytizing distinctly liberal expectations concerning femininity. Rodriguez's conversion into a humanitarian not only coincides with her transformation from a "party girl" (60) into a faithful churchgoer but also allows her "to be part of something bigger and more meaningful—something that gave me the feeling I was helping to save the world" (56). Within such a teleology, human rights again are configured as objects of sacred devotion and promise. Notably, this theological rhetoric is not unique to fiction but pervades much academic scholarship on rights. Paul Gordon Lauren's *The Evolution of International Human Rights* (1998), for example, characterizes human rights as a "revolutionary" "mission," "crusade," and "vision" dependent on bold actors in a "struggle" requiring "heroic efforts." Yet it goes without saying that such an illusion of divine calling masks desires that are deeply narcissistic, insofar as they both expiate Western guilt and secure the broader neoimperial mandate.[39]

Not surprisingly in the post-9/11 geopolitical climate, a preponderance of contemporary human rights bestsellers, like Mortenson's and Rodriguez's, conflate Islam itself with abuses of human rights, mirroring the tendency within political speech to collapse humanitarianism into the conjoined wars on terror and Islamic fundamentalism. The emergence of Mortenson's "mission" coincides with and becomes a means to combat the spread of madrassas in the late 1990s across Pakistan, institutions that the text inflammatorily describes as "hotbeds of extremism, growing like malignancies in these vulnerable valleys" whose "brainwashed...armies of extremism will...swarm over Pakistan and the rest of the Islamic world" (255, 244–45). Mortenson does claim that his primary goal is to impart a secular education to young women, and his narrative vehemently condemns post-9/11 U.S. military policy for its aggressive unilateralism. Nonetheless, *Three Cups of Tea* deploys both an inflated, Manichean rhetoric and deeply racialized imagery to render postcoloniality in terms of contagion and corruption assumedly deriving from the irrational, excessive appetites of radical Islam.[40] While Mortenson's aim of humanitarian uplift may be salutary, his description of Islam as a pestilence both sanctions militaristic self-defense against that scourge and portrays the postcolonial as a space of unreason, superstition, and the defeat of liberal ideals—once again, all things against which the West aims to define itself.

Khaled Hosseini's *The Kite Runner* (2003) and *A Thousand Splendid Suns* (2008) are even more fervid in their opposition to Islam and manipulation of that bias into a secular charge to eradicate it. While *A Thousand Splendid Suns* scripts the liberation of Afghanistan from the Taliban as a vindication of women's rights, as I will return to discuss, *The Kite Runner* indicts Western ineptitude in that region only to present the militarization of Afghanistan as the fulfillment of messianic promise. The novel's first-person, Westernized protagonist Amir frames his narrative as an epic quest to redress a "past of unatoned sins" that will teach him how "*there is a way to be good again.*" Amir's unexpiated childhood crimes, not coincidentally, correlate with the weaponizing of the Taliban in the 1970s, his personal misadventures thus allegorizing American foreign affairs. Furthermore, Amir's offense is one of inaction; he witnesses but fails to intervene in the homosexual rape of his best childhood friend. This acquiescence to cruelty facilitates the child perpetrator's adult evolution into a ruthless leader of the Taliban who is, what's more, a homosexual, pedophile, and rapist. *The Kite Runner,* as such, equates Islam itself with hypersexualized intemperance, all the while predictably mollifying the vicissitudes of fascination and horror that have long animated the colonial gaze. On one level, within Hosseini's allegory the onus to defend Afghanistan's profaned human rights permits Amir/America to compensate for his/its former negligence, which of course is inextricable from the novel's implicit apologia for the muscular occupation of Afghanistan.[41] Yet, on another level, it is once again the threat of specifically corporeal defilement that both ensures the explanatory authority of human rights discourses and fortifies the liberal body politic against a corresponding form of desecration.

Overall, the human rights bestseller recruits many well-documented codes and conventions of colonialist rhetoric. While the genre's humanitarian reformers are vested with divine license, their perpetrators are reduced to sheer barbarity and evil. To such ends, Makau Mutua has demonstrated how human rights discourses invoke a "higher morality" predicated on the polarized categories of "saviors," "victims," and "savages," and many bestsellers rely on precisely such metaphors both to valorize activism and to castigate the almost uniformly male villains in the humanitarian saga.[42] Similarly, David Spurr describes how the contemporary media enlists forms of "debasement," "abjection," and "negation" to impute to postcolonial peoples a moral void or total lack of ethical awareness, and these characteristics, too, map onto the genre of the human rights bestseller.[43] The global South is depicted as overrun with chaos and unreason, such as when Mortenson's narrative ruminates over the impracticalities he confronts in constructing schools throughout remote Pakistan. Many texts project full-fledged insanity onto the postcolonial world, a trope that emerges in Betty Mahmoody's *Not Without My Daughter* (1987), a nonfictional narrative that recounts her and her daughter's kidnapping by her Iranian husband. Not only does Mahmoody deride Iran as a "mad country" (391), but her husband's untreated insanity fuels his patriarchal privilege under Sharia and Iranian law, which together prevent Mahmoody and her daughter from legally contesting their captivity. By no means last, postcolonial regression is presented as entrapment outside historical progress and an appreciation for linear time. Much as Mahmoody despairs of how "time seemed to mean nothing to the average Iranian" (81), Ayan Hirsi Ali's autobiography *Infidel* (2007) caricatures the developmentally arrested, atemporal mindset of Muslim society. Ali describes her own grandmother as "in a sense, . . . living in the Iron Age" and berates 1970s Saudi Arabia as a "society [that] seemed fixed in the Middle Ages" (8, 43).[44] Of course, these almost clichéd statements rehash many tried-and-true imperialist stereotypes, along with their Orientalizing, homogenizing, and other racialized undercurrents. Nevertheless, we must continue to ask what new imaginative and ideological work those conventions perform when they work to verify human rights as a normative regime and discourse.

From one standpoint, we might analyze such tendencies through the lens of what Graham Huggan calls "the postcolonial exotic," a syndrome that Huggan ties to the packaging of cultural Otherness for Western consumption.

As Huggan puts it, the postcolonial exotic reflects "a pathology of cultural representation under late capitalism—a result of the spiraling commodification of cultural difference."[45] Insofar as postcolonial writers must "strategically self-exoticize" to self-market, for Huggan it is a relatively benign and, in any case, inevitable by-product of the publishing industry. However, something more than facile exoticism seems to govern human rights bestsellers, with their often overtly partisan agendas. Indeed, exoticism becomes newly troubling when it regulates the aesthetic depiction of abuses of human rights. Within the bestseller, not only does human misery become sensationalized but human rights violations are what seem to inspire the refraction of those victimized lives through the prism of Otherness in the first place.[46] In other words, if ubiquitous human rights violations are what produce the alterity of these societies, then the exoticization of those underlying abuses incites a certain fascination with them. And if the bestseller's allure lies in its representational exorbitance and hyperbole, what happens when assaults on human rights are aestheticized vis-à-vis those codes? In effect, human rights violations come to be rendered sublime—here in the classical sense that they elicit an alchemy of horror, wonder, and enthrallment.[47] Indeed, historical formulations of the sublime centrally attribute its power to the impression of a vast separation between viewer and object, and here, too, the perception of an insurmountable chasm between Western reader-observer and postcolonial victim seemingly compounds the success of the genre, further prompting the question of what exactly it works to commodify. While portraits of distant depravity may tantalize the genre's target audience, they do so to placate the insecurities of that readership, simultaneously verifying the liberal ideals through which it self-identifies. In turn, the liberal body politic comes to be constituted precisely by exorcising those realities that the genre limns as either threatening or exotic. Hence, what is often described as the ambivalence of colonial desire—which longs to variously master, repress, and be itself engulfed by the objects that excite it—not only plays out within the human rights bestseller, fostering its popularity, but also structures the contemporary imaginative landscape that lends symbolic authority to human rights.

Of the many exoticist motifs that the genre exploits, the veil has been conscripted into especially frequent service as a means to emblematize women's oppression. One could only begin to catalog the recent texts that enlist the veil accordingly, although among this chapter's case studies alone Azar Nafisi's *Reading Lolita in Tehran* (2003), Rodriguez's *Kabul Beauty School,* and Mortenson's *Three Cups of Tea* have almost identical cover images of younger women veiled and with lowered eyes.[48] Such pictures quickly signal those texts' preoccupation with women's rights, while reifying the prohibitions and constraints that oversee female sexuality in many Muslim societies. Within such an explanatory apparatus, the process of unveiling provides a transparent metaphor for both independence and enlightenment—thereby locating these texts within a distinctly liberal explanatory framework. Such a connection is finessed in Nafisi's memoir about a book club that she hosts for former Iranian students, providing a forum in which they can discuss censored literary classics. Nafisi deploys the veil throughout her text to denote the autonomy that their culture denies those young women:

> For nearly two years, almost every Thursday morning, rain or shine, they came to my house, and almost every time, I could not get over the shock of seeing them shed their mandatory veils and robes and burst into color. When my students came into that room, they took off more than their scarves and robes. Gradually, each one gained an outline and a shape, becoming her own inimitable self. (5–6)

Whereas compulsory veiling mutes the singular individuality of her students, its relinquishment almost inherently facilitates their self-fashioning, reclaiming their distinctive personalities. In this way, Nafisi figures the veil as an almost automatic affront to liberal subjectivity. And whereas this focus on the veil may seem to authenticate non-European and nonsecular cultural formations, it ultimately confirms the superiority of liberal norms surrounding both *bildung* and self-determination.

The centrality of the veil within many human rights bestsellers, moreover, ends up concentrating the very imperialist-paternalist gaze that the genre superficially pretends to deconstruct. While accessible, as an emblem the veil risks both homogenizing postcoloniality and reinforcing the genre's general tendency to essentialize, if not fully romanticize, victimization. It fetishizes an external token of women's assumedly uniform oppression, encouraging a reductive analysis of the veil's cultural politics as well as detracting from its ability to register ambivalence and contradiction. These texts consequently elide the veil's more contentious, variegated significations, submerging the tensions that beset it as a highly charged practice—one that connotes either subservience or defiance depending on circumstance and context. Questions of how the veil might operate *both* as a cipher for women's rights *and* as a powerful instrument for staging resistance are thereby foreclosed. Along parallel lines, such imagery negates the complex densities of cultural rituals as they are both inscribed on and actively inhabited by the embodied self, neglecting to address how the veil is experienced by women who freely choose to wear it. In turn, we might say that such reliance on the veil fails to capture what Saba Mahmood describes as "forms of corporeality that, while efficacious in behavior, do not lend themselves easily to representation, elucidation, and a logic of signs and symbols."[49] Indeed, while the practice of veiling might seem to demand that we attend to the ontological status of the body as it negotiates social norms, its appropriation as a superficial symbol short-circuits such modes of inquiry to merely entrench the diminished vision of the subject that liberal theories of political practice often disseminate.

Most human rights bestsellers further gender the different characters in the human rights saga along predictable lines. While their victims are overwhelmingly women and children, their villains are almost exclusively male, an opposition that neatly gratifies the joint fantasies of postcolonial innocence and misogynistic corruption. This formulaic dichotomy presents human rights as first and foremost tools for redeeming women from patriarchy, a gambit that within the bestseller proclaims and even purports to actuate cross-cultural feminist solidarity. Whereas postcolonial womanhood is exalted, postcolonial manhood is cause for derision, plagued by a misspent, disgraced virility that is framed as responsible for the postcolony's beleaguered human rights. While on the one hand postcolonial society is cast as rife with abusive tyrants, on the other it is suggested to be perverted by sexual desire run amuck, whether turned predatory or impotent. As in Hosseini's *The Kite Runner,* such ravenous yet defunct postcolonial manhood ultimately sanctions European interventionism, juxtaposing postcolonial atrophy with a contrasting brand of heroic yet domineering Western manhood. Such anxiety of sexual profligacy and license is, of course, classically imperialist, here again serving as a backdrop against which the ever-tenuous Western self-image can verify itself. The humanitarian mandate thus both paternalistically disciplines what it marks as the postcolonial condition and enforces an aggressive heteronormativity. And, as we have seen, it is precisely the specter of sexual perversion and profanation that solidifies the liberal social body and its integrity. Bodily excess and decay, as such, come to be symbolically expelled from the American/European body politic, at the same time as their menace renews the warrant for policing those borders.

Much as the human rights crusade ransoms a vacillating Western masculinity, the conceit of a debased postcolonial manhood consigns postcolonial women and children to a condition of chronic victimization and passivity. This device amplifies the sublime horror of human rights abuses with the implication that they foremost target innocence and purity—in a move that feminizes, eroticizes, infantilizes, and idealizes the global South and its suffering. We can, in turn, observe how the seemingly contradictory myths of postcolonial barbarity and purity here, too, operate in tandem to substantiate one another. The central threat driving Mahmoody's *Not Without My Daughter* is not so much Mahmoody's imprisonment in Iran as her daughter's unwitting absorption of that culture's backward norms controlling femininity. Likewise, the unspoken trauma that haunts *The Kite Runner* is the literal defilement of childhood sexuality, and its entire plot tracks its protagonist's attempted penance for that transgression. Ishmael Beah's *A Long Way Gone* (2008) contains an in-depth portrait of a child mercenary, whose indoctrination in liberal norms after he is released from conscription restores a desecrated youth. Far from last, Mortenson's desire to inoculate central Asia against radical Islam principally involves rescuing its young adults from Islam's corrupting seductions through a secular education. In each of these cases, the childhood being salvaged is transposed onto the postcolonial world as a whole, resurrecting yet another colonialist stereotype—here, of moral and other arrested development. Mortenson articulates related assumptions when he describes the village housing his first school as a site of "a rare kind of purity," causing him to "worry" about the incursion of Western values (112). In addition, such representational tactics smuggle in the view that these victims deserve salvation only if they exemplify such unspoiled virtue, even as they romanticize that condition for their jaded readers.

Yet the flip side of this fetishization of innocence is the eroticization of human rights abuse. The combined peril of female circumcision, nonconsensual marriage, spousal rape, and other sexual violence provides the narrative momentum and urgency for many bestsellers. Outrage at these offenses, however, is tempered by the fascination they equally cull, contributing to a complicated "metaphysics of gender violence" that is nourished by both intrigue and terror, or by the intertwined desires for ravishment and containment.[50] Such energies visibly motor Hosseini's *A Thousand Splendid Suns,* with its almost epic portrait of thirty years of Afghanistan's history. The novel follows the lives of two different preadolescent female protagonists, the second of whom is introduced when the first enters adulthood. Its narrative recycles an almost identical developmental course for both: youthful innocence and hope, nonconsensual marriage, violence and domestic abuse, and spent promise. These two self-mirroring plot trajectories not only vilify Islam but also dramatize the tarnishing of purity, sexualizing the human rights violation. Afghanistan's general plight is, by extension, conflated with such plundered female virtue, once again lending moralistic backing to the nation's military occupation after 9/11. Although Hosseini leverages a number of deeply exoticist tropes, this strategy is striking not in itself but because it divulges the centrality of the illusion of the idealized, essentialized body to the social meanings of human rights. By recurrently staging the infringement of bodily integrity, bestsellers like Hosseini's paradoxically corroborate that myth's symbolic authority as an enabling fiction for human rights, ratifying the liberal topography of the subject fettered to those norms. In other words, it is not that such popular texts are merely prurient, although that is clearly the case; rather, their engrossment with violated bodies illumines the broad symbolic architecture girding the liberal logic of human rights. In effect, precisely the predicament of being insufficiently integrated or dignified through reasoned self-determination is what renders the global South uniquely prone to undergo rampant human rights violations.

At the same time as they perform the vicissitudes of an ambivalence quintessentially symptomatic of imperial desire, many human rights bestsellers evince a gender politics that is equally divided. On the one hand, these texts display the self-congratulatory gestures that we might expect, celebrating a conspicuously liberal odyssey of women's emancipation. As we have seen, Nafisi's *Reading Lolita in Tehran* configures the veil as an inherently anti-individualist garment, the wearing of which automatically suppresses the wearer's unique identity and, by implication, agentive self-possession. Within many bestsellers, such liberal norms are further realized through a particular kind of consumerism, which is to say that Nafisi's fixation on attire is not anomalous. As we have seen, Rodriguez's humanitarian mission is organized around the bequest of beauty salons to the women of Kabul, a goal that similarly scripts women's freedoms in terms of compliance with a highly distinctive mode of self-production—in both instances, conformity with Western norms surrounding beauty, dress, and grooming. Such a premise also motivates Gayle Tzemach Lemmon's *The Dressmaker of Khair Khana* (2011), which announces its commitments in its very title. Of course, feminist theorists have long remarked on the self-undermining by-products of those culturally enforced prescriptions. Yet this recurrent slippage within the human rights bestseller between liberal self-fashioning and the fashion industry lends new force to the common complaint that liberal human rights norms are as much the progeny of capitalism as of the European Enlightenment. Chapter 4's discussion of Nawal El Saadawi will examine such a linkage in order to consider how financial measures of self-worth can act as decoys that secure consent to broader structures of oppression.

On the other hand, while these narratives superficially advocate for women's rights, they in fact cultivate nostalgia for an era prior to the encroachments of global modernity and its less equivocal social conventions. In this respect, their liberationist agendas mask a deep, albeit overdetermined conservatism that plays out in reactionary yearnings for highly traditional gender roles. In many instances, this tendency manifests itself in an absorption with the cult of domesticity and essentialized conceptions of uniquely women's work, which paradoxically are heralded as routes to autonomous self-realization. Most immediately, we might interpret this syndrome as evidence of a longing for less ambiguous expectations for women. But regardless of the feminist backlash this nostalgia may tap, it opens up the abiding contradictions inherent in liberal theories of selfhood, which credit only certain avenues to self-determination with legitimacy. These narratives reveal how the liberal onus to individuate only finds authorization to the extent that its expressions confirm a relatively limited—and, indeed, arbitrary and incoherent—set of norms regulating subjectivity and self-expression, which within the human rights bestseller have been overwhelmingly captured by what looks a lot like reactionary, right-wing ideology.

Such ambivalence about women's liberation is particularly apparent in Hosseini's *A Thousand Splendid Suns.* One of its heroines, Laila, becomes pregnant by spousal rape yet wrestles over whether to abort the fetus, an option she ultimately decides against—in the midst of war-torn, starving Afghanistan. She reasons, "The baby was blameless" in a world that already "had seen enough killing of innocents" (253). Despite Laila's near death in childbirth, the infant is extolled as "a blessing," occasioning a pro-life politics that works to idealize postcolonial purity. Yet this romanticized portrait of maternity is simultaneously framed as exemplifying individualistic self-fashioning, which for Laila surrounds a belief in her own inimitable uniqueness, or that she is *"going to be somebody"* (364; italics in the original). After the fall of the Taliban, Laila is freed to pursue her lifelong dream of a vocation, and she does so by founding an orphanage, a destiny that allows her literally and symbolically to adopt Afghanistan's forsaken youth. However, this sentimentalization of motherhood equally attributes postcolonial crisis to a breakdown in the moral standing of the bourgeois family. Overflowing with abandoned youth, Afghanistan's disorder is counterpart to a chronic failure of parenthood and collapse of the integral family unit, which signals a parallel fate against which the liberal body politic must be inoculated. Promoting an exclusively female succor, the novel concludes as a throng of unwanted but redeemed children "come running" to Laila; as it explains, "Some of them call her *Mother.* Laila does not correct them" (365). The narrative accordingly conducts a plea for the very consciousness manifested in Laila's actions—namely, humanitarian feeling. In sum, while *A Thousand Splendid Suns* purports to chart Laila's feminist emancipation—which is notably achieved by the U.S. invasion of Afghanistan—that *bildung* culminates with her accession to a collection of counterproductive and even self-defeating values.

While Laila's humanitarian *bildung* is actuated by her literal bestowal of aid, within other bestsellers the attainment of a humanitarian conscience stages a vindication of cosmopolitanism. Such a logic lauds human rights norms for purveying a visionary internationalism, as well as a recipe for surmounting ethnic, religious, national, and other differences through reasoned dialogue. Ishmael Beah's recovery and development in *A Long Way Gone* follows such a course, which is cemented by Beah's trip to New York City to join in "the United Nations First International Children's Parliament" (195). While celebrating the philosophy behind the UN, Beah recounts how these child diplomats jointly narrate their individual biographies to influence the UN's Economic and Social Council (199). Transforming respect for human rights into a multicultural success story, such an outcome extols a collection of distinctly liberal ideals: the role of storytelling in fostering humane sentiment, expectations for the democratic public sphere, and a distinctively cosmopolitan brand of civic participation. Much as the mock assembly allows youth from nations spanning the world to "cast our suffering aside and intelligently discuss solutions to the problems facing children in our various countries," reasoned deliberation fills those participants with "hope and promise" (198). A nearly identical defense of cosmopolitanism concludes the documentary *Born into Brothels,* winner of the 2004 Academy Award for Best Documentary Feature. In this case, the maturation of one child protagonist is consummated when he travels to Amsterdam for another version of a model U.N., here for child photographers. Like Beah's congress of underprivileged youth from around the world, the film's "World Press Photo" convention deputizes its child diplomats as their country's "representatives," advocating both photography's inherently democratizing propensities and a particular pedagogy of liberal reason.

In sum, the proliferating genre of the human rights bestseller indexes a number of interrelated phenomena. Most immediately, it gauges the multiplying anxiety of its main audiences in the aftermath of 9/11, revealing how the idiom of human rights can become opportunistic and self-serving. Both the discourses of human rights and appeals to humanitarian action can thus be seen to console narcissistic fears about the growing instability of Western hegemony. We might, then, conclude that the genre primarily offers a diversionary mechanism, or an imaginary stave against late imperial decline—and therefore is only marginally a statement of sincere concern for the postcolonial lives it depicts. Indeed, the increasing explosion of popular human rights causes and agendas itself works to consolidate a particular topography of the liberal subject, as well as to imaginatively quarantine those qualities seen to hazard it. The bestseller's recurring tropes, as such, inversely give shape to the myth of the integrated, dignified body that sustains contemporary discourses of human rights, even as they expose that idealized liberal body as alarmingly racialized and gendered. As a genre, the human rights bestseller accordingly vivifies far more than the tenacity of the countless stereotypes that it inherits from the classical rhetoric of empire. Rather, it also redeploys those biases to lend ideological coherence to liberal articulations of human rights. Within such a symbolic economy, the civil body politic is defined in terms of its antithesis to the violated, anarchic postcolonial bodies that populate these narratives, capturing how and why the fiction of individualist self-determination ironically requires for its very legibility the threat of bodies insufficiently mastered and subdued by liberal reason.

❧ CHAPTER TWO

Embodying Human Rights

Toward a Phenomenology of Social Justice

As I have argued, liberal human rights discourses
and norms, along with the theories of the human that sustain them, evince
significant ambivalence toward embodiment. On the one hand, within these
liberal cartographies of the subject, the body is treated as an entity that must
be mastered, integrated, and subdued through reasoned self-determination, a
project that casts rights-bearing subjectivity as dependent on the quarantine
of corporeal being and its subordination to the intellect. Liberal articulations of rights thus exhibit a highly dualistic architecture within which core
realities of embodiment come to be denied and repressed, contributing to
a remarkably unidimensional account of the subject. As a result, the liberal
subject entitled to rights is imagined in terms that are strangely abstract,
anemic, and decorporealized. On the other hand, the dual fictions of dignity and bodily integrity that incur legibility for human rights norms are
simultaneously consolidated by the specter of bodies being violated, broken,
and unmade. In the contemporary human rights imaginary, these profaned
bodies are frequently racialized and sexualized in overdetermined ways that
divulge the deep affinity between the languages of human rights and the
historical rhetoric of empire. All in all, liberal formulations of human rights
marshal a particular symbolic economy of the liberal social body, which sanctions concrete structures of oppression that find legalization in both law and
sociopolitical practice. The general aversion toward embodiment endemic to

liberal political thought has, in other words, provided the warrant for a spate of real-world discriminations. And given that many theoretical analyses of human rights display a comparative reluctance about embodiment, they only reproduce and entrench that exclusionary logic.

This chapter examines how a theoretical focus on embodiment might instead set the groundwork for remedying those exclusions, thereby enacting an imaginative recalibration of liberal mappings of human rights. It asks: How might a philosophy of embodiment begin to reverse liberalism's dualistic animus toward the body? Could embodiment be reconfigured to signal not servitude but instead experiential thickness, agility, and abundance? How might a more faithful rendition of human selfhood—one that takes embodiment seriously—augur a more inclusive liberal democratic public sphere, along with a conception of the body politic as permeable and diffuse rather than unified and nuclear? By validating the energies of corporeal being, might we arrive at a more capacious, robust, and versatile portrait of collective decision making and political life? In sum, might an account of human rights that foregrounds the body's talents and appetencies purvey a more faithful and productive model for elucidating the character of just coexistence?

In this chapter, I engage Maurice Merleau-Ponty's thought as one framework for negotiating and provisionally answering some of the interlocking debates about human rights that preoccupy this book. Above all, Merleau-Ponty's phenomenology of embodied perception implicitly verifies the body's many contributions to selfhood and social justice alike, countermanding the deep-seated anxiety about embodiment that haunts many liberal theories of politics. Instead of being reviled as a source of captivity and debasement, corporeal experience for Merleau-Ponty is composed of a reverberating matrix of vital intensities that facilitate the self's involvement with the surrounding lifeworld. Within such an ontology of the subject, mind and body are not divorced or antagonists but instead collaborate to foster not only individual selfhood but also communal belonging. For Merleau-Ponty, corporeal being inexorably intertwines the subject within their proximate milieu, in a mode of relationality that refocalizes debates about just coexistence by refracting them through determinations of reciprocity and interdependence. A phenomenology of embodiment thereby overturns the presumption of human mastery over the natural, animal, and object worlds, along with the dualisms that shore up those entitlements. Similarly, it exposes the liberal conceits of autonomous self-determination and reasoned self-abstraction as hollow and artificial, insofar as they elide the self's material enmeshment within a historically and contextually specific environment. In sum, Merleau-Ponty's philosophy gestures toward how a crucial fleshiness, density, and porosity might be returned to the dangerously idealized, and thus enfeebled subject that liberalism posits as the bearer of human rights.

In addition, Merleau-Ponty's insistence on the embodied and hence situated character of human judgment and perception is counterpart to an account of language as grounded and immanent, even while all meaning and insight remain fleeting and paradoxical. Despite his own concern with the many liaisons between discourse and power, Merleau-Ponty did not conceive of language as wholly captured or mediated. On the contrary, for Merleau-Ponty semantic experience remains to a degree secondary and subordinate to embodied cognition, causing those dual registers of experience to interact in a relay wherein embodied perception can creatively intervene within discourse. It is in this way that Merleau-Ponty's phenomenology gestures toward an itinerary for replenishing the increasingly wayward discourses of human rights. Whereas the languages of human rights have become progressively corrupt and impoverished, Merleau-Ponty explains how they might undergo transformation and renewal to become better aligned with social justice. Such a metric for tracking the fluid, dynamic movements of language thus accredits and endows the body with an active role in propagating significance. By no means last, Merleau-Ponty's philosophy further testifies to the preeminence of art and aesthetics, which he heralds as paradigmatically disposed to harness the body's perceptual rhythms and appetencies, in effect incarnating aesthetic experience. In this book I accordingly build on Merleau-Ponty's account of aesthetics to craft a defense of how narrative literature might redress the many foreclosures of human rights, within a process that I have described as an embodied politics of reading.

As I have suggested, one subtext of this book's reliance on Merleau-Ponty is to adjudicate recent disputes within postcolonial studies. At the field's current theoretical crossroads, debates about human rights can be seen to crystallize broader controversies facing theory, placing certain of its methodological blind spots into stark relief. Since this book aims both to reckon with the limitations of and to forecast a passage beyond those horizons, I self-consciously introduce phenomenology as one point of departure from postcolonial studies' reigning paradigms, and that focus notably participates within a wider embrace of phenomenology (along with other approaches to embodiment, materiality, and affect) occurring within criticism and theory far beyond postcolonial studies' particular ambit.

Moreover, my reliance on Merleau-Ponty to pursue the challenges to social justice facing the global South is by no means contrary to the spirit of his own politics. Although Merleau-Ponty's ideas about race were colored by his historical moment, he was deeply opposed to colonization.

Such a posture is evident in the classically anticolonial critique ventured in his author's preface to *Humanism and Terror,* wherein he maintains that "the material and moral culture of England presupposes the exploitation of the colonies" (xiii). Nonetheless, while Merleau-Ponty offers a provisional escape from the deadlock within postcolonial studies, we must remember that his thought is not an independent solution to those theoretical quarrels. Quite the contrary, taking Merleau-Ponty on his own terms would risk either mystifying embodiment or romanticizing more holistic ecologies of co-belonging. This chapter, then, does not propose a wholesale adoption of Merleau-Ponty's thought; rather it aims to develop a "historicized" or "neo-" phenomenology—that is, a phenomenology in self-aware dialogue with theory's advances over the many years since his historical moment.

Phenomenology's Heirs and Merleau-Ponty's Historical Moment

A brief detour through Merleau-Ponty's historical climate, contemporaries, and reception will clarify why a return to phenomenology at this theoretical juncture promises to be both timely and forward looking. The vast majority of Merleau-Ponty's work was produced in the 1940s and 1950s, before his premature and sudden death in 1961 at the age of fifty-three. Politically, he was active in the intellectual foment of postwar Europe and grappled with the atrophy of Soviet Marxism, although he questionably refused to denounce Stalinist terror.[1] Merleau-Ponty's primary philosophical influences were Edmund Husserl and G. W. F. Hegel, the latter of whom he deemed the first existentialist, an allegiance that renders Merleau-Ponty foundational to German phenomenology's migration into French letters.[2] Merleau-Ponty is also identified as having sown poststructuralism's seeds in the French academy. He was an early proponent of Claude Lévi-Strauss's structural anthropology, although Merleau-Ponty himself never took the "linguistic turn."[3] While his foremost interlocutor was Jean-Paul Sartre, their camaraderie was rivalrous. Merleau-Ponty understood his philosophy to conflict with Sartre's existentialism, in part because of what he interpreted as Sartre's dualism.[4] Likewise, Merleau-Ponty rejected the ennui and despair characteristic of Sartre's thought, instead emphasizing how wonder and meaning inform experience.

Despite his centrality to a highly transitional moment in Continental thought, Merleau-Ponty has not met with the intellectual heritage or following that might appear his due. In part because of his untimely death, he precipitously fell out of fashion within French letters; if anything, he became a type of whipping boy for many poststructuralists, even though he anticipates many of their basic critiques.[5] Multiple explanations might diagnose this almost uniform reaction against his thought, ranging from the allegation that his detractors misread him to the charge that such a disavowal is symptomatic of their own biases. Nevertheless, Merleau-Ponty has inspired a relative dearth of attention from intellectual historians and literary-cultural critics alike, although different currents of theory are presently witnessing a resurgence of interest in his philosophy, along with a larger "experiential," "materialist," or "anthropological" turn.

In the midst of this neglect, one field that has consistently been receptive to Merleau-Ponty is feminist and gender studies. Merleau-Ponty's focus on embodiment has provided a range of theorists with a scheme for validating women's ostensibly closer connections to the body. For one, Judith Butler has throughout her career engaged Merleau-Ponty, although I will not parse that complex dialogue.[6] Luce Irigaray's *An Ethics of Sexual Difference* and Iris Marion-Young's "Throwing Like a Girl" represent other seminal texts that enlist Merleau-Ponty to expatiate women's realities; however, both theorists ultimately decide that Merleau-Ponty fails to adequately grasp female sexual and other difference.[7] For example, Irigary celebrates how Merleau-Ponty both emphasizes "prediscursive experience" and transcends dichotomous thought, although only to conclude that he lends "an exorbitant privilege to vision" that diminishes his profit for explaining female embodiment.[8] As such, while gender studies has made frequent recourse to Merleau-Ponty during his absence from other theoretical conversations, he has nevertheless met with consistent criticism for offering a male-centered understanding of the body.[9] That said, even gender theory of late has renewed its investment in Merleau-Ponty, which for some concurs with his yield for evaluating other sites of sociopolitical marginalization.[10] The rest of this chapter now investigates four key aspects of Merleau-Ponty's thought in terms of their relevance to an imaginative refurbishment of liberal discourses of human rights: his phenomenology of embodied perception, his nondualist ontology, his account of language, and his philosophy of aesthetics.

The Anatomy of Embodied Perception

If Merleau-Ponty has been credited with two singular contributions to philosophy, they are his nuanced theorization of embodiment and his departure from the pervasive legacy of Cartesian dualism.[11] Above all, Merleau-Ponty contends with the corporeal nature of perception (or what is translated as "consciousness," although the use of that term is overdetermined). Rejecting an idealist account of thought, Merleau-Ponty instead traces its emergence through the body's material embeddedness within a phenomenal field. For the embodied subject, perception arises through an intersensory gestalt composed not just of vision but also of smell, color, affect, movement, and sound and other densities, reversals, and folds of experience.[12] This grounding of perception in the subject's corporeality aims to access the genesis of perception, or to register those elements of subjectivity that arise antecedent to— and hence must be explained as in part separate from, or not wholly regulated by—language, culture, and sociality.[13] It is in this respect that Merleau-Ponty anticipates, yet does not fully undertake, the "linguistic turn"; to the contrary, his ontology cautions against an excessive investment in textuality and discourse, instead exploring dimensions of consciousness that are not completely governed by language.[14] However, while Merleau-Ponty sets out to identify and elucidate the foundations of lived experience, his thought equally indexes the complex interchange between embodied cognition and the institutions of culture. Given that embodiment in its materiality ensnares the subject within history, location, context, and sociocultural convention, perceptual insight is rendered contingent, transitory, and multifaceted. Merleau-Ponty, as such, does not posit the transcendental, dehistoricized subject for which his critics have at times accused him. Rather, his cosmology and corresponding portrait of selfhood emphasize indeterminacy, flux, and contradiction, as human experience varies according to time, place, and circumstance.

Merleau-Ponty's focus on the embodied roots of perception importantly treats the body's different cognitive energies as interwoven in ways that are at once harmonious and paradoxical. Those faculties operate in concert, as Merleau-Ponty describes, "in a total way with my whole being."[15] He here posits that an essential mutuality coheres all experience, even while that union is shifting and heterogeneous. This conception of corporeal synthesis has, in turn, led theorists to argue that he envisions the body as a laboratory for the larger reciprocities that oversee the natural world as a whole.[16] Yet although phenomenological perception summons the totality of the embodied self, the insights it affords are necessarily ephemeral, entailing that they cannot be apprehended or contained within statements of objective, empirical fact. As he explains, "Our own body acquaints us with a species of unity which is not a matter of subsumption under a law."[17] Because consciousness is inexorably situated, its contours resist translation into truths that are transhistorical, evidentiary, or rule bound—thus defying legalistic, scientific, and analytic regimes of proof. Quite differently, embodied cognition remains hostage to the precarities of material existence, as well as to the vagaries of the individual's social-historical milieu.

Accordingly, we can observe why a notion of paradox is indispensable to Merleau-Ponty's thought. Indeed, Merleau-Ponty describes the paramount goal of phenomenology as to divulge the dynamic texture of the many paradoxes that animate an embodied consciousness, selfhood, collective existence, and ontology itself. Merleau-Ponty offers one especially illuminating statement of the phenomenological project that frames it thus. He deciphers the phenomenological method as "thoroughly to test the paradoxes it indicates; continually to re-verify the discordant functioning of human intersubjectivity; to try to think through to the very end the same phenomena which science lays siege to, only restoring to them their original transcendence and strangeness."[18] His paradox, as such, is not the disabling kind that political, legal, and scientific theory often seeks to purge or overcome; on the contrary, it is ontological, or residing within forces that are elemental to sheer being, to adopt his lexicon. In effect, Merleau-Ponty construes phenomenology's task as one of disclosure or unconcealment, even while the paradoxes it excavates will only deepen under scrutiny. Indeed, the fundamentally confounding nature of the quandaries that occupy Merleau-Ponty's phenomenology is what causes them to engender privileged philosophical insight, entailing that his paradox might resemble Derrida's *différance* or a Heideggerian "aporia." In any case, whereas scientific and other rationalisms domesticate truth, the phenomenological agenda—which, again, necessarily recruits embodied perception—is to disrupt and thereby rejuvenate sedimented knowledge, in the process "reveal[ing] th[e] world as strange and paradoxical."[19] To such ends, phenomenological inquiry strives to expose the fabric of "intersubjectivity," or the intimacy between the individual and the lifeworld that immerses perception. This commerce between self and world further mirrors the terrain of justice-ethics, even while those dual realms are sutured through dissonance and tension. Overall, Merleau-Ponty thus emphasizes both the frictions and solidarities that nourish coexistence, or how different lives interpenetrate one another in ways that are both fertile and "discordant."

Whereas other theorists commonly ascribe paradox to language, or to religious belief, or to the finite horizons of social justice, for Merleau-Ponty paradox is first and foremost localized as well as reified within the exigencies of embodiment. As a consequence, while a notion of paradox pervades his thought—once again, denoting the fiber of knowledge, interbeing, language, and ontology broadly speaking—the reverberating intensities of embodied cognition function as a microcosm of those overarching realities. In Merleau-Ponty's words, embodiment instantiates a "constitutive paradox" that "commands the visible for us, but it does not explain it, does not clarify it, it only concentrates the mystery of its scattered visibilities; and it is indeed a paradox of Being, not a paradox of man, that we are dealing with here."[20] While multiple dimensions of human experience accordingly converge within Merleau-Ponty's idea of paradox, they are made tangible to human consciousness through the contradictory rhythms and appetencies of one's experience of one's own embodiment. In effect, for Merleau-Ponty the phenomenal field that harbors and generates perception is composed of energies that echo those forces administering the larger lifeworld. It is by studying the phenomenology of embodied cognition, then, that philosophy can gain access to matters of ontology. Paradoxes that might otherwise appear overly theoretical or abstract can be rendered palpable and concrete through contemplation of the enigmas of one's immanent relationship to one's own corporeal being.

Let me now proceed to trace how Merleau-Ponty's phenomenology might inspire an imaginative remapping of liberal articulations of human rights. Importantly, Merleau-Ponty forswears the ability of "objective" or "scientific" knowledge to grasp the "fabric of brute meaning" that is at the heart of his ontology.[21] This disavowal of empiricism opposes two contrasting domains and conventions of understanding, one of which he aligns with scientific, instrumental reason and the other with phenomenological perception, embodiment, and aesthetics. Implicit in such a distinction is the view that form and style invariably influence both the content and the tenor of knowledge; a given mode of presentation will predispose the kinds of insight it can elicit. Moreover, Merleau-Ponty's wariness about empirical discourse implies a related suspicion of the grammar of the law. As I have argued, legal reasoning's bias in favor of rationalistic and evidentiary truth is, while necessary, not without casualties. And given that human rights as an explanatory regime is indebted to such legalistic habits of thought, Merleau-Ponty suggests why opposing genres of expression might correct the many foreclosures that trouble rights logic. To the extent that phenomenology provides an itinerary for reconstellating the dominant assumptions that lend descriptive authority to human rights, its yield directly involves the traffic between aesthetics and politics, pressing us to consider how and why different aesthetic genres might procure varying modes of awareness.

Merleau-Ponty's skepticism about "objectivity" is merely one component of his effort to dismantle Cartesian dualism. Given that the liberal logic of rights itself marshals dichotomous thought, we can here, too, look to Merleau-Ponty for a theoretical framework that might suspend such an orientation. In his critique of scientific reason, Merleau-Ponty notably challenges the opposition between perceiving subject and passive object. In addition to collapsing the mind/body divide, Merleau-Ponty subverts a series of corresponding binaries: interiority and exteriority, thoughts and feelings, culture and nature, public and private, and so forth. As chapter 1 considered, the liberal mandate to master embodiment through reasoned intellection is accompanied by such a continuum of hierarchies. The presumption that the rational faculties of the mind must wield sovereign authority over and thereby discipline material, physical being has provided a key justification for the exploitation of not only the natural world but also different human populations over history. A dualistic aversion toward embodiment has consequently licensed the mistreatment of peoples either imaginatively associated with or perceived to be captive to embodiment—which is to say that a particular breed of dualism has underwritten innumerable of global modernity's epidemic wrongs. In turn, Merleau-Ponty's critique of instrumental, appropriative reason is inextricable from the dual tasks of reclaiming embodiment and jettisoning some of modernity's most insidious ideological warrants for sociopolitical oppression.

And it is precisely by insisting on the corporeal, materialist genesis of both perception and selfhood that Merleau-Ponty's thought cancels liberalism's prejudice against embodiment. By repudiating the liberal denigration of corporeal being, his thought refuses the dualistic quarantine of mind from body. As we have seen, beyond how this wariness toward embodiment has sanctioned innumerable structures of injustice, it has authored a pauperized, constricted understanding of the subject. Liberal theories of the human tend to eclipse embodiment entirely, to depreciate the body's appetencies, or to aver the need for its management by reason. In whatever case, they hypostasize an idealized conception of the subject of rights that implicitly censors incarnate modalities of apperception and decision making—naturalizing a portrait of selfhood from which the body is strangely absent. At the same time, liberal political thought has tended to depreciate those perceptual faculties linked to the body, deeming affect, intuition, and the emotions untutored and unreliable. Received formulations of the liberal democratic public sphere, for instance, exhibit such animus toward the body. By enshrining reasoned self-abstraction as what vests political dialogue with legitimacy, such glorified definitions of democratic process discount activities that do not conform to such a standard, with the effect of both erasing the many realms of experience that emanate from embodiment and producing an account of politics that is idle, abridged, and unconvincing. All in all, liberalism evacuates its construction of the human of key faculties of selfhood that are indispensable not only to individual fulfillment but also to just co-belonging.

Merleau-Ponty, however, inverts this customary stigmatization of embodiment. Instead of elevating mind over body, he explores how embodied cognition furnishes insights that contest reason's exclusive authority, demonstrating the hazards of a narrow reliance on empiricist rationalism. Rather than to endow either body or mind with preeminence, Merleau-Ponty demonstrates how they cooperate to generate perception and allow the subject to negotiate the surrounding world. Whereas liberal theories of the human construe the body as an anarchic entity in need of government by reason, for Merleau-Ponty the self's visceral appetencies make crucial contributions to selfhood, which bear directly on ethical life. To enumerate merely a few examples among many, his phenomenology prompts us to consider how affective loyalties impact public choice; emotion can enhance the operations of reason; certain forms of decision making as well as attachment cannot be explained strictly vis-à-vis semiotic analysis; and, of greatest importance for our purposes, core dimensions of suffering resist inscription within the evidentiary protocols of the law. By valorizing the body's contributions to selfhood, Merleau-Ponty offers a basis for affirming those very dimensions of existence that have occasioned great anxiety within the liberal tradition. Within the aims of this study, his phenomenology accordingly alludes to how we might recast the liberal topographies of the human that lend intellectual coherence to human rights beyond their currently constricted ambit, with the goal of imaginatively enlarging the scope and force of human rights protections.

That said, Merleau-Ponty does not naively celebrate embodied experience or treat it as lacking ambiguity, although that ambiguity does not derive from a conception of the subject as fragmented, self-alienated, or immobilized by repressions in a psychoanalytic sense. On the contrary, he explains an embodied consciousness as animated by a matrix of conflicting, disparate, and ambulatory forces. Even while Merleau-Ponty here suggests how a vital fleshiness might be restored to the overly abstract, decorporealized, and purified subject of human rights, that quality is importantly messy, porous, and constantly mutating. We therefore confront another way in which his thought explodes the myth of the ideally dignified, inviolable, and sovereign liberal social body. When the human cannot be cleansed of the body's signature, liberal political thought has tended to decipher embodiment in strikingly artificial, antiseptic terms—as we have seen, as always already dignified and integrated. These twinned fictions have naturalized a highly sanitized as well as languid conception of embodiment that ultimately elides the complexity, density, and adversity of the human condition. Of deep irony, the symbolic connotations of embodiment that sustain human rights norms thus work to submerge core realities of corporeal existence—which are quintessentially manifested in the body's suffering, brokenness, and finitude.

Here, Merleau-Ponty's political views were notably inflected by a neo-Hegelian or Marxist dialectic, wherein certain instantiations of revolutionary violence become permissible. However, Merleau-Ponty's dialectic is a materialist (rather than spiritual or economic) one; indeed, he explains historical violence as simultaneously innate to and mirrored in corporeal existence.[22] For instance, *Humanism and Terror,* his most sustained discussion of politics, claims that the same "situated consciousness" that forges phenomenological perception breeds the compromises of political life. He explains, "We do not have a choice between purity and violence but between different kinds of violence. Inasmuch as we are incarnate beings, violence is our lot" (109). Whereas he elsewhere lauds an embodied consciousness for revealing "interbeing," he importantly does not mystify embodied existence by figuring it as devoid of aggressive or self-destructive tendencies. Here again, the body for Merleau-Ponty is neither ideally integrated nor purified; rather, even its affirmative energies are colored by antagonism and torment. This duality crystallizes another level of paradox within Merleau-Ponty's philosophy—namely, that corporeal perception is not a facile antidote to the depredations of political life. Although a phenomenology of embodiment registers the delicate equilibrium of collective existence, it also accounts for how embodiment innately disposes life to suffering and violence. This is why it is a misnomer to describe Merleau-Ponty as either a conventional humanist or advancing a straightforward ethics, and critics who dismiss his treatment of corporeality as overly enthusiastic or naive neglect how corporeal existence also ensnares life within relations that are inherently conflictual.

Given that the ontological condition of embodiment poses a constant reminder of the body's mortality and woundedness, embodiment itself might seem to represent something of a radical equalizer, one that eventually impinges on all expressions of freedom and consigns all beings to virtually identical fates. This universally shared servitude to the flesh offers another vantage from which to think about embodiment as inherently democratizing. In essence, the sheer inescapability of the body's wasting and frailty provides a powerful basis for rethinking interpersonal solidarity to countermand the presumption of atomistic self-interest that subtends liberal formulations of rights. Indeed, Merleau-Ponty himself cites the body's vulnerability precisely to rebuke the logic of individuation. As he explains, "At the very moment when I experience my existence...I discover within myself a kind of internal weakness standing in the way of my being totally individualized: a weakness which exposes me to the gaze of others."[23] For Merleau-Ponty, an awareness of one's own precarity simultaneously dispels monadic self-interest and orients the self toward the collective, a concurrence that in the preceding quote is magnified through the

use of the first person. An ontology of embodiment, in other words, necessarily acknowledges the self's chronic dependence on other lives, representing
a stave against egoism. Such a framework, in turn, rechannels debates about
social justice through questions of communal intertwining and embeddedness,
starkly diverging from the individualist calculi according to which theories of
rights are ordinarily plotted.

There is furthermore a sense in which embodied cognition can be
explained as more equitably disbursed than speech or reason, offering a
related though different type of leveling principle. While the capacity for
rational intellectual has offered a pretext for manifold discriminations over
time, emotion, sensory engagement, and imagination are arguably more uniformly distributed across populations (and even animal life). By the same
token, the inequities that do obtain within these affective, corporeal propensities are less clearly the baggage of preexisting privileges and entitlements. A
model of decision making that emphasized relational thickness and involvement versus objective detachment might therefore better account for how
those aptitudes valuably inform sociopolitical engagement, with the effect of
authorizing a wider scope of political actors as worthy, qualified participants.
As we can see, the inevitable barriers of citizenship are not alone responsible
for expelling certain lives from politics, as Arendt argued, but rather liberal
political thought's dualistic prioritization of reason and related ambivalence
toward embodiment must also be held accountable for those exceptions. An
analytic that verifies the body's contributions might thereby foster a more
vibrant as well as inclusive public sphere—and one less likely to perpetuate
the exclusions that human rights norms have failed to eradicate. In short,
if liberalism's neglect of embodiment is complicit with global modernity's
many injustices, Merleau-Ponty compels us to ask whether corporeal registers of affect and intuition might, paradoxically, interrupt the overly rationalistic, instrumentalizing logic that has permitted those harms. While neither
to minimize the chaotic drives that infuse corporeal being nor to suggest its
immunity to wrongdoing, the body's energies do not automatically co-opt
reason as a means of self-justification. To the contrary, they provide a type of
check on the corrosive tendencies of certain habits of abstract, quantifying
thought.

Nevertheless, while embodiment may represent a genuine universal, it
goes without saying that people's bodies are by no means equal but rather are
unevenly beset by maladies and afflictions, as well as enabled by exceptional
capacities. As a consequence, simply extolling embodiment will not tidily
equalize the metaphorical playing field. Instead, such a focus also requires
scrutiny of the handicaps and debilities that compromise bodies, charting

how they administer more totalizing effects. Taking embodiment as a theoretical starting point accordingly entails more than reclaiming its vital energies and defending their bearing on ethics-politics. In addition, a reliance on the analytic of embodiment requires that we probe how the nullification of bodily disparity in calculations of social justice has legalized structures of exclusion, subordinating some lives while enhancing others in ways that directly affect subject formation, at least as liberalism typically scripts that process. Of course, the body many be rendered innocuous or irrelevant for those who inhabit privileged subject positions—namely, for those who are white, male, straight, economically sufficient, and free of disabilities. For others, however, it chronically jeopardizes the very facets of selfhood that liberal thought likes to pretend can operate with relative independence. Affirmatively recasting embodiment as a ubiquitously shared site of disorder, flux, and brokenness would thus overwrite the stigma and shame that attach only to some bodies and not others. Such a recalibration of the symbolism of the liberal social body might thereby imaginatively undermine the ideal of corporeal symmetry, as it both effaces bodily difference and consolidates an array of negative stereotypes.

As may be clear by now, Merleau-Ponty's account of embodiment furnishes a basis for reconceptualizing just coexistence. For Merleau-Ponty, corporeal experience both derives from and reveals the self's immersion within all life, or what he calls the "flesh of the world." His posthumous "The Intertwining—the Chiasm" represents perhaps his most influential statement of how embodied perception fuses the self to other beings, as well as to inanimate objects. In this essay, he describes how the body, operating simultaneously as seer and visible object, undergoes a palpable "reciprocal insertion and intertwining of one in another" that engenders "intercorporeity."[24] Arising through both vision and "economies of touch,"[25] this synergy creates "reversibility," unleashing a "propagation of...exchanges" and a "fundamental fission," which "makes the organs of my body communicate and founds transitivity from one body to another."[26] Embodied modes of cognition, as such, not only divulge a collective equilibrium but also fuel kinetic energies that enmesh the self within "interbeing." Inciting what Merleau-Ponty's thought describes as something of an ethical charge, the phenomenal field that harnesses embodied perception naturally exteriorizes consciousness to generate a diffuse, shifting, and layered matrix of affective and visceral connectivities.

Other theorists have drawn on Merleau-Ponty's understanding of almost vitalistic interrelationality to theorize co-belonging in parallel terms. For example, David Michael Levin argues that for Merleau-Ponty embodied perception nourishes a "rudimentary, preconceptually formed, sense of justice."

According to Levin, Merleau-Ponty's "articulation of the intertwinings, trans-positions, and reversibilities taking place in the dimension of our intercor-poreality brings to light the body's deeply felt sense of justice—the natural, inaugural, and most radical grounding of the ideal of justice in the body of our experience."[27] Likewise, Diana Coole concludes that Merleau-Ponty's nondu-alist ontology offers "a project for a humanist politics after post-humanism."[28] Other theorists have instead addressed ethics rather than politics per se to adumbrate what Sara Ahmed calls "the social experience of dwelling with other bodies."[29] M. C. Dillon interprets Merleau-Ponty's notion of "revers-ibility" in such terms; for Dillon, touch reifies commonality but without the expectation of "coincidence," or "merging," that sight and intellectual knowledge presume.[30] The epistemological a priori of touch, in other words, does not culminate with the goals of identity, equality, or proportionality that inform liberal approaches to social justice and that, I have argued, smuggle in the many exclusions that enable the liberal public sphere. Rather, a focus on touch acknowledges the mobile, shifting forces that at times align and at others are imbalanced. Entailing simultaneous unity and paradox, the "intersubjec-tive" fabric of perception shows us to be, in Merleau-Ponty's terms, "tangled up in" one another through complex, layered, overdetermined contiguities.[31]

In sum, such a vision of how both selfhood and community are forged through shared beholdenness flouts a number of axioms that guide liberal topographies of the subject. In place of the atomistic, self-reliant individual, Merleau-Ponty unfolds a portrait of just cohabitation, envisaging humanity not as autonomous or radically free but instead as enmeshed within and reli-ant on the totality of being. Such an ontology configures subject formation as an odyssey not of rational self-determination but rather of the self's envel-opment within the haphazard rhythms of collective existence. Individuation, as such, becomes a hollow concept, given that subjectivity comes to be fash-ioned through a circuitous route of contingencies, fortuities, and "tangled" detours. In place of the rights and entitlements to which calculations of social justice are usually tethered, principles of obligation and responsibility would instead be controlling. Moreover, much as liberty becomes newly relative and contextual, Merleau-Ponty's insistence on the reciprocities that govern co-belonging refutes the presumption of human sovereignty over the animal, natural, and object worlds, thus opening up the ecological undercurrents to his phenomenology. If human welfare is inexorably yoked to all existence, *human* rights cannot antagonize that larger environment but must instead foster its intricate interdependence. Whereas liberal constructions of rights are generally both dualistic and human centered, such an ecology of social justice would instead purge debates about social justice of a certain kind of anthropocentrism.

To return to the body politic metaphor, Merleau-Ponty's notion of embodiment would further reconstellate its customary associations. His account of the embodied self's immersion in the lifeworld, as well as of thought's saturation by the perceptual field that embeds it, marshals very different assumptions from those that typically regulate the liberal social body's significations. As chapter 1 discussed, the body politic is generally imagined to be integrated and insular and, by extension, emptied of hostile and alien elements. Such a symbolic economy of the social body reinforces liberal theories of the human to produce an account of embodiment that not only consolidates the fiction of dignity subtending human rights but also secures the meaning and contours of our regnant national imaginaries. The myth of the ideally integrated human/social body thus buttresses the idea of the nation-state as nuclear and unified, a conceit that justifies both the policing of its borders and the ostracism of populations perceived to threaten that purity. However, Merleau-Ponty's assertion that to be embodied is to be not self-enclosed or sovereign or inviolable implicitly demands an imaginative repositioning of this topology of the body, natural and political. For Merleau-Ponty, the body is inherently porous and interpenetrated by other lives, its very essence to be infiltrated as well as constituted by external needs and demands. If we take his fragmented, dispersed body as an analogue for the nation, then it, too, becomes a space of permeability and flux. Akin to how individuals are interwoven with one another, so must the state be understood as comparatively suffused with claims and loyalties emerging from outside its geographical boundaries. Merleau-Ponty's figure of the "flesh" accordingly offers an imaginative vehicle for transcending the usual fixation on territoriality within discourses of nationalism to instead capture the multiform, fluid transnational circuits and flows that increasingly decenter the nation as a site of influence. Such a revised atlas of the body politic might thereby bypass the friend-enemy, host-parasite, resident-alien distinctions that frequently drive international relations. Whereas that binaristic logic compounds nationalism's exclusionary character, reconceiving the social body as a site of messy but fecund entanglements might both counteract the predatory tendencies of nationalism and better register the dynamics of globalization. In sum, these implications for the constitution of the body politic represent another way in which phenomenology might remedy certain of the exclusions that presently trouble liberal articulations of human rights.

A Nondualist Ontology

I have alluded to Merleau-Ponty's abandonment of dualism, but let me further explore what is widely regarded as the other revolutionary contribution of his oeuvre. Merleau-Ponty does not relinquish dualism to simply elevate body and matter over mind and thought. On the contrary, instead of positing the supremacy of either, Merleau-Ponty avers "the primacy of perception," effectively collapsing the distinction between immanence and transcendence.[32] His nondualist ontology thereby surmounts a continuum of the dichotomies that are foundational to analytic philosophy, legal reasoning, the scientific method, and liberal political theory alike. He subverts, among others, the bifurcation of subject/object, culture/nature, reason/emotion, public/private, interiority/exteriority, and human/animal. By dispelling these oppositions, his thought also forswears the many hierarchies they instate—namely, as they play out in the presumptions that civilization should exert dominion over nature, reason command the emotions, active subject manipulate passive object, public life wield authority over the private, and so on.[33] As such, his suspicion of specific brands of dualism bears intimately on questions of social justice. Moreover, this effort to depart from dualistic thought directly influences his philosophy of language. Since the forgoing binaries are ingrained within language itself, a core project of phenomenology is to denaturalize ordinary discourse, which the next section explores. Likewise, Merleau-Ponty disputes the apodictic precept of mind's mastery over body to implicitly challenge how reason, speech, writing, and language have, within the liberal tradition, come to demarcate the parameters of the human.

In chapter 1, I observed how the dualisms endemic to many liberal formulations of human rights and their supporting definitions of selfhood have provided an alibi for countless historical wrongs—with the effect of directly condoning manifold instances of imperialism, exclusion, and disenfranchisement. Within liberal explanatory regimes, the premise of reason's superiority permits the subordination of populations deemed subrational; the exaltation of public life consigns the domestic to inconsequence; and narratives of civilizational progress authorize the discipline and enslavement of peoples seen as developmentally arrested or existing in a state of nature. These and a collection of other hierarchical presumptions are basic to the philosophical architecture supporting liberal theories of the human—which is to say that liberal human rights norms often reproduce many of Western metaphysics' most damaging biases. Ironically, liberal articulations of human rights can thus work to fortify the very crimes that their standards on the surface aim to abolish, reinforcing rather than contesting the status quo. I therefore have argued that a dualistic reluctance toward embodiment subtends a number of the deepest paradoxes of human rights, and Merleau-Ponty's escape from the strictures of a certain species of dualism accordingly furnishes a theoretical itinerary for beginning to reverse those harms for which dualism has historically apologized. To the extent that modernity's institutionalized oppressions have been sanctioned by dualistic frames of reference, Merleau-Ponty purveys an alternate cosmology that instead might denaturalize those routine injustices.

Although Merleau-Ponty was relatively silent about the links between dualistic thought and structures of racism, he did defend his philosophy's relevance to ecology. Indeed, his late lectures posthumously collected as *Nature: Course Notes from the Collège de France* explicitly advocate for a nondomineering, anti-instrumentalist stance toward the natural world. Notably, corporeal experience itself nurtures this posture of respect; in essence, the perceptual field that actuates embodied cognition enfolds the self within a larger environment and thereby adumbrates its delicate balance:

> The nature within us must have some relation to the Nature outside of us; moreover, Nature outside of us must be unveiled to us by the Nature that we are.... By the nature in us, we can know Nature, and reciprocally it is from ourselves that living beings and even space speak to us; the concern is to collect outside of the radii that converge at the center [*foyer*] of Being. The deepening of Nature must clarify to us other Beings and their engagement in Being, this time directly. It is no longer a matter of ordering our reasons, but of seeing how all of this *holds together.* (206)

Akin to how Merleau-Ponty's notion of "intercorporeity" indexes the self's beholdenness to other human beings, Merleau-Ponty describes all nature as thus intertwined. These overlapping matrices of interdependence further divulge the essence of "Being," or ontology, and those dynamic patterns of symbiosis resist understanding via objective "reason"—a view that aligns with Merleau-Ponty's assertion that particular modes of aesthetic experience uniquely induce phenomenological insight. Merleau-Ponty accordingly collapses the human-animal and culture-nature binaries, undermining those justifications for the instrumental use and appropriation of nature. While Merleau-Ponty's focus on embodiment might seem to marshal its own form of anthropocentrism, he nonetheless describes human existence as reliant on nature—a relationship that, here again, is crystallized in the kinetics of embodied perception and how they parallel the overarching reciprocities that supervise the lifeworld.[34] Indeed, Merleau-Ponty lauds nature in particular as crucial to instigating phenomenological disclosure—which is to say that his politics are ancillary to a distinct comportment toward the environment. Yet by endowing nature with such exemplarity, he does more than jettison a key rationale for human domination over natural and animal life; on the contrary, he avers human responsibility to the environment, if only because human welfare is contingent on its cultivation. It is therefore no wonder that Merleau-Ponty has been espoused by proponents of deep ecology and other environmentalist philosophies, although such terms had not been coined at his death.[35] Similarly, we can ascertain why his thought might help to expatiate sociocultural worldviews, or what many refer to as indigenous epistemologies, that do not bifurcate nature from culture but instead treat them as holistically integrated.[36]

By the same token, this vision of the synergies overseeing nature overturns the dichotomy between active subject and passive object. For Merleau-Ponty, nature is not passive, inert matter awaiting manipulation and control; rather, it is congregated by mobile, vacillating stimuli that both generate and harness perception. As such, the material world exhibits its own quasi-agentive and fecund energies, unleashing almost vitalistic reverberations that exert a constant pull on consciousness. Precisely by restoring such dynamism to nature does Merleau-Ponty critique the scientific method, which he blames for inuring perception to those agile, vibrant forces. In general, he blames scientific reason and empirical modes of analysis for not only perpetuating the legacy of Cartesianism but also legalizing the structures of oppression that ensue from the scientific quest for mastery. For instance, he complains that science is "not an unmotivated instance." Unlike the philosopher, whose goal is "to see," the scientist strives to "find a foothold" for "intervening,"[37] an aim that, however, induces "alienation" in the observer. Merleau-Ponty thereby construes science as appropriative, instrumentalizing, and self-interested, and that colonizing mindset divests both science's own explanatory arsenal and its objects of inquiry of those properties that he instead recuperates as indispensable to ontology. By reducing matter to its use value, scientific rationalism eclipses the affective and visceral intensities that reside within and are propagated by the material world. In effect, Merleau-Ponty thus censures scientific discourse for both deadening and habituating perception, or for submerging the gestalt of incipiencies that make up the phenomenal field.

It is in opposition and in order to surmount this perceptual paralysis that Merleau-Ponty develops his phenomenology. Whereas instrumental reason mutes and discredits the body's interwoven faculties of perception—with the further consequence of impoverishing language—phenomenology seeks to rejuvenate those propensities. Here again, the interrelated goals of an embodied consciousness, of certain kinds of aesthetic experience, and of ethics-politics converge. For Merleau-Ponty, distinctly embodied modalities of aesthetic engagement can remedy the experiential aphasia wrought by scientific and empiricist thought. Merleau-Ponty thus forswears the "objectifying" impulses of science, for instance, as he explains that "to look at an object is to inhabit it, and from this habitation to grasp all things in terms of the aspect which they present to it. But in so far as I see those things too, they remain abodes open to my gaze."[38] Whereas science aims to control and regiment knowledge, for Merleau-Ponty the embedded observer is dependent on the haphazard vicissitudes of the material world. Physical matter is, as such, not secondary to human intellection but rather structures its genesis. Yet this relationship between subject and object does not render the former captive to the latter; instead, for Merleau-Ponty matter is pregnant with an affective density and richness that is fundamentally enabling. Such abundance incarnates human consciousness in a conversion that produces a prolific and "vertiginous proximity," in essence revitalizing human understanding in the midst of the torpor of empirical rationalism.[39] This conception of a profound symbiosis between material culture and human selfhood is one way that Merleau-Ponty offers a point of entry into theorizing objects or things. As he, for instance, relates, "The spirit of society is realized, transmitted, and perceived through the cultural objects which it bestows upon itself and in the midst of which it lives."[40] Such materialism represents another statement of how and why the self must be described as immersed within a specific historical and regional milieu, here again contravening the reigning logic of human entitlement and sovereignty that commonly organizes liberal formulations of human rights.

Along with this emphasis on the ontological freightedness of ordinary objects, Merleau-Ponty's phenomenology can be seen to contribute to a politics of the everyday—here, too, staging a departure from dominant expectations about human rights. Whereas contemporary human rights rhetoric can encourage sensationalism and hyperbole, Merleau-Ponty foregrounds the proximate and familiar. This attention to mundane experience counteracts the frequent tendency to characterize human rights abuses as singular, exemplary, or sublime, an impulse that emerges within both popular human rights discourses and many accounts of deconstructive ethics.[41] Moreover, while liberal political theorists such as Arendt often define political practice in terms of its separation from the private, Merleau-Ponty's reflections on materiality implicitly aver the importance of that latter realm. Although human rights may seem to acquire urgency only when put to the test in the dramatic theater of international diplomacy and law, Merleau-Ponty's phenomenology excavates realities of suffering that are inadvertently sidelined within such an emphasis on the macrocosmic and grand scale. The literary texts that occasion this book's case studies therefore similarly urge us to concentrate on commonplace, routine wounds in ways that compel us to rethink the social meanings of human rights beyond the compass of their liberal formations.

That said, Merleau-Ponty's emphasis on the situated, proximate nature of consciousness does not culminate with an uncomplicated embrace of the commonplace and familiar. On the contrary, for Merleau-Ponty routine practice also demands heightened scrutiny precisely because it has the propensity to domesticate and habituate injustice. In other words, quotidian experience, although it harbors paramount ontological significance, can equally serve to mask wrongdoing. We thus confront another reason why the agenda of phenomenology is commonly described as one of rupture or unconcealment. Given that oppression becomes normalized through repetition as well as ingrained within the very fabric of language, phenomenological perception aspires to subvert those gravitations and gain access to recognitions that effectively originate prior to being installed within custom. By "returning" to the building blocks of lived experience, phenomenology reclaims those rudimentary units of perception to enlist them as antidotes to the many patterns of cruelty that have haunted global modernity. And because such wrongs have come to be inscribed within the inner workings of language itself, the status of discourse is at the heart of the phenomenological project. On that note, let me now turn to an examination of the profit of Merleau-Ponty's philosophy of language for imaginatively recalibrating the different discourses of human rights.

A Grounded Account of Language

Although incurring less attention than his meditations on embodiment, Merleau-Ponty's phenomenology is grounded in a philosophy of language. Notably, Merleau-Ponty's thought here deviates from many poststructuralist accounts of semiotics, largely in that he does not privilege textuality and language. By extension, he refuses a strict constructivist account of subjectivity, and precisely for these reasons does he offer an apt lens for evaluating the doubled discourses of human rights. In fact, politics were by no means peripheral to Merleau-Ponty's thought; rather, the problem of how political opportunism corrupts language preoccupied him. In *The World of Perception,* a short text that compiles seven radio lectures delivered in late 1948, he indicts political speech in illustrative terms, complaining, "There is no longer a single word in our political vocabulary that has not been used to refer to the most different, even opposed, real situations: consider freedom, socialism, democracy, reconstruction, renaissance, union rights. . . . And this is not a ruse on the part of their leaders: the ruse lies in the things themselves" (80). For Merleau-Ponty, this syndrome is not unique to any specific idiom but rather infects politics itself. And since no political language is immune from such an eventuality, it cannot be guarded against by adherence to what Merleau-Ponty calls "noble ideologies" (81); in other words, the problem cannot be solved by substituting one explanatory regime or lexicon with another.[42] Through these reflections Merleau-Ponty grapples with the tendency of language to ossify and congeal, especially when deployed to sanction exploitative or disingenuous ends. When language's nexus with meaning becomes severed, its reservoirs further grow exhausted, preventing it from acting as an imaginative stave against wrongdoing.

Like many of his poststructuralist successors, Merleau-Ponty espouses a view of power as anonymous, pervasive, and diffuse. If individual interlocutors are unaware of the "ruse" to which they fall victim, it is because covert liaisons infiltrate all social institutions and practices, including the basic fabric of language. Such a conception of politics consigns isolated actors, despite their best intentions, to inadvertent collaboration with those pressures, even through mere resort to speech. This is a conundrum we will revisit multiple times throughout the literary case studies that follow, whether in terms of how the afterlives of apartheid have come to taint the English language in South Africa or how the dualistic architecture of language, broadly speaking, can foreclose dissent. In whatever case, Merleau-Ponty's philosophy of language suggests how the centripetal energies of discourse erode its affinity with justice. This is one reason Merleau-Ponty holds a fatalistic view of politics, calling it a "fundamental disease" that people can "never renounce."[43] Nevertheless, he equally champions linguistic malleability for engendering internal resistances within language, and he vests phenomenology with the onus to disrupt and thereby revitalize those mechanisms. Embodied perception, as such, serves as an indispensable corrective to the natural gravitations of language, promising to restore to politics its kinship with social justice.

Merleau-Ponty was thus highly attuned to the solidarities between language and power, and phenomenological insight gains urgency in part because of its ability to mine the hypocrisies that riddle political practice. Accordingly, his conclusions about political language in many ways parallel this book's approach to the paradoxes of human rights. Much as he despairs of the dualities that slant all "political vocabularies," human rights are increasingly rife with duplicity and contradiction. These tensions are especially pronounced within liberal human rights discourses and norms, as they marshal what I have described as an artificial and truncated picture of the subject. The fictions of selfhood that consolidate liberal articulations of human rights are, among many other liabilities, inordinately prone to ratify egoistic self-interest, to devalue registers of experience that elude rational intellection, and to entrench exceptions to their own ostensible protections. Yet while something about the idiom of human rights might seem to render that lexicon inordinately susceptible to misuse, Merleau-Ponty reminds us that any visible, charged, and compelling political grammar is liable to such infirmity. Indeed, the greater a term's descriptive currency, the more likely it will conspire with the machinery that authors injustice. If human rights are a "ruse," then their sheer popularity is what elicits their manipulation—meaning that this particular paradox of human rights is ironically a by-product of their discourse's very success.

Merleau-Ponty, however, explains vastly more than the relay through which political language recruits its own corruption and inelasticity. Rather, his philosophy of language equally tracks the polar operation—namely, how discourse undergoes desedimentation and is revivified, its somnolent reserves refurbished with meaning and significance, even if fleeting and episodic. This focus on linguistic flux and motility opens up another dimension of Merleau-Ponty's nonconstructivist account of subjectivity; here, Merleau-Ponty endows bodily perception with provisional access to immanent forms of understanding that are encountered before being fully submitted to linguistic containment or even intellectualization. Such an explanation of the juncture between perception and language clearly diverges from much poststructuralist theory to preserve a greater space for intentional intervention within the operations of discourse. We can, in turn, further grasp the implications of how Merleau-Ponty transcendends mind-body dualism; he envisages a perceptual field laden with a concatenation of variegated, mutating, and inchoate forces that the self first inhabits on a corporeal level. Phenomenological perception, as such, gains access to these synergies before they are processed either semantically or vis-à-vis the mind's faculties of interpretation. Such an embodied consciousness, that is, originates to a degree antecedent to language and acculturation; as Merleau-Ponty explains, "before being reason, humanity is another corporeity."[44] While such modes of cognition of course become arrested within and regimented by discourse, they nonetheless arise prior to and remain partially independent from the mediations of language, which is why they can productively destabilize preestablished constructions of reality.

A series of noteworthy consequences ensue from this theory of language. First, Merleau-Ponty avers that corporeal perception furnishes insight of paramount ontological importance despite (or, more accurately, because of) its supralinguistic status, even while cognition translates it into symbolic form. Second, since phenomenological disclosure occurs on a separate plane that is both partially unregulated by and capable of interceding within the preformed textile of language, experience is grounded rather than either wholly scripted or caught up in the infinite play of *différance*. Although the subject is not entirely self-founding, selfhood emanates directly from corporeal dimensions of engagement with the world, as they are untotalized by social convention and normativity. Simply put, Merleau-Ponty thus attests to species of meaning that, while evanescent and paradoxical, are self-present. An embodied consciousness "rediscover[s] a commerce with the world and a presence to the world which is older than intelligence," or, stated differently, "re-achiev[es] a direct and primitive contact."[45] Accordingly, we can discern why phenomenology is often construed as staging, although usually with reference to Husserl's thought, a reduction or return.

Third, and perhaps most important, embodied perception can work to rend the existing fabric of language, particularly when language has become sterile or diluted. Implicitly, then, language is not all-encompassing but beset with fissures and gaps that allow intervals for the subject's creative reinvention. Fourth, Merleau-Ponty preserves a modicum of individual authority over discourse.[46] Although language is "like an instrument with its own inertia, its own demands, constraints, and internal logic," one can seize that momentum. As Merleau-Ponty avers, language "nevertheless remain[s] open to the initiatives of the subject," entailing that it is protean, dynamic, and ceaselessly iterating while yet able to be harnessed by the intentional subject.[47] While such a theory of language might resemble aspects of Derridean *différance,* Merleau-Ponty postulates that certain realms of experience are not necessarily prone to those semantic deferrals and foreclosures. Particularly when discourse becomes laden with duplicities or overly rigid, phenomenological awareness can fracture and thereby reorient language toward alternate experiential registers, reinjecting it with meaning—albeit meaning that is, once again, transitory and evanescent. To apply Merleau-Ponty's philosophy of language to the predicament of human rights, his sense of language's labile, self-generating capacities suggests how human rights talk might be comparatively rejuvenated, a task that Merleau-Ponty notably vests with the actively engaged and perceiving subject.

In sum, Merleau-Ponty unfolds a relatively innovative heuristic for analyzing discourse, as well as for charting how individual perception can reinvigorate rote, decaying speech. When language petrifies because of either routine or misuse, the dual links between language-experience and language-meaning are eroded—a condition that paradoxically both frustrates and enables phenomenological disclosure. The inner workings of language inevitably cause its ties with social justice to deteriorate; as it becomes habituated, language naturally calcifies, obstructing facets of experience that are decidedly ethical and just. Here, too, we can grasp the relevance of phenomenology to politics. Whereas global modernity has aggravated the innate conservatism of political life, phenomenology aims to interrupt and reverse that gravitation toward the status quo. As such, Merleau-Ponty implicitly correlates individual alienation within the spent archives of language with the political lethargy of modernity, holding the depleted reservoirs of language in part responsible for the stagnation of politics. In doing so, even as he deprivileges writing and textuality, he implicitly suggests why politics must skirmish in the trenches of language, fighting battles over ideology on the level of discourse.

Above all, Merleau-Ponty correlates the fatigue and inertia endemic to political life with the tendency of language to congeal and thereby submerge "interbeing"—which is to say that politics itself can ironically deaden perception to the self's intertwining within the larger cosmos and its reciprocities. To be sure, language necessarily organizes consciousness; yet it also obstructs domains of experience that are invariably ethical, further illuminating why its operations require periodic suspension for phenomenological insight to emerge. That said, Merleau-Ponty simultaneously acknowledges why such encounters with interbeing can be unhinging, if not alarming, requiring their suppression within ordinary existence. Quotidian speech, although liable to mask injustice, helpfully covers over the "mysterious" elements of being, returning us here again to the centrality of paradox within Merleau-Ponty's thought. When phenomenological perception fragments ordinary habits of cognition, it exposes not consoling visions of wholeness and plenitude but instead life's fundamental perplexities—perplexities that centrally both inhere and are mirrored in the predicament of embodiment. Indeed, there is an important way in which Merleau-Ponty holds language itself responsible for the elision of embodiment, a condition that I have argued is generally silenced within the liberal intellectual tradition.

This agenda of rupture has led many theorists to characterize phenomenology as a technique for disclosure rather than a promotion of one formulation of truth over others. As a philosophy of practice, phenomenology treats such inspired modes of understanding as meritorious because they defy translation into normative schemes of value or fact, returning us to Merleau-Ponty's critique of the objectifying impulses of science. In contrast, phenomenology "stud[ies] the *advent* of being to consciousness," or the awakening of typically dormant registers of perception.[48] In *Sense and*

Non-sense, Merleau-Ponty delineates this constellation of aims: "Phenomenological or existential philosophy is largely an expression of surprise at this
inherence of the self in the world and in others, a description of this paradox
and permeation, and an attempt to make us *see* the bond between subject
and world, between subject and others, rather than to *explain* it as the classical
philosophies did by resorting to absolute spirit" (58). Merleau-Ponty accordingly describes phenomenology as an exercise in unconcealment aimed at
divulging the self's cohabitation with other beings; however, he simultaneously asserts that such relationality resists "explanation" vis-à-vis scientific
inquiry, reasoned objectivity, and propositional speech alike. This distinction
importantly segregates phenomenological awareness from genres of exegesis
that would solidify, rationalize, or purify "surprise" of its essential paradox.
By extension, Merleau-Ponty might seem to caution against related ambitions ingrained within the law. Not only does he warn against the pursuit
of empirical truth, protesting how that goal risks censoring vital dimensions of experience, but he interrogates rule-bound and normative claims to
universality. Instead valorizing situatedness and contingency, Merleau-Ponty
evinces significant wariness about the impetus to prescriptively codify trans-
cultural and transhistorical rules, given that such a project would quell the
layered indeterminacies that cohere the lifeworld.

This rejection of explanatory regimes typically employed to authenticate
knowledge, however, leaves Merleau-Ponty in something of a descriptive
and rhetorical vacuum. Indeed, Merleau-Ponty introduces his concept of
the "flesh" in such terms: "There is no name in traditional philosophy to
designate it" (139). Thereby marking key limits that confront philosophical
thought, Merleau-Ponty proceeds through an alternate lexicon that instead
enlarges the paradoxes, capturing the texture of the "surprise," on which
his ontology is predicated. Since analytic discourse would diminish those
vital qualities, Merleau-Ponty uses a style and manner of presentation that
we might conceive of as strategically confounding, or intentionally incommensurate to philosophical reason's conventional discursive arsenal. On the
one hand, this cognizance of philosophy's limits motivates Merleau-Ponty's
investment in aesthetic engagement and its exemplary capacity to instigate
embodied perception, as I will conclude by considering. On the other hand,
Merleau-Ponty develops a theological vocabulary of faith, commitment, and
divinity both to evade the shortfalls of empiricist rationalism and to expatiate the perceptual energies that he heralds as integral to his phenomenology.

As I have suggested, for Merleau-Ponty a consciousness of embodiment
displays not only life's matrices of interdependence but also the precarity
and finitude of all existence. These conjoined recognitions elicit a posture

of humility and respect—or, in place of rational certitude, something akin to trust. Merleau-Ponty describes such a disposition as an "act of faith" and "unreserved commitment which is never completely justified." Both fugitive and unverifiable, phenomenological perception flouts objective truth to instead demand a type of epistemological leap of faith. In Merleau-Ponty's terms, the "commitment" that phenomenology inspires "always assumes that one's affirmation surpasses one's knowledge, that one believes by hearsay, that one gives up the rule of sincerity for that of responsibility."[49] By invoking "responsibility," Merleau-Ponty relates phenomenological insight to justice and ethics, which he construes as equally governed by paradox. In effect, Merleau-Ponty's rhetoric of faith thereby indexes the nonevidentiary tenor of phenomenological understanding, as it rescripts doubt, fragility, and intellectual uncertainty to be fecund and enabling. The many ambivalences that pervade embodied cognition are therefore not, as within much post-Enlightenment metaphysical thought, impediments or embarrassing residues of human captivity that must be overcome. To the contrary, they both facilitate a phenomenological consciousness and signal its desired outcome.

In addition to this grammar of wonder and surprise, Merleau-Ponty employs a God-concept to designate the constraints of empirical rationalism:

> There is no means to think the two at once, for example, the separation and the union of the soul and the body. The contradiction is constitutive of the human. The domain of the human is always equivocal, his body is neither mechanized nor finalized from the point of view of the soul. It is not by thinking according to human being, but according to God that we can solidly think the elements of which human being is made. The incomprehensibility of God, which is nowise his unknowability and even less his irrationality, but "the formal reason of the infinitive," is indispensable for allowing us to resolve precisely the problem of "the ground of truth and the limits of our intelligence."[50]

Merleau-Ponty here underscores why the experience of one's embodiment is inherently "contradictory." Identifying that state as "constitutive" of the "human" yet "incomprehensible" within rational thought, he claims paradox as fruitful precisely because it confounds intellectual resolution and containment. By likening the enigmas of corporeal existence to the unfathomable aspects of a divinity, he endows those attributes with almost religious significance. Much as the notion of the divine reifies the limits of human cognition, a consciousness of embodiment crystallizes core perplexities that are near existential in their fiber. These tensions offer another point of entry into why the phenomenological project is predicated on rupture: insofar as such "constitutive contradictions" vivify the bounds of human intellection, they cannot be circumscribed within propositional thought. In order to elucidate them, Merleau-Ponty strives to capsize the existing fabric of language and the practiced conventions of interpretation that philosophy has naturalized.

This idiom of theology is largely expedient for Merleau-Ponty, geared to elucidate the features of phenomenological perception rather than religious belief per se. Nevertheless, it brings me to his thought's profit for interrogating assumptions about secularity, as they inform standard definitions of the liberal democratic public sphere and human rights. As chapter 1 considered, theorists have complained that the logic of secularity occludes affective, embodied dimensions of selfhood, whether they arise through interpersonal attachments, belief, or the basic experience of suffering. By defining civic participation in terms of reasoned deliberation, the secular thesis fails to apprehend the self's incorporation within community, minimizing the spiritualized allegiances that gird sociopolitical belonging. As William Connolly argues, secularism either "ignores" or "disparages" the "visceral register of subjectivity and intersubjectivity," entailing that "it forfeits some of the very resources needed to foster a generous pluralism."[51] Along similar lines, Saba Mahmood's work on "piety" challenges the secular emphasis on reasoned intellection by studying "the immanent form bodily practices take" as "the terrain upon which the topography of the subject comes to be mapped."[52] If the body, as these theorists suggest, inspires fidelities that elude secularism's artificial protocols, then Merleau-Ponty offers a lucrative framework for delineating such nonrationalist attachments that refuse to fully conform to what Mahmood calls a "semiotic ideology" of "correct reading practices."[53] While Merleau-Ponty's reclamation of embodied experience thereby corrects the body's erasure within liberal formulations of the human, he also suggests how political thought might recuperate the local, nonexceptional, and private components of social membership and coparticipation. Such realms of experience not only inflect religious belief and practice but also valuably underwrite many nonreligious social formations. Whereas determinations of rational choice govern most philosophical renditions of democratic process, Merleau-Ponty's defamiliarizing lexicon of faith and the soul contests that logic, demonstrating why his own jarring, paradox-laden style of analysis and a philosophy of embodiment are accomplices in an intimately related project.

Phenomenology and Aesthetics

Given how Merleau-Ponty prioritizes sensory perception, it should be no surprise that he assigns an exemplary role to art. Indeed, an exploration of

Merleau-Ponty's conception of aesthetic experience will refine and lend specificity to his account of embodied cognition. For Merleau-Ponty, art possesses a deep affinity with ontology—being variously disposed to expose the lifeworld's texture, to simulate phenomenological insight, and to trigger such disclosure. Certain modalities of aesthetic expression are thus uniquely poised to replicate the contours of phenomenological revelation; the artistic medium can paradigmatically "interrupt the normal process of seeing," furthering what Merleau-Ponty identifies as a cardinal goal of philosophy.[54] While the majority of Merleau-Ponty's writings on aesthetics address how painting can estrange the subject's ordinary habits of seeing, Merleau-Ponty also devoted meaningful attention to literature. For instance, he cites Proust as unrivaled in having demonstrated "the bond between the flesh and the idea, between the visible and the interior armature which it manifests and it conceals."[55] This book's succeeding chapters will look to literature for that very purpose of tracking how aesthetic experience can map the unfolding of an embodied consciousness, in the process suspending ordinary thought and discourse to excavate submerged registers of understanding.

Beyond his appreciation for Proust, Merleau-Ponty exalts poetry for "replac[ing] the usual way of referring to things...with a mode of expression that describes the essential structure of the thing and accordingly forces us to enter into that thing." In doing so, Merleau-Ponty characterizes phenomenologically generative art as more than merely opposed to ideational thought but rather itself infused with almost sensible properties. As he relates, certain kinds of aesthetic involvement are effectively internalized within the body. Art, in turn, holds a paramount ability to illuminate both the self's enmeshment within and perception's saturation by a phenomenal field. Moreover, such an understanding deciphers aesthetic engagement in terms that are suggestively egalitarian, given that Merleau-Ponty does not explain art vis-à-vis either privileged access to transcendental ideals or its derivation from orthodox cultural archives. Rather, he valorizes how aesthetic experience in its materialist genesis both emanates from and verifies the subject's commonplace interactions and surroundings.

Moreover, Merleau-Ponty correlates the features of phenomenologically compelling art with those of aesthetically vibrant species of discourse. For instance, he distinguishes between "the poetic use of language and everyday chatter." Whereas ordinary speech ossifies to become inert and inelastic, poetry works "as a creation of language, one which cannot be fully translated into ideas."[56] Precisely in being irreducible to propositional form, poetry guards against its own stagnation, at the same time claiming an exemplary ability to instigate phenomenological disclosure. Merleau-Ponty here lauds certain artistic genres and styles over others for their potential to thwart codification by the intellect as they instead catalyze phenomenological awareness. Unlike either evidentiary or analytic discourse, such aesthetically and ontologically fertile registers of presentation contain repositories of meaning that are inexhaustible because of their very ambiguity, rendering it interpretation's task to enlarge and imaginatively occupy those paradoxes, although only to preserve their strangeness. Within such a hermeneutic, phenomenologically conscientious art and language alike harbor the ability to surmount the pervasive alienation of political modernity, which Merleau-Ponty attributes to both the dominance of abstract rationalism and the sedimentations of language. Whereas these circumstances stifle corporeal dimensions of perception, certain forms of art can instead reactivate such faculties of engagement, serving as an antidote to modernity's progressive impoverishment of language, meaning, and experience.[57]

In short, this privileging of art aligns it with the central ambitions of phenomenology, as both aim to "formulat[e] an experience of the world, a contact with the world which precedes all thought *about* the world."[58] Once again, we see how Merleau-Ponty enshrines perceptual energies that originate prior to the mediations of the intellect. Indeed, art in this respect almost claims superiority over philosophy, being exempt from its dual agendas of persuasion and proof. Merleau-Ponty explains:

> Now art, especially painting, draws upon this fabric of brute meaning which operationalism would prefer to ignore. Art and only art does so in full innocence. From the writer and the philosopher, in contrast, we want opinions and advice. We will not allow them to hold the world suspended.[59]

Merleau-Ponty heralds art for its resistance to being either instrumentalized or subdued, and in this way do the primordial insights it unleashes work to disorient the perceiving subject's ingrained habits of cognition. Such textures of awareness are inherently antonymic to analytic reason, entailing that phenomenologically resonant aesthetic production will withstand appropriation to fulfill didactic or "operationalist" ends. No doubt Merleau-Ponty might here appear to subscribe to an arguably outmoded view of art's ideological neutrality and autonomy. Yet while such a fantasy of the unmotivated, "innocent" artwork should give pause, Merleau-Ponty nevertheless captures something crucial about the perceptual faculties that art can harness, as well as how its mechanisms of disclosure elude empirical or rationalistic systems of explanation. In turn, his philosophy of art is not entirely opposed to deconstructive accounts of literature's radical singularity, given that both laud art for eliciting forms of disclosure that yield distinct implications for justice and ethics. For Merleau-Ponty, aesthetic experience and phenomenological perception alike procure kinds of understanding that refuse to be drafted to fulfill any given political program or ideological agenda, which is precisely why they furnish recognitions that can be ethical. As such, they mine the fissures and foreclosures that dominant regimes of truth cover over, acting as a check against their colonizing tendencies.

These intransigent energies possessed by certain forms of art notably manifest themselves on the dual levels of content and form. Substantively, the fugitive, evanescent insights unleashed by phenomenologically productive art converge on the indeterminacy and ambivalence constituting human existence, as are quintessentially materialized in the condition of embodiment. Whereas scientific reason seeks to discipline and overcome such paradoxes, creative expression and phenomenological perception alike aim to amplify them. Particular genres and styles are thus especially prone to arouse such corporeal, paradox-laden modalities of responsiveness and the distinct cosmology they unfold. Within aesthetically rich texts, as this book's final chapter will especially consider, the varied elements of tonality, rhythm, sonority, metaphor, imagery, tactility, tempo, and aurality all collaborate to animate the body's many affective and visceral appetencies. Phenomenologically charged art consequently reveals the senses as interpenetrating one another in a type of gestalt, engendering and interweaving their mutual interactions. Much as Merleau-Ponty describes how bodily cognition incarnates a phenomenal field made up of a concatenation of mobile, shifting forces, certain kinds of literary engagement equally can lead the senses to collude in a "propagation of . . . exchanges" and a "fundamental fission."[60] Art, that is, can paradigmatically divulge and unfurl the tangled densities of embodied perception, verifying their experiential authority and intelligence. Here, too, the body's many reciprocities parallel those that supervise the lifeworld as a whole, with the internal dynamics of corporeal perception mirroring the patterns of intertwining that cohere all existence. It is in this respect, then, that an embodied aesthetic becomes profitable for theorizing social justice, given that it opens up the delicate interbalances that administer the lifeworld in its totality. By extension, such a hermeneutic brings into high relief the limits of both ideology critique and an exclusive focus on structure and form; quite differently, Merleau-Ponty's philosophy of aesthetics demands that we attend to the affective, corporeal synergies spurred by certain manners of aesthetic engagement.

In light of this celebration of art, it is not unusual or surprising that Merleau-Ponty's own writing evinces qualities that are highly aesthetic, if not fully poetic. Whereas he rejects the protocols of scientific rationalism, his rhythmic, lyrical prose itself simulates sensory perception and its erratic emergence. Indeed, we might look to the elements of Merleau-Ponty's own style to develop an account of phenomenologically generative aesthetic experience. Imitating how the senses conspire, Merleau-Ponty's language and imagery collapse multiple registers of bodily perception into one another. In extolling painting, for example, Merleau-Ponty praises it for expressing "space which the heart feels," an analogy that imbues emotion with tactile, visceral, and spatial attributes.[61] Judith Butler draws similar conclusions when she describes Merleau-Ponty's prose as "seek[ing], in its own rhythms and cadences, to cast language in the mold of the relation he attempts to describe."[62] Such incantatory language and impressionistic metaphors perhaps most visibly compose Merleau-Ponty's notion of the "flesh." As he relates, the vital fleshiness of the lifeworld is made "visible" through "a sort of folding back, invagination, or padding" that demands "a style, allusive and elliptical like every style."[63] Once again, matters of ontology and aesthetics are by no means separate but instead redouble and confirm one other. Merleau-Ponty delineates this concept of the flesh by endowing it with tangible qualities, and, in doing so, he not only testifies to its material basis but also suggests that its ideational content must enact a transposition of the senses. In sum, the very effort to theoretically grasp Merleau-Ponty's ontology requires both a channeling and an amalgamation of the multiform faculties of embodied perception.

It is for this reason that Merleau-Ponty directs us toward a relatively innovative conception of what a literary imagination might both foster and unveil. Critics have widely acclaimed the capacity of narrative literature to cultivate an ethical response, whether that response emerges from impressions of parity and likeness or instead radical alterity. However, the politics of reading implicit to Merleau-Ponty's thought both begins and ends with a phenomenology of embodied experience. For Merleau-Ponty, ethically salutary aesthetic engagement actuates the body's perceptual faculties, showing them to cooperate in ways that enlist the fullness of the self. This almost vitalistic fusion effectively replicates and thereby adumbrates the fabric of the self's immersion within the larger material and social environment that forges perception. Much as aesthetic involvement invigorates the senses to reveal how they collude, it divulges a parallel symbiosis that conjoins nature as a whole. To be sure, such a vision of palpable intertwining culminates in a cosmology that radically diverges from the tenets of empiricist rationalism, hence compelling Merleau-Ponty's theological idiom of faith and belief. Relatedly, his embodied politics of aesthetic engagement foregrounds the centrality of paradox to the tangled incipiencies that cohere the phenomenal field, self-hood, and intercorporeity alike. Such a notion of paradox rescripts it as fertile and generative, even while it gauges the body's inherent finitude and vulnerability. It is to such ends that Merleau-Ponty's embrace of particular modes of contradiction might be adapted to better reckon with the many paradoxes of human rights—especially given that they, too, ultimately surround the body's fundamental precarity and brokenness.

In sum, Merleau-Ponty offers an innovative as well as challenging explanatory prism through which to refract and thereby theoretically compensate for the missed opportunities of human rights. His thought, of course, does not independently offer a solution to those failures. Yet what he provides is an avenue for correcting key erasures that sustain the liberal subject entitled to human rights. If liberal topographies of the human envision that subject in terms that are truncated and anemic, his phenomenology reconstellates that imaginative terrain and its corresponding symbolic economy of the body—natural and civil. Above all, his thought recuperates those corporeal and affective layers of selfhood that liberal theories of social justice minimize and occlude. As such, Merleau-Ponty's attention to embodiment opens up why and how that condition's elision has apologized for modernity's many exclusions and other sociopolitical wrongs. And in remedying those omissions, he further gestures toward an itinerary for recasting human rights discourses and norms beyond liberalism's orbit. In particular, Merleau-Ponty's emphasis on the intertwining of all life in its mutual woundedness countermands the interrelated fictions of human mastery, freedom, autonomy, and dignity—along with the enabling myth of bodily integrity. We might, therefore, look to phenomenology to restore an experiential density—or what Merleau-Ponty might call "fleshiness"—to our reigning discourses of community and self-hood alike. This book's remaining chapters now set out to conduct precisely such a recalibration of the sociocultural meanings of embodiment by way of the heterogeneous energies of narrative literature.

❧ CHAPTER THREE

Constituting the Liberal Subject of Rights

Salman Rushdie's Midnight's Children

This book's literary case studies begin with Salman Rushdie, a writer who has personally lived out the nexus between free speech and human rights. Catapulted into the international limelight when Ayatollah Khomeini issued a fatwa in response to *The Satanic Verses* (1988), Rushdie and his career might seem to offer a parable for freedom of expression.[1] However, this chapter investigates not the real-world human rights controversy spawned by *The Satanic Verses* but rather *Midnight's Children* (1981), a novel that, although it garnered widespread literary acclaim, did not yet make Rushdie a global celebrity. Awarded the 1981 Booker Prize and then in 1993 named the "Booker of Bookers," *Midnight's Children* is widely understood to exemplify the theoretical preoccupations of postcolonial studies—not only manifesting high postmodernism's aesthetic difficulty, experimentation, and play but also verifying the poststructuralist emphasis on writing and textuality. Yet this chapter reads *Midnight's Children* against those grains to contemplate how it adjudicates the yield of liberalism as a theory of politics and selfhood, probing that broad framework's ability to negotiate the many challenges that have confronted both the incorporation of the postcolonial nation-state and the self-constitution of the liberal individual—a construct that, I have argued, lends crucial explanatory authority to human rights.

Midnight's Children conducts an epic sweep of the history of the Indian sub-continent over much of the twentieth century, above all recounting the first thirty years following postcolonial independence. As a saga of that tumultuous era, the novel has frequently been interpreted as a meditation on the "pitfalls of national consciousness," an approach that treats the misadventures of its first-person narrator and protagonist Saleem Sinai, born on the precise instant of independence, as an analogue for the fledging nations of India and, to a degree, Pakistan.[2] Indeed, *Midnight's Children* portrays both the trials of that strife-ridden transition and the unique texture of Indian nationalism; however, in doing so, it also mines the many values and expectations through which the newly sovereign Indian nation sought to define its legal and political culture. While Saleem's birth inaugurates postcoloniality, it simultaneously ushers in a particular vision of both national independence and individual liberty, and *Midnight's Children* charts the hazards as well as the promise of those conjoined bequests. Through his autobiographical narrative, Saleem endeavors to forge a cohesive identity that will equally capture the national self-image and ordain his own individuality, but he encounters a number of obstacles to those dual crucibles in self-determination, in particular, as his mandate to autonomously self-fashion conflicts with core ambitions of a liberal democracy.

The postwar era imagined by *Midnight's Children* occasioned more than the beginnings of decolonization: it also installed a new model and discourse of international governance—namely, human rights. While these two developments were neither synonymous nor seen to be innately politically or intellectually intertwined, in their proximity they jointly spawned a particular postwar political climate founded on a complimentary set of liberal commitments that have increasingly met with codification in both international and domestic law.[3] The official departure of the British from India occurred on August 14–15, 1947, a mere fifteen months and odd days before the adoption of the Universal Declaration of Human Rights (UDHR) by the United Nations General Assembly. Moreover, the Indian Constitution—ratified on November 26, 1949, and effective as of January 26, 1950—contains its own statement of rights. That charter of "fundamental rights" continues to serve as a prominent insignia of Indian nationalism, placing a belief in rights at the heart of India's legal and political culture. As a figure for the Indian nation, Saleem, too, experiments with the language of rights in devising his own identity, drawing on rights and related liberal vocabularies of selfhood to craft his emergent subjectivity. Yet while his odyssey of subject formation might appear to corroborate the descriptive authority of liberalism and its broad philosophical architecture, *Midnight's Children* ultimately indexes the contradictions and foreclosures that haunt rights logic, along with correlative assumptions about democracy, the rule of law, secularism, and the democratic public sphere.

As I have shown, liberal topographies of the human impose the burden of reasoned self-fashioning on the individual, and within *Midnight's Children* Saleem's exercise in self-determination mirrors the newly constituted nation's onus to self-legislate. That project is framed as a matter of written self-production, and it regulates Saleem's narrative on the levels of content and form. However, Saleem's efforts to comply with the many normative benchmarks that liberalism prescribes for the individual necessitate his quarantine and ostracism not only of core dimensions of his own experiences but also of certain characters that vie within his narrative for attention—in particular, his rival and nemesis, Shiva. In these ways does the novel indirectly indict the many privileges and exclusions that procure legibility for the logic of rights. Above all, those repressions play out in Saleem's deep anxiety about embodiment, a condition that he instead projects onto Shiva. In order to postulate himself as sovereign and independent, Saleem's textually inscribed subjectivity must exhibit discipline, order, and reasoned purpose—demanding that he master and deny his embodied faculties of cognition. However, his narrative simultaneously charts the casualties of that agenda, as such indirectly echoing many of Merleau-Ponty's complaints about dualistic and empiricist habits of thought. Moreover, in order to realize the premium on representative equality that accompanies rights, Saleem must expel Shiva, whom he reduces to an incarnation of the body's energies, from the "Midnight Children's Conference," an imaginary congress composed of the other children of independence. This consignment of Shiva to the ostensibly anarchic, ungovernable realm of the body reveals the deeply egoistic and self-serving undercurrents of Saleem's narrative machinations. These exploits, in turn, betray the interdictions that consolidate the symbolic economy of the liberal social body, showing how a purified metaphorics of corporeal integrity sanctions the expurgation of elements deemed captive to the body's drives and thereby legislates real-world exclusions. Nonetheless, as we will see, precisely by subtly deconstructing these assumptions does *Midnight's Children* initiate an imaginative recasting of the sociopolitical meanings of human rights, along with the dominant accounts of the subject tethered to those liberal norms.

Textually Inscribing the Subject of Rights

Human rights violations and the recovery from those abuses are central to the plot of *Midnight's Children*. A primary motive for Saleem's narrative outpouring is his attempt to reckon with the traumatic events that plague his adulthood. While the novel's vast narrative encompasses sixty years of Indian history, beginning three decades prior to Saleem's birth and concluding in his thirty-first year, the events that compel him to "write fast, faster than Scheherazade" (4) all involve violations of human rights. He loses his parents and most of his extended family in coordinated bombing attacks, inducing a bout of amnesia that coincides with Saleem's service in Pakistan's military during the Bangladesh liberation war. In combat, Saleem himself commits atrocities, and his narrative shifts from first to third person to reflect his psychic dissociation and trauma. Saleem thereafter deserts the military and regains his memory, only to undergo torture by Rushdie's fictional Indira Gandhi during the 1975–77 Indian State of Emergency, which legally suspended the civil rights enshrined within the Indian Constitution. Saleem's torture in particular imposes urgency on his narrative, with his recurrent characterization of his autobiographical self-inscription as a "struggle against cracks" (241). Here, Rushdie's subsequently published *Shame* (1983), a novel about political corruption in Pakistan, describes the torture of the dictator Iskander Harappa in terms that are instructive for reading *Midnight's Children* as Saleem's protracted recovery from such a fate. In *Shame,* the torture chamber is figured as an "inverse womb" that entails "*being unmade*" (Rushdie's emphasis, 244), whereas Saleem construes his entire narrative as "remaking my life" after its devastation (4).[4]

While *Midnight's Children* recounts these and other human rights violations, the text's separate relevance for theorizing the nexus between literature and human rights involves Saleem's efforts over the course of his narrative to conform to and thereby authenticate the many ideals that underwrite liberal formulations of human rights.[5] This undertaking is, first and foremost, a matter of reasoned and autonomous self-determination—an activity that is, from its inception, textually inscribed. The novel's premise is that we encounter Saleem in the midst of actively transcribing his autobiography from within the confines of a pickle factory, a metafictional device that tropes the many valences of constitutionalism. This conceit correlates Saleem's written self-incorporation into a rationally integrated subject with the Indian Constitution's drafting and codification, which, as I will show, Rushdie indirectly references. The novel's central metaphor for these parallel endeavors is pickling, or what Saleem calls "the great work of preserving" (37). To denote Saleem's age, *Midnight's Children* contains thirty chapters, each corresponding to a different "flavor" of pickle and phase of his life. Saleem explains the philosophy guiding these reciprocal feats of pickling and writing, "The art is to change the flavor in degree, but not in kind; and above all (in my thirty jars and a jar) to give it shape and form—that is to say, meaning. (I have mentioned my fear of absurdity)" (531). These goals accordingly cast Saleem's venture as a measured, deliberate, and calculable one, wherein his acquisition of substantive "meaning" finds a cognate in the aesthetic properties and structure of his narrative.

Along with this gambit of Saleem's self-codification, his biological genesis is recurrently likened to the elements of a text. For instance, his fetal evolution is reified through the visual signs and symbols of a manuscript. Saleem relates, "What had been (at the beginning) no bigger than a full stop had expanded into a comma, a word, a sentence, a paragraph, a chapter; now it was bursting into more complex developments, becoming, one might say, a book—perhaps an encyclopedia—even a whole language" (111). This motif of textuality is not coincidental; rather, it points to the necessary constitution of the rights-bearing subject through language, speech, and writing. The liberal individual in possession of rights is an always already textually and semantically constructed one, and that pretense certifies the role of reasoned intellection in the liberal subject's self-fashioning. It therefore evidences the dualistic anatomy of liberal articulations of rights, as well, from this book's perspective, as the fictionality of the idealized, truncated subject fettered to those norms. Saleem's self-authorship, as such, is crucial to his inauguration as a spokesperson not only for a distinctively liberal ontology of the subject but also for the institution of the contemporary nation-state—the sovereignty of both being dependent on equally performative and symbolic gestures of signatory self-founding. Saleem's self-constitution, however, is simultaneously depicted as both incessant and insecure, and that urgency manifests itself in the often frantic tone of *Midnight's Children*'s narrative. Overall, Saleem's ambivalence toward his own autobiography creates an indeterminacy within the text that betokens the simultaneously tenuous and utopian nature of such acts of self-authorization. Both Saleem's status as an exemplary liberal subject and the postcolonial state's legitimacy are inherently precarious; as such, even while Saleem's gesture of self-memorialization may aver its own permanence, it is shown to require perpetual renewal and reenactment.

This feint of Saleem's signatory self-founding thus creates an "undecidability" within the text over whether that act is merely "performative"—marking a preexistent, previously attained condition—or instead "constative"—in other words, creating a new, unprecedented reality. Here, Jacques Derrida's reflections on legal codification will help to elucidate the nature of this undecidability. Derrida argues that such uncertainty arises whenever a legal document or formal text attempts one of two complimentary statements, both of which are at issue in *Midnight's Children:* either postulating an individual right or declaring independence. For Derrida, this liminal zone between the performative and the constative is uniquely catalyzed in the act of signatory self-actualization. As Derrida maintains, "If it gives birth to itself, as free and independent subject, as possible signer, this can hold only in the act of signature. The signature invents the signer."[6] Derrida accordingly captures why displays of agentive self-inscription are indispensable to both authenticating and actualizing the sovereignty of the liberal individual and nation alike. Regardless of the reality that precedes the signature, the claims and entitlements that it formalizes only become legally and politically valid and enforceable vis-à-vis the deed of writing. As such, self-codification ceremonializes and thereby ratifies formerly incipient and uncognizable rights and privileges—which is why, within *Midnight's Children,* such a premise is vital to Saleem's ability to posit himself as a particular kind of subject. Yet, as I will maintain, the semiotic ideology implicitly naturalized through this maneuver equally predetermines the exclusions on which such a liberal constitution of the subject is erected.

Even as Saleem relates his emergence through the building blocks of language, that genesis also inclines him toward the universal. *Midnight's Children* begins with his assertion of infinite self-reference: "I am the sum total of everything that went before me, of all I have been seen done, of everything done-to-me. . . . To understand me, you'll have to swallow a world" (3). These designs on the "encyclopedic" have been deciphered as Rushdie's commentary on the hurdles of secular multiculturalism, or of India's obligation to realize its first prime minister Jawaharlal Nehru's call for "unity in diversity."[7] Akin to how Nehru lauds multiculturalism as the very philosophy that will lend ideological coherence to Indian nationalism, Saleem's yearning to encompass the vast heterogeneity of the Indian populace within his narrative inspires both its exuberance and scope. Yet that onus to universalize in addition creates a slippage or friction within the text, vivifying both the liabilities of Saleem's pursuit of universality and the contradictions fated to riddle such an enterprise. Although Saleem aims to incorporate what he calls the "wild profusion of my inheritance" (120–21), he simultaneously aspires for his narrative to follow a consistent, linear, organized trajectory. No doubt Saleem's objectives exist in tension, contributing to his narrative's divided tenor and warring perspectives.

On the one hand, Saleem relishes the expansiveness of his subject matter, which he associates with "the gift of inventing new parents for myself whenever necessary. The power of giving birth to fathers and mothers" (120). Here, he embraces his prolific heritage for facilitating both his agentive self-production and universal relevance. But on the other hand, the manifold diversity he subsumes within his autobiography induces a type of an identity crisis. His narrative cautions at the outset that the "consumed multitudes" "jostling and shoving inside of" him will mutate into "many-headed monsters" that cause him to become "grotesque" (4, 120–21). As we will see, these figures speak not only to the schisms that invariably fissure nationalism as an ethos but also to the foreclosures that afflict Saleem's itinerary of liberal individualist subject formation (4). He claims that his attempt to consti-tute national unity (as well as to assemble himself into a sovereign subject) demands the very multiplicity that he seeks within his narrative to reconcile and subdue. In this way, then, do Saleem's misadventures enact the inevitable rift between the singular subject and the universalizing energies of the col-lective, suggesting why those dual liberal tenets might be incongruous. Even while Saleem's narrative on the surface envisions the democratic nation as a melting pot, it dramatizes the failure of secular multiculturalism to harmo-nize multiplicity or discord.

One key image in the novel is widely cited to justify reading Saleem as an analogue for the Indian nation, his own crises paralleling the developmental woes of the newly autonomous state.[8] After his birth on the precise instant of independence, Saleem is "celebrated" in the newspapers and receives a letter from Nehru himself that "ratifie[s]" his birth. This letter hangs above his crib and is imprinted on his psychology. It informs him, "You are the newest bearer of that ancient face of India which is also eternally young. We shall be watching over your life with the closest attention; it will be, in a sense, the mirror of our own" (139). In this fictional letter, Rushdie quotes an actual essay that Nehru wrote shortly prior to independence in which Nehru applies the metaphor of a "mirror" not to the nation writ large but instead to endow the first Indian Constituent Assembly, or first Congress, with its primary responsibilities. So, if Saleem possesses a clear counterpart in Indian politics and history it is the first Congress, rather than simply the nation as a whole.[9] Of course, the fact that *Midnight's Children* contains its own imaginary "congress" raises further questions about the thrust of Rush-die's allusion to Nehru's words.

The Constituent Assembly was charged in the aftermath of indepen-dence with one highly symbolic task—namely, drafting India's Constitu-tion.[10] That document's central section, still widely deemed the "conscience of the Constitution," is its Charter of Fundamental Rights.[11] While "funda-mental rights" were present "in a very vague form" in Indian law prior to being thus enshrined, the mission of the first Congress was to devise the first comprehensive and authoritative statement of rights in the newly sovereign nation's legal code.[12] This task preoccupied the Constituent Assembly like no other; indeed, its members debated the subject of fundamental rights for a full thirty-eight days.[13] While the British legal system represents the most imme-diate influence on Indian law, the Congress's primary models for its Charter of Fundamental Rights were the United States' Bill of Rights and the French Declaration of the Rights of Man, which are together cited as the main precursors to the UDHR.[14] Moreover, one of the main questions that consumed the Constituent Assembly was whether the Constitution should have a due process clause governing property rights and personal liberty, although such a provision was eventually eliminated.[15] Hence, if Saleem's own draftsmanship can be aligned with particular duties imparted to the first Congress, he must codify a specific collection of rights intended to demarcate the meaning and parameters of individual independence relative to, and in potential conflict with, the demands of the collective. He is consequently faced with priorities that are not entirely consistent, requiring that he balance between his own self-interested prerogatives and the welfare of the populace as a whole.[16]

The historic words from Nehru read:

> The Congress has within its fold many groups, widely differing in their view-points and ideologies. This is natural and inevitable if the Congress is to be the mirror of the nation. But the Congress would cease to be an organization and a movement if there was not a common purpose and a common discipline binding together these varying groups and millions of individuals. That common purpose has been from the early days political freedom.[17]

Nehru here affirms a number of quintessentially liberal ideals. First, he defends the need for a rational "purpose" that will unite and "discipline" the disparate and anarchic masses. He aspires to principles that will be sufficiently persuasive as to integrate an otherwise fragmented populace, and he implicitly espouses secularism as such an ethos that might be held in "common" precisely in its emphasis on preserving difference. His thought progression can therefore equally be read as a project of incorporating the liberal body politic by simultaneously subduing and transcending dissensus—much as Saleem's imposition of meaning and purpose on his biography, subjectivity, and body alike is partner to a struggle against cracks. Nehru's quest for a "binding together" marshals the same symbolic economy of the liberal social body that Saleem sets out to consolidate through his activity of narrative self-inscription. Second, Nehru's rhetoric of purpose and discipline lauds reason as essential to such ends, echoing how rational intellection is seen to effectuate individual self-determination. Third, Nehru concludes by identifying the "common purpose" that might suture Indian nationalism as "political freedom," thereby paradoxically enshrining the importance of political equality, yet in terms that predicate it on the rights of the individual. In general, Nehru thus espouses constitutionalism as a route to ameliorating potential conflicts, and those conflicts in particular inhere between the simultaneous need to safeguard particularity and to forge universally "binding" principles and laws, the former of which can only occur through the latter. As chapter 1 explored, almost identical frictions beset standard theorizations of human rights, which also prescribe both the behest to individuate and abstract egalitarianism. In other words, liberalism consecrates *both* individuation *and* parity, or *both* the unique personality *and* social equality, yet Saleem's enterprise of self-constitution exposes the discrepancies between those dual mandates.

In particular, Saleem's narrative strives to execute Nehru's decree by way of his twinned pursuits of textual self-inscription and autonomous self-determination. Akin to Congress's "common purpose," Saleem aspires toward "meaning—yes, meaning—something" (4), which he opposes to his fear of "absurdity." Such an ambition fuels his narrative from the start; as he explains, "Even a baby is faced with the problem of defining itself" (147). This aim is thus a matter of agentive self-fashioning, or of what he calls "remaking my life" (4). Along the lines of Nehru's plea, such an odyssey of subject formation necessitates discipline and focus, for instance, as Saleem complains of "interruptions, nothing but interruptions!" within his narrative (214). By no means last of the resonances with Nehru's words, Saleem also construes his narrative as an exercise in "retain[ing] control" (531), even though that impetus renders him progressively megalomaniacal and convinced of his own egoistic "genius" and "greatness" (178). As I've suggested, Saleem's desire to impose a unified purpose on his identity, his narrative, and Indian nationalism alike is spurred by the specter of his dissolution—or his "falling apart," "literally disintegrating," and "eventually crumbl[ing] into . . . anonymous, and necessarily oblivious, dust" (36). Here, we can further grasp the symmetry between the constitution of the national body politic as nuclear and integrated, which occurs vis-à-vis the reason-based precepts of democratic political process, and the human as plotted within liberal cartographies of the subject, which together gain legibility from and furnish intellectual coherence to liberal discourses of human rights. Yet, as will become clear, both such enabling myths are dependent on the quarantine and repression of elements labeled alien and subversive—elements that are above all associated with embodiment.

Saleem's endeavors capture much about the texture of nationalism. While a fractured national self-image can incite internal hostilities and resentments, the delivery of a common purpose—whether through a constitution or other vehicle for legal-political myth making—can overcome preexisting and incipient divisions to assimilate a populace. By occupying the position of the first Congress, then, Saleem sets out to invent an inclusive and compelling account of the nation's origins precisely to cultivate such commonality. Yet *Midnight's Children* also contends with the casualties of that process. Saleem's agenda is simultaneously presented as a hyperindividualist, even narcissistic one; his enterprise of self-fashioning recurrently clashes with his concurrent goal of collective incorporation, even while his narrative casts those pursuits as inextricable. As a result, Saleem's dual commitments trouble and undermine one another, his effort to individuate jeopardizing the very cohesiveness, stability, and equality that he also pursues. In turn, we can here again observe how the liberal construct of the individual yields starkly different implications depending on whether it buttresses the Romantic fantasy of the self's inimitable uniqueness or the neutral impartiality valorized as formative of the democratic public sphere. In both cases—whether it represents a route to egalitarianism or a vindication of the untrammeled freedom of the liberal individual—Saleem's itinerary of subject formation requires him to self-abstract, and consequently to suppress, the faculties of his embodiment.

I should pause at this point to discuss *Midnight's Children*'s affinities with the Bildungsroman, especially since many critics have located the novel within that genre.[18] As chapter 1 addressed, recent scholarship has linked the intellectual history of human rights to the evolution of the Bildungsroman, as well as demonstrated the Bildungsroman's relevance to postcolonial nationalisms.[19] Indeed, Saleem's odyssey of subject formation does, in key respects, comply with the particular course of development that the Bildungsroman usually plots. As I will show, however, his narrative ultimately explodes those norms, testifying to the collapse of a particular vision of both postcoloniality and the liberal subject. In other words, while *Midnight's Children* quotes many conventions of the Bildungsroman, it ultimately invokes them not to fortify but rather to jettison the normative ideals for which they act as cognates. For example, while the Bildungsroman typically launches a plea for sociopolitical inclusion, Saleem is from the start tainted by privilege and entitlement, although *Midnight's Children* tracks his gradual abandonment of that myopic worldview. While liberal principles guide much of his narrative, its finale in particular renounces that facade of liberal *bildung* to expose the many exclusions and prejudices that both found such an articulation of the subject and are often naturalized within the genre.

Not only do Saleem's ambitions for his identity verge on being grandiose; Amina, Saleem's mother, also buys into the conceit of his preeminence. After learning of a contest sponsored by the *Times of India,* Amina believes that she will deliver Saleem on the precise stroke of independence. However, two children are in fact born simultaneously, and in the same hospital, no less, although Amina's class privilege ensures Saleem the accolade. As such,

Saleem's status as a harbinger of independence is from the outset contingent on his ostracism of other lives—in this case, the infant Shiva, Saleem's arch adversary. Amina's response to the birth further betrays the egoism intrinsic to the logic of rights. The narrative juxtaposes Amina's narcissistic reaction with other renowned words delivered by Nehru, not coincidentally also addressed to the Constituent Assembly:

> "Janum," my mother said excitedly, "you must call the papers. Call them at the *Times of India*. What did I tell you? I won."
>
> "...This is no time for petty or destructive criticism," Jawaharlal Nehru told the Assembly. "No time for ill-will. We have to build the noble mansion of free India, where all her children may dwell." (131)

Amina vocalizes the competitive individualism that Saleem himself comes to espouse, which might on the surface seem to starkly oppose Nehru's idiom of harmony and fellowship. Yet the proximity of these apparently competing sentiments ultimately discloses their affinity, belying the egalitarianism of Nehru's platitudes. Clearly, all India does not "dwell" in Saleem's relative position of advantage, and that disconnect highlights the imbalances on which rights, equality, independence, and related liberal tenets are founded. Before Saleem even embarks on his project of individualist self-fashioning, the sheer circumstances of his birth subvert the highfalutin ideals through which Nehru frames postcolonial independence, also foreshadowing the strategic exclusions that haunt Saleem's narrative. Despite the symmetry between these two births, equally heralding independence, Shiva's and Saleem's ensuing fortunes dramatize the material disparities and discriminations that come to be disbursed under the guise of abstract equality.

Along similar lines, Saleem's multiple and competing inheritances themselves foreordain contradictions within his identity and the many foreclosures that enable it, and these tensions further interrogate both Nehru's image for the nation and the assembly of liberal ideals sustaining it. Saleem's narrative is a manipulative one, and much of that subterfuge surrounds his biological, cultural, and political inheritances. While Saleem initially trusts that he is the natural son of his Muslim parents, the upheaval surrounding his perfectly timed birth allows a politically motivated nurse to reverse the fortunes of class and replace the destitute Shiva with Saleem, creating the rivalry that fuels his narrative. Hence, Saleem is not the biological offspring of his wealthy parents, as all believe, but instead the progeny of a more compromised liaison. As Rushdie's readers gradually learn, Saleem is the product of a clandestine affair between the impoverished Vanita, who dies in childbirth, and "the departing Englishman" William Methwold, who leaves India after England cedes control (104).

Accordingly, Saleem—as a figure for both the liberal individual and Indian nationalism—is a literal heir to the British empire. The residues of this bequest, moreover, populate the physical environment in which Saleem lives as a child. Saleem's de facto parents buy the very estate built by his British forebear, although in a purchase contingent on their willingness to retain Methwold's furnishings. This transfer of Methwold's estate to the Indian elite satirizes the common critique that the British infrastructure, government, and laws merely changed hands intact after decolonization, much as the new nation retained the figurative domicile of the English language. And in *Midnight's Children,* Saleem is literally steeped in the artifacts of the British empire. These relics make cultural claims on him, as for instance, is emblematized in the reproduction of Sir John Everett Millais's *The Boyhood of Raleigh* (1870) that hangs prominently above his crib alongside Nehru's prophetic letter. This painting equally informs Saleem's identity, and he labels it his own "special doom" (104), implicitly incriminating himself as an inadvertent conspirator with the imperialist ambitions of Raleigh.[20]

Likewise, Saleem's adopted family, while Muslim, has been thoroughly Westernized for generations, further rendering his cultural endowments overridingly European. The novel's expansive history begins with his grandfather Dr. Aadam Aziz, whom the reader encounters immediately after his return from Germany and in the midst of a spiritual crisis brought on by his medical education. As a result, Saleem's family is thoroughly secularized, although many of its women display almost cloying religious devotion.[21] Beyond this influence, his family's elite class status is what primarily vests Saleem with the privilege that insulates him from Shiva's type of dispossession. Practically speaking, Saleem's class advantage and economic security guarantee his rights, whereas Shiva instead wrestles with basic questions of survival that both functionally undermine his rights and preclude the relative luxury of Saleem's pursuit of reasoned meaning. *Midnight's Children* in this way, too, accentuates the material and other disparities that undercut the superficially universal, abstract ideals for which Saleem is a spokesperson. This paradox is recurrently highlighted in the narrative, for instance, as Joseph D'Costa, the revolutionary who unintentionally motivates the infant substitution of Shiva with Saleem, complains, "This independence is for the rich only; the poor are being made to kill each other like flies" (116). Saleem's very ability to exalt himself as a scion of independence and exemplar of liberal self-fashioning is thus exposed to be an effect of his family's prosperity, another way that formal equality is unmasked as a pretext for democracy's constitutive denials.

Along with his rhetoric of meaning, reason, and purpose, Saleem repeatedly appeals to legal constructs and terms of art to assert his prerogative, as well as to hypothesize the truth status of his narrative. He characterizes himself as a "witness" whose "reliability" is in doubt (70) and construes his narrative as a "confession" (511), while also levying it as "evidence" and "proof" (243, 506). Furthermore, the question of whether India can "give her approval to the rule of law" (303) is identified by Saleem as the moral of one of his highly allegorical digressions. This tale of murder and philandering involving the fictional "Commander Sabarmati" culminates with a widely publicized trial that Saleem deems "a theater in which India will discover who she was, what she is, and what she might become" (300), thus locating the rule of law at the fore of the emergent nation's self-understanding. Yet this and other legal technologies carry a highly ambivalent lineage in Indian history and politics. For instance, it has been demonstrated that the rule of law was perceived as a key implement in the civilizing mission of Western Europe, expected to instill a wide array of ancillary values tied to sociopolitical progress and advancement; by contrast, the absence of a legal code was interpreted as a handicap and sign of inadequacy.[22] Taken together, Saleem's appeals to the law are reminiscent of such a colonialist mindset, especially since he recurrently conscripts legal rhetoric to secure his privileges. Indeed, he explicitly defends his legacy against Shiva via the autocratic language of "rights" and "claims," even referring to the other midnight's children as his "birthright" (8, 323). It goes without saying that these opportunistic deployments of rights talk are highly disingenuous, given that they gird Saleem's dubious longings for power. And seeing as they directly disinherit Shiva, they also disclose the antagonistic as well as exclusionary anatomy of that logic.

In any case, Saleem's appeals to the rule of law are merely one component of his overarching attempt to script his narrative in compliance with a liberal trajectory of subject formation, an agenda that he intends will analogously impose reasoned self-determination on the national imaginary. The certitude and authority of the law accordingly seem to corroborate Nehru's call for "discipline"; in effect, the law's predictability and order both stave off Saleem's own dissolution and fortify the nation's sovereignty. Yet what is most revealing about Saleem's investment in legality, along with the broad collection of liberal precepts that control his narrative, is not his fixation on those standards per se but rather what they require him to censor and interdict. Saleem's exercise in liberal subjectification is counterpart to an antipathy to behaviors that he believes to hazard that itinerary. For instance, Saleem's emphasis on civic responsibility and law-abidingness entails an aversion toward forms of political upheaval and disarray, especially when violent or rebellious. This repugnance toward political dissent notably echoes historical tendencies within Indian political discourse to deride violence as illiberal and uncivilized. Dipesh Chakrabarty traces this bias, recounting how Nehru himself disparaged violence as "immature, childish."[23] Indeed, Saleem frequently vilifies the Indian populace in such terms, such as when he links political protest with excessive, immoderate rage and describes the masses as "hysterical" (82) and "filled with blood" (83). He dismisses the 1950s Bombay language riots with parallel disdain, commenting, "What grows best in the heat: fantasy; unreason; lust" (191). And these characterizations of popular politics notably inform Saleem's own nightmare of "annihilation-by-numbers" (284).[24] Importantly, Saleem here expresses scorn for those qualities that he aggressively defines himself in opposition against. In this respect, precisely his aversions and anxiety index the prohibitions subtending the mythology of the liberal individual. For instance, Saleem's feint of his own centrality compels him to guard against both anonymity and the fear of the multitude, even while the ethos of multiculturalism directly enables his basic identity.

Saleem evinces a related skittishness about sexuality, along with embodiment in general. This reluctance, above all, facilitates his self-constitution as a paradigmatically liberal subject, much as the conceit of textual self-inscription verifies a dualistic worldview that prioritizes the intellect. Merleau-Ponty's insights can here help to clarify why certain habits of discourse work to occlude embodied modes of cognition. Insofar as Saleem claims to record empirically and rationally verifiable truth, that feint necessitates his suppression of other "strange and paradoxical" realms of experience—the quintessential of which emanate from the appetencies of the body.[25] He therefore figures his sexual and other corporeal desires as automatic threats to his project of reasoned self-incorporation—much as political violence imperils the civic equilibrium seen to accompany the reason-based operations of liberal democracy. Overall, Saleem's squeamishness about sexuality and the body pervades his narrative. As an adult, he is fully impotent, a condition that materializes both his disgust toward embodiment and need to master those realities that he connects to its energies. To such ends, he frequently characterizes his own erotic desires as "unnatural" (361), and, indeed, they are often incestuous. His first experience of arousal is for his Aunt Pia; he is at length enamored of his sister; and, when visiting a prostitute, he admits to longing for his mother. Saleem thus exhibits a classically liberal ambivalence toward embodiment—one that, I have argued, ironically furnishes legibility to human rights. This reluctance is foremost naturalized through the dual fictions of bodily integrity and human dignity, as they collaborate to produce a vision of the human that is strangely bloodless and decorporealized. Throughout his narrative, Saleem, too, strives to quarantine and thereby transcend his corporeal being, with the outcome that he constructs himself in comparatively abstract, disembodied terms—even while his many qualms and aversions give the lie to that self-invention.

As chapter 1 demonstrated, the symbolic economy that lends ideological coherence to liberal human rights discourses and norms generally treats embodiment as a stigmatized source of moral atrophy and debasement, leading to the presumption that the body must be subdued and conquered through reasoned self-government. On the one hand, Saleem exorcises his fear of embodiment to such ends by projecting its excesses onto other characters in the novel—namely, Shiva, women, and the poor, all of whom he figures as captive to wayward, defiled, and otherwise repugnant bodies. On the other hand, Saleem's entire narrative can be plotted as his extended effort to defeat and surmount his own bodily condition—especially since his torture has presumably made him painfully aware of his corporeal existence. This endeavor also fuels Saleem's pretense of bodily self-enclosure and wholeness, although those illusions gradually unravel. As such, Saleem's hostility toward embodiment directs us again to the metaphorics of the liberal social body. Insofar as Saleem's fantasy of a self-integrated body solidifies parallel assumptions about the body politic, that fantasy justifies forms of social control and policing, or the expulsion of elements seen to compromise its unity and insularity. Whereas the success of Saleem's biographical self-constitution depends on his ability to forestall his (and the narrative's) dissolution, the nation-state must similarly combat parallel forms of sociopolitical anarchy. While for Saleem sexuality and violence especially imperil his quest for an ordered, reasoned subjectivity-narrative, he arraigns comparable energies for endangering the operations of democracy. Here again, Chakrabarty's insights into the historical role of the law within Indian politics can elucidate why Saleem's repression of his corporeality yields such implications. Chakrabarty explains, "The desire for order and discipline in the domestic sphere thus may be seen as having been a correlate of the nationalist, modernizing desire for a similar discipline in the public sphere, that is for a rule of law enforced by the state."[26]

Of central importance, Saleem's contempt for violence and sexuality alike condones his mistreatment of Shiva, whom he imaginatively relegates to those ostensibly destructive energies. For instance, he blames Shiva's "phenomenal fecundity" for rendering him "a notorious seducer; a ladies'-man; a cuckolder of the rich; in short, a stud" (473, 470), and he similarly relegates him to "terrifying, nonchalant violence" (250). This association of Shiva with nonutilitarian violence, of course, permits Saleem to strategically disassociate himself from wrongdoing, although Saleem's self-serving machinations simultaneously expose that gambit to be an ideological ploy. On one level, Saleem's smug distaste for violence betrays the entitlement that permits his lofty ideals, divulging the luxury of his worldview. Yet on another, by transferring the supposedly lawless appetencies of sexuality and violence onto Shiva, Saleem's self-serving tactics open up the broader logic through which an antipathy toward embodiment smuggles in real-world oppressions and exclusions. The eviction of Shiva from Saleem's narrative accordingly illuminates far more pervasive structures of sociopolitical ostracism and disenfranchisement, showing how the ideals superficially claimed by Saleem discount and penalize those qualities that they are defined in opposition to. In this respect, Saleem desperately needs the specter of Shiva's violence to consolidate his own identity; Saleem's preoccupation with Shiva's alleged dereliction and intemperance bolsters his own self-image as the author of a particularly liberal vision of postcolonial subjectivity and independence. So if the threat of Shiva grows increasingly pressing over Saleem's narrative, it is because his encroaching presence will unmask the fictionality of the many liberal norms through which Saleem self-identifies.

The Liabilities of Constitutionalism

At the same time as Saleem's activity of self-determination installs many contradictions within his narrative, those tensions index key challenges that beset legal codification as well as exegesis. A series of motifs in particular serve to reify the friction between the abstract universal and the singular particular—a friction that both is inherent in the universalizing ambitions of law and impedes Saleem's quest for encyclopedic relevance. One distinct pair of metaphors that defines the courtships of Saleem's grandparents and parents crystallizes this disconnect between fragment and whole. First, his grandparents' early romance is mediated by a perforated sheet. The doctor Aziz is allowed only glimpses of his future wife, Naseem, as he diagnoses her contrived maladies, entailing that he falls in love with a piecemeal and, hence, fabricated image of her. While in his mind she becomes "glued together by imagination" (22), he discovers that this invented composite does not correspond with reality, rendering his affections hard to sustain. By contrast, Saleem's parents, Ahmed and Amina, contend with the inverse relationship between part and whole. Amina is initially unable to overcome her love for her first husband, the revolutionary poet Nadir Kahn, so in order to generate desire for Ahmed she disaggregates him into incrementally palatable units. As the narrative explains, "She began to train herself to love him. To do this she divided him, mentally, into every single one of his component parts, physical as well as behavioral, compartmentalizing him into lips and verbal tics and prejudices and likes. . . . In short, she fell under the spell of the perforated sheet of her own parents, because she resolved to fall in love with her husband bit by bit" (73). Within these two courtships, the part is easier to tolerate than the whole, yet it far from guarantees that the sum of those ingredients will add up to admiration, and this discontinuity throughout the narrative stages a satirical critique of Saleem's (and Nehru's) expectations that multiculturalism as an ideology will ensure national unity.

Saleem as a child accidentally dons the perforated sheet of his grandparents' courtship while play-acting as a ghost, and that spectral object comes to emblematize his identity. He explains that the sheet "condemned me to see my own life—its meanings its structures—in fragments also" (119), although precisely those constraints drive his relentless efforts to self-incorporate. This discordance, moreover, returns us to the goals of legal codification. While I already examined the complexities of relying on constitutionalism as a means to forge national solidarity, this rift between part and whole also exhibits the snares of statutory authority and draftsmanship, which equally depend on the ability to register generalizable principles within a finite archive in terms that are sufficiently precise as to pertain to discrete situations. These challenges are especially pronounced within legal codes that, like a constitution or the UDHR, announce their universalizing ambitions—much as does Saleem for his narrative. Legal statements that purport to yield a comprehensive or universal purview must anticipate an infinite number of potential applications—or a plethora of "fragments"—yet resolve them without internal dissonance—that is, without creating exceptions to their bindingness and jurisdiction. In other words, to be valid, a law must produce both overarching consistency and isolated accuracy. Given that Saleem frames his narrative endeavor in parallel terms, he confronts hurdles akin to those plaguing legal draftsmanship—namely, to devise abstract, neutral principles that nevertheless will apply to a countless array of singular circumstances. As for legal doctrine, Saleem correctly describes those dual requirements as essential to his creation of authoritative "meaning."

Another way to elucidate this tension between fragment and whole is in terms of the consequences of error. Indeed, the Constituent Assembly charged with drafting the Indian Constitution contended with the fear that the rights incorporated therein would produce structural anomalies, causing certain to conflict with others and to inadvertently cancel those opposing provisions.[27] To avoid this risk, the Assembly adopted a "principle of accommodation" that would allow antonymic tenets to coexist without mutually nullifying one another.[28] Within his own narrative, Saleem, too, worries that isolated errors will either annul or disrupt his narrative's "chronology." After identifying a mistake, he meditates on its ramifications: "Does one error invalidate the entire fabric? Am I so far gone, in my desperate need for meaning, that I'm prepared to distort everything—to rewrite the whole history of my times purely in order to place myself in a central role?" (190). Within a legal document, error is an unavoidable, if not productive, by-product of the law's necessary abstraction as well as concision. However, Saleem's narrative can claim no such brevity, and the slippages and inconsistencies that infect it are more accurately symptoms of Saleem's strategic "distortion" of events to fulfill his egoistic aims. As such, Saleem's pursuit of encyclopedic relevance works to suppress certain kinds of heterogeneity (although his fantasy of multiculturalism simultaneously romanticizes that quality), as well as to license his manipulation of his audience.

Beyond the gap between fragment and whole, Saleem's "power of the nose" (8–9)—the source of his telepathy—illumines certain hazards of codification. Born exactly at midnight, Saleem is vested with the most rarified capacities of the midnight's children, which at first inclines him toward social justice. Saleem's heightened sense of smell serves overdetermined functions within his narrative: it facilitates his joint enterprises of pickling and narrative self-constitution, allows him to convene the Midnight Children's Conference, and governs his early intuitions about ethics. Yet while telepathy-smell might appear to represent a corporeal mode of perception, within Saleem's narrative it more accurately denotes his intellectual, rational habits of judgment and discernment—which is why that faculty's eventual destruction is partner to his relinquishment of a distinctly liberal worldview. Not surprisingly, Saleem's smell is therefore tainted by his many entitlements, revealing that sense to be, rather than a neutral arbiter, highly prejudiced. Saleem ironically claims to inherit this "power of the nose" from his nonbiological grandfather Aziz, who is saved by a great sneeze in Rushdie's fictionalized account of the Amritsar massacre. Saleem, however, does not acquire his olfactory abilities until, as an adolescent, he undergoes surgery to cure a chronic nasal blockage. Thereafter, Saleem's telepathic nose bestows on him insights so momentous as to bear on character, justice, ethics, and even ontology. Comparing his olfactory skills to his sister's exceptional voice, Saleem comments, "What I could smell, Jamila could sing. Truth beauty happiness pain" (361), along with "all the thousand and one drives which make us human" (363). Saleem explicitly associates smell with what he calls "fair-and-unfair," as it introduces him to "the bitter aroma of injustice" (425). As such, his telepathic powers play an adjudicatory role as they allow him to gauge the ethical fiber of both people and events.

However, Saleem soon grows conflicted about his olfactory sensibilities, especially when they force him to reckon with his embodiment. His sense of smell gradually "linger[s] on the uglier smells which invaded it" (361), eventually producing the "unspeakable" erotic scent of his sister Jamila. As a consequence, smell becomes an appetency that, like sexuality, Saleem attempts to subdue through regimented standards and proscriptions. In particular, he correlates his need for olfactory order with his overarching quest for narrative organization, as he explains of smell: "My overwhelming desire for form asserted itself, and I survived" (363). Saleem thus treats scents that emanate from the messy, ambiguous realms of embodiment as an automatic affront to his exercise in rational self-determination, again displaying a classically liberal discomfort over the body.

Saleem's longing for self-discipline is aggravated by personal crisis, in particular, as relations between India and Pakistan sour and his family is rent by those hostilities (363). Saleem's resultant disarray only exacerbates his penchant for control, inspiring within the narrative a type of parody of moral philosophy. With prose fluctuating between the first and third person to convey Saleem's inner turmoil, it relates:

> Saleem was working towards a general theory of smell: classification procedures had begun.... Only when I was sure of my mastery of physical scents did I move on to those other aromas which only I could smell: the perfumes of emotions and all the thousand and one drives which make us human: love and death, greed and humility, have and have-not were labeled and placed in neat compartments of my mind.
>
> ... Because I soon understood that my work must, if it was to have any value, acquire a moral dimension; that the only important divisions were the infinitely subtle gradations of good and evil smells. Having realized the crucial nature of morality, having sniffed out the smells that could be sacred or profane, I invented, in the isolation of my scooter trips, the science of nasal ethics. (363–64)

In his aversion toward embodiment, Saleem strives to "master" its appetites and subordinate them to rational principles, both instrumentalizing and policing the body's instincts. Saleem's "science," however, exposes the costs of that need to circumscribe the countless, fugitive, and variegated "drives which make us human." His impulse to disambiguate the "human" within a single, binaristic calculus—here, a Manichean polarity between "good and evil"—ultimately erases ambivalence. To be legible within Saleem's heuristic, a behavior must exhibit "the only important divisions," or comply with highly dichotomous, empirically verifiable characteristics. While this fantasy of objective knowledge furnishes a semblance of intellectual rigor, Saleem's metric in fact constricts the spectrum of human experience that he can conceptualize. Yet his narrative casts this as indispensable to his odyssey of self-determination, implicitly sanctioning that agenda for authoring a pauperized, anemic portrait of the human—one ironically divested of the layered densities of embodiment. To such ends, it is not accidental that Saleem enlists his nasal-telepathic powers to ends that are authoritarian and despotic, further revealing his narrative pursuits to be neither innocent of self-interest nor nonideological.

Democracy and the Midnight Children's Conference

As I have argued, Saleem's overlapping experiments in self and national constitution demand that he suppress and exclude key realities, many of which he projects onto his nemesis, Shiva, as well as the Indian masses. Saleem shields the other midnight's children from knowledge of this artifice, at the same time as he imposes on them his ambitions for unitary meaning, purpose, and order. As emblems for democracy and postcolonial independence alike, the children must conform to the ideals generally seen to cohere the liberal public sphere—including egalitarianism, rational deliberation, secularism, and, of course, the logic of rights. Born within the first hour of independence, each of the midnight's children is, like Saleem, endowed with a different magical propensity, varying according to their birth's proximity to midnight (260). Most immediately, these superhuman capacities register the exorbitant hopes for that transition, and Saleem, too, celebrates the children as "miraculous," "as though history, arriving at a point of the highest significance and promise, had chose to sow, in that instant, the seeds of a future which would genuinely differ from anything the world had seen up to that time" (224).

Yet precisely the magnitude of these aspirations for the children renders their significance overdetermined, much akin to the malleable discourses of human rights. As Saleem deciphers their "metaphorical content" (230):

> Midnight's children can be made to represent many things, according to your point of view; they can be seen as the last throw of everything antiquated and retrogressive in our myth-ridden nation, whose defeat was entirely desirable in the context of a modernizing, twentieth-century economy; or as the true hope of freedom which is now forever extinguished; but what they must not become is the bizarre creation of a rambling, diseased mind. (230)

Because the children lack an absolute, stable truth status, they serve as repositories for a spectrum of longings, anxieties, and motivations. Incarnations of the multitudinous and conflicting sentiments accompanying the birth of the postcolonial nation-state, their symbolic freight is directly proportionate to the intensity of the yearnings roused by that development. However, the sheer enormity of those desires projected onto the children compounds the likelihood of their exploitation and misuse, much as Saleem manipulates them. Indeed, Saleem himself imbues them with contradictory expectations, for instance, as he anticipates that they forecast a type of "defeat." In doing so, Saleem inquires whether the Schmittian loyalties inherent to the "mass fantasy" of nationalism are not also responsible for "retrogressive" and hence dangerous "myths" (125).

Seemingly to guard against this fear that the children and, by extension, the promise of independence are founded on illusions, Saleem holds them to the same standards that regulate his narrative, as he describes being "plagued" by their "purpose, and meaning" (261). It is in part to vest them with such a unifying agenda that Saleem convenes the novel's figure for democracy, or what he calls the "sabha or parliament of [his] brain" (259). In this forum, the children vie for what they collectively represent, proposing the alternatives of "collectivism," "individualism," "filial duty," "infant revolution," "capitalism," "altruism," "science," and "religion." This inventory of political philosophies concludes, "There were declarations of women's rights and pleas for the improvement of the lot of untouchables; landless children dreamed of land and tribals from the hills, of Jeeps; and there were, also, fantasies of power" (261). Through this series of competing justifications for the individual's inscription within the community, the narrative frames the children's identity crisis as one of democratic legitimacy.[29] Yet these different grounds are far from reconcilable; once again, sheer multiplicity is cast as an impediment to a compelling national self-image. The very diversity of those varied principles thwarts their integration into a universally binding ethos or creed, and that discord here again highlights the divisions fated to fracture the nation—divisions that *Midnight's Children* ironically explains as a direct outcome of secular multiculturalism.

In part because of these ideological factions, the midnight's children's federation does eventually dissipate, under circumstances that are at least partially beyond Saleem's control. While Saleem attributes their demise to the natural waning of the "principle" of "childhood" (294), or to overly credulous hopes for independence, their early harmony is eroded by deeper problems endemic to both liberal democracy and nationalism. In particular, the children are sundered by their own individual biases, which trump the dream of the collective. For one, Saleem blames conflict between Indian and Pakistan over Kashmir for amplifying religious schisms that incite more thoroughgoing political hostilities (291). Likewise, class and ethnic resentments besiege them, leading Saleem to label them "not immune to their parents" or to the "prejudices" of preceding generations (292). The children thus become a microcosm of the populace as a whole, their congress failing to prolong the initial buoyancy of the postindependence moment. Instead, as the narrative explains, "seized by atavistic longings, and forgetting the new myth of freedom [they] reverted to their old ways, their old regionalist loyalties and prejudices, and the body politic began to crack" (281). Rushdie here explicitly evokes the metaphor of the integrated and coherent liberal social body, yet that fragmentation is enacted on the level not only of the nation but also of Saleem's narrative, identity, and corporeal being alike. Moreover, while Saleem hopes that the "myth of freedom" will subdue those divisions, precisely the mandate of individual self-determination is revealed over and again throughout his narrative to impinge on the welfare of the collection. In fact, Saleem specifically indicts the logic of individualism for defeating his trial democracy. When he first encounters the children, they assert themselves in a cacophony of competing "I"s (192), and these "I"s only become more persistent and emphatic (214). Hence, at the same time as sectarianism and communalism undermine this experiment in democracy, egoistic self-interest equally precipitates that end.

It is Saleem himself, however, who bears primary responsibility for the children's eventual disbandment. When he first summons them, he strives for a "sort of loose federation of equals, all points of view given free expression" (252). And although their divergent ideological tenets might seem to crystallize democracy's natural limits, he encounters a practical dimension of that conundrum. Despite his feint of egalitarianism, the children "jostl[e] for space within [his] head," causing their many dialects to introduce "a language problem" (192). Although Saleem searches for "universally intelligible thought-forms which far transcended words," he is forced, as their sole translator, to mediate and consequently dominate their dialogue, which is to say that he himself subverts his facade of representative equality. Saleem as a result abandons his pretense of impartiality and succumbs to his epidemic desire for uniform meaning. He ultimately "refus[es] to distinguish the voices from one another," rationalizing why he must conflate their perspectives: "They were the very essence of multiplicity, and I see no point in dividing them now" (262). No doubt, such an excuse is a cop-out on Saleem's part, and even he admits to being seduced by "the lure of leadership" (260), as it sanctions his effective dictatorship over the children. That said, Saleem also surmises about their jealousy of his "education, or class-origins" (243) and disingenuously laments that "the midnight miracle had indeed been remarkably hierarchical in nature" (260). Yet both such ploys absolve him of the duty to level those class and other disparities, again underscoring the many exclusions—material and ideological—that undercut the abstract neutrality of the liberal democratic public sphere.

While the pitfalls of secular multiculturalism offer Saleem an alibi for his duplicity, he manipulates his narrative in other ways that expose the tyranny of his hyperindividualism and corresponding need for control. His "claim to be at the center of things" (272) is ancillary to an almost megalomaniacal obsession with his authorial prerogative, or his license to be his "own master" (37). The "heroic program of self-enlargement" (141) that informs his infancy comes to manifest itself in the aesthetics and form of his narrative; his narrative itself displays such a "spirit of self-aggrandizement," particularly in his goals for universal inclusivity and relevance (199). Saleem even admits to orchestrating the events that compose his plot, and he fantasizes about complete dominion over other characters' lives. His narrative relates, "Because the feeling had come upon me that I was somehow creating a world; that the thoughts I jumped inside were *mine,* that the bodies I occupied acted at my command; that...I was somehow *making them happen*...which is to say that I had entered into the illusion of the artist, and thought of the multitudinous realities of the land as the raw unshaped material of my gift" (199). The shared etymology of *auctoritas* and *auctor* here puns on the imaginative dictatorship performed by authorship. Nonetheless, Saleem's reasoned self-determination almost seamlessly transmutes into a domineering defense of his own entitlement; his pursuit of sovereignty knows no natural limits, leading it to become colonizing and all-consuming. Above all, these designs on "centrality" and "greatness" lead him to hide his own illegitimacy and Shiva's rightful claims on his inheritance. Despite a "concerted assault" from the children "on a broad front and from every direction" (341), he refuses to confess this secret, and it acts as the main catalyst for their undoing. In sum, if Saleem's narrative is an exercise in liberal individualist subject formation, then his recurrent appeals to purpose, autonomy, and reason indict those ideals for condoning fully calculative and egoistic behavior. His censorship of his true heredity illustrates why the liberal onus to individuate is guaranteed to sabotage the interests of the collective. Saleem's exploits thereby open up the inherent contradictions that riddle liberalism as an ethos, with its dual though conflicting premiums on individual self-fashioning and abstract equality.

Shiva and the Exclusions of Human Rights

As may be clear, Saleem's narrative erects a number of binaries, many of which cast Shiva as his dyad and alter ego. Although Shiva's very name, which alludes to the Hindu "god of procreation and destruction," points to the artificiality of Saleem's dualistic thinking (146), he refuses to interpret Shiva with complexity, instead treating him as little more than an envoy of pure violence. Not only is this polarity misleading; it also is the primary ruse that legitimizes Saleem's own authority. As we have seen, Saleem hinges the success of his autobiography and corresponding identity on the attainment of purpose and meaning, and he associates those qualities with the operations of the intellect. This construction of his own self-image, however, consigns Shiva to the undisciplined, primordial energies of the body, thereby discrediting his claims on Saleem. The logic that disenfranchises Shiva, as such, betrays the broader mechanisms through which rights logic with its dualistic organization instates a collection of interrelated exclusions. As chapter 1 considered, in their prioritization of the intellect, liberal human rights norms relegate certain lives to the stigmatized condition of embodiment and thereby permit their ostracism. Yet from a practical standpoint, Saleem's narrative reveals his class and other privileges to be directly contingent on Shiva's economic destitution, further divulging the material disparities that the explanatory regime of rights apologizes for. Saleem both reduces Shiva to abject poverty and suppresses that reality directly in order to safeguard his own entitlements. In turn, if there is a paradigmatic human rights claimant within *Midnight's Children,* it is Shiva, which is why Saleem's denial of subjectivity to Shiva is the interdiction that his narrative most aggressively enacts. Shiva's plight vivifies what is perhaps the core paradox of human rights—that their protections are fated to be disallowed to their most wanting and needful beneficiaries.

Shiva appears to be cognizant all along of his disenfranchisement and "exile" (324). As a child, he exemplifies the rage of the dispossessed. Saleem recounts his early memories of Shiva: "Gradually, down the years, we watched his eyes filling with an anger which could not be spoken; we watched his fists close around pebbles and hurl them, ineffectually at first, more dangerously as he grew, into the surrounding emptiness" (146). It is precisely Shiva's fury at his marginalization that for Saleem must be silenced—even while that reality is more accurately the status quo than the exception. Quite fittingly, Shiva himself exposes the luxury of Saleem's idealism, chastising Saleem: "When you have things, then there is time to dream; when you don't you fight" (293). If, as Shiva complains, Saleem's very designs on meaning are self-indulgent, Saleem's solipsistic retreat into the intellect is what permits him to overlook those brute conditions of survival experienced by most of the Indian populace. Saleem recalls Shiva's condemnation:

"Rich kid," Shiva yelled, "you don't know one damn thing! What *purpose,* man? What this in the whole sister sleeping world got *reason,*

yara? For what reason you're rich and I'm poor? Where's the reason
in starving, man? God know how many millions of damn fools living
in this country, man, and you think there's a purpose! Man, I'll tell
you—you got to get what you can, do what you can with it, and then
you got to die." (252)

Unmasking Saleem's inflated rhetoric of "purpose," Shiva derides Saleem's
faith in "reason" as an insignia of his elitism. Indeed, we have already seen
how Saleem's fixation on those qualities is highly narcissistic, diverting him
from oppression and effectively licensing his own abuses of human rights.
Shiva accordingly impugns the discourse of reason for not only failing to
check but more accurately fostering Saleem's egoistic self-interest, and, in
doing so, Shiva articulates an ambivalence about "reason" and other liberal vocabularies of selfhood that was common during and in the aftermath of colonization. As Partha Chatterjee explains, "For the colonized
middle-class mind, caught in its 'middleness,' the discourse of Reason was not
unequivocally liberating. The invariable implication it carried of the historical necessity of colonial rule and its condemnation of indigenous culture as
the storehouse of unreason, or (in a stage-of-civilization argument) of reason
yet unborn...made the discourse of Reason oppressive."[30] Saleem, as such,
levies an idiom that was not necessarily expected to reverse the structural
inequities entrenched under empire; on the contrary, that language was seen
to conspire with the derogatory stereotypes that furnished ideological supports for colonialism. And it is Shiva, ironically, who exposes Saleem's itinerary of liberal self-fashioning to collude with imperialism's larger ideological
apparatus, his dualistic privileging of the intellect displaying parallel biases as
those that warranted colonial rule.

   In addition to substantiating his class privilege, Saleem's binaristic patterns of thought disarm Shiva, writing off his claims upon him. In particular,
Saleem distinguishes his nasal faculties, which he associates with the intellect, from Shiva's superhuman propensity—an unusually large and powerful
pair of knees. In this way, too, Saleem defines himself in opposition to Shiva
by deeming Shiva hostage to corporeal being. In contrast to Shiva's knees,
Saleem insists on smell's impotence, bemoaning that "[a] nose will give you
knowledge, but not power-over-events" (352). This dichotomy between nose
and knees marshals a classically dualistic prioritization of mind and thought
over body and action. To similar ends, Saleem description of Shiva's physical
prowess as "grasping, choking" (488) dismisses it as excessive and ungovernable, while also differentiating it from his own pretense of order and discipline. This ploy of allying Shiva with rampant violence insulates Saleem from
everything he imaginatively transfers onto Shiva, implicitly absolving himself

of accountability for his own crimes. Of especial irony, Saleem's dualistic worldview further enables his illusion that he is Shiva's victim, as Saleem relates: "Shiva and Saleem, victor and victim" (497). However, such a conceit merely deflects attention from both his own machinations and Shiva's genuine disenfranchisement.

Although Saleem tangentially admits that he ostracizes Shiva—acknowledging that "throughout this narrative I've been pushing him, the other, into the background" (468)—Shiva's fate is never fully owned by Saleem. Rather, he continues to explain Shiva in terms of senseless and inexhaustible violence, downplaying the veracity of Shiva's underlying rage. While Saleem identifies Shiva as the "unspeakable name, the name of my guilt" (448), he refuses to overtly concede that he himself bears responsibility for Shiva's circumstances. Nevertheless, Shiva looms ever larger in the narrative, becoming so colossal as to demand his own "principle"—a principle that Saleem deciphers as "dooming us to flounder endlessly amid murder rape greed war" (342). In turn, although Saleem yearns to exert exclusive control over both his and India's destiny, he must increasingly acknowledge

> that Shiva, in short, has made us who we are. (He, too, was born on the stroke of midnight; he, like me, was connected to history. The modes of connection—if I'm right in thinking they applied to me—enabled him, too, to affect the passage of the days.) (342)

Saleem, in effect, is forced to credit Shiva with coauthorship of his narrative, if only because Shiva represents a necessary foil to Saleem's fantasies about himself. While Saleem scapegoats Shiva by displacing what he sees as the irrational, corporeal, and inhuman facets of existence onto Shiva's identity, that transference, of course, occludes how those very energies engender Saleem's own subjectivity. Saleem must, then, repress his "unspeakable" solidarity with Shiva precisely in order to secure the ruse of his own rightful entitlement.

Moreover, although Saleem superficially aligns himself with everything reasoned and emancipated—democracy, secularism, and equality, among other liberal values—his treatment of Shiva reveals the precariousness of those ideals, as well as how they require the specter of their presumed antitheses for their ideological coherence. As chapter 1 explored, the liberal social body is paradoxically consolidated by the menace of its own violation, much as the fiction of corporeal integrity is rendered persuasive by the threat of bodily desecration and abuse. In essence, Saleem must consign Shiva to a state of enslavement to the body in order to acquire legibility for his own subjectivity. Saleem's imaginative entrapment of Shiva within the body illumines how and why the consecration of certain properties as constitutive of the human necessarily leads to the maligning and policing of other, allegedly antonymic attributes. Saleem's disingenuous marginalization of Shiva (as well as, for that matter, of the reader) is therefore not incidental to but rather part and parcel of his goal of reasoned self-constitution, which is to say that his sophistries equally make manifest the exclusionary anatomy of the logic of rights. By opening up these foreclosures enabling the norms that Saleem recruits to posit himself as an exemplary liberal subject, *Midnight's Children* implicitly interrogates their larger philosophical architecture.

In sum, Saleem profits immensely from imputing all violence and depravity to the "principle" of Shiva. It is therefore Shiva who offers Saleem his primary alibi, one that not only pardons Saleem's own wrongs but also preserves the idealism of his generation. In a sense, then, Shiva also represents a necessary fiction. No doubt the transition to independence on the Indian subcontinent was overwhelmingly contaminated by violence—perhaps more so than any other decolonization process. Yet Saleem must imagine that event as a cause for optimism, demanding that he compartmentalize the internally rapacious violence of the partition, if not purge it from his narrative entirely. As such, Shiva comes to serve as a type of placeholder for those realities that Saleem must expel from his own identity in order to verify a particular vision of human and national emancipation.

"Rituals of Blood": The Enabling Violations of Human Rights

As we have seen, Saleem exorcizes his own intimacy with violence by deflecting it onto Shiva. However, he simultaneously becomes painfully cognizant that any hope embodied in the children—as figures for the nation-state, independence, and democracy alike—derives from their proximity to those many forces for which he blames Shiva. Saleem's narrative thus charts his gradual disillusionment as he reckons with the fact that his generation has spawned some of the most unthinkable violence of global modernity. As a consequence, Saleem confronts the knowledge that any "meaning" either he or the children possess must inhere within such entanglements, and this notion that violence can serve a confirmatory, generative role plays out on many levels in *Midnight's Children*. Most immediately, Saleem explains the national imaginary as activated and prolonged by cyclical enactments of its own almost ritual destruction, for instance, as he sardonically describes nationalism as a "mass fantasy" that "periodically need[s] the sanctification and renewal which can only be provided by rituals of blood" (124–25). Saleem here captures something essential about both the fictitious construct of the nation and the metaphor of the liberal social body. Much as the ideally integrated body politic is paradoxically corroborated by the menace of its violent unmaking, a parallel symbolic economy furnishes explanatory authority to human rights. Indeed, talk of human rights often appears parasitic on scenes of rights abuse, leading rights protections to appear most urgent when under siege. This is to say that the rhetorical currency of human rights is, albeit tragically, amplified by bloodshed and suffering, with human rights discourses thriving in a vicious relay with rights violations.

That said, the core paradox of the children is not this figural affinity with violence; rather, Saleem describes their ultimate "meaning" as deriving from their literal devastation, or "that they had come, in order to come to nothing" (348). Saleem thus contends with the anxiety that "the purpose of Midnight's Children might be annihilation; that we would have no meaning until we were destroyed" (262). For the majority of his narrative, "meaning" encodes his goal of reasoned self-constitution, as it is conducted on the intersecting levels of textual self-inscription, liberal subject formation, and national unity. However, the eventual fate of the children compels him to question those overriding ambitions. Within his narrative, the prophesied destruction of the children is carried out by Rushdie's fictionalized Indira Gandhi. Rushdie here rewrites the 1975–77 Indian State of Emergency, in which Gandhi enforced massive sterilization campaigns against peasants and indigent city dwellers alike.[31] However, Rushdie's Gandhi engineers the emergency specifically to disempower the children—much as it in actuality eviscerated the postindependence dreams of democracy, liberalism, equality, and human rights. Indeed, the historical emergency legally suspended the fundamental rights in the Indian Constitution, and in *Midnight's Children* that outcome is materialized through the children's sterilization, which Saleem refers to as "the smashing, the pulverizing, the irreversible discombobulation of the children of midnight" (492).[32] This assault also excises their magic, physically inscribing their violated rights on their bodies. The tragedy of their sterilization accordingly reifies more abstract repercussions of both legally condoned exceptions to human rights and the judicial failure to uphold those rights in the face of their infringement.[33]

As such, it is highly revealing that the children are sterilized, which effectively extinguishes a foremost indicia of their agency and individuality alike—namely, the capacity for "reproducing themselves" (505). This fate reinforces the linkage between sexuality and self-authorship that pervades *Midnight's Children*. One suggestion is that Saleem composes his autobiography in effort to compensate for his impotence, a condition exacerbated, if not directly wrought, by his torture under Gandhi's regime. Through-out, sexual vitality operates as a cipher for speech and self-narration, and the destruction of the children's reproductive organs is accordingly a synecdoche for more totalizing rights infringements, especially the wide-spread censorship instituted during the emergency.[34] Much as scholarship on human rights often regards speech as the nucleus of the human and, by extension, speech rights as paramount, the children's coterminous sterilization-silencing attacks the core of their humanness. Yet far more than their individual liberties are destroyed; rather, this fate also cripples their symbolic capacity to unify and energize the national imaginary. The "sperectomy: the draining-out of hope" (503) inflicted on the children is cast as a malady that plagues the Indian populace at large. Even as the children are rendered barren, that injury captures the emergency's analo-gous abrogation of both the original promise of independence and the commitments formalized within the Indian Constitution and its Charter of Fundamental Rights.

Even here, however, the children's fate also vivifies an inevitable by-product of legal codification and the frictions endemic to a secular democracy. While there is substantial scholarly disagreement over whether Gandhi's decrees in fact claimed constitutional backing, the conventional rationale for including emergency provisions in a constitution returns us to the inevitable schism between the individual and the larger community.[35] Emergency provisions like those Gandhi exploited typically gain justification through the belief that they provide a stopgap measure that will safeguard the collective in the midst of grave threats to its welfare.[36] Yet the children's devastation illustrates the inevitable costs of such willingness to forfeit or compromise individual rights to salvage the nation. If the children are the progeny of a particular vision of postcolonial independence and liberal rights, it is not entirely strange that they would be sacrificed to preserve the nation's equilibrium. Their steriliza-tion therefore seems to mark the demise—for better and for worse—of the distinctly liberal collection of norms Saleem strives to embody, and, indeed, the conclusion of Saleem's narrative does gesture toward a surrogate value structure that might replace them.

The novel's penultimate chapter, "Midnight," recounts Saleem's mutila-tion by Gandhi with accelerating panic:

> I don't want to tell it!—But I swore to tell it all.—No, I renounce, not that, surely some things are better left...?—That won't wash; what can't be cured, must be endured!—But surely not the whispering walls, and treason, and snip snip, and the women with the bruised chests?—

> Especially those things.—But how can I, look at me, I'm tearing myself
> apart, can't even agree with myself, talking arguing like a wild fellow,
> cracking up, memory going, yes, memory plunging into chasms and
> being swallowed by the dark, only fragments remain, none of it makes
> sense any more!—But I mustn't presume to judge; must simply con-
> tinue (having once begun) until the end; sense-and-nonsense is no lon-
> ger (perhaps never was) for me to evaluate.—But the horror of it, I can't
> won't musn't won't can't no!—Stop this; begin.—No!—Yes. (485)

On one level, Saleem's chaotic, stream-of-consciousness narrative simulates
the trauma and psychic breakdown induced by his torture; as his mental
equilibrium and physical well-being come under siege, his narrative similarly
falls apart. Yet on a deeper level, that dissolution also foretells the failure of
his itinerary of individualist self-fashioning. Whereas early on Saleem adopts
legalistic, evidentiary language to substantiate the orderly, reasoned dimensions of his subjectivity, his narrative's conclusion finds him beyond "sense-
and-nonsense," or divested of rational purpose. The frequently doubled
texture of his narrative thus anticipates his (and its) pending collapse into
fragments, again requiring that we align Saleem's interconnected goals for
his highly regimented biography, a rationally integrated subjectivity, and the
national imaginary—all of which are metaphorically conjoined within the
fiction of the impermeable, inviolable body. His torture's assault on his corporeal integrity jeopardizes each of these mutually imbricated imperatives
in parallel ways; in other words, it simultaneously induces and explains his
narrative's incoherence, his psychic rupture, the termination of his odyssey of
liberal self-determination, and the disintegration of the liberal body politic.

Although Saleem's torture precipitates his narrative and psychic atrophy,
however, he insists that it also divulges, at long last, the answer to his relentless
pursuit of "meaning" (504), and that answer magnifies yet another paradox
of human rights. Describing his "excision" by Gandhi, he observes that
if "it was at the house of the wailing women that I learned the answer to
the question of purpose which had plagued me all my life, then by saving
myself from that palace of annihilations I would also have denied myself
this most precious of discoveries" (488). So if Saleem's narrative represents a
crucible in the formation of the liberal subject of rights, that epiphany first
and foremost indexes the costs of such an itinerary of selfhood. It registers
both the cruelties that Saleem's ambitions have licensed and those domains of
experience that his privileging of reason has quarantined. These repressions
variously extend from his grandiose designs for the nation; his fantasy of his
own supremacy; and a particular symbolic economy of the liberal social body.

Each of those overlaid pursuits requires that Saleem deny and evade his own, as well as more ubiquitous, realities of suffering and vulnerability—entailing that Gandhi's "excision" ironically points to those foundational aspects of the human condition that liberal theories of selfhood must cover over. His dualistic disdain toward embodiment is only one symptom of how his onus to autonomously self-determine suppresses his own finitude and weakness. Yet precisely his experience of torture, it is suggested, interrupts and thus gives the lie to those distancing mechanisms.

Importantly, Saleem's torture further reminds us that respect for human rights does not arise ex nihilo; rather, the basic conditions that foster those norms' emergence lie in their violation. As Pheng Cheah frames this conundrum, there is no justice that is not a "justice-in-violation," no appeal to human rights that arises from a pure, uncompromised, unsullied state.[37] To state things differently, no achievement in the name of human rights is exempt from the production of corresponding denials of rights protections. Saleem's self-serving machinations, as such, present us with the residues and remainders that are guaranteed to trouble human rights in their claims to universal jurisdiction. By extension, we might ask whether Saleem's coming into appreciation for human rights represents, to draw on Gayatri Spivak's language, an "enabling violation" for the liberal subject.[38] On the one hand, Saleem's exercise in reasoned self-determination is premised on the active disenfranchisement of other lives, most notably Shiva's. It therefore dramatizes the symbolic, material, political, and ideological foreclosures that lend explanatory authority to human rights, at the same time illustrating why the individual in conformity with their dictates is paradoxically inaugurated through such exclusions. Yet on the other hand, Saleem must first experience the infringement of his own rights—as well as the annihilation of the subjectivity his entire narrative has labored over—before he can fully grasp the "meaning" of the irreplaceable work that human rights indeed can do. He himself must become a victim before he can comprehend the essence of either what he heralds as a scion of independence or the invaluable safeguards of human rights. Given that the failure of the midnight's children is what compels Saleem to renounce his chronic egoism and self-interest, it is precisely this failure that ushers in a less bold and significantly more realistic approach to what human rights might portend.

The Collapse of Individualist Self-Fashioning

As Saleem's narrative nears its end, his fears that "memory cracks beyond hope of reassembly" and that "fadings, and gaps" will overtake him become all the more persistent (442). And indeed, this anxiety that his overlapping experiments will meet with psychic and formal breakdown eventually does comes to fruition—and in a denouement that leads Saleem to repudiate the liberal norms he has otherwise sought to verify. Drawing toward his narrative's finale, Saleem relinquishes his designs on politics to instead focus on the domestic; he agrees to marry Padma, his muse, and becomes increasingly invested in his adopted son, Aadam. He likewise jettisons his goal of authoritative "purpose," instead "conclu[ding] that privacy, the small individual lives of men, are preferable to all this inflated macrocosmic activity" (500). Thus forswearing universal relevance, he explains that "refus[al] to take the larger view": "We are too close to what-is-happening, perspective is impossible, ... right now we're too close to the cinema-screen, the picture is breaking up into dots, only subjective judgments are possible" (500). Saleem here abandons his facade of abstract neutrality to confront both his own contingence and the singular, localized realities that he had formerly elided. No longer postulating his narrative as "proof" or "evidence," he similarly concedes to his own fallibility, admitting of his autobiography, "The process of revision should be constant and endless" (530). However, Saleem does not present these moderated aims as a resignation or defeat. Quite the opposite, he impugns the falsity of his earlier pretense of mastery, idealism, and "greatness." Confessing to the narcissism that fueled such an agenda, he relates, "I hear lies being spoken in the night, anything you want to be you kin be, the greatest lie of all" (533). By no means last, as he foregoes his totalizing ambitions, Saleem instead claims to embrace "small[ness]" and "privacy" (500). Simply put, Saleem disavows the principles that have guided his narrative not in a vacuum but by gesturing toward a surrogate foundation for a markedly different topography of social justice and human rights.

Near the end of *Midnight's Children,* Saleem also grows preoccupied with a sense of pending death, although even that eventuality fills him with "profound relief" (515). In utter weariness, he describes his own face: "Now prematurely aged, I saw in the mirror of humility a human being to whom history could do no more, a grotesque creature who had been released from the preordained destiny which had battered him until he was half senseless" (500). Throughout his narrative, liberal self-fashioning has acted as the "destiny" that he here blames for rendering him "senseless"—a fitting condemnation in light of this book's argument that liberal cartographies of the human occlude the texture of sensory, affective engagement. Moreover, Saleem derides the exorbitance of his identity for being "grotesque," thereby acknowledging both the self-aggrandizing and self-indulgent nature of his twinned pursuits of individual and narrative mastery. Of even greater importance, in the process of eschewing his illusions of sovereignty, he substitutes them with "humility," here too representing a striking departure from the ideals governing most of his narrative.

Saleem does imagine his own collapse at the end of *Midnight's Children,* and that fate in addition implodes the liberal body politic.[39] Saleem's disintegration, without question, signifies a failure on multiple levels—of a particular vision of postcoloniality, of the wild hopes surrounding independence, of democracy in the aftermath of Gandhi's emergency, and, moreover, of the liberal norms subtending the logic of rights. However, his fate is simultaneously cast as a celebration of sorts, given that it induces him to accept a markedly unprecedented conception, for Saleem, of human selfhood as well as community. In particular, the apocalyptic conclusion of the novel depicts Saleem as overwhelmed and succumbing to the demands of the collective, which it notably inflicts on his corporeal being. Saleem awaits his demise ready to "explode, bones splitting breaking beneath the awful pressure of the crowd" (533). He gives in to the violence and the tumultuous energies of the masses, which most of his narrative deplored. In doing so, he abjures his elitist self-enclosure to instead accept kinds of intermingling and porosity, vividly describing himself as "a broken creature spilling pieces of itself into the street" (533). Beyond this graphic imagery, Saleem's fate is deeply sexualized. At the same time as he anticipates his own marriage, his narrative employs overtly erotic language to register the fracturing of his subjectivity: "I am being buffeted right and left while rip tear crunch reaches its climax, and my body is screaming, it cannot take this kind of treatment any more" (533). Here, the very realms of experience that Saleem sought to control and negate engulf him on a carnal level, forcing him to contend with the messy dimensions of his own embodiment. If this cataclysmic conclusion reifies the exhaustion of liberalism as an ideology, then the violence it has authored over the course of Saleem's narrative comes to be exacted on his own body. Once again, Saleem's corporeal being at once symbolizes the state of affairs in the national body politic, both denoting the decline of a particular vision of the nation as ideally integrated and magnifying the violence of the many exclusions sustaining such a metaphor. Whereas liberal theories of the human depend on the fiction of the impermeable, self-enclosed, sovereign subject, the penetration of Saleem's physical being ultimately marks the hollowness of those ideals.

Saleem's abdication of the liberal onus to self-determine thus wreaks violent wounds; however, that surrender simultaneously enables his fusion with the exuberant, chaotic rhythms of the collective. Rushdie concludes the final paragraph of *Midnight's Children* with a passage that poetically captures such synergies:

> Yes, they will trample me underfoot, the numbers marching one two three, four hundred million five hundred six, reducing me to specks of voiceless dust, just as, in all good time, they will trample my son who is not my son, and his son who will not be his, until the thousand and first generation, until a thousand and one midnights have bestowed their terrible gifts and a thousand and one children have died, because it is the privilege and the curse of midnight's children to be both masters and victims of their times, to forsake privacy and be sucked into the annihilating whirlpool of the multitudes, and to be unable to live or die in peace. (533)

Saleem envisages himself inundated by "numbers," or by the infinite human complexity that he has aggressively sought to suppress. The public "whirl-pool" here cannot be ordered, reasoned, or integrated into a unified ethos, as Saleem aspires for his encyclopedic narrative. His terminal vision is therefore not a vindication of the liberal democratic public sphere or of impartial civic deliberation; on the contrary, Saleem's immersion in the collective rescinds those standards that have overseen both his individual and the nation's self-founding. Saleem is further rendered anonymous and "voiceless," another salient reversal in a novel that recurrently correlates individuation with self-authorship. Overall, *Midnight's Children*'s conclusion stages a disincorporation, a deconsolidation, and a deconstitution—or a renunciation of the very logic that organizes the vast majority of its narrative. Saleem becomes both victim and offender, both cursed and privileged, and both alive and dead—seemingly, at last, acclimating himself to paradox. Needless to say, this end also explodes the dualistic architecture that has supported both his ostracism of Shiva and his illusions of self-importance. In turn, *Midnight's Children* leaves us with a picture of independence *from* the mythology of liberal self-determination that Saleem strives to realize. And with that in mind, we should additionally note that its narrative concludes on the exact anniversary of Saleem's birth—as such, on another "Independence Day"—although one that inaugurates a very different vision of both individual and collective emancipation.

Conclusion: The Empty Jar

In light of such a violent conclusion, *Midnight's Children* might seem to leave us with a bleak forecast for the postcolonial nation-state, for Indian democracy, and for liberal theories of politics and selfhood alike. And indeed, its narrative does in many ways caution against the boldness and triumphalism that frequently colors those vocabularies of freedom. But the final passages of *Midnight's Children* also offer up two images that we might equally take to presage the vital promise of human rights. First, the narrative returns us to Saleem's pickling motif, albeit only for Saleem to discard that enterprise and the many kinds of codification it denotes. Saleem here relinquishes his interrelated desires for his autobiography's unity, order, and vast reference, conceding, by contrast, that "the future cannot be preserved in a jar; one jar must remain empty" (532). For Saleem, the contents of this final jar must instead remain open to "revision" that is "constant and endless" (530), reconstellating Saleem's figure for narrative self-constitution seemingly to index those aspects of both individual and collective experience that resist preadjudication and inherently flout universalization. Accordingly, we might interpret Saleem's empty jar as a metaphor for justice itself, since the essence of justice, too, is to be perpetually under negotiation, revisionary, and residual.

Along similar lines, we might take Saleem's empty jar to occasion a meditation on the intertwined opportunities and constraints of human rights. The enormous potential of human rights inheres precisely in the fact that their discourses defy containment or arrest; rather, to be persuasive, their imaginings of social justice must mirror the incalculable heterogeneity of human existence—again, for better and for worse. As aspirational, visionary languages, human rights must remain fluid, capacious, and malleable—which is to say that, like Saleem's jar, they are empty vessels, the very openness of which creates their conditions of possibility. That said, Saleem's concluding recognitions do not compel him to destroy his existing jars; he does not entirely forego his designs on authoritative meaning and truth. However, if we playfully read Saleem's thirty jars as uncanny analogues for the thirty articles of the UDHR, then as metaphors they caution that our available definitions of human rights must equally include a vacant, interstitial term that could technically be filled with anything—with the unordained, the unforeseeable, the unprecedented. Saleem's empty jar, as a result, gestures toward what Werner Hamacher calls the "right to have rights"—that is, "a principally open right" that "does not belong to the catalog of rights . . . because it is the unconditional condition of all rights, therefore legally uncodifiable."[40] Perhaps, then, Saleem's empty vessel portends the sort of fluid, protean protections that might surmount the many exceptions endemic to liberal theories of the human, the jar's sheer lack of binding, prescriptive content an antidote against those exclusions. This is all to say that while Saleem's terminal jar might appear to mark a tragic incompleteness, it simultaneously registers the fertile generativity required to navigate the uncharted terrain of the future.

Second, as his narrative closes, Saleem increasingly reflects on the outlook for his adopted son, Aadam, who is suggested to forebode another alternative to Saleem. Yet Saleem importantly refuses to weigh in on Aadam's significance, merely surmising that "new myths are needed; but that's none of my business" (527). Nonetheless, his narrative introduces Aadam—with a name clearly lauding his status as another inaugural subject—as something of a corrective to the folly of Saleem's generation. Aadam is also born during the onset of a midnight, although a radically different one from Saleem's—namely, the midnight of Gandhi's emergency and her suspension of the rule of law. In this sense, he, too, signals the urgency of human rights, although here under the shadow of Indian democracy's downfall rather than expectations about its buoyant future. Moreover, his temperament diverges strikingly from that of his adopted father; in place of Saleem's exorbitant ambitions, Aadam is endowed with "humility" (515). In place of Saleem's prolific narrative outpouring, Aadam also refuses to speak, and that reticence is seemingly a by-product of overly large ears that have exposed him to too much. As Saleem admits, Aadam belongs to a generation that "would grow up far tougher than the first, not looking for their fate in prophecy or the stars, but forging it in the implacable furnaces of their wills" (515). It is in opposition to his own inflated, self-reflexive idealism that Saleem attributes to Aadam realism—a mindset that will assumedly orient his concerns much closer to the ground, or to the material, local, mundane problems of social justice. Indeed, it is further noteworthy that Aadam is Shiva's biological son, given Shiva's fine gauge for inequity and intolerance of Saleem's privileged pursuits. Hence, it is through the figure of Aadam that *Midnight's Children* tentatively sketches the contours of an emergent topography of human rights—one that precisely in its "humility" might be better disposed to negotiate their many paradoxes.

CHAPTER FOUR

Women's Rights and the Lure of Self-Determination in Nawal El Saadawi's *Woman at Point Zero*

> In countries of the South the issue of human rights raises the question, How far can we talk of human rights without a new conception which extends them to the economic, social, cultural, racial and religious fields as well as to women and youth?
>
> —Nawal El Saadawi, 1992

Of all the controversies over human rights, those surrounding the status of women's rights perhaps most vividly illumine how and why rights discourses are prone to overdetermination. Indeed, one need merely cite recent contentions about the veil to demonstrate the exceptionally, even explosively charged tenor that debates about women's rights often assume, especially when they mutate into related disputes over secularism. To be sure, from one vantage point, the beleaguerment of women's rights in many societies—within the North as well as the global South—is troubling and persistent. There is little doubt that advocacy for women's rights represents one of the most important tasks on the human rights agenda. Yet appeals to women's rights simultaneously provide a frequent pretext for international policing, one often cloaked in a rhetoric of postcolonial regression and lack. Women's rights campaigns are especially susceptible to the neoimperial and paternalistic undercurrents that animate much contemporary human rights reportage. In turn, the polarizing thrust of these and other disagreements has led many theorists to take women's rights as a prototypical "test case" for adjudicating the basic universality of the rights paradigm, or for interrogating rights as both a legal-philosophical construct and a discursive regime.[1] For instance, Susan Moller Okin famously put the question in such terms by asking whether the precarity of women's rights in many societies forces us to conclude that "multiculturalism is bad for women."[2]

We might further examine these tensions to index why the disparate values subsumed within the logic of human rights frequently appear self-canceling and internally contradictory. On the one hand, we have seen how liberal cartographies of the human define the subject in terms of reasoned self-determination, positing the autonomous and self-contained individual. On the other hand, human rights norms are equally understood to enshrine the right to cultural self-determination and thus to imagine the subject as embedded within a larger community. However, cultural rights have at times been impugned for prioritizing the collective over the individual in ways that dangerously subordinate the interests of women to the group's needs. No doubt, this complaint comes to appear quite trenchant in light of how women's lives and bodies have, over history and throughout the world, been policed under the assumption that they are repositories for a culture's shared practices and beliefs.[3] Indeed, it is precisely in response to such realities that theorists like Okin venture arguments that, however misleading, treat "culture" as virtually synonymous with patriarchy and the oppression of women—thereby capturing why anxieties about the cultural imperialism of human rights often appear newly salient when debates about women's rights are on the table.[4]

Yet what these at times inflammatory conversations further illustrate are significant casualties that have accompanied the expanding currency of the international languages of human rights. The growing popularity of rights talk is partner to that idiom's increasing malleability, entailing that the vocabulary of human rights can find itself deployed to justify competing ideological and political commitments at once. Such a syndrome has been particularly acute in relation to quarrels over women's rights, wherein discourses of women's rights both represent a crucial tool for auguring social and political advancement and evidence the frequently reactionary undertones of such concerns.

Both the fragile status of women's rights and the conflictual relationship between the individual and the collective preoccupy Nawal El Saadawi's *Woman at Point Zero*. Yet El Saadawi also directs us to consider a historical moment before the languages of women's rights incurred international preponderance and legitimacy. First published in Beirut in 1973, the original text of *Woman at Point Zero* was composed prior to the historic developments that fueled the women's rights movement—and thus when the grammar of women's progress and liberation was still mobile and in transition. While 1975 was declared International Women's Year by the United Nations, the Convention on the Elimination of Discrimination Against Women (CEDAW) was not adopted by its General Assembly until 1979, and it did not come into force until 1981. Likewise, it was not until the 1985 Third World Conference on Women in Nairobi that violence against women became a major international issue.[5] We might therefore conceive of *Woman at Point Zero* as documenting an era when the discourses of women's empowerment were still in contest and under negotiation. El Saadawi's protagonist Firdaus—an Egyptian prostitute on death row for the offense of murder—appeals over the course of her autobiographical narrative to an assorted collection of liberal tenets, including "respect," "self-determination," and "freedom," as she attempts to fashion her self-worth. In this respect, El Saadawi's narrative actively searches for a language through which to promote concerns that have subsequently been formalized and consolidated under the designation of *women's rights*. *Woman at Point Zero* accordingly experiments not so much with the idiom of rights alone as with corresponding liberal vocabularies of selfhood, weighing their effectiveness for explaining and redressing women's distinct experiences of injury.

While the novel's central narrative grasps at these germinal discourses of women's liberation and progress, El Saadawi later supplemented *Woman at Point Zero*'s original text with an author's preface to the 1983 English edition. This addendum overtly enlists the language of rights, retrospectively framing Firdaus's entire narrative as a testament to the "need to challenge and to overcome those forces that deprive human beings of their right to live, to love and to real freedom."[6] As such, this preface in its own way tracks the ascendancy of human rights discourses over a relatively finite span of time. In hindsight appealing to the newly minted language of human rights, El Saadawi draws upon it seemingly to corroborate the experiences of a protagonist who might otherwise be written off as a pariah, thereby averring the acumen of that evolving idiom. Firdaus's actual biography, however, more accurately dramatizes the foreclosures and contradictions that haunt human rights as an explanatory regime; her narrative chronicles how the liberal ideals that support human rights inure her to her own social and political subjugation. Moreover, although Firdaus's narrative follows a trajectory of *bildung* that, on first blush, might seem to verify a liberal cartography of the human, it simultaneously marshals aesthetic codes that implicitly countermand such an itinerary of subject formation. The self-image that Firdaus devises over her narrative is riddled with ambivalences that together expose not only the hollowness of the values prescribed for her by a misogynistic culture but also the pitfalls inherent in liberalism's descriptive arsenal. Ironically, much as the act of murder awakens within Firdaus long-overdue feelings of "pride," prostitution is the only profession that affords her a semblance of autonomy, freedom, and "honor." When all is said and done,

Firdaus's rhetoric of freedom and choice acts more as an alibi for her chronic oppression than a vehicle for her meaningful empowerment, with *Woman at Point Zero* staging a pointed critique of liberalism's reigning assumptions about human flourishing.

At the same time, the novel portrays how dimensions of Firdaus's subjectivity exceed and defy such liberal mappings of the subject, even while El Saadawi's rhetoric might seem to confirm their authority. Firdaus's stream-of-consciousness narrative repeatedly lapses into visceral, ecstatic, and affective measures of expression, overwhelming the referents within which El Saadawi encases it. In effect, Firdaus inhabits and experiments with two different aesthetic and linguistic registers of selfhood, their corresponding vocabularies warring against and unsettling one another. Although Firdaus's conspicuously liberal rhetoric might appear to imply a liberal account of the human, her yearnings for emotional and physical intimacy overturn the erasure of embodiment that generally underwrites such norms. Firdaus's desires flout the conceit that bodily integrity is a necessary predicate to human dignity, as her narrative proceeds through language, imagery, and an aesthetic that are deeply corporeal in their fiber. Thus exploding the impermeable, self-enclosed, sovereign subject of rights, her biography unfolds an ontology of social justice grounded in porosity of self, embodied suffering, and interpersonal beholdenness. It is in this sense that *Woman at Point Zero* opens up the liabilities accompanying liberal discourses of human rights, marking why they will fall short of certain kinds of injury. These reservations about rights logic consequently redirect us to a question I have already posed by way of Merleau-Ponty's phenomenology: why might corporeal domains of apperception and cognition beget an alternate topography of human rights—one better geared to contend with the many aspects and implications of embodiment?

The formal properties of *Woman at Point Zero* further probe the appropriate mode and genre for representing violations of human rights, laying bare the competing demands that regulate rights narration, especially when it documents abuses of the "Third World woman." *Woman at Point Zero* is a realist novel that claims empirical, even legal authority. El Saadawi frames Firdaus's story not once but twice—in the Author's Preface with its retrospective reliance on human rights and within the original text. In the latter case, the novel's internal proxy for El Saadawi, a "doctor" who encounters Firdaus in a women's prison awaiting execution, both introduces Firdaus and defends El Saadawi's decision to reproduce her story. Yet while El Saadawi's frame narrator presents Firdaus as a "real woman," El Saadawi categorizes *Woman at Point Zero* as fiction. Similarly, although this narrator purports to transcribe Firdaus's spoken autobiography, Firdaus herself insists that language and "words" are inadequate to convey her experiences. Overall, while El Saadawi levies Firdaus's life as a parable seemingly designed to proselytize for women's rights, Firdaus's actual narrative complicates that very agenda. *Woman at Point Zero*'s quoting of the generic and discursive conventions germane to human rights witnessing is, as such, counterpart to its strategic enactment of their limits, and precisely by dramatizing those limits does it incarnate the reading experience to adumbrate an alternate fabric of just co-belonging.

The Mixed Opportunities of Human Rights

El Saadawi has experienced an unusually long and prominent career, due to her activism as much as her literary production. El Saadawi began her professional life as a medical doctor in rural Egypt, which she recounts in *The Hidden Face of Eve* (1977) and her memoir, *Walking Through Fire* (2002). Her preceding *Memoirs of a Woman Doctor* (1960) and *The Hidden Face of Eve* together garnered El Saadawi the reputation of being the first to introduce into Arab letters "the issue of sexual oppression of women connected with everyday customs and the prevalence of deviant behaviours such as incest that victimized women in the family."[7] Much as *Woman at Point Zero* broadcasts its political commitments, El Saadawi's writing frequently displaces the boundaries between medical treatise, memoir, sociology, fiction, and activism.[8] Indeed, precisely by challenging those artificial barriers does *Woman at Point Zero* raise important questions about both the aesthetic conventions and ideological presumptions that further the consciousness-raising ends of human rights narration.

While El Saadawi entered medicine with the belief that it would empower her, she faced repeated gender discrimination and a pervasive neglect of women's health issues within the Egyptian medical community. She served as director general of the Health Education Department of the Egyptian Ministry of Health from 1966 to 1972, only to be dismissed from that post for her feminist politics. She was thereafter imprisoned along with numerous other Egyptian intellectuals and dissidents in 1981 by Anwar el-Sadat, which she recounts in *Memoirs from a Women's Prison* (1983). After abandoning the practice of medicine, El Saadawi cofounded the Arab Women's Solidarity Association only to have its Egyptian chapter forcibly closed in 1991. In the meantime, her writings have incited multiple death threats by fundamentalist as well as terrorist organizations, forcing her into exile in the United States in the late 1990s.

El Saadawi's reception has also been striking.[9] Arab and Western scholars alike have rebuked her for catering to a foreign readership and gratifying neo-Orientalist stereotypes about the oppression and "exotic" cultural life of "Third World women."[10] Her writing has likewise been assailed for its overtly political and sociological content, or for didacticism that sacrifices sophistication and complexity.[11] Such an allegation, however, directly contravenes El Saadawi's own understanding of her novels and their audiences. El Saadawi explains that her "frame of reference is my village, Arabic, Egyptian culture, history, and my struggle in my country" and chides Western critics for the failure to "imagine that there is a Egyptian writer who writes without being anchored in the west. Or as if there is nothing called original thought except in the west."[12] In the meantime, she has been attacked by Arab scholars for her radical message and audacious feminism.[13] Understandably, her mixed "celebrity" in the West has only further "delegitimized" her with such readers.[14] Other critics have instead treated El Saadawi's corpus as, in Amal Amireh's words, primarily "an interesting subject for a reception study." Amireh both critiques how Western critics have responded to El Saadawi by "rewrit[ing] both the writer and her texts according to a scripted first-world narrative about Arab women's oppression" and berates El Saadawi's willingness to "compromise" her publications by packaging them for such consumption.[15]

Although *Woman at Point Zero* has earned its share of credit on postcolonial syllabi, El Saadawi's novels have not met with the volume or spirit of academic scholarship elicited by Salman Rushdie, J. M. Coetzee, and Arundhati Roy, and we might explain this deficit as resulting from her failure to entertain the dominant stylistics and motifs that postcolonial studies has naturalized.[16] Whereas prevalent strains of postcolonial criticism have often preferred an aesthetic of defamiliarization, El Saadawi asserts that the literary can render empirical truth and a concrete politics.[17] Likewise, if postcolonial scholars have favored texts that "write back" to the Western canon, a project undertaken by this book's other three writers, El Saadawi maintains that her primary audience is a local one. It is thus in opposition to the tropes of nomadism, movement, and cultural crossing that El Saadawi contends with realities of cultural confinement and captivity. Although El Saadawi has inspired isolated analysis that draws on poststructuralist theory, it remains worth asking whether and why *Woman at Point Zero* may be something of an outlier relative to the other, Booker Prize–winning authors considered in this book.[18] If, as critics allege, postcolonial theory has at times elided the material conditions of survival within the postcolony, then El Saadawi's situated, locally invested aesthetics and politics provide a fruitful occasion to revisit the field's overriding dispositions.

Beyond these more academic debates, El Saadawi has self-consciously reckoned with the doubled nature of human rights discourses. While on the one hand she welcomes the label of "human rights activist," on the other she decries the opportunistic ways that human rights talk is manipulated to buttress Western self-interest.[19] El Saadawi makes frequent recourse to both human rights and related liberal constructs such as "freedom," "dignity," and "respect," as for instance in the Author's Preface. Similarly, when discussing her imprisonment under Sadat, El Saadawi condemns her incarceration without trial as a "tyranny" and "an abuse of human rights."[20] She has elsewhere endorsed codifying human rights as a mandatory safeguard of international law, and *The Hidden Face of Eve* (1980), her in-depth study of women in the Arab world, positively cites the Universal Declaration of Human Rights as a meaningful corrective to marriage laws in Muslim countries, which "give a husband an uncontested right to refuse his wife permission to leave the house, go to work, or travel" (190).[21]

In the midst of this rhetoric, however, El Saadawi in her political commentaries laments how human rights talk, despite its immense opportunities, poses serious problems, in particular, when neoimperial deployments of that idiom pollute and detract from its insurrectionary promise. For example, *The Hidden Face of Eve* advocates for women's rights while also criticizing how neoimperial foreign policy drafts that language to license the militarization of the global South, in particular, during the Gulf War (48). For El Saadawi, the rhetoric of "peace, development, justice, equality, human rights, and democracy" obscures economic and political wrongdoing. As she comments, "The media and the international information order concealed the real economic reasons behind the Gulf War (oil) behind a false morality built on phrases such as 'human rights,' 'democracy,' 'liberation of Kuwait,' etcetera" (20), and El Saadawi notably censures fundamentalist regimes for a comparable misappropriation of the language of human rights.

The text of *Woman at Point Zero* stages precisely such concerns about the slipperiness of the multiply coded idiom of human rights, both affirming its continued profit and accounting for its risks. Even while El Saadawi deplores how human rights discourse can apologize for duplicity, she mobilizes that very language to plot Firdaus's development. As such, the text underscores not only the dualities inscribed within the idiom of human rights but also the fictionality of the assumptions that it marshals. In effect, *Woman at Point Zero* simultaneously borrows from and contests the varied discourses of women's freedom and self-determination that were increasingly proliferating at the time of its composition. By holding those ideals up to scrutiny, it reckons with those aspects of selfhood that they occlude, as well as with how they actively misguide Firdaus.

Over the course of her narrative, the human rights abuses inflicted on Firdaus are legion: she is held in servitude, forced into sexual slavery, compelled into marriage without consent, subjected to prolonged intrusions of privacy, denied remuneration in exchange for her "work," and the list goes on and on.[22] All in all, the sheer scope and volume of these offenses indict Egyptian law for failing to safeguard her person. Hence, Firdaus's realities seem to ratify the common diagnosis that the legal, political, and economic order itself is structured to chronically undermine women's rights and freedoms: indeed, Firdaus's abuse is undoubtedly "part of a larger socio-economic and cultural web that entraps women."[23] Given that the majority of these rights infringements are committed by private actors, her circumstances in addition recall the frequent criticism that human rights law privileges public, state-sponsored crimes while neglecting harms that occur within the realm of the domestic.[24] Yet most central to her narrative is the violent experience of genital excision that Firdaus undergoes as a child, which the final section of this chapter considers in depth. While this event exacts a profound trauma, her narrative figures that injury as indispensable to her self-conception, and in ways that are suggested to be generative and even enabling. In particular, Firdaus's erotic life cannot be deciphered without reference to this violation of her corporeal integrity and human rights—a recognition we encounter as Firdaus first falls in love with a female schoolteacher, then is forced into a tyrannical marriage, finds herself twice conscripted into prostitution, and is eventually self-employed as a prostitute.

Striving to overcome these specific violations of her human rights as well as a broader climate of oppression, Firdaus salvages a tenuous sense of self by drawing on a liberal grammar of "respect," "self-determination," and "freedom." However, her reliance on such an explanatory apparatus ultimately serves to expose the falsity of those ideals, subverting their descriptive and philosophical authority. The devastating consequences of Firdaus's resort to such liberal vocabularies of selfhood become evident on multiple occasions, but two instances in her narrative are especially revealing. First, during her initial period of self-employ as a prostitute, Firdaus allows the notion of "respect" to guide her decisions. A male friend and periodic client one day tells her, "You are not respectable" (70), and Firdaus cannot dismiss his condemnation. As her narrative relates, these words "clung to me cold and sticky like spit, like the spit of an insult echoing in the ear" (72), and the onus to have respect ultimately motivates Firdaus to renounce her whole lifestyle out of the belief that it cannot live up to such a standard. Here, even Firdaus's deep suspicion of men does not alert her to the patriarchal origins of this accusation, with its proprietary undercurrents and disciplinary policing of her sexuality. The myth of "respect"—with that term's clear affinities to "dignity"—secures her acquiescence to a misogynistic basis for social control and causes her to misread circumstances that are vastly more complicated, given that her existence as a prostitute represents a state of relative autonomy and liberation. The idiom of "respect" is consequently shown to be a dangerously malleable one, all too readily invested with coercive content.

It is not accidental that this episode problematizes the assumptions about bodily integrity implied by her friend's use of the term *respect,* mirroring how the construct of dignity sustaining human rights is underwritten by a related conception of the impermeable body. In effect, an idealized conception of bodily inviolability is what both shames Firdaus and allows prostitution to be labeled deviant, even while that baseline proscription is revealed to conflict with Firdaus's own perceptions of her enhanced agency and worth. Her friend's epithet transforms this common though submerged link between respect and corporeal integrity into a basis for disciplining Firdaus, turning what should operate as a shield into a weapon of active disempowerment. Rigid, purified ideas about embodiment accordingly provide the warrant for Firdaus's continued social, political, and economic disenfranchisement, illuminating the mechanisms through which those dual premiums smuggle in concrete structures of oppression. While El Saadawi's activism against female circumcision no doubt testifies to the urgency of precisely such protections, sanctimonious views about bodily integrity caution about how that standard can readily become compulsory and punitive.

Along with this appeal to respect, the rhetoric of freedom populates Firdaus's narrative. However, her reality often resembles something closer to an individualist nightmare than a vindication of such an ideal. In a type of epiphany that she undergoes after being romantically jilted, she finds herself walking through the midnight streets in a dystopic dream state of "estrangement from everything":

I was a like a woman walking through an enchanted world to which she did not belong. She is free to do what she wants, and free not to do it. She experiences the rare pleasure of having no ties with anyone, of having broken with everything, of having cut all relation with the world around her, of being completely independent and living her independence completely, of enjoying freedom from any subjection to a man, to marriage, or to love; of being divorced from all limitations, whether rooted in rules and law in time or in the universe. (87)

Firdaus here experiences a peculiar fantasy of self-transcendence, which she relates in conspicuously liberal terminology. In a vision of total sovereignty (which tellingly demands a shift to the third person), she imagines herself beyond the law and all social constraints. Her vision takes atomistic individualism to the extreme, as she claims to relinquish all forms of dependence on her surrounding community. Yet, while this passage deploys the liberal axioms that Firdaus otherwise strives to fulfill, that appeal seemingly demonstrates not their veracity but rather their oversights and contradictions. In effect, Firdaus's rhetoric resembles mere wordplay that superficially rewrites coerced decisions to code them as free. While Firdaus claims to have attained radical freedom, her narrative invites us to read that assertion as an instance of false consciousness, and, as such, *Woman at Point Zero* courts the very paternalistic interpretations of Firdaus that El Saadawi elsewhere repudiates. Although this disconnect may vivify why liberalism will fail to comprehend her plight in a nondomineering way, we can nonetheless wonder what El Saadawi achieves by plotting Firdaus's development in an idiom of which she is deeply suspicious. That said, this language of freedom and independence equally divulges the latent biases that render that grammar of self-assertion exclusionary. Since for Firdaus such aspirations are fated to remain illusory, her appeals underscore the constraints imposed on her by her society—which consign Firdaus to posit her subjectivity within a discourse fated to do little more than point to her inadequacy.

In addition, Firdaus attempts to stipulate her individual worth through the rhetoric and logic of financial valuation. Firdaus, it goes without saying, is well aware of how women in her culture are bartered as property. She begins her childhood memories by describing her father's financial double-dealing, which involved both knowing "how to sell a buffalo poisoned by his enemy before it died" and skill in the "exchange" of women (12). Later, her beloved uncle callously forces her into an undesired marriage simply because Firdaus will fetch a "big dowry" (37). Although she revolts against this commodification of women, Firdaus is highly conscious of her own class status, which she construes as a hybrid of competing insignia depending on whether one looks to attire, education, or birth, although the final establishes her as "lower class" (12). Firdaus's work as a "successful prostitute" in particular magnifies this contradiction: she outwardly resembles "respectable upper-class women" and is financially secure, but she remains by profession and birth a pariah. Such class indeterminacy does not lead to increased social mobility for Firdaus but instead alienates her from all milieus.

Despite her awareness of her culture's social hierarchies and how they facilitate the objectification of women, Firdaus recurrently hypostasizes her identity through financial self-valuation and consumer choice, allowing fiscal autonomy to furnish the impression of control over her larger circumstances. After fleeing her husband, Sheikh Mahmoud, Firdaus is astounded at the psychological impact of economically asserting her tastes. When she first meets Bayoumi, who later forces her into prostitution, he inquires whether she "preferred oranges or tangerines," a question that "no one had asked [her] before" (47). This opportunity for consumer self-definition is revelatory for Firdaus and becomes integral to her, albeit transitory, glimpses of autonomy. Subsequently, a similar logic of financial calculus engenders her sense of self-ownership when she is a self-employed prostitute. After escaping Sharifa, a high-class madam who effectively enslaves her, Firdaus unwittingly prostitutes herself to survive the night and earns an unexpectedly large sum. Notably, her first act after being paid is to order a roast chicken at a restaurant, which triggers a response so visceral as to induce her to reminisce about her early encounters with "piastres," or coins.[25] Firdaus recalls how, when she was a child, the first money that was "mine to do with what I wanted" represented financial independence, or the ability to "buy what I wanted" (65). The different foods that Firdaus purchases in both childhood and adulthood are thereafter imbued with supersensory properties akin to the chicken's "strange, powerful sweetness" (65), signifying the potency of those acts of self-definition. After eating the chicken, Firdaus next exercises her newly acquired skills of financial self-determination to refuse a potential client. She informs him of her reasoning: "Because there are plenty of men and I want to choose with whom to go" (68). While these perceptions of agency embolden her, Firdaus's belief in economic self-fashioning also blinds her to the systematic exploitation that forces her into prostitution in the first place, allowing capital's seductive aura to mask the decorporealizing logic that entices her into the dual activities of self-barter and self-commodification.[26]

The madam Sharifa secures Firdaus's consent through an alternate but complimentary scheme of entrepreneurial self-definition. When Sharifa first meets Firdaus, she chides her: "You failed to value yourself highly enough. A man does not know a woman's value, Firdaus. She is the one who determines her value" (54–55). Yet by persuading Firdaus that she can autonomously stipulate her own self-worth, Sharifa cloaks how she directly conscripts Firdaus into prostitution—again displaying how financial self-abstraction not only mystifies Firdaus's predicament but also facilitates ends that are highly opportunistic. Indeed, the illusion that Firdaus can self-determine here incurs more than her willing debasement; rather, it eclipses the fact that she submits to a condition of virtual slavery. To the extent that the "speculative reason" that enables Sharifa to dupe Firdaus is equally endemic to the logic of financialization and of human rights, it reveals them to be interrelated tenets within a distinctly neoliberal system for appraising and organizing human affairs. As such, they jointly conspire to elicit Firdaus's ideological servitude, luring her into a bargain that is nothing short of dehumanizing.

That said, Firdaus herself marshals such a rhetoric of self-possession throughout her narrative, perhaps most visibly when she rationalizes her decision to leave a "respectable" job in business and return to prostitution. Ironically maintaining that the latter profession is "better," she cites the disproportionate end of the exchange assumed by the corporate employee: "She pays the price of her illusory fears with her life, her health, her body, and her mind. She pays the highest price for things of the lowest value" (76). While we might deride Firdaus's calculus for its reductive Marxism, precisely this fantasy that economic self-abstraction offers a viable route to both measuring and proving her self-worth is what, as we will see, Firdaus violently rejects at her narrative's conclusion. Nevertheless, for its duration she conflates more amorphous kinds of fulfillment with what she arbitrarily designates as their financial correlates, and this gambit shows how her fantasy of entrepreneurship conditions her to profoundly unjust arrangements. It is from this vantage that Firdaus's double bind reifies the ephemerality of neoliberal economic barometers for gauging selfhood. As long as Firdaus concentrates on a token of her autonomy that is both abstract and variable—namely, her price as a prostitute—she successfully suppresses other, more substantial though less quantifiable indicia of her well-being.

Firdaus's reliance on economic valuation accordingly brings to mind debates about whether rights logic is anatomically indistinct from or instead can be separated from that of capitalism.[27] Much as human rights discourses and systems of finance capital often collude to transact cycles of postcolonial dispossession, Firdaus's reasoning urges us to probe the circumstances that permit such liaisons. Akin to how programs of "development" mortgage the global South to Northern profit centers and other technologies of neoimperial control, Firdaus's rhetoric of fiscal self-determination acts as a decoy that lures her into her own systemic oppression and disenfranchisement.[28] The speculative reason germane to finance capital both blinds her to her real needs and solicits her consent to glaring patterns of exploitation. Indeed, Firdaus's reliance on economic calculus is especially perplexing in light of El Saadawi's own politics. El Saadawi is a self-avowed Marxist and has publicly railed against how the materialism of Western feminism institutes merely another, equally insidious form of "veiling," for instance, as she hyperbolically deems Western women "victims of cultural and psychological clitoridectomy."[29] The fact that Firdaus recurrently postulates both her independence and her progress through consumer choice and monetary gain raises a series of questions: Do her claims merely highlight her alienation, subtly critiquing the "capitalist" ideology that seduces her? Or does her rhetoric, while deceptive, implicitly ratify the common argument that women's fiscal gains must precede other political and social advancements? Does El Saadawi here endorse the view that financial self-reliance represents a necessary predicate to more comprehensive rights and freedoms for women, even while that goal carries certain costs?[30] Is Firdaus's grammar of economic worth a necessary antidote to and vehicle for overcoming her cultural climate, wherein capitalism is intrinsic to the patriarchal machinery that commodifies women in order to enforce their subjugation? Or conversely, by confronting us with the casualties of such habits of analysis, does her narrative enact a plea for alternative vocabularies and measures for calibrating selfhood?

In sum, Firdaus's narrative indicts the explanatory arsenal of liberalism for furnishing values that fully conspire with patriarchy. While within her retrospective autobiography it is unclear when and how that discourse is unmasked to her as illusory, it symbolically yields throughout much of her narrative the impression of her relative improvement. This irony that Firdaus's perceptions of empowerment are furnished by the very ideological framework that legislates her subservience creates a friction within the text that returns us to El Saadawi's own strategic endorsement of the language of human rights. Although such liberal vocabularies of selfhood clearly mislead Firdaus, her continued reliance on them nevertheless suggests that they may offer a meaningful vehicle for her self-actualization. As a consequence, Firdaus (and, for that matter, El Saadawi herself) cannot simply jettison the language of rights upon having identified its submerged violence; on the contrary, it remains enormously potent and compelling, despite its liabilities.

The Embeddedness of Human Rights Narration

The formal properties of *Woman at Point Zero* also dramatize key dilemmas that beset human rights advocacy, documentation, and reportage. Although El Saadawi deciphers Firdaus's life in terms of the emergent language of human rights, both her authorial framings and Firdaus's actual autobiography are rife with aesthetic and other formal contradictions. In addition to El Saadawi's author's preface, the text of *Woman at Point Zero* contains a separate prelude that sets forth the circumstances behind El Saadawi's contact with Firdaus, her reactions to that encounter, and her various motives for publishing Firdaus's story. However, these introductions together reflect strikingly divergent attitudes toward Firdaus. Most immediately, by doubly framing Firdaus's story, El Saadawi problematically implies its need for authorization, even while she bookends it with almost exhortatory statements of its independent political merit. While the preface's bold assertion of the "need to challenge and to overcome those forces that deprive human beings of their right to live, to love and to real freedom" (iii–iv) champions Firdaus's life as a crucible for human rights, the ambitions of El Saadawi's mediating narrators are at odds with both the content and texture of Firdaus's narration.

El Saadawi's preface and the novel's internal narrator recurrently aver Firdaus's truth status. The novel begins with the sentence "This is the story of a real woman" (1), with the first person I reinforcing its alleged factuality. This entrée concludes on a similar note, maintaining that Firdaus was "no dream" and that "the woman sitting on the ground in front of me was a real woman" (7). El Saadawi is assumedly aware of how the cult of authenticity regulates the marketability of minority literatures, as well as how the imprimatur of Western critics determines academic reception; that said, she authorizes Firdaus's story.[31] This defense of the empirical veracity of Firdaus's life further probes the evidentiary requirements that govern literary human rights advocacy. Overall, *Woman at Point Zero* underscores multiple tensions that literature aimed at human rights consciousness-raising confronts. For one, such narratives must profess their own truth in order to combat material, pressing scenes of injustice, and that onus is often partner to the demand of mimetically realistic, verifiable portrayals of those underlying realities. Even more, human rights narratives must postulate the representative, generalizable status of their victims in order to certify the normative, universalizable character of the principles they presumably yield. However, much as El Saadawi's statements about Firdaus appropriate her as a mouthpiece for all Arab women, such gestures risk casting their subjects as synecdoches for larger populations, with the effect of homogenizing and essentializing those underlying lives. At its outset, then, the novel quotes many of these common devices in order to interrogate them.

The narrator's insistence that Firdaus is a "real woman" further locates the novel within the genre of the testimonial.[32] Eva Paulino Bueno notes that testimonial narratives often begin "with memorable statements of the authors' commitment to the cause of their communities," as does El Saadawi's framing.[33] The etymology of the word *testimonial* itself confirms the genre's juridical ambitions. Early secular uses of the word *testimony* carried a specifically legal meaning, denoting "personal or documentary evidence or attestation in support of a fact or statement; hence any form of evidence or proof."[34] That said, precisely the testimonial's evidentiary aspirations have rendered it an apt forum within which to challenge dominant views about fact. For instance, Shoshana Felman argues that testimony produces a "crisis of evidence," insofar as it "does not offer... a completed statement, a totaliz-able account of [the narrative's] events."[35] According to Felman, because the testimonial disputes legalistic orders of truth, its ideological commitments, while law based, typically do not endorse but rather unsettle the law's pre-tense of certitude. We should in addition observe that the genre has often inspired a fraught politics of reception, in particular, when it invites dubious fantasies about the "Third World woman." As Wendy Hesford and Wendy Kozol observe, while "much of women's human rights discourse depends upon the testimony as a juridical concept," the genre's key difficulty is "how to avoid reproducing the spectacle of victimization while also not erasing the materiality of violence and trauma."[36]

Indeed, El Saadawi's dual framings do invoke what might resemble neoim-perial tropes, courting precisely such prurient appetites for distant suffering. Firdaus's story is narrated from a prison cell and replete with reminders of her physical incarceration. Prison in turn comes to function as a transparent metaphor for the predicament of all Arab women, akin to how the motif of "unveiling" repeatedly signifies Firdaus's self-realizations.[37] This symbolic commentary might seem to exploit self-congratulatory, condescending ste-reotypes about Middle Eastern women's degraded realities, providing fodder for critics who deride El Saadawi for self-exoticism. However, that location simultaneously deconstructs liberal assumptions about freedom, agency, and constraint—even while Firdaus requisitions such a grammar of selfhood. As Barbara Harlow notes, because of the "authoritarian control of the 'power of writing'" enacted by physical confinement, even ordinary speech "contest[s] that other control" and can become resistant.[38] The space of the prison, that is, alters the coordinates determining what forms of communication are insur-rectionary, arguably politicizing all speech. To such ends, Firdaus's captivity is ultimately not inhibitory but instead facilitates her narrative outpouring, unfettering her imagination and will. These material constraints paradoxically incite her autobiography, with the effect of challenging core assumptions that subtend liberal articulations of human rights—namely, that corporeal self-possession, privacy, and autonomy must precede the intellect's free exercise.

Along with the metaphor of prison, El Saadawi's Author's Preface exem-plifies the sort of gesture that has incurred skepticism from her academic audiences, although here, too, things are significantly more complicated. Superficially, the preface mollifies its readers' assumed desires for displays of barbarism and depravity; El Saadawi encounters Firdaus in a world of "sudden gloom" and "overall harshness," with "women, lurking behind bars like animals, their white or brown fingers twisted around the black metal" (ii). Such a description invites being projected onto Firdaus's entire society, much as, as chapter 1 argued, the human rights bestseller conflates Islam itself with social oppression. However, El Saadawi implicates herself in these seemingly loaded responses by foregrounding her own fascination with Firdaus. She acknowledges an enthrallment with "the idea of 'prison'" (i) and admits that Firdaus becomes "even more compelling" when she discovers her to be a murderer awaiting an especially graphic, inhumane punishment—"sentence of death by hanging" (ii). This accentuation of her own intrigue refuses to sanitize it by performing neutral or sanctioned disinterest. Given that she exhibits the very curiosity she elsewhere impugns in Western audiences, such framing tactics raise the question of whether and why El Saadawi might undermine her own reliability. In other words, by attributing such sentiments to her proxy, does El Saadawi implicitly apologize for the narcissistic self-reference that inevitably fuels human rights advocacy? Or does she instead qualify her investment in Firdaus to emphasize how such reactions can problematically compromise human rights witnessing? In whatever case, these quandaries remind us that certain kinds of suffering preclude objective detachment, instead arousing visceral registers of engagement from the observer—even while those responses may be haphazard and unpredictable.

In addition to such engrossment, El Saadawi's framing narrator evinces a different though related type of ambivalence about Firdaus's evidentiary merit. Despite the preface's almost didactic tone, this proxy internal to the text of the novel succumbs to a crisis in confidence. Rather than to feign detachment, this narrator describes her interest in Firdaus as stemming from a combined bodily, emotional, and spiritual identification and attraction. She relates how, when she first learns about Firdaus's refusal to seek clemency, she personalizes that silence, allowing it to erode her self-assurance. Suddenly, her professional work appears "in jeopardy" and her "whole life seem[s] to be threatened with failure" (3). Conversely, when Firdaus is willing to talk mere hours before her execution, the narrator is overtaken with something bordering on romantic passion, which she had "only known once before, many years ago" in a love affair (6). Before Firdaus even begins to speak, the narrator enters a dreamlike state—one thereafter mirrored in Firdaus's own ecstatic trances (7). As such, there is little question that this narrator's connection with Firdaus is fully corporeal in its intensity, if not outright erotic. However, El Saadawi characterizes that enthrallment as resistant to being reduced to a single factor or inscribed within a psychologically normalizing symbolic economy—meaning that something far more than sheer sexual longing is at issue.

In fact, this narrator's absorption with Firdaus arises on multiple, inconsistent levels. Even before her autobiography's inception Firdaus is endowed with paramount importance, yet this assertion paradoxically attenuates the initial categorization of her life in terms of the liberal ideals associated with human rights. Whereas liberal theories of political practice prioritize reasoned neutrality, El Saadawi's enchantment with Firdaus derives from far different energies. Along similar lines, although liberalism valorizes self-abstraction through the intellect, *Woman at Point Zero*'s narrative harnesses and affirms corporeal and affective faculties of participation. Given that El Saadawi's engrossment with Firdaus emanates from precisely such countervailing channels of engagement, we might say that the narrative incarnates its own aesthetic to reveal what Merleau-Ponty calls the self's "intertwining" within other lives, and, in doing so, it heralds those intersensory registers of involvement as indispensable to cultivating a different kind of respect for human rights.

Both framings of Firdaus's narrative likewise reject scientific, and by extension legal, knowledge and truth for being insufficient to comprehend Firdaus. In her nonfictional writings, El Saadawi has argued that those protocols of analysis are highly gendered. For instance, she criticizes medical practice for its "one-dimensional" vocabulary that not only is alien to women's realities but also exacerbates their marginalization.[39] Not coincidentally, such an accusation censures the primary idiom modernity has brought to bear upon the body—namely, medicine—for harboring feeble, impoverished explanatory reserves. In effect, *Woman at Point Zero* thereby develops an opposing hermeneutic of embodied interpretation to compensate for medicine's pauperized descriptive arsenal. Whereas medical discourse objectifies the body, effectively diminishing vital dimensions of experience, El Saadawi's contrasting language of embodiment instead amplifies the body's dynamic, regenerative propensities. El Saadawi's divergent idiom of the body thus not only is richer and denser than that of scientific empiricism but also, as we shall see, captures the concatenation of protean and interwoven energies that animate embodied perception.[40]

El Saadawi's Author's Preface explains that she originally pursued Firdaus to include in a sociological study, *Women and Neurosis in Egypt,* but Firdaus's narrative refused to be circumscribed therein. Unlike her other case studies, Firdaus "remained a woman apart," who "vibrated within me" (iii), and this visceral imagery further contests the generic codes as well as taxonomic categories endemic to a scientific treatise. Although El Saadawi here avers Firdaus's exemplarity, she simultaneously exposes her own investment in Firdaus to derive from murkier, even self-interested motives, which she additionally distinguishes from the sorts of grounds that typically support scientific inquiry. Her internal framing narrator chastens herself: "Subjective feelings such as those that had taken hold of me were not worthy of a researcher in science" (5). Such a statement enlists empirical certitude to quell her epistemic and emotional unmooring; she invokes science seemingly to manage her overwhelming response to Firdaus. Likewise, when this narrator initially encounters Firdaus, she reminds herself, "I was a researcher in science, a psychiatrist, or something of that kind" (6). While on the one hand this yearning for impartiality aims to subdue Firdaus's provocation, on the other it characterizes scientific and other positivistic brands of knowledge as incommensurate with Firdaus's existential realities. El Saadawi thus contrasts these different habits of discourse and thought in terms that recall Merleau-Ponty's critiques of the objectifying, appropriative, and instrumentalizing impulses of science, which for Merleau-Ponty only induce alienation within the observer.[41] Much as Merleau-Ponty lauds how phenomenological insight can cultivate a "vertiginous proximity" between object and observer,[42] El Saadawi's reflections on science mark the deficiencies of empiricist rationalism while at once celebrating embodied modalities of cognition.

Akin to how her frame narrator's affective reactions subvert El Saadawi's initial political call to arms, Firdaus's narrative resists being conscripted to fulfill a clear-cut ideological agenda. Here, too, it produces a dissonance between its aesthetic properties and the content that El Saadawi retrospectively imposes on it, and this dissonance further queries the standard expectations informing human rights reportage. Firdaus's narrative is dense with diametrically opposed inclinations, which also magnify the competing and at times volatile desires at stake within narratives of human rights. While her story follows a linear progression, Firdaus often describes her memories as dreams or euphoric states. The first of such trancelike episodes occurs when she recalls learning to walk, an event that thereafter symbolizes her ensuing quests for emotional and other intimacy. She remembers being "buffeted by contradictory forces that kept pulling me in different directions" (17) and then mesmerized by "two eyes," here her mother's:

> Forever sinking and rising, sinking and rising between the sea and the sky, with nothing to hold on to except the two eyes. Two eyes to which I clung with all my might. Two eyes that alone seemed to hold me up. To this very moment I do not know whether they were wide or narrow, nor can I recall if they were surrounded by lashes or not. All I can remember are two rings of intense white around two circles of intense

black. I only had to look into them for the white to become whiter and the black even blacker, as though sunlight was pouring into them from some magical source neither on earth, nor in the sky, for the earth was pitch black, and the sky dark as night, with no sun and no moon. (17)

The narrative's rhythmic, incantatory prose and stark, minimalist imagery deracinate Firdaus's hallucinatory memory from context and place, as she imagines herself exiled "between the sea and sky." The passage's intense lyricism is almost vertiginous, a sensation assumedly induced for Firdaus by her mother's emotional and physical abandonment. The imagery itself lacks concrete, stable referents, denoting the psychic upheaval accompanying her vision, which concludes near apocalyptically. If this passage can be taken as representative of an embodied aesthetic, it unleashes, in Merleau-Ponty's terms, a "propagation" and "fundamental fission" of synergies that "found transitivity from one body to another," which here generate such a symbiosis between El Saadawi's proxy and Firdaus.[43]

Significantly, this sequence in Firdaus's narrative immediately precedes her mother's emotional betrayal, entailing that Firdaus's memory conflates the welcome liberty attendant to learning to walk with the pain of being forsaken. This elision, again, deconstructs conventional notions about individual freedom. Firdaus relates how, at her father's request, she "replaced" her mother in the task of washing his legs every evening, at which point her mother "was no longer there." As such, she seems cognizant that her own desertion is counterpart to her mother's parallel neglect by her husband, which is mirrored in her mother's evacuated eyes—as Firdaus observes, "No light seemed ever to touch the eyes of this woman" (18). Many of Firdaus's near-delirious memories thereafter mourn and revisit this loss, which is notably overlaid by guilt. In particular, almost identical eye imagery reemerges every time she approaches intimacy with another person. While on certain instances such encounters are triggered by romantic attraction, on others Firdaus conspicuously seeks a maternal presence. For instance, shortly following her mother's early death, Firdaus first becomes enamored of a boarding school teacher named Miss Iqbal. One night when Firdaus is alone outside, Miss Iqbal stumbles upon and sits down beside her. Firdaus begins crying, and when Miss Iqbal empathizes, Firdaus lapses into a comparative state of euphoric rapture with Miss Iqbal's eyes. Firdaus describes this vision in nearly identical language: she is mesmerized by "two rings of pure white, surrounding two circles of intense black" fueled by "some unknown magical source" (29). After this episode, Firdaus becomes obsessed with and believes herself in love with Miss Iqbal, although that feeling is unreciprocated.

Much as Firdaus's thwarted desire for Miss Iqbal replays her alienation from her mother, Firdaus's romantic union with Ibrahim follows a similar cycle of intense attachment succeeded by disappointment. When Firdaus temporarily leaves prostitution, she works as a corporate secretary and becomes sexually, and from her perspective romantically, involved with Ibrahim, a labor agitator at the company. In a striking repetition of her rendezvous with Miss Iqbal, Firdaus meets him one night while sitting outside after business hours crying in a courtyard of the offices. Her ensuing hypnosis through Ibrahim's eyes is conveyed in highly reminiscent language—as drowning in "two rings of pure white" that radiate "from some unknown, mysterious force" (78). Subsequently, a friend presses Firdaus about Ibrahim, accusing her of "living in a dream world" (80), and that prodding compels Firdaus relive the incident, although her memory becomes jumbled and "confused," impeding her ability to "distinguish between the faces of my mother and my father, or Wafeya and Fatheya, or Iqbal and Ibrahim." In effect, Firdaus's unfulfilled intimacy with her mother, friends, and lover alike merges into a single ecstatic yearning that both motors and complicates her pursuit of economic self-determination.

Importantly, Firdaus's trances seem to reside in the prediscursive; her longings rail against and test the limits of verbal and especially reasoned self-presentation. Such moments arise when she succumbs to an overwhelming euphoria rooted not in the intellect but in bodily sensations—hence her appeal to "magic" to elaborate them. Her visions accordingly refuse to be couched within scientific, legalistic, or other normalizing frames of analysis; when encouraged to characterize them as manifestations of erotic "love," Firdaus denies her feelings rather than to contain them within that clichéd, unidimensional framework. Given that these corporeal appetencies are deeply formative for her, her narrative in addition brings to mind Merleau-Ponty's insights into how certain modes of expression are uniquely geared to adumbrate and thus engender embodied perception. Indeed, Firdaus's narrative resorts to such viscerally charged registers of explanation precisely when she contends with the "tangled" dynamics of interpersonal co-belonging. Even when platonic, Firdaus figures these solidarities in corporeal terms, apparently to capture both their intensity and the affective fiber of the underlying reciprocities that she grasps at. Firdaus's recognitions at these moments ensue from radical self-surrender, or kinds of self-obliteration that explicitly controvert liberal presumptions about bodily self-possession and inviolability. These central incidents arise when Firdaus relinquishes her autonomous self-enclosure. In other words, self-loss, even when paired with suffering and vulnerability, does not detract from but rather fosters both her ecstasies and larger pursuit of self-realization. Thus eluding liberalism's usual expectations about human flourishing, Firdaus's subjectivity is informed by a significantly murkier economy of attraction and desire wherein pleasure is imbricated with pain. While we might be tempted to dismiss these appetites as masochistic, it is nonetheless through the infringement of her bodily impermeability, integrity, and self-possession that Firdaus finds intimations of meaning and fulfillment. As a consequence, the contours of her selfhood, while she may be tormented, do not map onto what I have described as a liberal topography of the human, and, in this respect, they point to the explanatory poverty of those articulations of the subject.

This motif of vision that signals Firdaus's pursuits of intimacy is, as such, highly overdetermined; as a metaphor, vision variously denotes her exposure to male predation, her epiphanies of self-realization, and her newly attained self-confidence. When as an adolescent Firdaus flees rather than marry the aged Sheikh Mahmoud, she finds herself alone at night stalked by "two eyes, nothing but two eyes" (42). In this context, "two eyes" are so "frightening" as to cause Firdaus to return and submit to an oppressive marriage. In one sense, then, vision portends a misogynistic and objectifying threat to her security. Yet Firdaus's own facility of sight provides a catalyst for her experiences of self-actualization. One key way that Firdaus asserts herself is through eye contact and directness of vision. Her ability to deliver an "unwinking gaze" not only effectuates her confidence but also empowers her within others' perspectives. Taken together, these competing figurations of vision metonymically mirror the novel's layered troping of "the veil"—a similar device that at once symbolizes freedom from male intrusion, self-discovery, and sociopolitical constraint. Thus additionally like the novel's prison metaphor, *Woman at Point Zero* manipulates the veil's resonances in ways that might elicit complaints of exoticism from El Saadawi's critics. That said, Firdaus both nourishes and communicates her social worth through visual confrontation—more so than through spoken words. And these multiple associations of vision index the preeminent role that embodied and affective, as opposed to purely rational and linguistic, dimensions of selfhood play in constituting her subjectivity. While vision is often seen to conspire with a Cartesian privileging of mind, for Firdaus sight entails those facets of her selfhood that cannot be subsumed within the neoimperial measures of progress that she elsewhere employs. Her recurrent focus on the ontological freight of sight accordingly opens up the fissures in her endeavors to self-fashion vis-à-vis the logic of economic self-determination and worth. While Firdaus, of course, does eventually resort to speech to communicate her story, even the frame narrator claims that Firdaus is compelling not because of the authority of her spoken words but rather because she draws El Saadawi into a trance-like enchantment that forestalls translation into the empiricist languages of medicine and science.

To related ends, Firdaus's refusal to appeal for clemency speaks to the unavailability of human rights or other legal protections for women in her society. Firdaus desists from defending herself within any and all formal institutional channels of redress, evincing little faith in legal or other forms of political advocacy. No doubt this silence testifies to the functional non-existence of legal remedies and safeguards for women in her society. Her abstention from speech, then, might be taken as a principled disavowal of the state organizations that have systematically eviscerated her rights and securities. Yet her silence also denounces language itself for not only fore-closing all available avenues of relief but also producing her basic predica-ment—in other words, for simultaneously discounting and authoring her disenfranchisement. Her refusal thus elucidates why the dualistic order of the law is predisposed to dismiss both the terms of Firdaus's sociopolitical exclusion and the texture of her embodied suffering. Firdaus's final, bitterly angry words conduct such a wholesale renunciation of speech, as her nar-rative concludes: "I spit with ease on their lying faces and words, on their lying newspapers" (103). With the plural "their," Firdaus decries language's patriarchal construction of reality; however, her abrogation is at once far more totalizing. We have already considered how the neoliberal rhetoric of self-determination has provided little more than an ideological decoy for Firdaus, effectively colonizing her consciousness, and here she further rejects the machinery of politics and law for being constitutively stacked against her. Her concluding epiphany seems to recognize that the primary idioms through which she could have decried her oppression—namely, lib-eral discourses of freedom and rights—are destined not only to license her continued subservience but also to misread her basic plight, compounding her sense of futility and marginalization.

The concluding episode in Firdaus's biography similarly dramatizes the extent of her ideological servitude to a neoliberal explanatory regime. Whereas for most of her narrative financial self-valuation procures the impression of self-worth, this vision explodes that false criteria. After mur-dering a pimp who forces her into his employ, the act for which she is executed, Firdaus vows to leave prostitution, until a man in a "luxurious car" ignores her rebuffs and offers her a huge sum. After receiving the money, Firdaus reaches unprecedented awareness. She figures this final revelation as removing "the last, remaining veil from before my eyes" and begins liter-ally ripping up the money (98). This epiphany discloses to Firdaus "the true enigma" of her existence, or what she calls "savage, primitive truths" (98). While her narrative fails to define these "truths," the fact that Firdaus forbears from verbalizing them is itself revealing. In a way, her destruction of the money stages a wholesale abdication of the symbolic order that has administered her self-conception. Having trusted economic calculus as an accurate indicator of her fulfillment, she eschews that illusory gauge in a gesture of sudden demystification that impugns her entire value structure. However, this leaves her in something of a semantic and conceptual vacuum, and it is therefore not surprising that her behavior verges on suicidal. Indeed, she volunteers to her final client that she is a murderer, essentially soliciting her own death sentence. Whether or not that decision can be explained as a principled defiance of an unjust culture, it does augur a strange type of liberation for Firdaus. Whereas most of her narrative implicitly endeavors to verify the different tenets that underwrite liberal theories of the human, she ultimately realizes that those mandates have provided alibis for her subservience and policing, habituating her to its inevitability. As a consequence, she responds to this linguistic treason by refusing to substitute the worldview she relinquishes with an alternate system of valuation.

There is accordingly a sense in which Firdaus's position of complete destitution at the end of her narrative renders her a type of martyr. And, indeed, Firdaus herself claims to possess feelings of "pride," "superiority," and "courage" that, until that point, have eluded her (11, 102). Despite confronting something of a rhetorical abyss, she finds that state emboldening. She comes to discover the extent to which the neoliberal measures of selfhood she has trusted have colluded with patriarchy in shoring up her society's exclusions, and she jettisons that explanatory framework in its entirety. However, she does not encounter a total void. On the contrary, she additionally draws upon what we might call an embodied register of self-presentation. This competing grammar of selfhood is affectively and viscerally charged, and it refuses to be colonized by the discursive apparatus of liberalism, instead overwhelming that language's false barometers. This chapter's final section now turns to explore that alternate ontology of the human.

Sexuality, Pain, and the Human

Firdaus's relationship to her embodiment, in particular, her sexuality, enacts her narrative's most pointed rebuke to the truncated, anemic vision of the human tethered to liberal formulations of human rights. Her narrative recounts her memory of her childhood circumcision, and it charts her prolonged coping with the many psychological and other residues of that assault. This injury, however, does not suppress or curtail Firdaus's sexual appetites; rather, it paradoxically enlivens them. Firdaus's experience of her erotic life thus contravenes the notions of privacy, bodily integrity, and consent that typically regulate how liberal political thought accounts for embodiment, censuring those standards for enforcing an overly purified conception of the body. Likewise, her experiences of love and intimacy, romantic as well as platonic, refute the corresponding logic of dignity, freedom, and self-determination. The core attributes of Firdaus's embodied and affective selfhood—precisely in being multiform, protean, and messy—are shown to variously defy and exceed the liberal terminology that her narrative elsewhere requisitions. While Firdaus borrows from that vocabulary in an effort to stipulate her self-worth, the most formative moments in her autobiography instead emanate from sacrifice and vulnerable self-exposure. Rather than being subsidiary or secondary to the exercise in reasoned self-abstraction that might structurally appear to organize Firdaus's narrative, her embodied faculties of engagement engender species of meaning and fulfillment that liberal mappings of the human, with their dualistic anatomy, will fail to capture.

Female genital excision has become one of the most polarizing issues within debates about women's rights. The practice is extremely prevalent. One study concludes that it is performed on approximately 5 million girls each year and that between 80 to 120 million women currently alive have been subjected to it. Common within Muslim, Christian, and indigenous communities alike, it extends across socioeconomic classes.[44] While the 1993 Vienna Declaration declares that it violates human rights, it has continued with little, if any, abatement.[45] Accordingly, for many theorists it represents a type of litmus test for resolving contentions over the cultural relativism of human rights.[46] For instance, Françoise Lionnet describes the procedure as, for human rights norms, "an ideal test case, since it apparently illustrates absolute and total cultural conflict between the rights of the individual to bodily integrity and the individual's need to be satisfactorily integrated into a community."[47] Indeed, even the correct terminology for the procedure has inspired heated disagreement. Nahid Toubia surveys the antithetical sentiments that surround the label *circumcision,* which on one hand "implies a fallacious analogy to nonmutilating male circumcision" and on the other allows "a recognition of the terms of reference of the communities in which it occurs."[48]

As Lionnet's observations suggest, female circumcision/female genital mutilation (FC/FGM) also directs us to the ambivalences that haunt bodily integrity as an ideal and a construct.[49] Opposition to the practice, it goes without saying, confirms the merit and crucial importance of that standard; however, popular discourses surrounding FC/FGM simultaneously divulge the problematic assumptions often embedded within idealized conceptions of bodily integrity. Not surprisingly, FC/FGM has generated substantial furor, in part because the procedure is prone to incite a type of lurid fascination, which I will return to consider. Yet precisely because it provides an unusually troubling (and, for Western critics, distant) image of the violated body do conversations about FC/FGM consolidate expectations about the body's integrity, as a result furnishing legibility to liberal articulations of human rights. If FC/FGM represents an ideal test case for women's rights, it is not merely because it crystallizes the friction between communitarian and individualistic cultural formations. Rather, opposition to the practice also lends coherence to the equation between bodily integrity and dignity that sustains liberal human rights norms. In other words, advocacy aimed at abolishing FC/FGM—while without question valuable—reinforces the liberal fiction of the self-contained, impermeable subject, which I have argued shores up the discursive authority of human rights. In effect, the specter of the female body violated by FC/FGM paradoxically fortifies the symbolic architecture of the liberal body politic, acting as a foil to the West's self-image as unified, sovereign, and self-contained. Needless to say, by highlighting this imaginative work performed by opposition to FC/FGM, I aim not to condone it but rather to illustrate how it naturalizes a particular metaphorics of embodiment that has helped to authorize a continuum of sociopolitical exclusions, as chapter 1 analyzed.

Within Egypt, FC/FGM has met with widespread condemnation, and such efforts to prevent it gained prominence in the 1990s. That said, much of that early foment was not framed in terms of public health or human rights but instead its status under Islamic law. Yet, as Ann Elizabeth Mayer discusses, Muslim scholars have historically differed greatly about whether FC/GFM is required or even allowed by Islamic religious codes.[50] Such an approach notably mirrors Egypt's reluctance to ratify human rights instruments without first establishing their conformity with Quranic doctrine. For instance, the Cairo Declaration of Human Rights in Islam (1990) did little to incorporate human rights principles into Egyptian law, instead merely "affirm[ing] that all rights were subject to Islamic law."[51] This legal stance toward FC/FGM changed in 2008, however, largely in response to a widely publicized death of an eleven-year-old girl from the ritual in late 2007. That case led to the criminalization of the process within Egypt, in a ban that cites both its physical and psychological damage. Nonetheless, penalties for violating the law remain relatively light, and recent studies suggest that the practice continues largely unmitigated, despite its official prohibition.[52] For instance, it was not until August 2009 that an actual arrest was issued for violation of the policy.[53]

El Saadawi has over the duration of her career conducted a vigorous and sustained campaign against FC/FGM, an agenda that she construes in terms of both human rights and corporeal integrity. For instance, she describes it as a "cruel rite" that "deprive[s] millions of women all over the world of one of their basic human rights: the right to bodily integrity."[54] In the midst of these efforts, however, El Saadawi has critiqued the Western preoccupation with FC/FGM, complaining that Western feminists "tend to depict our life as a continued submission to medieval systems, and point vehemently to some of the rituals and traditional practices such as female circumcision" in order to create in themselves a "feeling of superior humanity."[55] This is a charge that has been widely echoed in scholarship about the practice. Reina Lewis and Sara Mills indict the "obsessive focus" on FC/FGM, which "runs the risk of perpetuating a longstanding prurient interest in a sexualized 'African' female body and of distracting attention away from other pressing women's health issues in the developing world."[56] Similarly, Nahid Toubia castigates media discussions of FC/FGM for "treating African and Asian women in a condescending manner."[57] These tensions, once again, gauge the paradoxical role of the construct of bodily integrity in human rights advocacy. While bodily integrity represents a necessary baseline, objections to how activism can fetishize FC/FGM also evince an awareness of how that ideal can be recruited to naturalize a sanitized conception of embodiment that directly licenses paternalistic patterns of international oversight and policing. Ironically, precisely because representations of FC/FGM problematically arouse the most sensationalistic and exoticizing tendencies of contemporary human rights rhetoric, they also place the casualties of liberalism's conventional figuration of embodiment into high relief. However laudable and productive, this focus on FC/FGM exposes the body imagined to be in possession of rights as highly abstract and unrealistic.

The especially fraught status of FC/FGM—a practice ritualized within many cultures and quickly labeled barbaric by Western critics—also heightens the stakes of its artistic portrayal, and *Woman at Point Zero* sheds important light on those dilemmas. While El Saadawi both confronts and condemns Firdaus's circumcision, the narrative omits a graphic, explicit, or complete rendition of Firdaus's experience of the procedure. Instead, Firdaus recalls her memory in simple, pared-down prose that departs from the tone and imagery composing most of her narrative. Casting her mother as the agent of her violation, Firdaus recollects:

> First she beat me. Then she brought a woman who was carrying a small knife or maybe a razor blade. They cut off a piece of flesh from between my thighs.
>
> I cried all night. Next morning my mother did not send me to the fields. (13)

This abrupt, comparatively unemotional passage starkly diverges from the vertiginous, hallucinatory prose recounting Firdaus's recurrent immersion within "two eyes." Its muted tenor avoids magnifying or cultivating fascination with the assault. Yet that minimalism also represents a disavowal of the narrative's imaginative task, which it instead places on the reader. Its curt, abbreviated sentences interrupt the prose's momentum, forcing a concentration on Firdaus's suffering. Paradoxically, narrative withholding here vivifies the practice's violence and lingering immediacy, with descriptive reticence conveying the egregious nature of Firdaus's harm.

Significantly, the narrative construes the procedure as merely one component of a beating and hence a punishment, being conducted shortly after her mother's emotional abandonment. That continuity assumedly instills in Firdaus an awareness of her culture's loathing for the female body, which stigmatizes her sexuality as an inherent cause for guilt and penalization. Moreover, such a linkage between maternal rage and FC/FGM connects it, while enforced by women's networks, to patriarchy's pervasive control and denial of independence to women. Her mother feels replaceable vis-à-vis her husband, and she exorcizes that fear by inflicting it on Firdaus's body. We might say, then, that El Saadawi explains Firdaus's experience of FC/FGM as a direct by-product of the hierarchical organization of the household, which is only compounded by her society's disallowance of economic self-sufficiency to women. Moreover, the fact that the violation is carried out by a collective of women subverts the frequent impulse to romanticize female solidarity; quite differently, this detail implies significant skepticism about communitarian alternatives to human rights. Indeed, FC/FGM exemplifies the type of practice that can lead the bonds formalizing the community to tyrannize the individual, depriving its unitary members of freedom in the name of collective obligation. To such ends, Firdaus's status as a prostitute checks a related tendency of Western feminism to, as Chandra Talpade Mohanty puts it, "discursively colonize" by "producing/representing a composite, singular 'Third World woman.'"[58] There is a way in which her profession strategically impedes the impulse to read Firdaus as either an iconic victim or an essentialized prototype of all Muslim women. In sum, it is by preserving these multiple tensions surrounding FC/FGM that *Woman at Point Zero* offers a complicated portrait of why that practice has been difficult to abolish.

Along related lines, Firdaus is painfully cognizant of her community's internal disciplinary violence. She is forsaken throughout her life by women, who prove just as unreliable as men. Beyond her mother's abandonment, Firdaus is forced into an unwanted marriage by her uncle's wife, deserted by Miss Iqbal, and exploited by Sharifa. Firdaus's world is devoid of female alliances of support; on the contrary, her autobiography follows her extended efforts to wrest herself from the collective's inhibiting demands. After fleeing Sharifa, Firdaus overtly characterizes her community in such terms, reifying its prohibitions: "How many were the years of my life that went by before my body, and my self became really mine, to do with them as I wished? How many were the years of my life that were lost before I tore my body and my self away from the people who held me in their grasp since the very first day?" (68). Firdaus here inscribes her more amorphous struggles for autonomy on her own body, seemingly to denote their magnitude.

Although Firdaus's circumcision is narrated in exceptionally sparse prose, her subsequent mourning for that loss emerges diffusely and even cyclically throughout her narrative. In particular, the suggestion is that she relives this injury every time she becomes entranced with "two eyes." After her circumcision, Firdaus tries fruitlessly to undergo sexual pleasure, and, despite her disappointments, her narrative adopts a tone that is almost euphoric. While aroused, Firdaus cannot concentrate on sensations she nonetheless remembers; as she explains, "I closed my eyes and tried to reach the pleasure I had known before but in vain. It was as if I could no longer recall the exact spot from which it used to arise, or as though a part of me, or of my being, was gone and would never return" (15). As Firdaus grieves an absence for which, being relatively uneducated, she might realistically have lacked a referent, her desire is manifested in the same incantatory, lyrical aesthetic that conveys her pursuits of emotional intimacy. Firdaus thereafter characterizes her yearnings for gratification as a prostitute by relating such a vacuity: "Yet it seemed to go back even further than my life, to some day before I was born, like a thing arising out of an ancient wound, in an organ which had ceased to be mine, on the body of a woman who was no longer me" (56). This imagery of an "ancient wound" vivifies the texture of both her sexual longing and its frustration, even as her language of violation and dispossession amplifies that injury. Moreover, Firdaus here does not segregate pleasure from pain; rather, it seems, she is not conditioned to regard pleasure and pain as antonymic or exclusive. Instead, she imaginatively collapses those energies into one another, with the effect of destabilizing artificial, idealized conceptions of both dignity and bodily integrity. As such, her experience of her own embodiment implicitly contests the liberal assumption that corporeal pain must be compartmentalized and mastered as a route to individual self-fashioning.

All in all, Firdaus's quests for emotional and erotic intimacy controvert a number of the core philosophical presumptions that underlie liberal constructions of the human and of human rights. As we have seen, Firdaus's sexual appetites repeatedly externalize themselves in behaviors that flout purified conceptions of bodily integrity and self-ownership. Indeed, the importance that Firdaus places on bodily inviolability, along with her views about what constitutes abusive treatment, fluctuate based on context, seemingly to underscore those values' relativity as social goods. A gesture that from one person is hostile in identical form but under different circumstances becomes exciting, and her attitudes toward her clients reflect such inconsistencies. Likewise, when as a child Firdaus is alone with her uncle who raises her after her parents' deaths, he touches her leg with his hand "traveling up my thigh... with a grasping, almost brutal insistence" (14–15). Firdaus, however, does not interpret these advances as unwelcome but instead tries to experience them as erotic. She claims to enjoy her uncle's overtures—in an interaction that would hastily be labeled predatory from most perspectives. Standard notions of consent do not register for Firdaus; her longings are instead inscribed within a very different economy of the pleasurable, one that apparently operates without reference to the liberal conceit of the self-enclosed, sacrosanct body. The most axiomatic expectations that underwrite human rights norms—namely, that bodily integrity represents an essential predicate to human dignity and to an individual's possession of rights—at times seem plainly foreign to Firdaus. Rather than safeguarding her inviolability, Firdaus on multiple occasions longs to have her corporeal integrity invaded. Of course, we might here again be tempted to deride these desires as self-sabotaging mechanisms through which she copes with either the trauma of her circumcision or her broad climate of oppression—in other words, as further evidence of false consciousness. Yet her narrative ultimately denaturalizes both privacy and the liberal fiction of the self-contained, autonomous subject—demonstrating why those norms fail to speak to crucial dimensions of her experience and subjectivity.

Talal Asad's *Formations of the Secular* interrogates the views about agency and pain that commonly subtend human rights discourses through a lens that can further help to illumine Firdaus's realities. In particular, Asad examines how secularization narratives script both historical progress and "self-empowerment" as exercises in "replac[ing] pain by pleasure—or, at any rate, by the search for what pleases one" (68). Within such a plotting of the subject, the "principle of individual freedom," Asad argues, endows certain categories of lives with humanity based on whether their cultures have successfully eliminated "wasteful pain" (111–24). Opposing this liberal logic, Asad instead maintains that pain can enable "modes of living a relationship" and become socially meaningful; he thus reclaims corporeal pain as potentially "agentive" rather than an automatic insignia of failure and passivity. From within Asad's analytic, Firdaus's relationship to suffering can be seen to reverse liberalism's blanket aversion toward pain, given that it enables her to meaningfully bond with others. Yet liberal formulations of human rights would denigrate those very desires, confronting us once again with the explanatory deficit that besets such vocabularies of the human. Not only do liberal articulations of selfhood lack the hermeneutic versatility to calibrate Firdaus's ambivalent longings, but their dualistic prioritization of mind would negate the corporeally animated dimensions of her experiences, especially to the extent that they are colored by suffering. Whereas liberal human rights norms quarantine and depreciate embodiment, Firdaus attributes paramount significance to her embodied faculties of engagement and apperception. That the experiences they purvey are overlaid by pain suggests that Firdaus's deepest expressions of selfhood stem less from rational self-preservation than from perceptions of shared need and woundedness. Firdaus's suffering—whether sexual pain or the "tears" she sheds with Ibrahim and Miss Iqbal—directly triggers her quests for interpersonal mutuality, along with the more diffuse recognitions those incidents afford. Yet liberalism's pervasive anxieties about embodiment are only intensified when the body can be deemed a site of anarchy and insurrection—as pain quintessentially entails—meaning that these encounters of Firdaus's, too, would be labeled regressive and self-undermining.

In this respect, we might again enlist Merleau-Ponty both to elucidate the anatomy of embodied suffering that Firdaus's narrative unfolds and to comprehend why it stages a rebuke to the abstract, bloodless human fettered to liberal definitions of human rights. Merleau-Ponty, too, seeks to reclaim the body's faculties of perceptual and other involvement, affirming their indispensable role in facilitating human selfhood, community, and fulfillment alike. These corporeal appetencies bear directly on matters of justice-ethics, as they orient the self toward the surrounding lifeworld. Chapter 2 extensively considered the relay through which embodied perception fosters what I described as an ecological approach to social justice. Above all, an embodied consciousness discloses the self's embeddedness within a materially grounded phenomenal field composed of layered densities, and those experiential folds channel the body's many energies, in effect incarnating both mind and sub-jectivity. Not only does such corporeal engagement cause the senses to col-laborate but those embodied modes of awareness themselves cooperate in ways that mirror the fabric of collective intertwining. In turn, a phenome-nology of embodiment can adumbrate the character of more comprehensive solidarities that congregate all life and matter, divulging the self's reciprocal dependence on other beings. Building on such an ontology, then, we might say that the embodied dimensions of Firdaus's experience both nourish and oversee her attempts at intimacy. Her embodiment does not detract from her appreciation for ethics-justice, as liberal political thought typically presumes, but rather directly nurtures such commitments. Ironically, her pursuits of freedom and individuation are what more accurately lure her away from just co-belonging to produce her isolation.

Firdaus's reflections on romantic love—although a subjective measure of fulfillment, one not as riddled with sexuality's interwoven economies of plea-sure and pain—likewise elude the calculi of autonomy and self-determination that Firdaus elsewhere recruits. As with other kinds of intimacy, Firdaus imagines love to require a relinquishment of the ego. Although she is reluc-tant to confine her inchoate attractions to that unidimensional, sterile met-ric, she retrospectively deciphers her attachments in such terms. Yet, even here, her ideas about love emanate from corporeal pain and self-sacrifice. For instance, while she concedes to "suffering" "humiliation" by Ibrahim, she paradoxically interprets that disappointment as somehow essential. Indeed, her meditations on love are precisely what expose the poverty of the neo-liberal measures of self-worth that deceive her. She explicitly distinguishes "love" from the experiential horizon of the prostitute:

> With love I began to imagine that I had become a human being. When I was a prostitute I never gave anything for nothing, but always took something in return. But in love I gave my body and my soul, my mind and all the effort I could muster, freely. I never asked for anything, gave everything I had, abandoned myself totally, dropped all my weapons, lowered all my defenses, and bared my flesh. But when I was a pros-titute I protected myself, fought back at every moment, was never off guard. To protect my deeper, inner self from men, I offered them only an outer shell. (85–86)

Firdaus's description is striking in that she associates romantic love and pros-titution with antithetical circuits of exchange. For Firdaus, prostitution is rationally based in a scheme of equivalence, self-abstraction, and cost-benefit analysis. This decorporealizing logic reduces Firdaus's existence to quantifiable gains and losses, mortgaging her happiness to such speculative tokens of valuation. The objectifying framework that she requisitions as a prostitute distances her from her underlying actions—which is to say that such reasoning all too successfully achieves the self-abstraction she seeks. Notably, Firdaus's description enacts these tolls corporeally, as she explains that only in love does she achieve genuine porosity of selfhood. The ruse of financial self-determination accordingly not only masks her subservience but also solidifies a particular metaphorics of embodiment that corroborates the liberal fiction of the impermeable, self-contained sovereign subject.

Conversely, romantic love does not compel Firdaus to refract her choices through the distorting prism of quantifiable self-interest. For Firdaus, love instead extends from unrequited, vulnerable self-exposure, or the willing breach of her facade of autonomy and inviolability. Predicated on self-loss, risk, and irrational abandonment, love transgresses and supersedes the axiomatics of neoliberalism, subtly arraigning them for duping her, as well as marking the exclusions that support their architecture. Firdaus, as such, deciphers love as fundamentally incommensurate to the fantasy of agentive self-fashioning that her lifestyle as a prostitute ironically vindicates—meaning that El Saadawi depicts the prostitute, not the lover, as the paragon of the tragically fleshless, decorporealized subject in attainment of the liberal norms accompanying human rights. Yet if the prostitute represents the most apt spokesperson for those liberal ideals, El Saadawi indicts that explanatory regime for significantly more than its paucity. In addition, El Saadawi implicitly sanctions it for legislating a matrix of interlocking structures of servitude and oppression. Indeed, Firdaus's literal and figurative prostitution comes to stand for the natural outcome of the onus to self-abstract through reasoned intellection, and it is in this way that El Saadawi reproves that mythology of the subject for directly conspiring with both capitalism and patriarchy, dual institutions that together collude to entrench a contempt for embodiment. While on the one hand women's stigmatized reduction to the body justifies misogyny, on the other liberal individualist subject formation scripts progress as the gradual transcendence of one's embodied state, rendering its overcoming a predicate to the subject's entitlement to rights. Thus confronting a double bind, Firdaus must sequester and subdue her embodiment in order to stipulate her self-worth, even while the act of prostitution does so by exploiting the very condition her culture consigns her to. It is in this respect, then, that *Woman at Point Zero* mines the contradictory and impossible demands that liberalism's ambivalence toward embodiment creates for the individual.

To conclude, I should return to observe how Firdaus's insights into love play out on the level of aesthetics. Firdaus's glimpses of fulfillment, despite being thwarted, importantly defy both intellectualization and translation into the liberal grammar of selfhood that she intermittently subscribes to. As such, they mark the limits of such an itinerary of the subject. As I have maintained, El Saadawi refuses to circumscribe Firdaus's realities within the rigid, formulaic diagnostic categories offered by medicine, and her reservations about that unidimensional genre of analysis equally apply to the language and the protocols of the law. The most generative moments in Firdaus's autobiography are devoid of evidentiary or empirical weight in a legal or scientific sense, and for this reason do they necessitate her corporeally vibrant registers of self-presentation. Stylistically, Firdaus's narrative is highly cyclical and repetitive, despite being encoded within the grammar and form of liberal *bildung*. Likewise, her narrative displays aesthetic properties that are imagistic and impressionistic, simulating her trancelike and affectively charged reactions. *Woman at Point Zero* is thus itself saturated with corporeal intensities, in effect incarnating the embodied habits of cognition through which Firdaus approaches her world. By itself harnessing and thereby inciting an embodied reading experience, *Woman at Point Zero* implicitly attests to such an aesthetic's merit. Such an embodied politics of reading unfolded within the narrative obeys neither the semantic conventions nor the ideological dictates that buttress liberal articulations of human rights. *Woman at Point Zero*'s narrative instead catalyzes the fugitive rhythms of embodiment, even while those energies war against the liberal idiom that El Saadawi simultaneously deploys to interpret Firdaus. While it would be nonsensical to expect a legal term of art to speak to all facets of existence, *Woman at Point Zero* documents those attributes of Firdaus's selfhood that the liberal doctrine of human rights works to censor, distort, and discredit. Indeed, the complexity of Firdaus's embodied grounds of self-justification would appear unintelligible, if not ridiculous, from within the dualistic worldview that informs both legal decision making and standard definitions of the liberal democratic public sphere.

It is therefore not accidental that Firdaus describes her anti-individualist pursuit of love as the one avenue through which she can "become a human being" (84, 85). Such a cartography of the human starkly diverges from the one Firdaus attempts to conform to throughout most of her narrative. This competing odyssey of the human instead requires her to forfeit rational calculation, along with her many "weapons," "defenses," and entitlements. Notably, the narrative's language here bears uncanny resemblances to what we will next encounter in J. M. Coetzee's *Disgrace*. In *Disgrace*, Coetzee similarly equates rights with "weapons" to contest their liberal logic, highlighting its socially atomizing repercussions. Social justice in both texts is not achieved in a fictional state of rightful, reasoned self-sufficiency but instead is incarnated—by no means incidentally for Firdaus—in the "baring" of one's "flesh." This appeal to the "flesh" of course echoes Merleau-Ponty's lexicon, and in both instances that term indexes a type of interpersonal solidarity and intertwining that emerges from the vulnerability of embodiment. Such a notion of the "flesh" thus captures those most contingent, injured, and permeable aspects of selfhood, and such an emphasis on embodied precarity and woundedness equally challenges the liberal premium on freedom and self-determination. Ironically, then, it is through such ruminations on love—the most idealized of human sentiments—that *Woman at Point Zero* reveals the many idealizations that guide liberal formulations of human rights to be so woefully damaging and misguided.

❧ CHAPTER FIVE

J. M. Coetzee's *Disgrace*

The Rights of Desire and the Embodied Lives of Animals

> "Yes, I agree, it is humiliating. But perhaps that is a
> good point to start from again. Perhaps that is what
> I must learn to accept. To start at ground level. With
> nothing. Not with nothing but. With nothing. No
> cards, no weapons, no property, no rights, no dignity."
>
> "Like a dog."
>
> "Yes, like a dog."
>
> —J. M. Coetzee, *Disgrace*

Much as the language of human rights can
serve as a powerful means to censure injustice, it is also believed to contain
the political ideals, legal mechanisms, and idiom for enacting healing—both
on an individual and a national level—after a pervasive legacy of rights violations. While narration is key to human rights witnessing, it is equally central
to bringing the language of human rights to bear on recovery and reconciliation. By compelling a reckoning with formerly silenced (and in extreme
cases unspeakable) wrongs, public acts of storytelling can variously convey
the magnitude of the harms inflicted on a society's former victims, repair
their humanity in the eyes of the larger world, and induce a kind of moral
catharsis within a populace. Indeed, narration is widely seen as indispensable
to confronting the past, making sense out of it, initiating recovery, and restoring a culture's basic respect for human rights.

Within South Africa's project of rehabilitation after apartheid, public
theaters of human rights narration played an especially prominent role.
The South African Truth and Reconciliation Commission (TRC) not only
captivated the international human rights community like few other human
rights tribunals but also was seen to augur a general prognosis for the descriptive authority of human rights, both as a discourse and a legal-political
paradigm. The TRC's inquiries focused on excavating "gross violations of
human rights," a term defined in the Promotion of National Unity and

Reconciliation Act of 1995, and proceeded with the expectation that the widespread circulation of stories about human rights abuses under apartheid would incite the South African nation to confront those injustices, inspiring both public contrition and rapprochement. As such, these globally monitored proceedings have commonly been read to adjudicate the basic legal and political legitimacy of human rights discourses and norms, betokening their promise as well as constitutive failures. Similarly, the 1993 South African Interim Constitution and 1996 Constitution have been heralded as "human rights manifestos," and the nation's transition beyond apartheid labeled "arguably the most historical event in the human rights movement since its emergence."[1]

In *Disgrace* (1999), J. M. Coetzee makes the TRC's experiment in human rights—in particular its agenda of uncovering stories of violation and holding them up for public scrutiny—a central issue. Located explicitly in postapartheid South Africa, *Disgrace* contends with both the ongoing residues of apartheid and the law's circumscribed ability to repair those offenses. The novel's commentary on the TRC primarily extends from the two criminal sexual assaults that fuel its plot, both of which magnify the vexed status of race in postapartheid South Africa. Whereas its white, late-middle-aged protagonist, David Lurie, commits the first offense—a seduction informed by questionable consent that nevertheless incurs a highly punitive trial—the succeeding violation involves a shockingly brutal gang rape of Lurie's daughter, Lucy. This second assault, however, meets with a conspicuous lack of legal vindication—in a dereliction of justice that haunts Coetzee's characters throughout the novel's plot. While *Disgrace* thereby wrestles with apartheid's damaging afterlives within South Africa, its plot simultaneously examines broad errors and biases that afflict the operations of law in general. Beyond the friction between its necessary abstraction and the concrete suffering within which the law intervenes, *Disgrace* decries the law's excessive reliance on procedure, its denial of nondominant epistemologies, the disembodied principles that inform its rules, and its ready enlistment to service injustice—limitations that collectively render it a blunt tool for negotiating the murkiness of human affairs. Regardless of these deficiencies, however, Coetzee's characters experience a profound longing for, in his words, the "necessary fictions" that law purveys.

While *Disgrace* self-consciously addresses the TRC's particular oversights, it also interrogates the legal term that was at the crux of its inquiries—namely, *human rights*. In doing so, it challenges the philosophical and practical wisdom of using the language of rights either to condemn wrongdoing or to instigate sociopolitical recovery. Overall, rights talk causes intense ambivalence in *Disgrace,* and its characters invoke the rhetoric of rights to justify and describe multiple kinds of malfeasance. Perhaps most visibly, in an attempt to excuse his own misbehavior, Lurie claims to possess sexual "rights of desire" (89)—a plea that is highly loaded within the context and history of South Africa. Through Lurie's opportunistic manipulation of the discourse of rights, *Disgrace* charts the hazards of relying on such an intrinsically charged, self-politicizing idiom, demonstrating why the language of rights is inordinately prone to sanction injustice when endowed with privileged legal and political standing. Although Lurie's self-defense resonates hollowly, it nevertheless offers crucial insight into the tendency of rights talk to lend free reign to predatory, atomizing self-interest. Lurie at the beginning of the novel represents, like Saleem Sinai and Firdaus, a spokesperson for the broad expectations about selfhood that underwrite liberal articulations of human rights, and his character's exploits dramatize the many inequities that shore up such fantasies of individual sovereignty and entitlement. In turn, *Disgrace* grapples with the deep irony that the TRC's efforts to facilitate recovery relied on an intellectual framework that also helped to apologize for apartheid's wrongs.

At the same time that it contends with the casualties of the discourse of human rights, *Disgrace* proposes a series of alternatives to rights logic, seemingly in response to both its rhetorical imprecision and latent biases. For one, it contemplates a communitarian ethic with notable affinities to the indigenous African value structure known as *ubuntu* (often seen to have merged with human rights within the TRC proceedings), although it engages such a vision of human solidarity only to expose its limits. *Disgrace* also looks to the animal world for a surrogate approach to social justice, and over the course of the novel its human characters progressively comprehend their own predicaments with reference to animal being. Not only does animal life dispel the dualistic fantasy of a unique human dignity; animals also exist in full captivity to their own mortality and corporeal being—that is, in a condition of mutual vulnerability and dependence that *Disgrace*'s human characters paradoxically come to emulate. Becoming "like a dog," a phrase that Lurie applies to decipher Lucy's plight after her rape, is accordingly lauded as a posture that might better aid South African recovery by surmounting the many foreclosures that sustain liberal mappings of the human, as they above all trouble the idiom of human rights.

The Writer and South Africa

Somewhat ironically, South African apartheid provided many critics with an exemplary scenario for debating the responsibility of the socially engaged writer to protest political oppression. Arguably one of the last nations to repudiate official, state-sponsored and legally codified practices of race-based persecution, South Africa was for much of the twentieth century an international pariah. Apartheid (the name of this official policy means "separate-ness" in Dutch) was formally enacted in 1948 and remained in place until 1990. It entailed the racial classification of peoples and resulted in a range of laws and prohibitions: barring interracial marriages, creating "whites only" jobs, segregating medical and educational facilities as well as public transportation, and refusing the vote and participation in government to nonwhites. During the apartheid era approximately 3.5 million black South Africans were relocated and 9 million were denationalized through the establishment of "homelands." Blacks were required to carry "passes" in white-only districts and were prohibited from political protest, the penalty for which often included indefinite detention and torture. The era was also marked by a series of conflicts that met with brutal suppression, the most well known being the Sharpeville massacre (1960) and the Soweto uprising (1976).

The dismantling of the apartheid government was as gradual as the policy was prolonged. On February 2, 1990, President F. W. de Klerk lifted the ban on the oppositional African National Congress (ANC) and ten days later released Nelson Mandela from prison. Following agreement by its major political parties, South Africa conducted its first fully democratic elections on April 27, 1994, and elected Mandela its new president. In the same 1993 Interim Constitution that authorized the elections, the last apartheid parliament instructed the incoming government to create procedures for granting amnesty for acts "associated with political objects and committed in the course of the conflicts of the past." This directive was framed by general reflections on the Interim Constitution's goals, which identified itself as an "historic bridge" between a "deeply divided" past to a renewed future aimed at the "promotion of national unity." In the document's words, "There is a need for understanding but not for vengeance, a need for reparation but not retaliation, a need for *ubuntu* but not for victimization."[2]

After extensive public consultation and debate, the TRC was convened on July 19, 1995. In its organization and structure it differed from previous truth commissions in other national contexts.[3] Most immediately, the TRC solicited an unprecedented volume of reports; altogether, more than twenty-two thousand victim statements were procured and over seven thousand amnesty applications filed.[4] Equally unusual was the scope of its media coverage; hearings were open to the general public and covered nightly on television with near-endless press analysis.[5] Despite mesmerizing, in addition to South Africa, much of the world, the TRC's proceedings were tarnished by seemingly innumerable missteps, errors, and omissions—which *Disgrace* revisits and subtly critiques. Perhaps the greatest source of controversy was the TRC's notorious "truth for amnesty" provision, a "bargain" added in the postamble to the Interim Constitution that gave precedence to uncovering "truth" about apartheid over penalizing its perpetrators. Effectively exonerating the worst apartheid era offenders, this clause inverted the priorities of other human rights inquests, including the Nuremberg trials.[6] Taken together, the many problems that compromised the TRC, along with the ordeals experienced by South Africa in ensuing years, have led some to dismiss postapartheid reconciliation as largely a failure. For instance, Achille Mbembe concludes, "South Africa today is still a nation composed of too many black people in possession of almost nothing—no meaningful foundation for social and economic autonomy."[7]

Within such a climate, artists and intellectuals have assumed an exceptionally politicized role. In the 1960s and 1970s, government censors adopted an increasingly partisan, conservative agenda, imposing aggressive regulations that policed even marginally controversial speech.[8] In turn, prominent artists were forced to navigate the fraught terrain between self-inoculation against censorship and moral responsibility for South Africa's oppressed populations. Many writers thus overtly thematized the burden of writing under censorship and consequently either were forced into exile or suffered imprisonment. Although Coetzee himself escaped direct interference, some have seen his stylistic obliqueness and frequent use of allegory as a deliberate ruse to evade such intrusion.[9] That said, phases of his career exhibit a conspicuous preoccupation with the impact of censorship on literary production, something he examines both in his nonfictional essays and more codedly in his fiction, for instance, the novel *Waiting for the Barbarians* (1980). However, Coetzee has not decried censorship as uniformly stifling; rather, he insists that the specter of government recrimination can paradoxically invigorate certain kinds of creativity.[10]

Under the apartheid laws that suppressed all dissent, even disinterested speech was often viewed as collusive, leading neutrality, or mere indifference, to be taken as an effective endorsement of that regime.[11] With sheer apathy thus deemed suspect by opponents of apartheid, it is not surprising that many South African writers favored self-consciously political writing that overtly depicts specifiable events in South African history. For instance, the 1977 murder of Steve Biko, the prominent black activist, by the South African police spawned a substantial literary response, including Coetzee's indirect portrayal of the incident in *Waiting for the Barbarians*. These elevated stakes within South African letters have also influenced debates about the relationship of aesthetics to politics, in particular, whether mimetic realism is best suited to the depiction of South African political reality. Within such an atmosphere, Coetzee's often defamiliarizing, experimental writing has inspired the complaint that he irresponsibly dehistoricizes and dislocates his novels from their politically laden, identifiable contexts. Perhaps most memorably, his fellow Nobel Prize laureate Nadine Gordimer implicitly derided Coetzee's use of allegory in his early novels, which for Gordimer reflected a "desire to hold himself clear of events and their daily, grubby, tragic consequences."[12] For his part, Coetzee disparages the conventions of realism for what he sees as their separately problematic ideological undercurrents. Describing Naguib Mahfouz's writing, Coetzee denounces the "heavy intellectual baggage" of the realist novel, calling it the appropriate genre for "Europe's merchant bourgeoisie."[13] Gordimer's remonstrance, moreover, moved Coetzee to a self-justification that will prove revealing in this chapter's analysis of *Disgrace*. While Coetzee rebukes Gordimer for being overly prescriptive, regretting that "discourse about what people *are* writing in South Africa slides so easily nowadays into discourse about what people *ought* to be writing," he also defends his refusal of the content-based strictures "imposed on the writer by society." Instead, he explains that he favors material "constitutional to the writer" involving a "transcendental imperative" that surpasses any given historical milieu.[14]

These quandaries about the politics of aesthetic form are especially instructive in light of the remarkable influence that *Disgrace* has had beyond the literary realm. Its portrait of the complicated South African political landscape has been, for some readers, so vivid that its fictional events have been levied as authoritative fact.[15] For example, in an oral report made by the ANC to the South African Human Rights Commission in 2000, *Disgrace* was offered as "evidence" of the contemporary status of South African race relations.[16] And, to further make the point, the novel has been credited with coining a term—the "Lucy syndrome"—as a cipher for "white guilt" in South African discourse.[17] With the potency of its diagnosis of postapartheid tensions thus in mind, let me now take a deeper look at *Disgrace* and the insights it affords into both the proliferating discourses and the philosophical architecture of human rights.

Principles, Agency, and the Law

The plot of *Disgrace* is driven by a series of almost Shakespearean reversals—all of which bear on the status of the law in South Africa, a common trope in Coetzee's fiction. Above all, we might explain this theme's prevalence as a by-product of living and writing in a nation that enlisted the rule of law not only to conceal but also to mandate gross violations of human rights. Such

unease over legality permeates *Disgrace*. Whereas on the one hand its characters exhibit an undue faith in the rule of law and legal procedure, on the
other they repeatedly jettison legal intervention, even when in dire need of
the law's assurances. Both responses can again be interpreted as remnants of
the complicated and compromised function of the law under apartheid.
Overall, much of the plot's momentum builds on either definitions of crime
or the unavailability of legal rectification. The law, despite its complicities,
is thus shown to play a pivotal role in both constituting social reality in
postapartheid South Africa and securing for Coetzee's characters their basic
perceptions of self.

The majority of *Disgrace*'s plot unfolds in the aftermath of its two crimes.
Lurie, the protagonist, assumes antithetical roles in these offenses, acting in one
as perpetrator and in the other as victim. These changes inspire the dynamic
and even dialogic relationship between Lurie and his daughter, Lucy, over the
narrative, which specifically emerges in their attitudes toward legal enforce-
ability. Despite the fact that each undergoes a reversal in response to the second crime, which finds them unexpectedly the objects of racially motivated
aggression, they hold opposing views about the merits of legal remedy. These
fluctuations underscore a chronic impasse in both the explanatory idiom and
diagnostic categories that law makes available, especially within the vexed
postapartheid legal arena. Nevertheless, while the novel displays how apartheid's remainders continue to sully the law's operations within South Africa,
it also investigates broad oversights that trouble legal reasoning. Along the
way, it deconstructs a number of basic tenets that gird liberal, contract-based
systems of law: the premium on evidentiary proof, the neoliberal myth of
self-possession, and the belief in measurable legal restitution.

Lurie commits the novel's first offense. Melanie Isaacs is a young female
student in his Romantic poetry class whom he coercively seduces into a short-
lived affair. By categorizing Melanie—"the dark one" (18)—as Coloured, *Disgrace* places, in addition to gender politics, postapartheid South African race
relations at its fore. Melanie eventually lodges a complaint, requiring Lurie
to participate in a widely publicized disciplinary hearing, and that hearing
conspicuously quotes many of the questionable facets of the TRC, while also
peripherally satirizing academic political correctness. Lurie scoffs at the hearing, refuses to defend himself, and rejects the disciplinary committee's request
that he sign a statement acknowledging the nature and scope of his wrongdoing. The narrative presents a range of explanations for why Lurie repudiates these demands, all due, as he claims, not to "challenges in a legal sense"
but rather to "reservations of a philosophical kind" (47). Here, Lurie offers
his first of many contradictory statements about whether the law should

embody "principles," or higher ideals, although at this point he opposes his own dubious principles to those of the law. This stance, although Lurie soon abandons it, seemingly impugns the apartheid regime's manipulations of law, which exploited its value-neutral facade to institute policies of racial oppression. Given that the principles Lurie opposes to law are, like apartheid's, decidedly not on the side of justice, his appeals appear to ratify the need to segregate law from changeable ideologies. Whereas it is often bemoaned that the law's formal abstraction sunders its affinity with justice, Lurie's self-serving justifications paradoxically stage a defense of insulating the rule of law from the sway of passing agendas.

In addition to Lurie's "philosophical reservations," the narrative's commentary on his disciplinary hearing alludes to widely held objections to the postapartheid reconciliation process.[18] For instance, when Lurie complains of "the gossip-mill...turning day and night, grinding reputations" (42), Coetzee brings to mind anxieties about the TRC's sensationalized media coverage. Believing that he experiences prurient scapegoating, Lurie describes spectators "circl[ing] around him like hunters who have cornered a strange beast and do not know how to finish it off" (56). Here, the narrative invokes the allegation that the TRC's rhetoric of "healing" transformed the need for public purgation and catharsis into a communal pillorying.[19] The demand that Lurie comply with a particular "package" involving "confession" and "abasement" in exchange for exculpation similarly parodies the controversial "truth for amnesty" provision that legally absolved severe apartheid offenders (56).[20] Likewise, as he visualizes himself under the "cross of righteousness" (40), Lurie bewails what he perceives as his trial's religiously inflected moralism, from which he, however, abstains: "Before that secular tribunal I pleaded guilty, a secular plea....Repentance belongs to another world, to another universe of discourse" (58).[21] This reservation, too, revisits another widely noted criticism: that the TRC's leaders, Chairman Archbishop Desmond Tutu, the country's most senior Anglican clergyman, and Deputy Chairman Alex Boraine, a Methodist minister, were foremost members of the clergy who imposed on the TRC their personal religious inclinations. To such ends, the TRC's vocabulary of "repentance" and "forgiveness," mocked by Lurie in *Disgrace,* has commonly been faulted for representing a religious grammar of confession and "atonement."[22]

Despite Lurie's sweeping condemnations of his trial, the second crime in the novel induces a polar reversal on his part, leading him instead to lament the law's abbreviated scope and protections. This violation occurs shortly after Lurie is dismissed from his university post and arrives on his daughter's smallholding farm in the rural Eastern Cape. Lucy, a self-identified lesbian, lives alone farming and boarding dogs after the breakup of a commune. This location is itself loaded, insofar as that region witnessed some of the most brutal violence of the apartheid era.[23] One afternoon, three black South African males approach the farm, force entry, shoot and kill the boarded dogs, and steal Lurie's car and other valuables. They hit Lurie over the head, causing him to lose consciousness, and lock him in the bathroom, thus barring him from the violation that, while it haunts the remainder of the narrative, remains unspoken and unrepresented: the brutal gang rape of Lucy.[24] Yet Lurie is denied access to Lucy's injuries not only because of his physical removal but also because of Lucy's refusal to narrate them. She says to her father, *"You don't know what happened"* (134) and insists that the rape is her "business" alone (133).

The assault on Lurie and his vicarious anguish over Lucy's harms precipitate a sudden shift in his views about law. In contrast to his former disparagement of its jurisdiction over his own life, Lurie seeks both legal retribution and the law's symbolic verification of Lucy's injuries. As he explains, "I am Lucy's father. I want those men to be caught and brought before the law and punished. Am I wrong? Am I wrong to want justice?" (119). Now aspiring for the law to incorporate "principles" for meting out justice, he embraces rather than derides its normative function, asserting that society "can't leave it to insurance companies to deliver justice" and that there must be "a principle involved" (137). Whereas before he deplored the public censure of his own misdeeds, now his personal sense of victimization compels him to pursue the law's role in the production of social values. From the standpoint of the novel, Lurie's about-face enables Coetzee to stage something of a debate over the law's bearing on political transformation. It should be noted, however, that both of Lurie's contradictory statements are equally symptomatic of an apparent luxury, rendering them potential proxies for the views of apartheid's ruling class. His initial belief in his own immunity clearly reflects such privilege, even while his overly credulous faith that the law will rescue him is a relic of his elite status.

Nevertheless, Lurie's experience of legal disenfranchisement compels him to solicit the outward contrition of Lucy's rapists, seemingly vindicating the TRC's goals as well as exposing the social advantages that girded his former pretense of disinterest. Shortly after the attack, he identifies the youngest of Lucy's rapists, an adolescent, at a party on the farm of their neighbor Petrus. When the boy "does not appear to be startled" by Lurie, the magnitude of Lurie's outrage registers itself viscerally: "his throat is thick with rage" and "his whole body shakes with violence." As Lurie accosts the boy, his widely overheard though ignored words of accusation fail to ameliorate his ire; rather, he seeks the boy's outward repentance, as he beseeches Petrus, "But let *him* tell you what it is about. Let *him* tell you why he is wanted by the police" (132). Ironically, Lurie here pursues the very display of penitence that he earlier scorned as unseemly and excessive. Although we might discredit that reaction as yet another insignia of Lurie's apartheid era prerogative, only when he no longer wields entitlement can he fathom the predicament of those historically denied the law's protections. Newly dispossessed, Lurie finds himself alienated from and beyond representation within the grammar of the law, and this marginalized state forces him to endorse its promulgation of principles, as well as their affirmative role in auguring a more just world. Lurie's vicissitudes thus disclose his initial dichotomization of principles and law to be an intellectual gambit only available to those wholly within the law's circumference—a gambit that, moreover, neglects how law, in the real world, procures both punishments and rewards.

Lucy, too, undergoes a reversal in her attitude toward law, but in the opposite direction. Before the attack, she chides Lurie for his insipid self-defense—"Shouldn't you be standing up for yourself?" (88)—and failure to recruit the law to his benefit. Following her rape, however, in one of the novel's many manifestations of rights talk, Lucy claims "the right not to be put on trial like this, not to have to justify myself" (133), echoing sentiments strikingly similar to those she earlier disparaged from her father. Yet in this case, she appeals to rights to inoculate herself from law rather than to condone wrongdoing. Lucy adamantly rejects the law's capacity to ameliorate her injury, and that position seems, on many levels, to extend from an awareness of its especially damaging entanglements within South Africa. Through Lucy's refusal to lodge a formal complaint, Coetzee calls to mind the fury unleashed on the victim in rape allegations, as well as the relative silence surrounding rape in the TRC hearings. Accordingly, the narrative invites us to read her forbearance as an unwillingness to allow her violation as a white woman to assume precedence over the spate of identical assaults inflicted on black South Africans during apartheid.[25] Lucy, in this way, seems aware that the circulation of her story of abuse could not possibly serve a conciliatory end. Whereas incendiary narratives of black-on-white sexual violence conscripted the law into racial policing under apartheid, she seemingly opts for silence precisely to quell the interracial hatred that apartheid capitalized on.[26]

Although Lucy abstains from legal speech, she invokes a similar law-principle binary as her father. Lucy, however, disavows not only the institutions of the law but also supralegal ideals, spurning both for being deficient relative to her behavior. When Lurie chides her for imprudently remaining on her remote farm following the attack, she explains her choice: "It was never safe, and it's not an idea, good or bad. I'm not going back for the sake of an idea" (105). Implicitly refuting her father's artificial dichotomy between principles and law, Lucy instead espouses a third term—namely, that of pragmatic decision making—to guide her actions. When Lurie rebukes her via the vocabulary of legal reparations—"Do you hope you can expiate the crimes of the past by suffering in the present?"—Lucy rejects his very logic. She accuses him of "misreading" her, insisting on the specificity of her predicament: "Guilt and salvation are abstractions. I don't think in terms of abstractions" (112). Here, Lucy avers not that her harm is entirely beyond representation but rather its incommensurability to a particular mode of quantifying, rationalistic, and disembodied analysis that is exemplified both in the law's abstract egalitarianism and in her father's solipsistic philosophizing. Lucy's antipathy to "abstraction" thus is partner to the recognition that the law's machinery is doomed to distort her basic plight and thereby depreciate the posture of vulnerable acceptance that her character exhibits.

As Coetzee presents it, the law's discursive conventions and protocols alike divorce it from the realities faced by both Lurie and Lucy. For example, Lurie's expulsion from his professorship is framed as the consequence of overreliance on legal proceduralism, or a blind faith in the rule of law. Dr. Rassool, the chair of his disciplinary committee, quiets her apparent anxieties about Lurie's charge by insisting that rigid adherence to formality will guarantee fairness. She assures Lurie: "It's always complicated, this harassment business, David, complicated as well as unfortunate, but we believe our procedures are good and fair, so we'll just take it step by step, play it by the book" (41). Seemingly deflecting her own doubts about the cogency of the allegations, Dr. Rassool appeals to the rule of law to legitimate the substantive questions that the hearing will adjudicate—an appeal that resonates with particular hollowness in South Africa. In contrast, Lurie's ex-wife Rosalind voices a scathingly unromanticized view of legal process that unmasks Dr. Rassool's belief in its procedural soundness. Berating Lurie for his disingenuous adherence to "principle," Rosalind chides him, "That may be so, David, but surely you know by now that trials are not about principles, they are about how well you put yourself across" (188). Although Lurie defies the committee, Rosalind cynically reminds us that compliance was wholly within his capacity—and thus an option disallowed the majority of South Africans. Once again, Lurie's casual disdain is marked as highly privileged, whereas Rosalind points to how apparently impartial legal standards in fact smuggle in concrete discriminations, given that the ability to gratify law's technical requirements is directly predetermined by class, gender, and, especially in South Africa, race.

Lucy's refusal to submit her violation to either a court of law or law enforcement authorities offers a related point of entry into the law's many exclusions and errors. Lucy raises the question of whether certain injuries—those informed by violence, pain, suffering, and abuse—are fated to defy the law's rhetorical, formal, and other truth-authorizing prescriptions. Theorists of trauma and pain have long maintained that trauma produces psychic fragmentation, disequilibrium, and incoherence, whereas the law favors evidentiary proof, propositional fact, and reasoned judgment. When it intervenes in response to those kinds of injuries, its truth-finding mechanisms risk censoring trauma's affective dimensions, ironically exacerbating the isolation and other emotional wounds of a victim. Through Lucy's silence, *Disgrace* accentuates the limits of legal process, suggesting that the empiricist and dualistic bias of the law would not only eclipse her psychic devastation but also, in rendering that injury legally actionable, require her to relive the assault. Lucy's withholding of her rape from the law, then, further probes whether the TRC's impetus to impose legal-political intelligibility on traumatic harms might have been misguided, if only because it reawakened the abuses of apartheid's countless victims.

Following the attack, Lurie and Lucy debate the basic possibility of narrating Lucy's harm, the perils of publicizing that story, and the law's fraught role in sanctioning particular instances of speech while suppressing others. For Lurie, each of these matters bears directly on what he perceives as Lucy's agency and self-possession, which he sees as mutually constitutive. The language of property and ownership abound in Lurie's thinking, and that proprietary logic reveals his indebtedness not only to competitive individualism but also to a strikingly colonialist mindset. Imagining gossip about Lucy, Lurie presumes an intimate connection between speech and self-possession, fearing that "like a stain," the story "is spreading across the district. Not her story to spread but theirs: they are its owners" (115). Lurie understands the rapists' mission in similarly economic terms, calling them "debt collectors, tax collectors" seeking "booty; war reparations; another incident in the great campaign of redistribution" (158). Although Lurie longs for the law's symbolic vindication, he fixates on remedies that are financial or otherwise affirm property's paramount status, and this prejudice ultimately leads him to discount alternate means to Lucy's (and South Africa's) recovery (110, 137). Indeed, Lurie's insistence that financial restitution offers the only meaningful route to redress represents an ideological barrier to the types of sociopolitical restructuring that might have prevented Lucy's rape. Lurie's preoccupation with property rights, as such, summons another denunciation of the TRC— that its failure to reallocate wealth held by whites under apartheid enfeebled South Africa's rehabilitation process.

Unlike her father, Lucy refuses to play the game of property rights, suggesting that the logic of financial calculus will fail to map onto either her injuries or her self-conception. She instead labels her rape a "purely private matter" (112) and insists to Lurie, "What happened to me is my business, mine alone, not yours" (133), condemning his desire to appropriate it.[27] As we have seen, Lucy's wish to preserve the "purely private" status of her harm countermands her father's proprietary worldview—a worldview that equally filters events through the lens of lingering black-white resentments in order to minimize his own wrongdoing. She therefore safeguards her rape with full awareness of South Africa's exceptionally charged social landscape, as well as the hostilities her story risks reactivating. Yet her demurral also resonates far beyond the particular context of South Africa. Indeed, Lucy protests a distinctly liberal mindset that is both quintessentially colonial and recurrently displayed by her father, whether in his defenses of property rights, his atomizing self-interest, or his hyperrationalism. She thus disavows the notion that the law must be founded on a social landscape composed of competing claims and entitlements. And by repudiating such a viewpoint, Lucy implicitly impugns it for both fostering the discriminations of apartheid and impeding reconciliation. Moreover, by shielding her violation from the public gaze, she rejects another basic tenet of the TRC—that formerly submerged human rights violations could become matters of public property without incurring deleterious results. It is in place of such an antagonistic model of political process that she instead displays a posture predicated on quiet forgiveness, humble acceptance, and just cohabitation, as I will return to later to consider.

The Impasses of Rights Logic

On one level, *Disgrace* is thus explicitly concerned with the ambivalent postapartheid legacy of the law in South Africa. Yet on a broader level, it simultaneously raises pointed questions about the language of rights in general and how rights-based theories of justice predispose human affairs. The idiom of rights reverberates throughout the text, whether in Lucy's appeal to "the right not...to have to justify myself" (133), the disciplinary committee's charge that Lurie has violated his student's "human rights" (57), or Lurie's own disingenuous defense that he possesses "rights" to seduce his student. While vivifying the slippery malleability of rights talk, *Disgrace* also reckons with damaging oversights that beset liberal discourses of rights and their accompanying assumptions about human selfhood. It asks whether rights logic is doomed to promote a highly anemic, sterile conception of the human—one that censors vital realms of experience while enshrining other, less salutary faculties. Along the way, *Disgrace* interrogates the TRC's mandate to uncover "gross violations of human rights" under apartheid. Much as the TRC's enlistment of the language of human rights rendered that grammar unusually visible, reports on the status of human rights have, in intervening years, only continued to dominate assessments of postapartheid national healing, further demonstrating the many perils of relying on human rights rhetoric to gauge more amorphous kinds of progress and recovery.[28] Overall, Coetzee problematizes the idiom of rights in order to dispute its ability either to nurture societal rapprochement or to discourage misconduct.

Indeed, the TRC's construal of *human rights* was not uncontroversial. The TRC significantly amplified that term's standard definition to include crimes not covered by former truth commissions in other national locales. In addition to offenses such as "killings, disappearances, and torture," the TRC broadened the scope of human rights violations to incorporate "severe ill treatment," a potentially vague, ambiguous term that not surprisingly spawned heated contention.[29] Akin to how the TRC's definition verged on overexpansiveness, the disciplinary committee asks Lurie to concede in a public statement, "I acknowledge without reservation serious abuses of the human rights of the complainant" (57). This application of the label *human rights* to Lurie's offense clearly registers the dangers that can ensue from the proliferation of human rights discourses and their ever expanding currency. Of course, Lurie's mistreatment of Melanie likely would have fallen under the TRC's inquiries, and *Disgrace* thereby seems to echo the fear that its demarcation of human rights was overly broad, forsaking critical precision and casting its inquiries too sweepingly. In this respect, the narrative confronts what Michael Ignatieff refers to as "rights inflation," a syndrome wherein imprecise appeals to the language of rights forebode that term's descriptive obsolescence. Here, too, we might ask whether the constant monitoring of human rights as an overall barometer for national health and prosperity hazards a parallel sacrifice of that term's explanatory purchase as a diagnostic.

Moreover, alleging that a person has committed human rights violations is an unusually powerful epithet, through which *Disgrace* dramatizes another liability of the dilated scope of the TRC's definition—namely, punitive excess. Precisely because of its potency the language of human rights carries heightened stakes, as are manifested in Lurie's penalty. While not to downplay his wrongs, the indictment levied by the disciplinary committee is incredibly toxic and damning, calling into question its proportionality relative to Lurie's underlying offense. We might thus ask whether the severity of his punishment turns him into something of a scapegoat, presenting us with

another casualty of reliance on the idiom of human rights to enact reconciliation. When a regime's victims are elevated in power, the risk is that they will
merely perpetuate the animosities of their former oppressors.[30] Once again,
the hearing's controversial politics here come to the fore, insofar as Lurie is
ultimately condemned by the committee chair, Dr. Rassool, a black female,
newly vested in postapartheid South Africa with the authority to levy such
allegations of infringed human rights. This dynamic within the narrative, too,
queries whether Lurie's hearing might commence a cycle of vengeance that
will only feed preexisting appetites for reprisal.[31] All in all, *Disgrace* cautions
that rights talk is not only a forceful idiom but also a volatile one just as likely
to exacerbate tensions, especially when deployed to license retaliatory judgments and decision making.

That said, while Lurie's fate might be a by-product of judicial activism,
there is no doubt that his treatment of Melanie prolongs and is enabled
by the race-based injustices of apartheid. As such, *Disgrace* illustrates why a
vast history of abuse facilitated by power differentials and legally entrenched
rights deprivations might render otherwise negligent behavior fully criminal.
Lurie's first two sexual liaisons in the novel are with nonwhite women—a
telling detail that confirms his ongoing privilege, as well as the extent to
which he retains a mindset endemic to apartheid.[32] Indeed, Rassool overtly
identifies Lurie as an heir to that entitlement by alluding to "the long history
of exploitation of which this is a part" (53). By aligning Lurie's malfeasance
with South Africa's other systemic oppressions, Rassool summons the untold
human rights violations that collectively shore up Lurie's very capacity to
abuse. In another venue Lurie's penalty might have bordered on punitive
excess, but its extremity, within the context of South Africa, is implied to
be necessary to reverse the institutionalized biases from which Lurie profits immensely. Given that Lurie unquestionably benefits from the historical
wrongs of his forebears, *Disgrace* ponders whether he should be held accountable in the present for that complicity. Much as apartheid transformed mere
quiescence into consent, Lurie's failure to disavow his accumulated prerogative may be enough, within the location of South Africa, to establish his guilt.

By no means last, Lurie's offense brings to mind the long-standing complaint that human rights inquests have disproportionately neglected sexual
violence against women. Indeed, critics have argued that the human rights
enforcement community has failed to devote sufficient attention to violations, paradigmatically rape, that are overwhelmingly inflicted on women.[33]
For instance, Catherine MacKinnon argues that "because male dominance
is built into the social structure, social force is often enough" to perpetuate systemic deprivations of women's rights.[34] Since the TRC hearings, too,

procured a relative dearth of rape narratives, we might ask whether such an allegation similarly pertains to those proceedings. In whatever case, by enlisting the rhetoric of human rights to denounce a form of rape, *Disgrace* invites us to applaud the application of that label to Lurie's offense as an overdue enlargement of the scope of human rights protections. Indeed, even Lurie concedes the proximity of his offense to rape, identifying it as "not rape, not quite that, but undesired nevertheless, undesired to the core" (25), and his eventual plea to Melanie's father further attests to his recognition of the seriousness of his actions.

The "Rights of Desire"

As we have seen, the disciplinary committee's charge against Lurie dramatizes a number of the hazards that have accompanied the growing preponderance of human rights discourses. Yet Lurie's defense of his actions simultaneously illuminates a different but related pitfall of rights talk—the ease with which it can be usurped to justify malfeasance. Lurie does just this when he invokes his "rights of desire" in effort to exonerate his mistreatment of Melanie; as he maintains, "My case rests on the rights of desire. . . . On the god who makes even the small birds quiver" (89). This appeal conspicuously juxtaposes Lurie's disingenuously self-serving rights of seduction with the disciplinary committee's accusation, a move that highlights not just the astonishing fluidity of the language of rights but also how it readily comes to sanction egoistic and even obstructionist behavior. This aspect of Lurie's hearing, too, recalls the warring discourses of rights that haunted the TRC proceedings. Akin to how Lurie recruits the language of rights to rationalize his predatory behavior, some of apartheid's most notorious offenders conscripted that idiom in attempt to inoculate themselves against the TRC's authority.

Yet beyond this allusion to the TRC, Lurie's self-defense opens up more foundational problems that afflict liberal articulations of human rights. It goes without saying that Lurie is, at times, an unlikable protagonist, and his character has provoked strong critical reaction, much of it focused on the thorny politics of the novel's two sexual offenses and the relationship between the two crimes.[35] Does the narrative underscore their similarities or instead their differences, in the latter case entailing that we should interpret Lurie's infraction as less serious an offense? Whatever the case, Lurie's appeal to his "rights of desire" evidences a decidedly colonial mindset—in other words, the very thinking that legitimized apartheid. Beyond how his erotic attractions ensnare him within such a heritage, Lurie's fetishization of property rights reflects a

classically imperialist compulsion toward insatiable acquisition, which paradigmatically manifests itself in his attitude toward the land. Displaying a posture
common within both South African letters and other imperialist writing, Lurie
feminizes the land, for instance, as he romanticizes Lucy's role as caretaker of
the pastoral landscape. In his 1987 Jerusalem Prize acceptance speech, Coetzee
explicitly links such longings to the appetites that fueled apartheid, which was
animated by an interrelated erotic yearning for unspoiled, uncharted territory
and the anxiety of contamination. As Coetzee explains, "[Apartheid's] origins... lie in fear and denial: denial of an unacknowledgeable desire to embrace
Africa, embrace the body of Africa; and fear of being embraced in return by
Africa."[36]

In spite of all of this, Lurie's character is astutely able to observe how others
are captive to their South African inheritances, although while utterly failing
to diagnose his own behaviors as such. He patronizingly reduces Lucy's rapists to "history speaking through them," a "history of wrong... [that] came
down from the ancestors" (156), but he cannot admit that he, too, fulfills a
corresponding lineage. If anything, Lurie's almost allegorical interpretations
of his and other characters' interconnected roles serves to divert him from
self-scrutiny. And in this respect, Lurie's hyperacademic intellectualization
of events is part and parcel of what we might deem a quintessentially liberal
worldview. If Lurie is an invariably unlikeable protagonist, those alienat-
ing aspects of his personality derive directly from the extent to which he
exhibits the self-enclosure and other hypocrisies that are, in extreme form,
apologized for within liberal theories of the subject. For one thing, Lurie is
beholden to the conceit of his own self-sufficiency and autonomy. When
describing his love life at the beginning of the novel, his narrative acknowledges his "need to be alone" (2), and after the attack he bristles when he and
Lucy must depend on the beneficence of others, especially their neighbors
and fellow farmers, the Shaws. Furthermore, Lurie recurrently rationalizes
events, a symptom of his dual beliefs in the priority of reasoned intellection
and possibility of redemption through the life of the mind. His investment
in "principles" similarly privileges abstract thought over either pragmatic
or affective modes of cognition—a divide that is especially apparent in his
disagreements with Lucy, who rebukes his ideational thinking for distancing
him from the real world. Even Lurie himself eventually concedes that his
retreat into "the comforts of theory" (98) after the attack is an avoidance
mechanism. By no means last, the opera that he immerses himself in toward
the novel's conclusion incurs an almost identical function, as I will return to
later to consider. Lurie initially intends for this opera to depict the life of
Lord Byron, with whom Lurie, an expert in Romantic poetry, identifies in

light of Byron's elite disdain for social conventions, eventual exile, and almost self-defeating individualism.

Even more, Lurie's biases play out in a classically dualistic disdain toward embodiment. Whereas on the one hand he superficially claims the supremacy of his selfish "rights of desire," on the other he is deeply uncomfortable with the body's rhythms and appetencies. Beyond his illusion of prowess as a "womanizer" (7), he is almost Victorian in his sensibilities. In the very first sentence of the novel we are told that Lurie "has, to his mind, solved the problem of sex rather well" (1). Weekly liaisons with a prostitute keep his sexual life "functional, clean, well regulated" and in "compartments" (5, 6), purveying a "moderated bliss" (6) that allows him to subordinate the body's needs to his academic pursuits. In addition to being an inconvenience, bodies (both his own and those of others) inspire shame and derision. Indeed, his reactions to Lucy's body border on offensive. When he first encounters her within the narrative's trajectory, he is startled by changes she has undergone, observing that "she has put on weight" and become "ample" (59). His ruminations, however, do not stop with this immediate surprise, and he on multiple occasions analyzes her bodily condition. Lurie surmises: "*Ample* is a kind word for Lucy. Soon she will be positively heavy. Letting herself go, as happens when one withdraws from the field of love" (65). Bev Shaw is the object of similarly demeaning thoughts, for instance as she is condescendingly described as "a dumpy, bustling little woman with black freckles, close-cropped, wiry hair, and no neck. He does not like women who make no effort to be attractive" (72). At once, Lurie is preoccupied with his own corporeality, most conspicuously, as his waning sexual vigor leads him crassly to speculate about self-castration (9). As he maintains that "desire [is] a burden we could well do without" (90), the start of the novel finds Lurie caught up in a protracted endeavor to evade and deny his carnal being. While his defense of sexual rights might appear to render him a proponent of embodiment, even this appeal is informed by the expectation that the body will cause "disgrace" and therefore demand discipline.

Lurie follows the paean to his rights of desire that is intended to excuse his treatment of Melanie with a lengthy description of a dog owned by some former neighbors. He deciphers its predicament for Lucy:

> "It was a male. Whenever there was a bitch in the vicinity it would get excited and unmanageable, and with Pavlovian regularity the owners would beat it. This went on until the poor dog didn't know what to do. At the smell of a bitch it would chase around the garden with its ears flat and its tail between its legs, whining, trying to hide."

He pauses. "I don't see the point," says Lucy. And indeed, what is the point?

"There was something so ignoble in the spectacle that I despaired. One can punish a dog, it seems to me, for an offence like chewing a slipper. A dog will accept the justice of that: a beating for a chewing. But desire is another story. No animal will accept the justice of being punished for following its instincts."

"So males must be allowed to follow their instincts unchecked? Is that the moral?"

"No, that is not the moral. What was ignoble about the Kenilworth spectacle was that the poor dog had begun to hate its own nature. It no longer needed to be beaten. It was ready to punish itself." (90)

Leaving aside Lurie's apparent willingness to exonerate his own "instincts" through this appeal to nature, he seems convinced that with embodiment comes humiliation and torment. His liberal, rights-based thinking is accordingly revealed to entrap him within a mindset that can only imagine the body to be a burden—or an entity that will either detract from rational subjectivity, incite embarrassment, or remain hostage to anarchic needs. As we will see, Lurie gradually abandons such a jaundiced understanding of corporeal being, but this hostility toward embodiment permits him to evade certain painful and humbling realities surrounding, above all, his own weakness and vulnerability.

In sum, *Disgrace* not only leaves us with an intensely bleak view of the ramifications of rights talk but also construes the pervasive aggression experienced by its characters as, in extreme form, intrinsic to the liberal logic of rights. This chapter's final section will examine how that social landscape directly ensues from the types of dualistic antipathy to embodiment that also lends coherence to liberal formulations of rights, which is why Lurie's overcoming of his abhorrence of embodiment enables both his relinquishment of his egoistic self-enclosure and recognitions that the narrative holds up as overridingly just. Nonetheless, Lurie's character over much of the novel offers a case study in the risks of rights-based thinking, and the novel thereby asks to what degree his egoistic views mirror the ideological edifice that apologized for apartheid. Indeed, Lurie's hyperindividualist investment in the authority of rights is closer than a distant cousin to the mindset that rationalized the race-based exclusions and other prejudices of the apartheid era. As such, not only Lurie's privileged indifference but also his reliance on a particular language of rights marks his complicity with apartheid thinking. Although Lurie himself is less than fully cognizant of the extent that he remains in league with apartheid's enabling assumptions, his recurrent neglect of the full implications of his behaviors is also highly incriminating.

Lurie's predicament in this way brings us to another deep irony of the TRC—that it used an idiom and evaluative prism with troubling affinities to the core logic that was requisitioned to authorize the policies of apartheid. *Disgrace's* implicit censuring of rights talk for condoning Lurie's malfeasance is thus partner to a parallel inquiry into whether that reasoning should be held accountable for having legislated the many wrongs of the apartheid era. By introducing Lurie as a spokesperson for a particular formulation of rights, the narrative asks whether and how his unique oversights and biases pervade rights logic broadly speaking. To the extent that postapartheid reconciliation has been a morass, *Disgrace* further questions whether those failures arose in part because the TRC enlisted a value structure with noteworthy resemblances to some of apartheid's most insidious ideological warrants. The narrative, in turn, contemplates whether the TRC, in employing the language of human rights, paradoxically perpetuated an intellectual framework of which it should have been suspicious. These may be some of the most profound paradoxes of human rights—namely, that their liberal philosophical architecture can support the very exclusions that are their foremost target.

Returning to Lurie's defense of "rights of desire," *desire* is another unusually loaded term within South African law and politics—one especially redolent for understanding literary and other artistic production. Under the Publications Act of 1975, in place until 1990, the legal category that controlled all censorship was the term *undesirable,* and it regulated both fictional and nonfictional writing based on whether it was seen to cultivate illicit desire. Within the act's definition of the "undesirable," it censored publications that were deemed "obscene or offensive," as well as prejudicial to "security, welfare, peace and good order"—in other words, an extraordinarily broad, amorphous category of texts.[37] While Coetzee has written extensively on the many repercussions of censorship in *Doubling the Point* (1992) and *Giving Offense: Essays on Censorship* (1996), he, too, construes censorship in terms of its nexus with desire. Explaining the censor's task as the tracking of desire, Coetzee himself cites in *Giving Offense* the 1975 act for the idea that "an eager appetite for the books or pictures or ideas under interrogation is precisely what the censor seeks to curb. . . . What is undesirable is the desire of the desiring subject" (viii). For Coetzee, censorship ramifies beyond the simple suppression of speech to further enjoin the basic human interest in a given subject matter. He dismisses these ambitions, however, as ultimately naive, since they collapse under the circularity of their own logic. By erecting a prohibition, censorship creates an appetite not only for defying that law but also for the object and guise of its transgression. In turn, the sheer act of labeling as taboo a subject matter (rather than the content of that subject matter) is what engenders a desire for it.[38]

"Desire" for Coetzee thus simultaneously encodes the illicit, egoistic energies that fuel creativity and the ethical sensibilities that can be aroused by art. In *Doubling the Point,* Coetzee also describes creativity as animated by a dynamic interchange between passion and inspiration. Explaining how writing unleashes dormant desire, he comments, "Writing shows or creates (and we are not always sure we can tell one from the other) what our desire was, a moment ago" (18). This suggests how desire for Coetzee elucidates the reciprocities between passion and aesthetic experience that are necessarily harnessed by creative vision. These permutations of desire in addition bear on the status of the artwork in *Disgrace.* Indeed, Lurie is a champion for not only desire's predatory dimensions but also its generative, transformative, and even potentially redeeming properties. Lurie's opera, which this chapter's final section turns to, accordingly represents a type of laboratory for testing the many vicissitudes of desire, as they are inextricably linked in *Disgrace* to an imaginative remapping of the terrain of social justice.

Language and the Law

In the first half of *Disgrace,* Lurie's foibles divulge certain perils and prejudices of rights logic, but as the plot unfolds we see his gradual escape from that value structure and attempt to replace it with something different. In particular, as Lurie contends with his own constitutive woundedness, he strives for a workable means of just coexistence. Although his experience of dispossession leads to this soul searching, that process awakens a sense of solidarity with South Africa's many excluded populations, both human and animal. Lurie, however, confronts epistemic barriers that prevent him from fully inhabiting such a marginalized, nondominant viewpoint. On the one hand, he is trapped within dualistic, reasoned-based patterns of thought that disavow the overwhelming reality of corporeal and other suffering. On the other hand, he encounters representational constraints that derive from the contaminated status of English and its hyperpoliticization within South Africa. As a consequence, he must address apartheid's residues within English as well as his own complicity with those biases before he can fully own his personal wrongdoing. Much as Lurie's beholdenness to empiricist modes of discourse impedes his ability to fathom the injuries of South Africa's historically aggrieved populations, the narrative presents language itself as inadequate to grasp Lurie's own perception of vulnerability, which extends above all from an emerging consciousness of the ontological condition of embodiment. Lurie's development over the course of *Disgrace,* then, is intimately tied to his quest for alternate registers of expression that might at once surmount and replenish the attenuated reservoirs of the English language.

In his other novels, Coetzee has frequently depicted characters who, like Lurie, are barred from full self-revelation in speech. Yet in *Disgrace,* the narrative's predominantly realist mode entails that those foreclosures are wrought in large part through Lurie's own perspective. While this device enacts Lurie's chronic solipsism, it also reveals the ways that language naturally censors certain subject positions—and along lines that fairly predictably track society's social and political exclusions. Unsurprisingly, Lucy's African neighbor Petrus is inordinately victim to the biases and other repressions installed within language, and his viewpoint is perhaps most conspicuously denuded within the narrative. It is Lurie's inability to comprehend Petrus, however, that leads him to ponder the many obstructions built into language. Lurie surmises:

> Doubtless Petrus has been through a lot, doubtless he has a story to tell. He would not mind hearing Petrus's story one day. But preferably not reduced to English. More and more he is convinced that English is an unfit medium for the truth of South Africa. Stretches of English code whole sentences long have thickened, lost their articulation, their articulateness, their articulatedness. Like a dinosaur expiring and settling in the mud, the language has stiffened. Pressed into the mould of English, Petrus's story would come out arthritic, bygone. (117)

Lurie here bemoans how apartheid and its legally sanctioned wrongs have perverted English, so much so as to prevent it from communicating core realities. To record such linguistic stagnation, Lurie stumbles over multiple conjunctions of the verb *articulate*—a word not coincidentally laden with invidiously racist connotations—none of which suffice. While he bewails that decay, his fixation on such a charged word nevertheless displays his lingering thralldom to apartheid era habits of thought, much as his ruminations are tainted by "suspicion" of Petrus and yearning for "the old days" (116–7). Lurie engages in similar musings when Petrus applies the word *benefactor* to Lucy, which Lurie finds "distasteful" not because of Petrus himself but because "the language he draws on with such aplomb is, if he only knew it, tired, friable, eaten from the inside as if by termites" (129). However, this resignation begs the question of whether Lurie's lament isn't something of an ethical cop-out. Indeed, "English" is the only medium of which he can conceive, and, by ascribing fault to language alone, he forsakes personal responsibility to remedy its omissions. Lurie does evince tentative sympathy for Petrus's plight when he despairs that, even after South Africa's comprehensive project of restoration, English still remains an exhausted archive fated to perpetuate an apartheid worldview and license Petrus's oppression. Nevertheless, Petrus disproportionately suffers the effects of this inertia, exposing how speech deprivations can directly pave the way to rights infringements.

While Lurie bemoans the violence that apartheid has inflicted on speech itself, he encounters more foundational limitations of language when he attempts to express his trauma after the attack. Much as Lucy insists that her rape resists symbolic containment, Lurie cannot obtain psychological clarity or closure. He attests to the assault's lingering immediacy by citing what speech cannot convey: "The day is not dead yet but living. *War, atrocity:* every word with which one tries to wrap up this day, the day swallows down its black throat" (102). Notably, Lurie employs vivid bodily imagery seemingly to overwhelm language in its poverty, marking why propositional discourse and abstract ideals—his customary genre of thought—will fail to register such a profound affront. In this respect, Merleau-Ponty's reflections on scientific and legalistic regimes of thought can help to elucidate the consequences of Lurie's entrapment within reason-based, empiricist styles of discourse. In his usual habits of cognition, Lurie enlists language for intellectual control, or to "lay siege to" otherwise unnerving experiences, stifling their "paradoxes" and "discordances" and providing him with the illusion of mastery over those circumstances.[39] Such an illusion, however, becomes increasingly hard for him to sustain after the attack. While Lurie here grapples with the failure of speech to capture his trauma, he also reckons with the casualties of his own instrumentalizing relationship to language, seemingly admitting to realities and recognitions that it has foreclosed.

These debilities that beset speech come into especially high relief within the grammar of the law, returning us to its exceptional compromises under apartheid. Importantly, Petrus's peculiar legal status triggers Lurie's meditations on the "unfit medium" of English, compelling him to admit to the discriminations inscribed within the legal order. He struggles to define Petrus's new role in the postapartheid social world:

But though Petrus is paid a wage, Petrus is no longer, strictly speaking, hired help. It is hard to say what Petrus is, strictly speaking. The word that seems to serve best, however, is *neighbor*. Petrus is a neighbor who at present happens to sell his labour, because that is what suits him. He sells his labour under contract, unwritten contract, and that contract makes no provision for dismissal on grounds of suspicion. It is a new

world they live in, he and Lucy and Petrus. Petrus knows it, and he
knows it, and Petrus knows that he knows it. (117)

This repetition of the phrase "strictly speaking" displays Lurie's tendency to
recruit language to discipline and manage forms of ambiguity and complexity.
In this instance, he clings to rote legal definitions seemingly to mask his hostility toward the novel arrangement reached by Lucy and Petrus, again highlighting the law's many liaisons with the reasoning that supported apartheid.
It is, moreover, significant that these juridical categories govern property
rights, a further demonstration of the links between contract-based theories
of justice and apartheid's enabling logic. By reminding us of Lurie's relative
social clout, *Disgrace* indicts the legal order itself for prolonging his apartheid
era privileges and hierarchies, deterring their reversal and reform. Yet Lurie's
investment in this particular vision of law is counterpart to his broader need
for intellectual order, impulses that together excuse his onus to scrutinize both
the underlying practices and substantive values naturalized by the law's established precedents and protocols. When Lurie subsequently considers Lucy's
willingness to enter into an "alliance" or "deal" with Petrus that, through her
marrying him, would ensure her safety on the farm, he again disingenuously
blames the rule-bound inflexibility of law for his own dearth of imagination,
concluding that "legally it's not workable" (204). Much as Lurie refuses to
envision an alternative to English, his cavalier defense of an especially antiseptic conception of law apologizes for his own egoistic entitlements.

Disgrace thereby indexes the depth of apartheid's toxic residues within
South African legal discourse, while Lurie's hypocrisies simultaneously interrogate rights-based theories of social justice in general. Such an evaluative
prism induces Lurie to erroneously envision Lucy and Petrus as independent,
self-interested subjects motivated by antagonism and, hence, "suspicion." The
fiction of the rights-bearing subject, that is, obscures the mutual indebtedness
that more accurately binds Lucy and Petrus within the postapartheid social
landscape, illustrating why rights logic will eclipse core dimensions of social
coexistence. As such, neither Lurie's idiosyncratic failings nor the particular
afterlives of apartheid can be entirely blamed for his self-enclosure; rather,
Disgrace indicts liberal vocabularies of selfhood, along with their imprint on
the law, for hampering South African rapprochement. As Lurie's reasoning
divulges, contract- and rights-based systems of justice are fated to perpetuate
the myth of the monadic, self-reliant liberal individual, misreading social
formations that do not corroborate such cartographies of the human. Insofar
as Lucy's accord with Petrus instead aims to forge an emergent species of
just cohabitation, it defies liberalism's conventional explanatory framework.

Precisely Lurie's shortsightedness, then, shows why such counterindividualist ideals will appear incoherent and "not workable" within the law's standard grammar, betokening little more than radical destitution.

That said, Lurie gradually abandons his reliance on the interrelated fictions of self-ownership and the abstract authority of rights, and that shift enables his sense of solidarity with other beings. Correspondingly, his growing awareness of the latent cruelties that reside within language far beyond the rarefied lexicon of law fosters his desire to transform English into a more democratic register of communication. In sum, his progressive relinquishment of a hyperindividualistic worldview is directly linked to his quest for an alternate, uncompromised vehicle of description and analysis. In the same breath as Lurie dismisses English as an "unfit medium" for South Africa, Coetzee's narrative relates, "The real truth, he suspects, is something far more—he casts around for the word—*anthropological,* something it would take months to get to the bottom of, months of patient, unhurried conversation with dozens of people, the offices of an interpreter" (118). Lurie here advocates a method of truth disclosure strikingly similar to that employed by the TRC.[40] On the one hand, his appeal to the "anthropological" foregrounds the socially constructed and contingent nature of all such "truth," with its dependence on history, location, and other accidents of circumstance. On the other hand, Lurie yearns "to get to the bottom of" such fortuities and to annex forms of meaning that might surpass the variables of place and context. While he frames this as a dual problem of volume and testimony, he is also seduced by the prospect of meaning that is "authentic" (214, 118). Here again, we might invoke Merleau-Ponty's account of phenomenological perception. Much as Lurie grasps at insights that are not reducible to empiricist modes of discourse, Merleau-Ponty comparatively describes an embodied consciousness as affording clearings in language that "rediscover a commerce with the world and a presence to the world which is older than intelligence."[41] And to such ends, Coetzee's reflections on the "transcendental imperative" of the writer here, too, bear on Lurie's pursuits. Indeed, Lurie seemingly aspires for a type of cognition that might evade both the polluted archives of English after apartheid and the many obstructions that language naturally harbors—obstructions only multiplied by Lurie's atomizing worldview.

For Lurie it is the composition of his opera that ultimately permits him to escape both the constraints of language and his formerly egoistic mindset. The opera is increasingly central to the conclusion of *Disgrace,* above all providing a forum for Lurie's imaginative experiment in ethics. Precisely because its plot is "going nowhere," with "no action" and "no development," Lurie imbues his opera with extraordinary, near-existential freight (214). As he anticipates, "somewhere from amidst the welter of sound there will dart up, like a bird, a single authentic note of immortal longing" (214). He concedes that this exemplary "note" will be ephemeral and fleeting, yet he also imagines that it will evade the innumerable liabilities of English to purvey "immortal" significance. Of course, the overridingly Romantic texture of Lurie's yearnings invites us to reject them as a symptom of his solipsistic self-indulgence. Nonetheless, *Disgrace* productively considers whether certain kinds of artistic experience might remedy the enervated condition of discourse by momentarily furnishing what Merleau-Ponty refers to as "a direct and primitive contact" with instantiations of meaning.[42] *Disgrace,* in turn, entertains a vision of linguistic renewal—or of expression uncorrupted by the many cruelties and distortions that infect even commonplace speech. Particularly in light of the many imperialisms and other structures of exploitation that global modernity has licensed in part by inscribing them within language, Lurie's opera probes the capacity of art to surmount those injustices and intermittently redeem language from its impoverishment.

Social Justice and the Embodied Lives of Animals

As I've suggested, Lurie's absorption with his opera and fatigue with his customary intellectual mechanisms for approaching the world are intimately related developments. Moreover, the subject matter of Lurie's opera is itself of utmost significance; its evolving plot tracks his character's entrance into what we might, with reference to Merleau-Ponty's thought and in the context of this book, call a phenomenological consciousness of embodiment. This emergent awareness of a fundamental, universally shared predicament of embodiment compels him to jettison the liberal mythologies of selfhood that have supported his monadic self-interest and predatory worldview. As Lurie questions his routine, practiced ways of interpreting the world, he experiments with surrogate philosophical bases for deciphering just coexistence, and he importantly evaluates these alternate cosmologies in terms of whether they will surmount the many oversights and exclusions that problematically sustain liberal topographies of the human.

One such alternative that Lurie contemplates is a brand of communitarianism. A particularly long-standing philosophical reservation about human rights is that they erroneously prioritize the individual's needs over the larger community, failing to cultivate relations of obligation and interreliance. For instance, Iris Marion Young argues along such lines that the ideal of "self-determination" elides those components of selfhood that arise through reciprocities and commitments.[43] In turn, critics have maintained that rights logic demands either replacement or supplementation with a value structure that instead foregrounds the collective. To such ends, Gayatri Spivak not only understands rights as antonymic to and "underived from" notions of "responsibility" but also concludes that they should be appended with norms concerning commitment and duty.[44] Not surprisingly, the viability of such a communitarian ethic received significant debate within the TRC, largely in reference to the indigenous ethic of *ubuntu*. *Ubuntu* is widely regarded as community oriented in its tenor and commonly defined to connote "humaneness, or an inclusive sense of community valuing everyone." In fact, some have suggested that *ubuntu* complements or even supplants the ideals of human rights.[45] This is a view that Desmond Tutu, a key proponent of *ubuntu*, implicitly endorses when he explains, "A person with *ubuntu* is open and available to others, affirming of others, does not feel threatened that others are able and good, for he or she has a proper self-assurance that comes from knowing that he or she belongs in a greater whole and is diminished when others are humiliated or diminished, when others are tortured or oppressed."[46]

Indeed, the 1993 South African Interim Constitution cites *ubuntu* as critical to the South African restoration process. According to chapter 16, titled "National Unity and Reconciliation," there is "a need for understanding but not for vengeance, a need for reparation but not for retaliation, a need for *ubuntu* but not for victimization."[47] Scholars, however, have differed over the precise philosophical relationship between *ubuntu* and human rights, especially whether its values merely fortify or instead offer correctives to human rights norms. In keeping with Tutu's view, many, including Martha Minow, understand the concept to furnish ideals that are virtually indistinguishable from those underlying human rights.[48] In contrast, others argue that *ubuntu* is incommensurate with rights logic, a position that implicitly questions whether the TRC's constitutional mandate subtly problematizes the notion of rights. For example, Mark Sanders contrasts *ubuntu* with human rights, claiming that the former is grounded in "responsibility, not the rule" and predicated on a nonegoistic view that selfhood "com[es] into being in a response to and for the other." For Sanders, who draws on deconstructive ethics, *ubuntu* provides a "communitarian alternative to human rights" that supersedes the static, rule-bound approach to justice intrinsic to theories of rights.[49]

Disgrace does not explicitly cite *ubuntu*, but its ubiquity in South African political discourse would seem to render it a subtext of Lurie's search for an alternative to liberalism. Lurie's own flirtation with communitarianism coincides with his disavowal of his congenital egoism, such as when he is forced to depend on others after the attack. As Lurie finds himself "trying to accept disgrace as a state of being," he weighs the prospect of becoming "a good person" (216), and he similarly recasts his relationship with Lucy in terms of "visitorship, visitation: a new footing, a new start" (218), foregoing his customary paternalism. Yet while he adopts what may resemble communitarian commitments, he is allergic to what he derides as an overly facile trust in other people. Here, Lurie's dismissal of his debt to Bill Shaw is instructive:

> Bill Shaw believes that, because he and David Lurie once had a cup of tea together, David Lurie is his friend, and the two of them have obligations towards each other. Is Bill Shaw right or wrong? Has Bill Shaw, who was born in Hankey, not two hundred kilometres away, and works in a hardware shop, seen so little of the world that he does not know there are men who do not readily make friends, whose attitude toward friendships between men is corroded with scepticism? Modern English *friend,* from Old English *freond,* from *freon,* to love. Does the drinking of tea seal a love-bond, in the eyes of Bill Shaw? Yet but for Bill and Bev Shaw, but for old Ettinger, but for bonds of some kind, where would he be now? On the ruined farm with the broken telephone amid the dead dogs. (102)

Although Lurie pays tribute to the community's support, he intellectualizes that recognition, citing etymology as well as philosophizing over the meaning of friendship. Clearly, these mechanisms both avert the emotion at hand and reaffirm Lurie's pretense of superiority. He cynically ironizes the prospect of a "love bond," counteracting his superficial endorsement of "obligations," "friendship," and "bonds." Overall, Lurie's overtures toward other people are invariably colored by such displays of condescension and reluctance—which is to say that whatever version of communitarianism he adopts, it is a strange one indeed.

Lurie's interactions with animals, however, are far less wary or vexed. Genuine camaraderie with other humans may elude him, but his growing affection for (and solidarity with) animals directly precipitates the transformations we see in his character over the final portion of the novel. As such, the human-animal bond is the one that for Lurie seems to exert the most pressing claims. It is, paradoxically, from animals that he learns both to show greater decency toward other people and to accept his own vulnerability. As the narrative progresses, he engages with animals in various forums: at the animal clinic helping Bev Shaw, on Lucy's farm, and, perhaps most important, by transporting the clinic's euthanized dogs to the incinerator for cremation. In the process, he develops an unexpected kinship with these animals. For instance, although "he does not know how," Lurie experiences a connection with two sheep that Petrus is preparing to slaughter for a party celebrating his new land ownership (126). This affinity, however, perplexes Lurie, being neither "one of affection" nor due to their singularity. As he explains, "It is not even a bond with these two in particular, whom he could not pick out from a mob in a field. Nevertheless, suddenly and without reason, their lot has become important to him" (126). Lurie's recurrent language of "bonds" notably deciphers their attachment in terms of "imprisonment," a "restraint of personal liberty," and, in a legal sense, the creation of a mortgage or debt— thus as an attachment that directly flouts the conceit of autonomous self-possession otherwise espoused by Lurie's character, as well as that underwrites the liberal subjectivity tethered to rights logic.[50] Moreover, Lurie distinctly frames this fellowship as extending from an awareness that is independent from, if not counter to, reason, which is to say that it harnesses a dimension of cognition that is more ontological—affecting him on the level of his being—than purely epistemological.

Lurie attempts throughout the terminal sections of *Disgrace* to make sense out of this communion with animals, and he recurrently does so in ways that recall classical philosophical disagreements over the legal status of animals, along the way quoting a number of the usual grounds for denying both subjectivity and rights to animals.[51] In this respect, parts of *Disgrace* are reminiscent of Coetzee's more overtly philosophical *Elizabeth Costello,* and, indeed, in both these texts Coetzee rehearses such justifications with the ultimate effect of challenging them, along the way illuminating broad errors that trouble liberal theories of selfhood and rights.[52] In fact, the predicament of animals as discussed within the novel's dialogue discloses some of the deepest deficiencies of liberal rights logic, demonstrating not only why it is inadequate to explain animal being but also how its corresponding assumptions about human life are anemic. While Lurie at first holds the dominant view that an absolute gulf separates human from animal, he gradually revises that position, coming to share Bev Shaw's opposition to how animals are relegated to being mere "things," even while they "do [humans] the honour of treating us like gods" (78).[53]

Much as Bev Shaw decries the objectification of animals, Lurie eventually renounces his views about their inferiority, and, in doing so, he indicts Cartesian dualism for providing the intellectual warrants for that mindset. Again lamenting the death of the two sheep, Lurie probes his own desire to rescue them:

> When did a sheep last die of old age? Sheep do not own themselves, do not own their lives. They exist to be used, every last ounce of them,

their flesh to be eaten, their bones to be crushed and fed to poultry. Nothing escapes, except perhaps the gall bladder, which no one will eat. Descartes should have thought of that. The soul, suspended in the dark, bitter gall, hiding. (124)

While squeamish about the dietary consumption of animals, Lurie playfully collapses the Cartesian divorce of the intellect from the body. He rejects the premise that animals lack a soul—the very conceit that has authorized their captivity. However, of greatest importance is the thought progression that brings Lurie to such a conclusion. He contemplates the materiality of their "flesh" and its destruction, which the passage vivifies with the visceral image of "bones" being "crushed." It is by imagining the plight of animals that Lurie immerses his consciousness within the phenomenology of not only animals' but also his own embodiment. This graphic reckoning with the carnal immanence of the flesh is accordingly what compels him to relinquish his formerly dualistic construction of reality. For Lurie, the body's eventual demise is fraught precisely because it cannot be quarantined or purified through reason; its physical decay resists being mastered or expunged by the machinations of the intellect, thus subverting his customary approach to such troubling matters. Much as the intellect's prioritization has led to the denigration of animal life, Lurie seems to acknowledge how that bias has comparatively contributed to the erasure of vital dimensions of human selfhood, above all the embeddedness of human cognition within embodiment. As I have considered vis-à-vis Merleau-Ponty's thought, this immersion of perception within material existence divulges the self's intertwining within and dependence on the surrounding milieu—an awareness that, at last, appears to descend on Lurie. In sum, even while the lives of animals permit Lurie to reckon with his own corporeal being, their fates expose a central lacuna within liberal rights logic—namely, its failure to adequately account for how the self's corporeal faculties are vital to human (and animal) welfare.

In his grieving for the two sheep, Lurie's internal dialogue overturns another traditional basis for proving the inferiority of animals: the notion that they lack full consciousness of death. Lurie at first ratifies such a view, wondering, "Should he mourn? Is it proper to mourn the death of beings who do not practise mourning among themselves?" (127). However, his subsequent actions dispute such a presumption, and Lurie instead treats animals as though their deaths cause suffering of the same magnitude as humans'. As he aids Bev at the clinic euthanizing unwanted dogs, the animals are depicted as fully aware of their pending deaths: "The dogs in the yard smell what is going on inside. They flatten their ears, they droop their tails, as if they too feel the disgrace of dying" (143). Lurie here not only endows animals with the complex self-awareness inherent to "disgrace" but also portrays that sentiment as emanating not from the mind but instead from the corporeal elements of their being. The dogs "smell" their fates, which they communicate through physical rather than linguistic signs, and those visceral modalities of expression are what create the occasion for an ethical response on Lurie's part. Lurie's engagement with the dying dogs contests both the liberal precept that rational, deliberative thought necessarily precedes moral action and the common prioritization of the gaze or look, an emphasis that organizes many poststructuralist approaches to ethics. Quite differently, his interactions with animals affirm the merits of the corporeal dimensions of his involvement. These embodied registers of expression, moreover, are heralded as something that animals and humans have in common, adumbrating a vision of interspecies solidarity that undermines the anthropocentric privileging of the human.

Importantly, Lurie does more than merely philosophize about his fellowship with animals. Rather, he also puts these recognitions into practice, perhaps most memorably as he assumes responsibility for "disposing of the remains" of the euthanized dogs, a task he understands as "sav[ing] the honour of corpses" (144, 146). Lurie in this way identifies an ethical obligation to animals extending beyond the parameters of life itself. Akin to his fondness for the sheep, the narrative furnishes no rational basis for these actions, on the contrary, characterizing them as "stupid, daft, wrongheaded" (146). At once, Coetzee draws on a religious idiom of "gods," "honour," and "salvation" to elucidate Lurie's commitments, much as the novel's concluding scene depicts Lurie almost Christ-like carrying a lame dog "in his arms like a lamb" (220).[54] This appeal to the language of theology is important on a number of levels. Most immediately, Lurie's behaviors stem from knowledge that is more faith based than propositional, reasoned, empirical, or ideational. In this respect, his character's transitions again bring us to Merleau-Ponty's phenomenology, in particular, his use of a God-concept to elaborate "the separation and the union of the soul and the body"—a paradox that he deems "constitutive of the human" and that similarly seems to motivate Lurie's turn to a spiritualized lexicon.[55] As such, Lurie's rhetoric of belief undermines not only the dualistic architecture of rights but also the secularism thesis, another staple of liberal democratic thought. Within the logic of secularity, political decision making acquires validity only when religious commitments can be sequestered from public life, yet Lurie's theological vocabulary challenges that basic premise. Quite differently, it captures the fabric of countervailing fidelities that, while they might defy established standards governing democratic legitimacy, are nevertheless suggested to be indispensable to just coexistence. In effect, Lurie's language of the "soul" and "belief" countermands the idea that entitlements and rights should provide the primary metric for distributing goods and liberties, and his metamorphoses in this way further open up the limits of liberalism as an explanatory paradigm.

Beyond Lurie's kinship with animals, his character evolves in other important ways that manifest an affectively charged, embodied engagement with experience. Whereas early on, Lurie makes recourse to abstract "principles" to detach from things, he finds that his attempt to "hold to the theory and to the comforts of theory" (98) resonates with increasing hollowness, no longer permitting him to short-circuit his own affective involvement. As he confronts his own vulnerability, philosophical maxims and their distancing effects fail to succeed, and he must instead wrestle with both his enmeshment in his material surroundings and his contingency. On one level, he learns to submit himself to other lives, human and animal. As he comforts the dying dogs, he finds that "his whole being is gripped by what happens in the theater" of the operating room (143). Neither dissociating from nor rationalizing their deaths, he gives himself over to the dogs' suffering, inhabiting it not just cerebrally but instead with his corporeal faculties of participation. At the same time, he deciphers his own reflexes in embodied terms. For instance, he magnifies his horror at the attack through a series of corporeal metaphors: as having "shocked him to the depths"; as causing him to feel like "inside him, a vital organ has been bruised, abused—perhaps his heart"; as forcing him to encounter "what it will be like to be an old man"; and, finally, as compelling him to imagine that "he is bled dry... he is bleeding" (107). While reifying his psychological damage to lend it physical referents and tangible shape, such images simultaneously attest to a growing sense of the ontological import of embodiment.

In fact, the entire trajectory of *Disgrace* can be read to trace Lurie's progressive coming to terms with his own embodiment, a development that enables him to relate justly and nonegoistically with other beings. His attitudes toward the body change markedly over the novel, from his reviling what he sees as its excess to his embracing its weakness. Whereas we initially encounter Lurie regimenting his sexual needs to create the illusion of autonomy, he slowly accepts his inherent woundedness and precarity. No doubt the postattack narrative of *Disgrace* is haunted by such visions of corporeal brokenness, for instance, as he imagines being "stretched out on an operating table... laid open... from throat to groin" with his internal organs scrutinized by a surgeon (171). Lurie's reflections, however, denote far more than his own self-involved crises. On the contrary, he invokes the body as presenting something of a leveling principle, one that opens up the symmetries that oversee all existence. At one point he chides Rosalind in revealing terms: "'I'm going to end up in a hole in the ground. . . . And so are you. So are we all'" (189), citing the body as a kind of perverse cipher for such universalizing realities.

Much as animal life seems to trigger many of Lurie's recognitions, Lucy similarly looks to nature as a type of laboratory for reconceiving human co-belonging in a more radically inclusive frame. In one of the most moving dialogues of the novel, which is also this chapter's epigraph, she defends her pending marriage to Petrus by citing to the predicament of animal being. As she explains to her father:

> "Yes, I agree, it is humiliating. But perhaps that is a good point to start from again. Perhaps that is what I must learn to accept. To start at ground level. With nothing. Not with nothing but. With nothing. No cards, no weapons, no property, no rights, no dignity."
>
> "Like a dog."
>
> "Yes, like a dog." (205)

Imaginatively divesting herself of the instruments of domination that secured her apartheid era privilege, Lucy blames weapons, property, and rights for collectively subsidizing the fiction of human dignity. As we have seen, that fiction is underwritten by the parallel conceit of bodily integrity, and those dual myths conspire not only to gird liberal articulations of human rights but also to reinforce the species divide.[56] Lucy therefore renounces these many insignia of human mastery to advocate parity within not only the human community but also the natural world. While such a dream of reverting to a milieu untarnished by apartheid's wrongs is, of course, wishful thinking, the fact that she correlates human dignity with these other, more tangible markers of oppression is highly revealing. It is not accidental that her catalog of entitlements culminates with dignity, given its important work in con-solidating liberal articulations of human rights. Whereas Lurie dismisses her choice as embarrassing dehumanization, for Lucy it represents "start[ing] at ground level," or in a state of radical reciprocity prior to class, race, gender, and other social stratifications. As she eschews dignity, then, she identifies its role in the enabling logic of conquest—whether of one race over another, of human over animal, of mind over body, of culture over nature, or of men over women.

Lurie maintains a far more complicated, if not tormented, attitude toward postapartheid South Africa than Lucy does, but he increasingly emulates her comportment of patient acceptance. In the novel's penultimate passage, after Lurie has moved from the farm, he visits Lucy to discover her working in the field and, before announcing himself, quietly observes her. Instead of his berating her "ample" physical being (59), as he earlier does, his gaze rests on "the milky, blue-veined skin and broad, vulnerable tendons of the backs of her knees: the least beautiful part of a woman's body, the least expressive, and therefore perhaps the most endearing" (217). Such an attitude represents a striking departure from where the novel first introduces him. Here, he regards the human body not as an object of appropriative desire or in need of discipline but as something to be relished in its abiding fragility. Although Lurie both sentimentalizes and aestheticizes Lucy's connection to the land, a particularly problematic move in South African letters, he simultaneously locates the moment's paramount existential freight in its very mundaneness—in the fact that he studies a most unobtrusive part of Lucy's body while she performs merely "ordinary tasks" (217). Moreover, Lurie does not reduce Lucy's situation on the farm to one of dangerous exposure; instead, he celebrates her perseverance as evidence that she is "solid in her existence" (217). Along related lines, his reflections on Lucy's pregnancy from the rape inspire not his typical solipsism but instead a reckoning with his own inconsequence. He meditates on the cycles of life and reproduction within which he no longer participates, thinking, "So it will go on, a line of existences in which his share, his gift, will grow inexorably less and less, till it may as well be forgotten" (217). Rather than arrogating Lucy's pregnancy to ordain his own Romantic, heroic self-completion, he interprets it to forecast his irrelevance—as well as, we might say, the irrelevance of the liberal norms for which he has been a spokesperson.

Although Lurie's heirs are far from transparent metaphors for art, he similarly minimizes his aims for his opera. While he invests himself in its composition with heightened ardor, the opera, too, stages Lurie's gradual acceptance of the aging and wounded body. With this new focus, Lurie discards his original intent to portray the life of Lord Byron, formerly a type of alter ego, and discovers that his protagonist must be Byron's scorned lover, Teresa, a figure largely subsumed under Byron's towering identity. Lurie explains his newfound interest in Teresa: precisely because she is "beyond honour" (209) and no more than a "plain, ordinary woman" (182) her life presents a fitting emblem for the human condition. Not only has her story been erased from the dominant historical record but she is also unexceptional, and Lurie seemingly adopts her viewpoint because of its very proximity and familiarity. Indeed, he projects his own spiritual enfeeblement onto Teresa, inscribing their shared injuries on their mutually broken bodies, as he envisions them: "The halt helping the lame, for want of better" (183).

This image of the "halt" and "lame" additionally alludes to the young dog whose fate preoccupies the novel's conclusion. As Lurie isolates himself at the clinic writing his opera, he experiences "a particular fondness" for one dog—"a young male with a withered left hindquarter that it drags behind it"—although, however, "he has been careful not to give [it] a name" (215). As with Teresa, Lurie displaces his own brokenness onto the dog, construing its plight as a hallmark of human existence. Yet of perhaps greatest significance, Lurie aspires to incorporate this lame dog into his opera. When he performs music in its company, he imagines that it avails itself of such an outlet, to "the point of singing too, or howling" (215). Lurie's fantasies about the dog, in turn, work to test the representational bounds of art, in particular, its capacity to surmount propositional, empirical discourse.[57] Lurie thinks:

> Would he dare to do that: bring a dog into the piece, allow it to loose its own lament to the heavens between the strophes of lovelorn Teresa's? Why not? Surely, in a work that will never be performed, all things are permitted? (215)

Thus conceived as occupying a type of separate sphere, art permits Lurie to challenge liberal norms concerning action, will, and self-expression, which are typically evaluated through the lens of rational deliberation. By valorizing the dog's propensity for nonintellectual though affective and corporeal engagement, Lurie's opera implicitly controverts the dualistic biases that cohere liberal definitions of selfhood. As such, Lurie's opera offers a forum for renegotiating the contours of justice and ethics alike, affirming very different dimensions of selfhood than those conventionally verified by liberal theories of politics. As opposed to reasoned speech and value-neutral self-abstraction, Lurie's opera incarnates the dog's visceral registers of being, harnessing the perceptual rhythms of its flesh.[58] Lurie's opera accordingly lauds such corporeal faculties, while also presenting music as a relatively democratic medium disposed to transcend the many hierarchies that, as Lurie recurrently complains, are installed within English.

Disgrace, however, does not conclude with a facile apologia for the salvific powers of art. Despite the opera's ostensibly more just and inclusive ethical-political domain, its composition reinforces Lurie's deep-seated myopia—secluding him from other people and excusing his retreat from other obligations—and the narrative thus invites us to read his growing immersion within that imaginative space as an ethical failing. To such ends, it might appear that *Disgrace* subtly reminds us of deep impediments to art's ability to affect the real world, even while the opera purveys insights that for Lurie are redemptive. By serving as Coetzee's own metafictional self-commentary, then, the opera returns us to the novel's own fictional status.

Likewise, in the midst of its theological rhetoric of "salvation" and "grace," *Disgrace* culminates with the overwhelming necessity of loss. Lurie ultimately "gives up" the lame dog—he himself executing its death sentence—and the novel aggressively preserves the moral ambiguity of that decision, refusing to resolve the question of whether Lurie's actions are self-interested. While Lurie deems its death an act of "love," the narrative foregrounds the violence of that end. Lurie thinks, "Something happens in the room, something unmentionable: here the soul is yanked out of the body; briefly it hangs about in the air, twisting and contorting; then it is sucked away and is gone" (219). Such vivid corporeal imagery underscores the death's ontological freight, while averring that it is actively experienced on multiple levels by the dog itself. Moreover, the narrative does not sanitize this killing by presenting it as a reprieve from bodily suffering and captivity, which might render it ethically permissible. Instead, by framing it as "unmentionable," it is presented as something that cannot be intellectualized, consecrated as something that cannot be abstracted or purified through reason. We might therefore say that the dog's killing defies legality, normalization, and universal relevance. It will never be equal or just or dignified or proportionate—as will no death, outside a purely fictional state. By challenging such calculations, *Disgrace* suggests why liberal discourses of rights may be incommensurate with the very dilemmas with which it leaves us—as well as unsuited to the dynamic structures of embeddedness and equilibrium that enmesh them.

Conclusion

As I have tried to show in this chapter, Coetzee's *Disgrace* dramatizes core paradoxes that haunt the proliferating discourses of human rights. Most notably, the novel mines the ambivalences of human rights rhetoric within and in the aftermath of the project of South African reconciliation, offering one explanation for why rights logic has failed to meaningfully reverse the many injustices of the apartheid era. Yet it also condemns what it casts as more systemic failures afflicting the liberal mappings of selfhood that consolidate dominant discourses of human rights, and it exposes how their norms work both to license predatory self-interest and to entrench historical structures of exclusion. It is seemingly in effort to remedy the countless liabilities of such liberal constructions of rights that *Disgrace* contemplates alternative approaches to social justice. While Coetzee weighs the efficacy of the communitarian ethic of *ubuntu,* however, the novel's foremost insights into just coexistence ironically emerge as its characters meditate over the predicament of animals and their apparent beholdenness to the flesh. By thus foregrounding the relationship of embodiment to social justice, *Disgrace,* I have argued, illumines how a phenomenological consciousness might facilitate an imaginative repositioning of the discourses of human rights, and it explores the vital work performed by art in inciting such an endeavor. Let me now turn to this book's concluding literary analysis, of Arundhati Roy's *The God of Small Things,* to further chart how aesthetic experience might unfold an embodied politics of reading.

❧ CHAPTER SIX

Arundhati Roy's "Return to the Things Themselves"

Phenomenology and the Challenge of Justice

We be of one blood, Thou and I.

—Rudyard Kipling, *The Jungle Book,* quoted in Arundhati Roy, *The God of Small Things*

As a writer, one spends a lifetime journeying into the heart of language, trying to minimize, if not eliminate, the distance between language and thought. "Language is the skin on my thought," I remember saying to someone who once asked what language meant to me. At The Hague I stumbled on a denomination, a sub-world, whose life's endeavor was to mask intent.

—Arundhati Roy, on whether water should be labeled a basic human right

       This book has wrestled with many of the foreclosures haunting the liberal cartographies of selfhood that guide dominant human rights discourses and norms. Above all, such mappings of the human have been defined by their profound ambivalence about the ontological condition of embodiment. As they ordain reasoned, autonomous self-fashioning, liberal formulations of the subject variously elide and diminish crucial dimensions of corporeal being and experience. This aversion toward embodiment has helped to author countless of the exclusions that have historically compromised and only now continue to trouble the universality of human rights. In turn, I have argued that greater theoretical attention to embodiment might gesture toward reversing those omissions, minimizing the innumerable failures that have beset the globalization of human rights. This book's attempt to reclaim and endow the body's faculties of apperception with interpretive authority has, moreover, required that we contemplate how particular modalities of aesthetic expression can procure phenomenological insight, contributing to what I've referred to as an embodied politics of reading. It is within such a hermeneutical project, then, that we might begin to undertake an imaginative repositioning of political thought's customary assumptions about the natural and civil body, returning vital corporeal energies to the strangely bloodless, idle, and unconvincing liberal subject of rights.

This book's final chapter now turns to Arundhati Roy's *The God of Small Things* (1997) to trace the contours of precisely such an embodied aesthetic, along the way making a case for how it might nourish a compelling vision of just coexistence. As we will see, the formal and stylistic properties of *The God of Small Things* both mirror and engender the philosophical quandaries that animate the novel's plot. As with this book's other literary object lessons, *The God of Small Things* despairs of the beleaguered status of human rights, in this case within postcolonial India. Its narrative indicts what it identifies as a widespread contempt for human rights in Indian juridical and political culture, which it variously detects within a biased legal code, patriarchy, the caste system, and the many by-products of globalization, of which Roy is a scathing critic. In Roy's view, globalization has exponentially multiplied both human and ecological suffering around the world, and *The God of Small Things* overtly critiques the tourist industry, environmental neglect, and numerous other symptoms of both late capitalism and popular culture. As Roy censures neoimperialism for the ongoing exploitation of the global South, the novel further reckons with more ubiquitous patterns of injustice that cannot be attributed solely to empire's residues. In particular, it explores the basic anatomy of human cruelty, investigating how habits ingrained within the human psyche can inure people to wrongdoing. While no doubt exists that imperialism's afterlives have exacerbated human rights abuses around the world, within *The God of Small Things* injustice is also spawned by routine gender discrimination, local class resentments, and even the cauldron of family life. As such, the novel directs us to scrutinize historically and geographically specific lineages of oppression, even while it conducts a broad meditation on the nature and genesis of human brutality.

On one level, these offenses are cast as intrinsic to political existence and, by extension, language itself. In this way, *The God of Small Things*'s narrative is absorbed with many of the same dilemmas that preoccupied Merleau-Ponty. Indeed, there are key ways in which the novel lends itself to being read to fictionally probe and thereby illuminate central insights that we have already obtained from Merleau-Ponty. Overall, *The God of Small Things* decries multiple instances of political opportunism and malfeasance, evincing conspicuous cynicism about the ability of the institutions of law and politics to counteract human iniquity. By documenting the extensive toll wrought by self-interest on ordinary speech, it further tracks the mechanisms through which hypocrisy comes to infect even commonplace, otherwise innocent language—depleting it of meaning and eroding its affinity with social justice. Yet while the novel portrays how injustice takes up residence within the very fabric of discourse, it equally sets out to mine the descriptive, affective, and imaginative reserves that language can nevertheless harbor. This odyssey of perceptual disclosure is enacted within the features of the narrative's own highly distinctive aesthetic. Roy's narrative stages creative intrusions into discourse that has become rote and ossified, both magnifying the consequences of that semantic impoverishment and showing how language might be revivified. In this way, the novel demonstrates how the proliferating discourses of human rights might similarly be restored, in an imaginative project singularly performed within the realm of literature.

Perhaps most important, *The God of Small Things*'s aesthetic harnesses distinctly corporeal registers of discernment, revealing the body's perceptual energies to interpenetrate and mutually reinforce one another in something of a gestalt. Within such an embodied experience of reading the senses collaborate in ways that parallel the reciprocities overseeing the lifeworld as a whole—which is to say, Roy's aesthetic purveys recognitions that it presents as invariably just. Although the narrative frames those insights as fleeting and provisional, they unfold a vision of the self's material enmeshment within not only other human lives but also the natural and the object worlds. Within the novel, this collective intertwining notably corresponds with a parallel conception of interspecies cohabitation, or what we might call *deep ecology*. All in all, Roy's devotion to the basic ingredients of lived experience attempts its own type of return—namely, to quote the rallying cry of the phenomenologists, "a return to the things themselves." For Roy, however, such a phrase first and foremost signals the "small things" that her title both vests with near theological significance and claims as central to its ontology of social justice.

Moreover, Roy's peculiar cosmology productively countermands many of the expectations that underwrite liberal articulations of human rights. Whereas liberal topographies of the human quarantine and negate embodied experience, Roy's aesthetic celebrates the body's appetencies, affirming their merit. Likewise, whereas liberal accounts of the public sphere confer legitimacy on politics only when deliberation can be defended as carried out by rationally disinterested actors, *The God of Small Things* divulges the perils of such models for evaluating political process. Its narrative instead documents the horrific crimes licensed by reasoned self-abstraction, in particular, when intellectual disengagement is prized over affective faculties of participation and involvement. That said, the novel does not facilely romanticize its portrait of corporeal being. To the contrary, it extensively confronts the phenomenality

of violence, immersing its perspective in the excruciating throes of bodily suffering. Yet this very aesthetic experiment, I argue, is paradoxically necessary to
restore the disavowed fleshiness to liberalism's dangerously pallid, unidimensional, and lifeless subject of rights. *The God of Small Things* thus reconfigures
liberalism's usual metaphorics of embodiment to claim touch, blood, and the
flesh as vital sites of interpersonal connection and mutuality, overwriting the
typical priority attributed to vision and the intellect. It goes without saying
that this troping of touch is a loaded gesture in a novel that takes the caste
system's myth of untouchability as one of its central targets.

Apart from what this chapter describes as the novel's embodied aesthetic,
The God of Small Things stands out in its relatively constricted plot. Its action
follows a series of tragedies that befall a single Indian family, the Kocham-
mas. And while its dense, circuitous story line spans more than twenty years,
ranging between 1969 and 1993, it mainly recounts two abbreviated periods
of time: mere weeks in the late 1960s, and in the early 1990s apparently
only days. The vast majority of these events are retrospectively focalized
through the perspective of its child protagonists, the fraternal twins Rahel
and Estha. Only seven years old during the traumatic past, Estha and Rahel
in the narrative present are adults newly reunited after those twenty intervening years, which compels them to revisit their family's devastating history.
Their memories especially surround the accidental drowning of their young
cousin, Sophie Mol; the violent murder of their family's servant Velutha; and
the banishment and premature death of their mother, Ammu. Those fatal
occurrences are set in motion, as the narrative gradually discloses, by a clandestine love affair between the divorced and socially ostracized Ammu and
"untouchable" Velutha. When that liaison is discovered, the ensuing scan-
dal catalyzes explosive anxieties about caste, class, and gender that together
prompt the many human rights violations within the narrative. While on
one level these abuses are both precipitated and legislated by larger historical, political, and economic forces, on another the petty resentments rife
within the Kochamma family proximately incite them. In this respect, Roy
casts the domestic as a mere microcosm of the grand-scale turmoil of the
nation-state, impugning the private as by no means exempt from the many
state-sponsored crimes of global modernity.

A highly political novel, *The God of Small Things* invites analysis alongside
Roy's nonfictional writings. In the intervening years since it received the
1997 Booker Prize, Roy has failed to capitalize on *The God of Small Things*'s
remarkable, unprecedented success by publishing another work of fiction.[1]
She has similarly barred a film version of the novel, which is not surprising,
in light of her exceedingly negative views of the global media. These two

principled refusals testify to Roy's acute sensitivity to the volatile reception of creative production, to its inevitable commodification, and to how even politically conscientious art can be appropriated to service the status quo. Although she has disappointed an eager audience, however, Roy has willingly exploited her literary celebrity through prolific activism.[2] Since the novel's publication, Roy has been a spokesperson for issues ranging from water rights to nuclear disarmament, even while fervently disparaging the crisis-driven reportage of the media. Environmental welfare is one of her most consistent agendas—one that is also at the forefront of *The God of Small Things*.[3] By no means least, we should note Roy's vigorous criticism of the rhetoric of liberty and rights, which she blames for distorting the initial mandate of postcolonial independence. In her estimate, that idiom has merely "consecrat[ed]" the "old order" of power as it existed under colonization. Roy has further applied such suspicions to the language of the law, bemoaning how "the cold, contemporary cast of power is couched between the lines of noble-sounding clauses in democratic sounding constitutions."[4] In effect, Roy here complains that the legal codification of otherwise valuable ideals by no means insulates them from abuse; on the contrary, the law's imprimatur can just as readily conscript those principles to fulfill disingenuous ends, a syndrome that we shall see pervades *The God of Small Things*.

Beyond the Postcolonial and the Postmodern

The God of Small Things brings us full circle to reconsider the dominant currents within postcolonial studies. It exhibits conspicuous weariness with many of the literary-theoretical tropes that have organized postcolonial criticism, and this rejoinder emerges perhaps most visibly in the ways it quotes and rewrites *Midnight's Children*.[5] If the crisis within postcolonial studies in part derives from its prevailing hermeneutical orientations, *The God of Small Things* indexes why they have become outmoded, occasioning a case study in the types of interpretation they have foreclosed. *Midnight's Children* for many represents a paradigmatic postcolonial text, and *The God of Small Things* undertakes an extended quarrel with Rushdie's epic novel, on the levels of style and content. Whereas *Midnight's Children* is postmodern, Roy spurns Rushdie's irony, mimicry, play, and performative excess as well as his pop cultural pastiche and allusions to Bollywood, in effect renouncing *Midnight's Children*'s rhetorical and other extravagance.[6] Even as it censures Rushdie's self-aggrandizing vision of artistic creation, Roy displays significant ambivalence about popular culture. In opposition to Rushdie's implicit celebration of globalization for heightening intensity and inspiring an almost dizzying interconnection, *The God of Small Things* indicts it for producing polar opposite effects, a critique to which I will return. Roy's narrative instead evinces substantial wariness about the postmodern mediatization of experience, which it arraigns for pauperizing meaning and understanding. In contrast, Roy's aesthetic itself recuperates dimensions of perceptual engagement that Rushdie's satirical posture precludes and derides. In place of its forebear's at times glib exuberance, the novel's tone is often muted and wistful, while itself invested in forms of aesthetic experimentation. Whereas *Midnight's Children*'s scope is encyclopedic, Roy's novel announces its countervailing commitments through its very title. Although Saleem Sinai is recurrently exonerated by the fantastic and supernatural, Roy's characters find no such escape, instead remaining trapped within the inexorability of the present. And, far from last, whereas Saleem's magical propensities emblematize the immense promise of postcolonial self-determination, the Kochamma family has internalized a sense of malaise and defeat; they have long forgotten the highfalutin ideals that occupy Rushdie's narrative. In effect, Roy gives us the jaded generation of Saleem's son Aadam—a child who initially refuses to speak but instead "listened, and memorized, and learned."[7] Much as Aadam signals a moment that harbors no illusions about postcoloniality, Estha, too, has been rendered mute in the face of the many tyrannies his era has authored.

It is not surprising that Roy would stage a departure from Rushdie, given that his legacy has loomed large for a generation of Indian novelists. Yet the parallels between the two novels are not only striking in their own right but also crucial to understanding what is at stake within Roy's narrative.[8] While the climactic onset of independence lends velocity to *Midnight's Children*'s plot, *The God of Small Things* was published in 1997, on that transition's fiftieth anniversary, and it equally commemorates its momentousness. As I have maintained, much of *Midnight's Children* depicts the overwhelming optimism of early expectations for postcolonial self-rule, even while Saleem's apocalyptic murder-suicide at the end of the novel reifies the atrophy of the constellation of values that independence inaugurated. Saleem's fate therefore enacts an implosion of the body politic, although one that problematically reinforces that particular metaphor's associations with corporeal integrity, purity, and self-enclosure. Within *The God of Small Things,* the specter of premature death similarly mourns the countless disappointments of Indian nationalism, but through a very different symbolic economy of embodiment—one that instead opens up the liabilities of Rushdie's analogue for the nation. These correspondences and the degree to which both texts return us to the unfinished business of independence are further emphasized by the ages of the novels' different characters, along with their respective authors. Both Roy and Rushdie were in their early thirties when they composed their Booker Prize–winning novels. Moreover, not only does Ammu die at thirty-one, which is

Saleem's age at the end of *Midnight's Children,* but Roy's twin protagonists are also thirty-one in the narrative's adult present. Finally, while Saleem is delivered during the atrocity of partition, the twins are born "amid news of a lost war" and thus are equally ensnared within the internally predatory temper of postcolonial nationalism (213).

While replete with a spate of such incidental allusions, *The God of Small Things* also revisits Rushdie's pickling metaphor.[9] *Midnight's Children's* gambit is that Saleem transcribes his history within the factory Padma Pickles, and he recurrently likens the writing process to the chemical "preservation" of pickles. In *The God of Small Things,* the Kochamma family is likewise in the pickling industry, and much of its plot occurs in or around their small rural business. However, this family-owned company, incorporated as "Paradise Pickles & Preserves," is eventually driven under by local communist agitation, an outcome that parodies the economics of the global publishing industry (as well as, we might conclude, the institutional demands of academe).[10] Moreover, that figure for literary production yields very different resonances within the two novels. Saleem's "great work of preserving" (37) is a monumental task, on which the future of the entire Indian nation depends. His grandiose pursuit of "meaning" bears macrocosmic consequences, inciting both the frenetic mania and egoistic self-interest of his narrative. In contrast, Roy's pickles entail no such exorbitant prospects. Her characters doubt "whether [they] would ever master the art of perfect preservation," and their pickle jars chronically "leak," turning their labels "oily and transparent" and leaving the pickles a "little on the salty side" (159). In effect, Roy cautions against *Midnight's Children's* totalizing aims, while further construing historical memory as a messy, haphazard process—if only because its residues will ceaselessly spill over into and contaminate the present. While each of *Midnight's Children's* thirty-one chapters corresponds to a different jar and hence a given year in Saleem's life, the past in *The God of Small Things* cannot be so neatly compartmentalized. Roy's narrative is neither linear nor divisible into discrete eras; rather, its characters' memories constantly erupt into the mature present, defying emotional containment.

Roy further distinguishes her novel's purview from Rushdie's, in particular, differentiating the "Small God" of the local and day-to-day from her precursor's designs on the "Big God" of national history. *The God of Small Things's* narrator bewails how "personal turmoil," its own métier, is submerged by

> the vast, violent, circling, driving, ridiculous, insane, unfeasible, public turmoil of a nation. That Big God howled like a hot wind, and demanded obeisance. Then Small God (cozy and contained, private and limited) came away cauterized, laughing numbly at his own temerity. (20)

Opposing its scope to Rushdie's, *The God of Small Things* despairs of how the consuming theater of Indian politics eclipses personal crisis, which will always pale in comparison with the nation's vast tragedies. In effect, it thereby impugns *Midnight's Children*'s epic reach for both sanctioning and occluding the many private injuries that fail to affect the national imaginary. It is precisely to jettison *Midnight's Children*'s thematic ambit, then, that *The God of Small Things* excavates the local, domestic, and mundane. In place of Rushdie's enthrallment with the nation's sublime founding myths, Roy salvages the indigenous, ecological, and particular—or what the novel calls "the whisper and scurry of small lives" (4). In effect, *The God of Small Things* inverts the ambitions and compensates for the foreclosures of *Midnight's Children*'s bold and at times self-congratulatory agenda. This reduced compass furthermore entails a very different conception of self-hood and community from the one Saleem espouses. Whereas *Midnight's Children* recounts Saleem's misadventures in individualist subject formation, *The God of Small Things* interrogates the exclusions that enable such an itinerary of self-determination. In this chapter I accordingly argue that Roy's aesthetic forges an opposing portrait of sociopolitical coexistence that implicitly contests Saleem's fixation on rights and entitlements, demonstrating why such a focus constricts and impedes core aspects of just cohabitation.

Roy's omniscient narrator repeatedly offers a type of metacommentary on the plot's events, elucidating their broader, often philosophical significance. This narrator at one point overtly meditates on the relentless logic of historical progress, anthropomorphizing history as a ruthless, inflexible force that "negotiates its terms and collects its dues from those who break its laws" (54). It is thus in contrast to such energies that its own narrative arrests the momentum of time, in another apparent rebuke to the accelerating pace of *Midnight's Children*. While this impetus to halt time's passage is reflected in the novel's circumscribed temporality, it is also poignantly symbolized in seven-year-old Rahel's toy watch, the painted hands of which are fixed at the arbitrary hour of ten to two. Roy's narrative returns to this image on multiple occasions, seemingly both to imbue the passing increments of the everyday with paramount ontological merit and to vouchsafe the affective freight of ordinary objects. The randomness of this frozen instant further underscores the irreversibility of historical change, reclaiming a tragedy erased within the sweeping telos of national history. In this way, Roy's particular figure for historical memory pointedly critiques *Midnight's Children*'s valorization of the epochal, widely memorialized midnight of independence, with all the violence it unleashed.

The Problem of Human Language

The tragic developments that haunt the plot of *The God of Small Things* derive from highly specific crimes suggested to be rife within Indian society and politics. However, these historically and geographically discrete injustices occasion a broad rumination on the nature and origins of human cruelty. Many of the concerns of the novel are quintessentially postcolonial; it laments everything from the disenfranchisement of the global South to its characters' Anglophilic self-loathing. That said, it does not exclusively scapegoat the bequests of empire for sowing current postcolonial crisis. Rather, it figures the central offenses that impel its plot—in particular, the harms spawned by the caste system—as innate to legalistic thought, showing how they are installed within the basic fabric of language. Gesturing transhistorically, the novel's narrator surmises "when" "it all began" (32):

> It could be argued that it actually began thousands of years ago. Long before the Marxists came. Before the British took Malabar, before the Dutch Ascendancy, before Vasco de Gama arrived, before the Zamorin's conquest of Calicut. Before three purple-robed Syrian bishops murdered by the Portuguese were found floating in the sea, with coiled serpents riding on their chests and oysters knotted in their tangled beards. It could be argued that it began long before Christianity arrived in a boat and seeped into Kerala like tea from a teabag.
>
> That it really began in the days when the Love Laws were made. The laws that lay down who should be loved, and how.
>
> And how much. (33)

Rehearsing the long history of conquest on the Indian subcontinent, the narrative refuses to privilege British domination or even European influence. On the contrary, its expansive summary converges on indigenous practices and taboos, locating the inception of exclusionary thinking within a precolonial past. In addition, it overtly attributes the myth of "untouchability" to legalistic patterns of thought, suggesting how the caste system's rigid hierarchies anchor and control even mundane language. We might recall here *Disgrace*'s anguish over the "tired, friable, eaten" status of English (129); *The God of Small Things* similarly contends with the corruption of commonplace speech through legacies of malfeasance. Its plot dramatizes how such semantic colonization precludes neutrality, naturalizes deep structures of wrongdoing, and implicates the individual within those histories. Of course, these reflections on linguistic decay are far from original or unprecedented; nonetheless, they lend context to the narrative's sense of its own aesthetic, which self-consciously intercedes within such a cycle of degradation and impoverishment.

This double bind of language is crystallized for Roy's child protagonists by the occurrences that follow Velutha's murder, which abruptly cause "childhood [to] tiptoe out" (303). After the discovery of his affair with Ammu, Velutha is falsely accused by Baby Kochamma, Ammu's aunt, of sexual assault—a doubly criminal offense because it transgresses caste lines. As a direct result of that allegation, Velutha is brutally, near-fatally beaten by local policemen. While he lies on the brink of death, Baby Kochamma enlists the twins to help cover up her treachery. With threats of law and criminality, she dupes Estha into incriminating Velutha. Estha does no more than utter the word "yes," but that concession is enough to consign Velutha and his victimization to historical erasure, rendering Estha his de facto executioner. Through a speech act that would be innocent under most circumstances, Estha inadvertently condones Velutha's murder. However, Estha is misled not only by Baby Kochamma but also by the duplicities latent within discourse itself. The narrative insists that the children "both knew that they had been given a choice" (302), and, as a result, Estha's dilemma represents a classic instance of what Slavoj Žižek calls a *choix forcé*—an impasse that in Estha's case arises because of both the coordinates of his predicament and the legalistic economy of ordinary language.[11] Given that either answer of yes or no would have framed Velutha and embroiled Estha within his fate, forswearing to answer was Estha's only viable exit. His predicament, in turn, illustrates how the very order of dichotomous thought secures consent to the functional inevitability of its polarized terms. It is consequently not so much the content of Estha's response that makes it a betrayal; rather, his failure to conceive of an escape from Baby Kochamma's dilemma is what inculpates him.

This rigid binary of yes versus no further denies Estha room for ambivalence, foreordaining that his answer will both fall short of the complexity of his circumstances and submerge their ambiguity. And precisely because Estha's quandary is an extreme one that begets devastating results, it magnifies the real-world discriminations widely smuggled in through language's dualistic architecture. That exclusionary organization is, moreover, presented within the narrative as incommensurate with the children's instinctive modes of interpretation, implying that their trauma extends not only from the violence they witness but also from how the order of discourse deprives Estha of an avenue for opting out. By filtering large portions of its narrative through a child's perspective, *The God of Small Things* scrutinizes these impasses inscribed within language, capturing why and how they stifle dissent. On the one hand, and as the following section will discuss, a child's viewpoint allows the narrative to stage periodic disruptions of habituated speech, portraying how language might operate without obeying the legalistic operations that mislead Estha. On the other hand, it simultaneously tracks how language acquisition administers and constrains the children's available repertoire of responses, rendering their choices captive to language's artificial order and rules. For instance, the narrative recounts how Rahel and Estha are instructed at an early age about the "Edges, Borders, Boundaries, Brinks and Limits" that regulate speech (5). This catalog and use of capitalization foreground the fictionality of those arbitrary strictures, even while the passage's imagery reifies the real-world cruelties and oppressions licensed by such semantic regimentation.

While Estha's forced choice exposes such pitfalls, it also marks the epistemic violence that accompanies his entrance into knowledge of the complicities intrinsic to speech. Rather than negotiating them, however, Estha surrenders language in its entirety. Guilt at forsaking Velutha seemingly inspires this attempt to inoculate himself against the covert biases that infect language. In turn, we might compare him again with Rushdie's Aadam, who similarly reacts to an overexposure to suffering by retreating into silence. Yet this disavowal for Estha exacts an inordinately high cost—his radical self-enclosure and isolation. Estha is depicted in adulthood as a pathetic figure withdrawn from all meaningful human intercourse, construing his solution to the double bind of language as far from viable. While his Bartleby-like passivity safeguards him against inadvertent wrongdoing, it constitutes an ethical dead end. By abjuring speech, Estha foregoes the ability to intervene within discourse and thereby counteract its centripetal tendencies. In this respect, his posture of resignation further resembles that of Coetzee's Lurie, who similarly attempts to fend off personal responsibility only to guarantee his own irrelevance as well as inertia. In any case, Estha exemplifies one possible response to what Merleau-Ponty calls the "ruse" that blights language—that of passive resistance. That stance, however, ultimately renders Estha a casual bystander to language's hidden cruelties and thus a cautionary figure. And it is precisely in opposition to such an eventuality that the novel offers up its own aesthetic—one predicated on no less vigilance while being equally invested in creative remedy and renewal.

Much as *The God of Small Things* imaginatively confronts this aporia, Roy has inveighed against related perils of political discourse throughout her nonfiction writings. She complains of how the contemporary geopolitical climate has produced "a writer's bad dream," giving rise to "the ritualistic slaughter of language as I know and understand it."[12] Roy applies this critique with particular earnestness to the global media, which she reproaches for "cloud[ing] the particular facts of [a] particular story" and working "to mask intent."[13] Within the terms of Roy's grievance, both political rhetoric and public reportage finesse truth to render it consumable; however, in doing so, they lay siege to meaning and suppress complexity, rather than conveying the range and intricacy of the issues they purport to communicate. This impoverishment of popular discourse has only been exacerbated, in her view, by global capital's expanding influence. For instance, Roy castigates how the United States culled support for its post-9/11 invasion of Iraq by "cynically manipulating people's grief" and "pillaging... even the most private feelings for political purpose," the impact of which was "to cheapen and devalue grief, to drain it of meaning."[14] Such disingenuous ends plunder language's ethical and affective reserves, and here Roy wrestles with a syndrome akin to the one that afflicts human rights. She decries how, much as appeals to rights rhetoric are often highly opportunistic, the machinery of politics naturally recruits and thereby contaminates ordinary speech to consolidate its interests.

The God of Small Things condemns how such obstructionism is especially endemic to the law. I have repeatedly observed how the law's dualistic architecture works to disarm dissent, at the same time as it preys on a logic that underwrites broader structures of sociopolitical discrimination. Ammu's premature death from tuberculosis, for example, is determined by gender biases within the Indian legal code. As the narrative obliquely relates, her lack of "Locusts Stand I" permits her family to legally disinherit and abandon her, the law essentially decreeing her death as a pauper (56). However, only readers versed in either Latin or Anglophone legal speak will translate this phrase, skewed to simulate a child's miscomprehension, as *locus standi,* or "legal standing"—the right to bring suit in a court of law. Under this juridical requirement, an individual can be party to a suit only after demonstrating sufficient connection to and harm from the action at hand. Since the Indian rule of primogeniture barred the bequest of property to women, Ammu is denied *locus standi,* or a legally cognizable right to contest her divestiture. Instead, Ammu's brother, Chacko, is sole heir to the family's estate, his claim superseding even his mother's. Through its repeated references to "Locusts Stand I," the narrative subtly impugns India's patriarchal legal system for authoring Ammu's dispossession and banishment. By encasing its allusions to this arcane rule at once within Latinate, child speak, and capitalization, it reproves legal argot for shoring up the status quo, as well as eliding questions of both causality and intent. Ironically, precisely by deterring the reader's comprehension of this rarefied concept, the narrative reveals how the legal order secures its authority, here further attenuating the rights of an already marginalized person.

Much as the law refuses Ammu "Locusts Stand I," Chacko enlists a com-paratively malleable political discourse to ensure his patriarchal and caste-based privileges. While on a Rhodes scholarship at Oxford, Chacko imbibes an academic Marxism, with which he still identifies as an adult. However, Chacko is little more than an armchair Marxist who finagles that ideol-ogy to deflect attention from his exploitative management of the family's pickle factory. Indeed, the narrative parodies Chacko's politics by deeming them a "cocktail revolution" (64), and he plies Communist jargon not only to thwart local labor agitation but also to procure sexual favors from his female employees. Insisting that they address him as "Comrade" and attend trade union classes, Chacko recruits Marxist rhetoric to cloak his manipu-lative designs and, assumedly, to silence critique. Likewise, Mammachi, the matriarch of the Kochamma family, deploys an equally duplicitous idiom to apologize for Chacko's predatory behavior, which she euphemistically labels "Men's Needs," another phrase that is capitalized to highlight its fal-sity. All in all, Mammachi and Chacko conscript language to fulfill glaringly self-interested aims, and the recurrence of such incidents throughout the novel bemoans how such assaults on language simultaneously serve to mystify social relations, legalize disparity, and shield personal responsibility. Of course, none of these insights into the mortgaging of language through its misuse are unprecedented. That said, within *The God of Small Things* they explain the narrative's primary relationship to that syndrome, which is to interrupt and reverse those liaisons between language and power through its own aesthetic.

In addition to Chacko's hollow Marxism, hypocrisy infects the local Communist Party, which profits from the caste system by "work[ing] from *within* the communal divides, never challenging them, never appearing not to" (64). The local leader and novel's stereotypical politician, Comrade Pillai, is something of a Judas figure. Pillai has the opportunity but neglects to avert Velutha's murder, which he rationalizes as the "Inevitable Consequences of Necessary Politics" (15). On the eve of his death, Velutha pleads to Pillai for help, but Pillai cites Communist Party doctrine as the pretext for inac-tion. He justifies himself thus: "The Party was not constituted to support workers' indiscipline in their private life" (271). This reasoning draws on abstract, disengaged principles in order to override and obscure the challenge of the particular. Notably, Pillai also appeals to a well-entrenched dualism to negate his responsibility—namely, the binaristic divide between public and private. Fittingly, however, Velutha is not the only casualty of Pillai's ability to divorce his "private" allegiances from his "public" duties; in fact, he later inflicts such logic on his friend Chacko in order to sabotage the family's pickling business. It is by turning Chacko into an "abstract functionary" and a "theoretical construct" that Pillai can "keep his conscience clear," even while he destroys Chacko's livelihood (115). Here, Pillai's capacity to erect a "disjunction between the man and his job," engaging in private business with Chacko while publicly labeling him "the Management" (115), imposes on Chacko the very double-dealing that facilitates Chacko's own misdeeds. In both instances, the strategic misappropriation of language not only is deceitful but also directly corrodes Chacko and Pillai's ethical sensibilities, conditioning them to realities that might otherwise be unconscionable.

Imaginative Language and the "Small Things"

It is in contradistinction to these liabilities of political and legal discourse that *The God of Small Things* crafts its own aesthetic. Indeed, the very fluidity that allows the manipulation of language allows it to harbor great promise, auguring internal resistances and its capacity for rejuvenation. In this sense, Roy's study of the many liaisons between speech and injustice is partner to the novel's own aesthetic enactment of precisely such inverse movements of linguistic renewal. Roy's narrative performs intrusions into rote discourse that are tantamount to what we have seen Merleau-Ponty identify as a central goal of phenomenological inquiry. We might, in turn, conceive of *The God of Small Things* as striving to undo various forms of semantic colonization, suspending that process to implicitly challenge how it shores up the status quo. Whereas Pillai and Chacko hold language hostage to power, *The God of Small Things* rescues language from that ideological servitude, its narrative both critiquing and suspending the conservative gravitations that can render speech inelastic. It thereby reclaims the imaginative potential of language, heralding in particular its own species of aesthetic enchantment as an antidote to the interrelated tragedies represented by the deaths of Estha, Ammu, and Velutha. Importantly, this discursive revitalization is shown to both depend upon and invigorate distinctly corporeal registers of engagement, displaying how aesthetic experience can harness the body's many affective and other sensory faculties with the result of verifying their crucial bearings on social justice.

Such a relay of linguistic disruption and enrichment is achieved by focalizing significant portions of the narrative through the children's perspectives, which allows it to track, in Merleau-Ponty's terms, the "*advent* of being to consciousness."[15] While refracted through the mature present and commented on by an omniscient narrator, much of Roy's narrative mimics a child's untutored, receptive perception. It accordingly dramatizes a type of semiotic defamiliarization that feigns a state of confusion prior to linguistic mastery. This device, on the one hand, divulges how discourse becomes contaminated and deceptive, particularly when in league with power and oppression. As such, Roy capitalizes words and phrases that either are recruited to fulfill such ends (such as "Men's Needs") or magnify deeper tyrannies inscribed within language (for instance, "Edges, Borders, Boundaries, Brinks and Limits"). Many of these capitalized terms are, further, misspelled (again, "Locusts Stand I"), accentuating how language is rendered opaque when affixed to such specious referents. Capitalization in the narrative thus often flags language that requires heightened suspicion.

On the other hand, such misspellings and emphases simultaneously denote the polar opposite relation—that is, a child's grasp of language prior to its sedimentation into predictable patterns, prompts, and referents. In effect, the narrative's miscues and jarring, unexpected allusions simulate the experience of language before its standardization, or prior to its arrest within recognizable signs and conventions. Although the reader may initially confront them as mistakes or mistranslations, these devices paradoxically multiply and enlarge the associations implied by the text. While discordant, these allusions convey revelation and discovery, capturing the passage from obscurity to insight that accompanies language acquisition. We might, then, analogize the texture of a child's unschooled reception of language to phenomenological disclosure, given that both follow a parallel course from perplexity to expanded awareness. To return to "Locusts Stand I," that phrase's abrupt, declarative tenor and harsh tonality register the aggressive, punitive repercussions of the underlying legal term of art, at the same time as the visceral imagery of large bugs is colorful, even playfully humorous. These combined visual, aural, and even tactile intensities actuate multiple dimensions of sensory engagement, showing those faculties to collaborate within embodied cognition. In short, that single phrase illustrates how a particular kind of literary imagination can fruitfully propagate meaning, essentially enticing the reader to collude with the text's own curiosity and delight. By portraying a child's entrance into language, *The God of Small Things* charts the doubled movements of discourse, performing a type of dialectic between language's centripetal tendencies and its potential for reinvention and restoration.

To dislocate the reader's preformed expectations about language, Roy tampers with spelling, grammar, standard word order, the relationship between signifier and signified, and other principles of usage. Terms incessantly become unmoored from their established definitions, while sentence structure and other such regularities are inverted and otherwise askew. This overarching experiment with language causes the novel's prose to resemble something closer to poetry, wherein meaning equally arises through sonority and the arrangement of words on the page. As the family awaits the arrival of Chacko's ex-wife, Margaret, and daughter, Sophie Mol, the narrative lilt-ingly describes the airport's "tall iron railing that separated the Meeters from the Met, the Greeters from the Gret" (135), using rhyme, alliteration, rhythm, meter, and lyrical repetition. While these properties emerge from gram-matical slippages and other syntactical errors, they imbue already charged imagery with heightened emotion and even pleasure. Indeed, the foregoing cadences convey the same tentative expectancy and exuberance that they relate in Roy's characters. Yet those missteps, misplaced capitalizations, and other inconsistencies at once enact alienation within language, rendering it foreign and even disquieting. Interrupting the pace of its own prose, these devices require the reader to concentrate on certain words versus others, channeling both emphasis and significance. This simultaneity of astonish-ment and perplexity induces a sense of cognitive vertigo and disorientation, reinforcing the conceit that the narrative's retrospective events are observed from afar.

Perhaps most important, these various devices incarnate the reading expe-rience, animating deeply visceral, embodied registers of understanding. Roy's aesthetic thereby charts how perception emanates from the embodied self's immersion in a phenomenal field, and, in doing so, it testifies to how certain literary genres can both replicate and incite such phenomenologically reso-nant habits of awareness. This activity within the narrative takes place on an incremental level, wherein even isolated words catalyze such a consciousness. While certain words, like "sturdy," are "terrible" in their associations for the children, others, such as "twinkle," have "crinkled, happy edges" (53). The affective qualities of words thus refuse to be distinguished from their refer-ents; on the contrary, the phonetics of language are conflated with the physi-cal responses that particular notions and ideas evoke. The symbolic valences of language, Roy implies, cannot be evacuated of their corporeal energies; rather, even ostensibly ideational concepts are shot through with affective intensities. In effect, the narrative captures how the self's intellectual and corporeal faculties of knowing penetrate one another, creating synergies that mirror the collaboration between the senses. For instance, the word "later" is "a horrible, menacing goose-bumpy word. Lay.Ter. Like a deep sounding bell in a mossy well. Shivery, and furred. Like moth's feet" (139). Here, too, sound, touch, vision, and even smell conspire to elicit the foreboding kindled by an otherwise mundane word, mimicking how the senses intertwine as they modulate perception and endow language with texture, color, volume, inflection, and even temperature. This incorporation of rhythm, punctuation, rhyme, and alliteration also delays the velocity of the narrative's prose, as it, for instance, lingers over the magnitude of what "later" communicates. We might therefore say that the novel's aesthetic refuses to disarticulate percept and concept, instead unfolding the variegated, shifting commerce between mind and body as they cooperate to generate perception and furnish experience with meaning.[16] To such ends, Roy's portrait of language acquisition explicitly challenges dualistic philosophies of mind, given that it depicts embodied cognition as both prefiguring and organizing certain kinds of intellection.

By a similar token, within *The God of Small Things* perception and especially memory actively inhabit and are triggered by the physical, object world, representing one way in which the narrative celebrates the faculty of touch. Key realities, particularly painful ones, take up residence in commonplace things; for example, "the Loss of Sophie Mol" materializes itself "like a quiet thing in socks. It hid in books and food. In Mammachi's violin case" (17). This reification of grief within material culture indexes its visceral fiber, suggesting how it defies both rationalization and predictability. Likewise, the memory of Velutha's brutal murder is not only instigated by particular senses—being recurrently foreshadowed through references to "History's smell"—but similarly inheres within random objects. For instance, the affective caliber and pervasiveness of his memory "lurk[] forever in ordinary things. In coat hangers. Tomatoes. In tar on roads. In certain colors. In the plates at a restaurant. In the absence of words. And the emptiness of eyes" (54). This catalog with its lyrical prose figures consciousness as saturated with the phenomenal incipiencies that enmesh the embodied subject. Inexorably situated as well as fettered to the body, cognition is presented as contingent on things, which predetermine both its emotional fiber and its episodic emergence. It is on the level of aesthetics, then, that *The God of Small Things* contests the Cartesian presumption of distance and mastery over the passive, inert object world, instead capturing the concatenation of mutating, fecund forces that render material culture vibrant and generative.

Much as it depicts perception as materially and corporeally grounded, *The God of Small Things* also wrestles with the embodied self's captivity to the fortuitous rhythms of time, which render perception ephemeral in additional ways pertaining to phenomenological insight. At the same time as Rahel's toy watch heralds the day-to-day, it symbolizes an impossible desire to stay time's passage. This desire, of course, is particularly acute because of the narrative's preoccupation with the irreversibility of the premature deaths that overtake three of its characters. At once, its lament over the abbreviated span of childhood seemingly underlies this fixation, along the lines of how the forced choice of language precipitates Estha's untimely maturation. Such ambivalence concerning temporality notably plays out in the narrative's own disjunctive, cyclical, and disorienting chronology. It simultaneously condenses and elongates time, marking both the past's irretrievable distance and its vertiginous proximity, for instance, as it sporadically leaps into the mature present. On one level, these dislocations track the psychic contours of traumatic memory, which erupts in response to similarly arbitrary circumstances. Yet on another level, such vicissitudes effectuate a phenomenology of time—or what Achille Mbembe calls "*time as lived,* not synchronically or diachronically, but in its multiplicity and simultaneities, its presence and absences, beyond the lazy categories of permanence and change beloved of so many historians."[17] By intermingling past and present, the novel resists standard expectations about linearity and progress, instead vivifying the inherently paradoxical quality of time's elapse.

As I have been arguing, Roy's aesthetic self-consciously conducts its own experiment in the creative refurbishment of language and, along with it, the literary imagination. It is therefore not surprising that its plot looks to a fictional art form in order to reflect on the stakes of its own aesthetic venture. In particular, it returns on multiple occasions to contemplate the traditional Keralan Kathakali dance form, which spawns its meditations on both the casualties of globalization and art's transformative capacities. Deriding the tourist industry, it despairs of how the actors must "hawk...their stories" for those audiences (219), causing them to become "collapsed," "amputated," and "slashed" (121). The implication, of course, is that such graphic imagery applies not only to the dramatic routines but also to the actors' comparatively truncated, diminished lives. Nonetheless, the narrative embraces Kathakali as something of a spiritual bulwark against the encroaching tides of global culture—a characterization that notably extends from what it identifies as Kathakali's embodied caliber. Indeed, the narrative's description of the Kathakali artist self-consciously dispels dualistic assumptions about mind:

> The Kathakali Man is the most beautiful of men. Because his body *is* his soul. His only instrument. From the age of three it has been planed and polished, pared down, harnessed wholly to the task of storytelling. He has magic in him, this man within the painted mask and swirling skirts. (219)

The narrative here lauds Kathakali for fusing body and spirit, or for fully engaging the affective, corporeal faculties of the self. Moreover, it immediately thereafter juxtaposes Kathakali performance with Velutha's murder, which it instead reproves for being sanctioned by instrumental reason and "savage economy" (224).

That said, the narrative puts pressure on what might appear a naively ideal-ized portrait of Kathakali. Indeed, it is skeptical of the impulse to romanticize art either as a facile stave against the corrosive by-products of globalization or as an uncomplicated relic of an idyllic past. Although it valorizes Kathakali for its embodied aesthetic—implicitly likening its properties to its own—it underscores the violence that lurks even within such corporeally engaged art. While on the one hand Kathakali might seem to vindicate art's redemptive properties, on the other the content of one particular Kathakali performance configures it as a type of laboratory in human evil. Here, the narrative's ostensible defense of Kathakali almost seamlessly occasions an examination of the structure of human brutality. In the mature present that instigates Estha's and Rahel's memories, they find themselves in the audience of a spontaneous nightlong dramatization of the epic Kathakali myths. This protracted per-formance is not artificially curtailed to placate tourist audiences, and it thus permits the actors to fully inhabit their ceremonial roles—even while that absorption is incited by both "humiliation" and being "stoned out of [their] skull" (218, 221). Yet even this unadulterated, uncensored performance is not immune to the exclusionary thinking that the narrative elsewhere holds responsible for global modernity's many cruelties. One of its story lines recounts the origins of the "Love Laws" in a progression that first chal-lenges but ultimately preserves their authority (222)—in effect, naturalizing the very order of legality that legislates Velutha's murder. This, of course, is a telling detail in a novel whose entire plot decries the violence of the caste system. The precolonial past, as such, is presented as far from exempt from empire's many institutionalized wrongs, which is to say that neither indigene-ity nor art are panaceas for those ills. Even while certain genres of aesthetic experience might intermittently overcome the affective paralysis such ills have wrought, the narrative suggests that art, too, cannot inoculate itself against the contagion of global modernity's most lethal ideologies.

Moreover, the nightlong Kathakali performance culminates with its own gruesome murder, which an ensuing passage correlates with Velutha's death. However, the narrative is strikingly evasive about this act of violence, lapsing into a dreamlike aura that compounds its indeterminate truth status. In one sense, the murder is suggested to be a ceremonial completion of an epic story that "fulfill[s]" a "vow" (223), and the actors are similarly described drinking and bathing in the victim's "fresh blood," framing it as a ritual or sacrament (224). Yet the narrative also insists that "it was no performance," and this pre-tense is substantiated by intensely visceral imagery, for instance of "gurgling blood bubbles pale pink between his teeth" (224). It also foregrounds the "madness," "frenzy," "brutality," and "anarchy" that accompany the act, which the performers continue to exorcize by going "home to beat their wives" (224), further suggesting that this symbolic murder transgresses the line separating art from life, bringing the fragility of that divide into high relief. Such a slippage between the Kathakali murder's literal execution versus its strictly imaginative enactment reproves the temptation to approach art as a failsafe antidote to other sociopolitical harms. In the end, the novel productively curtails its own desires for redemption, even while it may appear to harbor such ambitions for its own medium.

Toward a Phenomenology of Embodiment

Simply put, *The God of Small Things* unfolds what I have referred to in the larger context of this book as an embodied politics of reading, affirming the relevance of such an aesthetic to matters of social justice. Above all, this aesthetic emerges through the narrative's phenomenologically charged language and imagery, which harness corporeal modalities of apperception to illuminate their merit. Its embodied aesthetic incites an almost ontological awareness, particularly as it adumbrates both the many paradoxes that govern existence and the parallel symmetries that cohere the lifeworld as a whole. To pursue these paradoxes, Roy's narrative converges on the dual verities of human finitude and sexual experience, ruminating over the many enigmas that haunt those intertwined realms of existence. No doubt this focus might appear to require a predictably psychoanalytic account of the "death drive" and its connection to sexual desire; however, these connections more accurately elaborate a vision of just codependence, or a distinctly ecological sense of interspecies fellowship and cohabitation. This conception of reciprocal vulnerability is forged through the narrative's sensory immersion in the phenomenality of both egregious violence and exquisite sexual longing, an aesthetic project that is brought to fruition as well as mirrored in the novel's layered metaphorics of touch, blood, and the flesh. Hence, it is by incarnating these corporeal dimensions of aesthetic engagement that the narrative illustrates why a nondualist phenomenology of embodied cognition might provide a starting point for an imaginative remapping of our dominant understandings of social justice and human rights.

The God of Small Things fully crescendos toward, first, Velutha's murder and, thereafter, the socially taboo love that precipitates it. These events are adjacent and, as such, symbolically aligned, although the retrospective narrative inverts them rather than follows their actual chronology. Its four concluding chapters consecutively render Velutha's murder, Estha's betrayal, his subsequent traumatic separation from Ammu and Rahel, and, finally, the initial rendezvous

between Ammu and Velutha. This succession amplifies the emotional intensity of the concluding segments of the novel, bringing them to what it itself
describes as "unaffordable heights" (318). A painstaking rendition of Velutha's
brutalization opens this terminal sequence. While the narrative inventories
his wounds with precision so scientific as to mimic a coroner's report, that
graphic detail neither sensationalizes nor sanitizes the murder. Rather, it
relentlessly probes that atrocity in order to almost phenomenologically submerge its perspective within the body in pain. To begin, however, I must
underscore what this lengthy passage does not do. First, it does not dramatize
the mind's intellectual limits to comprehending atrocity, a recurrent impulse
in human rights witnessing. Likewise, its descriptive excess does not excite an
exhilarating or exoticizing aesthetics of the sublime, as we repeatedly encountered in the human rights bestseller. On the contrary, it forestalls both such
distancing devices to instead cast open the anatomy of violence with agoniz-
ing, exhaustive clarity, scrupulously confronting its impact on the lived body.
In a way, Roy's narrative provides too much specificity and information—far
more than would be available to an actual observer.

For instance, one paragraph adopts the rhetoric and viewpoint of a medical practitioner, enumerating the fractures in Velutha's skull, his body parts
that are paralyzed, and his sites of internal bleeding, among a litany of other
devastating wounds (294). This passage superficially feigns scientific detachment, although this objectivity creates a disconnect between the narrative's
tone and the enormity of his trauma. Moreover, its laborious itemization of
Velutha's injuries culminates with an image that recurs in the novel's final
scene, in that case, however, to evidence sexual desire. At the very end of
this belabored catalog of Velutha's abuse, before a section break, the narrative
plainly relates, "He had goosebumps where the handcuffs touched his skin"
(294). Its almost aggressive documentation of the damage to Velutha's body
accordingly does not conclude by scrutinizing a graphic wound or other
insignia of atrocity. Rather, it registers the magnitude of his suffering through
almost exquisite detail, and the delicacy of such imagery is what captures so
very much about the ontological condition of embodiment. Despite lying on
the brink of death and in physical agony, Velutha's body remains sufficiently
alive as to be susceptible to the cold of metal pressed against his skin. Not
coincidentally, the narrative's imaginative concentration on the phenomenality of violence thus builds to verify the ontological status of touch, in a
haunting snapshot that magnifies both the deep fragility and extraordinary
resilience of the body.

While his trauma is assiduously documented, Velutha's own subjective experience of the assault is omitted. Instead, the attack is focalized

through two very different witnesses: his "Touchable" policeman assailants and young Rahel and Estha, who are accidental bystanders. The mercenary policemen's viewpoint receives the most attention within the narrative; however, that perspective is visibly distorted, largely by its encasement within the codes and formulas of popular culture. The policemen descend on Velutha "like Film-policemen," executing the "Surpriseswoop" with "Headlines in their heads" (291), and these cinematic tropes enable their mental dissociation from their actions. Insofar as these generic conventions inure them to wrong, Roy indicts the global media for eroding their moral aversion and conditioning them to violence—in another potential rebuke to *Midnight's Children,* whose plot is overlaid with celebratory allusions to Bollywood. These references introduce the policemen as performers of sorts, thereby aligning Velutha's beating with the Kathakali myth that occasions the novel's meditations on art. Even as both performances occur on a type of "stage" (224), the underlying murders represent almost ritual exorcisms of primal terror that both symbolically and in practice serve to inoculate the body politic against forms of boundary crossing and perceived defilement.

However, the narrative at once underscores the radical divergences between these two crimes. While the Kathakali drama escalates into a "frenzy" of "madness" (224), the police are entirely devoid of emotion, which casts them as emissaries of global modernity itself. Indeed, their actions comply with the standardized, calculated logic of economic neoliberalism; they proceed "with economy, not frenzy. Efficiency, not anarchy. Responsibility, not hysteria" (293). In place of their experiencing the "abyss where anger should have been" (292), such as fueled the Kathakali performance, the only sentiment they are endowed with is "fear." Yet theirs is not the fear of dispossession and obsolescence faced by the Kathakali actors; instead, it is explained as the anxiety of power in its "pursuit of ascendancy" and "complete monopoly" (293). Roy's omniscient narrator overtly links that mindset to a continuum of other dualisms and their attendant oppressions, including "civilization's fear of nature, men's fear of women, [and] power's fear of powerlessness," as well as "Men's Needs," a phrase that subsumes Chacko's behavior within those habits of exploitation (292). Overall, the policemen's capacity for "aesthetic distance"—in other words, to retreat into the mind and jettison the body's appetencies—is what permits them to carry out their strategic and orderly aggression. We might, by extension, interpret them as ambassadors for specifically instrumentalizing reason; no doubt it is precisely by suppressing their corporeal faculties of involvement that they intellectually quarantine the suffering they transact. Hence, the temperament they exemplify exposes the dark underside of both the dualistic logic and emphasis on empirical ratio-nalism that organizes liberal formulations of human rights.

It is in opposition to such cold-bloodedness that the narrative instead lingers over Velutha's injuries. As it shifts from their onslaught to his actual abuse, it reverts to the children's vantage, registering in corporeal, affectively charged terms the repercussions of the assault. The narrative here enlists not only visual imagery but also sounds, smells, and physical sensations; it employs intensely tactile and aurally resonant words, such as "thud," "grunt," "crunch," and "gurgle," while observing details like blood's "sourmetal smell." This experiential immediacy on one level explains the children's subsequent trauma, simulating their sensory shock. Yet on another level, its excruciating study of the anatomy of violence indexes far more than the extremity of the children's distress. Rather, the novel's imaginative absorption with atrocity also, albeit paradoxically, is essential to its unique vision of social justice. In effect, the novel contrasts its own aesthetic with the comportment exhibited by the mercenary policemen, whose capacity to abuse Velutha is directly facilitated by their hyperrationalism. Precisely their beholdenness to overly mechanistic, appropriative, and empiricist habits of thought dulls the faculties of responsiveness that might have impeded Velutha's murder. It is from this perspective that the narrative's phenomenology of embodied literary engage-ment enacts a pointed rejoinder to such an outlook. Whereas the policemen's mindset implicitly evacuates thought of affective and corporeal vitality, the narrative restores those fertile intensities to perception, and, in doing so, it gestures toward how such an embodied consciousness might counteract the impassivity that holds the policemen captive. It itself enlists and thereby dem-onstrates the viscerally dense, vibrant language required to account for the body in pain—which is to say that the novel's disturbing portrait of death directly serves to reawaken suppressed perceptual energies that are invariably just. In effect, Roy's narration of Velutha's murder critiques liberal rationalism for having denuded and impoverished irreplaceable components of selfhood while reanimating those very sensibilities.

This is all to say that the narrative endows the policemen with the very animus toward embodiment that this book has sought to impugn by track-ing how it incurs legibility for liberal constructions of human rights. As I have argued, liberalism posits as the bearer of rights a dangerously truncated, bloodless subject, and it is exactly by turning Velutha into such an abstrac-tion that the policemen become psychologically equipped to enforce his murder. It is therefore in direct opposition to such callousness that we should interpret both *The God of Small Things*'s aesthetic and its rendition of Velutha's death: as a strategic reversal of that disdain and countervailing attempt to reincarnate the subject of human rights with an essential fleshiness. If liberal topographies of the human variously repress and essentialize the body, and if that ambivalence has warranted global modernity's routine exclusions, then the narrative's rapt concentration on Velutha's dying, broken, bloodied body paradoxically returns to the liberal social body its disavowed materiality and embodiment. The narrative's extraordinarily raw image of the wounded, violated, and profaned body is one that cannot be purified or sanitized, short-circuiting the mechanisms through which embodiment is typically managed and subdued. In fact, the narrative absorbs itself with those very facets of self-hood that neo-Cartesian dualism brackets off, while at one demonstrating the perils of their successful expungement and disambiguation through reason. It amplifies, rather than intellectually minimizes or elides, the precarity and messiness of embodiment as a site of being—and with painstaking exactitude that resists being distilled into philosophical principles, ideals, or theorems. In short, the novel's excruciating depiction of Velutha's horrific death is not introduced as a moral warning or passing foray into subject matter that must be handled with caution. On the contrary, this sustained contemplation of the phenomenality of the suffering, dying, vulnerable body is levied as a vital corrective to—and thus an imaginative exercise that might interrupt—the emotionally closeted, decorporealizing attitude of the policemen.

The narrative similarly does not cleanse violence of its ontological import by treating it as either somehow aberrant or an episodic reversion to sub-human, precivilizational tendencies. Quite differently, it characterizes the violence of Velutha's murder and, to a degree, the nightlong Kathakali performance as by-products of a mindset that liberal rationalism and scientific empiricism have fostered. It explicitly resists the kind of apologetics for atrocity that facilely dismiss it as a fitful eruption of animalistic or regressive appetites. Ruminating over the Kathakali ritual, it concludes, "Certainly no beast has essayed the boundless, infinitely inventive art of human hatred. No beast can match its range and power" (225). Here, Achille Mbembe's reflections of the phenomenology of death might further help to decipher its import in *The God of Small Things*. As Mbembe comments of the postcolony, death "embraces all substantiality—indeed, to the point where it has penetrated almost everywhere and virtually nothing escapes it." This "substantiality" of death, however, inheres not so much within its negativity, or how it nullifies existence. Rather, for Mbembe human mortality also compels the question "What does it mean to partake of human existence?"[18] In this respect, death claims a strangely life-affirming status, orienting us toward the enigma of what it means to be alive in a robust, energetic way. Both Mbembe and Roy thus differently imply that a phenomenological grasp of human mortality—in all its terror and unfathomability—can paradoxically enable perception to inhabit a consciousness of what Merleau-Ponty calls the "flesh of the world." Indeed, as I have suggested, this metaphorics of blood, flesh, and touch pervades *The God of Small Things,* ultimately collapsing both the ominous and generative valences of these figures into a reverberating symbolic economy that overwrites liberalism's customary denigration of embodiment. With this in mind, we again might levy Merleau-Ponty's spiritualized lexicon to analyze both Velutha's graphic death and this recurrent imagery of "blood." Immediately before Ammu embarks on her fatal affair, Rahel quotes to her a line from Kipling's *The Jungle Book:* "We be of one blood, Thou and I" (312). Consanguinity is here invoked as a cipher for human—and, if we look to Kipling, interspecies—solidarity. However, even within Kipling's famous text, Mowgli follows by explaining, "My kill shall be thy kill if thou art ever hungry." Hence, even blood as a figure for just cohabitation is overlaid by the violence of survival that it simultaneously connotes.

Nevertheless, it is in light of the foregoing that Velutha's death yields a clear profit for thinking about social justice—although not within the different rubrics of ethical recognition or sympathy or trauma, at least as they are usually conceived. While the narrative copiously catalogs his wounds, it eliminates his subjective reaction, failing to inscribe his injuries or pain on his face. This omission is noteworthy in that it refracts the challenges of ethics-politics not through theory's customary analytic prisms but rather through the phenomenology of his embodiment. Thus, contra what is frequently associated with Levinasian ethics, the narrative does not enshrine the look or reciprocal gaze as a catalyst for ethical exchange and responsibility. Whatever plea is enacted by Velutha's suffering does not prompt an intellectual response but instead extends from the throes of his carnal being; his plight accosts the reader on a visceral level that thwarts the heuristics of either empathetic identification or Otherness.[19] Along similar lines, the sheer facticity of his suffering forestalls a retreat into dualistic assumptions about the priority of mind. Velutha's wounded body—along with the evils it comes to emblematize—cannot be abstracted, or objectively reconciled, or sequestered, or idealized, or transcended. In this respect, the narrative contends with the body in pain without relying on deceptively dualistic assumptions about corporeal integrity or the self-contained, reasoning subject. In sum, Roy's narration of Velutha's death variously defies deconstructive theorizations of ethics, established models for deciphering trauma, and liberal mappings of the subject, suggesting how each of those frameworks has naturalized overly sanitized accounts of embodiment that inadvertently reproduce Western metaphysics' long-standing anxieties. And it is relative to the descriptive paucity of these regnant paradigms that Velutha's death returns the lived body to the subject of human rights. The narrative overwhelms us with relentless, gory detail that verges on being offensive precisely to impair the sort of intellectual response that might neutralize that outrage.

In addition to presenting its layered metaphorics of blood, the narrative correlates the phenomenal texture of violence with that of sexual desire. Of course, this basic link is far from striking or original; however, the imagery that erects it works to enlarge the narrative's evolving symbolism of touch. In particular, this parallel between graphic death and erotic longing is reinforced through the snapshot of the goose bumps that consummates the narration of Velutha's attack. Shortly after this passage, the concluding scene of the entire novel contains a flashback to Ammu and Velutha's initial liaison, in a chapter fittingly titled "The Cost of Living," given that their desire foreordains both their fates. As Ammu and Velutha part ways, the narrative relates how Ammu's touch leaves "a trail of goosebumps on his skin." Compounding the passage's already elevated emotion, this imagery is further elaborated through succeeding similes with intensely aural, visual, and tactile properties: "Like flat chalk on a blackboard. Like breeze in a paddyfield. Like jet-streaks in a blue church sky" (321). Even as the motif of "goosebumps" refers to Velutha's pending murder, these lyrical connections hearken back to Sophie Mol's funeral, during which Rahel contemplates the church ceiling "painted blue like the sky, with drifting clouds and tiny whizzing jet planes with white trails" (7). In turn, the narrative's intertwining allusions not only conflate those multiple losses but also collapse them into the anatomy of sexual desire, thus directing us to consider the constitutive paradoxes of embodiment, or how the body's inextricable resilience and vulnerability both mirror and illuminate the tangled reciprocities that supervise the lifeworld as a whole. In doing so, this final image also contemplates the synergistic energies of what Sara Ahmed calls "economies of touch."[20] Indeed, while the central crime in *The God of Small Things* indicts the logic of untouchability—a logic that equally underwrites the caste system and the many sociopolitical exclusions that haunt liberalism's philosophical architecture—this concluding scene affirms touch as a critical site of ethical exchange and incipiency.

It is from within such a framework, then, that we must explain the narrative's concluding reflections on erotic experience. While its final passage celebrates touch as a vital site of co-belonging, it nevertheless foregrounds the many paradoxes of embodiment that quintessentially emerge in desire. On the one hand, much as it lauds touch for fostering just cohabitation, sexuality amplifies the fugitive energies incited within such corporeal circuits of exchange. In a way, sexual experience consummately mingles and intertwines separate bodies, disclosing the inherent porosity of the boundary between self and Other. On the other hand, the corporeal basis of violence simultaneously checks the narrative's valorization of touch as a surefire route to ethics. Indeed, the last word of the entire novel—"tomorrow"—comments on the circularity of desire, or how it is animated by its own frustration. In an affectively wrenching progression, the novel abruptly ends with the promise that Ammu and Velutha extract from one another after their first rendezvous, yet the very word "tomorrow" underscores its futility.

No doubt similar tensions are crystallized for Ammu during a dream sequence that descends on her in an unusually vivid afternoon nap. In this dream, Ammu envisions herself journeying through a shadowed forest guided by a one-armed man, whose limitations are inscribed on his body, in particular, as his single arm leaves him "no other arm with which to fight the shadows that flickered around him" (205). Beyond his physical constraints, this imaginary lover is further impaired:

> He could only do one thing at a time.
> If he held her, he couldn't kiss her. If he kissed her, he couldn't see her. If he saw her, he couldn't feel her. (205)

These handicaps offer a powerful image of the foreclosures and contradictions that riddle desire, especially insofar as it represents a primary font of embodied experience. As such, the impediments that afflict Ammu's imaginary man denote far more than her idiosyncratic disappointments. Rather, they also gauge the limits of theories of selfhood that segregate the body's varied capacities from one another, whether because of a latent dualism or as a result of the conventional prioritization of vision. While Ammu's imaginary lover may reify her deep cynicism, as a figure for the tangled energies of embodiment he also exemplifies why the effort to compartmentalize and thereby censor the self's different appetencies will necessarily forfeit vital opportunities for just and ethical engagement.

The Politics of Environmental Justice

As we have seen, corporeal being within *The God of Small Things* offers a prototypical reminder of the self's basic inherency within other beings, registering the extent to which all existence—human, animal, and natural—thrives in delicate interdependence. To related ends, this collective intertwining is partner to a deeply ecological conception of social justice. *The God of Small Things* depicts human welfare as inexorably embedded within and therefore reliant upon both natural and animal being. Much as the material environment enmeshes the subject within a phenomenal field of perception, a vision of interspecies cohabitation predicated on human symbiosis with the surrounding lifeworld is adumbrated within the narrative. Within such a framework, the fortitude of nature bears intimately on justice and ethics, and we can observe how such a cosmology diverges markedly from liberal political thought's typically anthropocentric paradigms. Notably, the novel overtly holds globalization to blame for defiling the natural environment, and those ecological ravages are figured as part and parcel of global modernity's other wrongs, including its many assaults upon human rights.

While Roy is a scathing critic of almost all guises of globalization, she is most impassioned when attacking its devastating impact on the environment. In *The God of Small Things,* the carnage it wreaks on the natural world is widely apparent, and the narrative links the sapped emotional lives of its characters to this adulteration of the environment. In the twenty-plus years separating the twins' traumatic past from their mature present, the local river has become "thick and toxic" with the "smell of shit," leaving it "choked" with "its spirit spent" (119), as is related in a chapter whose title ironically quotes popular tourist brochures for Kerala: "God's Own Country." This metaphor further correlates ecological blight with the depletion of language; much as the river's life-sustaining properties have been polluted, so, too, has the fluid nexus of language with meaning been severed. As we have seen, the incursions of global culture attenuate the policemen's ethical faculties, akin to how the tourist industry truncates both the Kathakali performances and their actors' lives. In short, the contamination of the river by industrial waste represents merely one among many ways that globalization desiccates the local environment, throwing its equilibrium out of balance.

Whether or not one agrees with Roy's dire assessments of globalization, her sense of the delicate harmony sustaining life permeates *The God of Small Things,* wherein nature is frequently anthropomorphized as a participant in the novel's unfolding plot. For instance, before introducing its human characters, it offers a prolonged description of the local environment:

> May in Ayemenem is a hot, brooding month. The days are long and humid. The river shrinks and black crows gorge on bright mangoes in still, dustgreen trees. Red bananas ripen. Jackfruits burst. Dissolute bluebottles hum vacuously in the fruity air. (3)

This evocatively lush, rich imagery and language effectively endow nature with agency, the prose echoing its tonality, rhythms, colors, smells, and other tactile as well as aural properties. Indeed, the narrative uses words so vivid and turbulent as to halt its pace, elongating these intersensory reverberations.

It actuates and thereby imbricates multiple dimensions of perceptual engagement, causing those affective faculties to collude to engender what we might
term a phenomenological consciousness of the environment. The novel's
own aesthetic, as such, both illuminates and nourishes Roy's political commitments, and these synergies offer another point of entry into why particular species of phenomenologically resonant art are uniquely disposed to
expatiate the texture of such an ecology, which propositional and empirical
genres of analysis would instead quell and obscure.

Along similar lines, the different characters' attitudes toward nature provide a barometer for their overall ethical-imaginative fiber. Much as a casual
indifference to Velutha's embodiment enables the policemen to execute his
murder, a dualistic neglect of nature conspires with that mindset. Among
the many neo-Cartesian biases that sanction his death, "civilization's fear
of nature" is prominently included, allying nature's instrumental use with
countless other oppressions. As they lay siege to Velutha, his assailants are
oblivious to the millipedes crushed by their boots, as well as to other animal
life "running for cover" at their approach (289). While one policeman briefly
mulls "the dynamics of dragonfly sex," this imaginative digression is abbreviated as "his mind clicked to attention and Police Thoughts returned" (289).
Insofar as such a disregard for nature is deeply anthropocentric, the narrative dramatizes the psychological and moral costs of that human-centered,
myopic worldview. In effect, the pretense of human mastery over nature is
reproached for not merely shoring up the species divide but also exhausting
Roy's characters' imaginative reserves. The policemen's animosity toward the
environment is merely one facet of a corresponding resentment of human
weakness, and, conversely, the narrative suggests that greater appreciation for
ecological welfare might have interrupted their ability to carry out Velutha's
ruthless killing.

In contrast with such contempt, the natural environment purveys for other
of Roy's characters profound meaning and consolation. Much like Coetzee's
Lurie, these characters come to terms with their different predicaments by
contemplating the delicate harmonies of nature. Throughout their affair,
Ammu and Velutha project their plight onto a small spider living in the
abandoned house where they meet—not coincidentally, the same house that
later is witness to Velutha's murder. Rather than openly acknowledge the
risks they court, they displace their anxieties onto the spider. As the narrative
explains, "They linked their fates, their futures... to his" (320). During their
nightly unions, they debate his "frailty," "smallness," his need for "camou-
flage," and his "shambling dignity" (321), heralding those insignia of his vulnerability as cause for "love." While the spider may be a repository for Ammu

and Velutha's own disquiet, the narrative nevertheless relates that transference in terms that describe its own allegiances. As it comments, because "they had nothing. No future," Ammu and Velutha "stuck to the small things" (320), and that solicitude for "smallness" is further construed as "put[ting] their faith in fragility" (321). Here, then, Roy's narrative almost self-reflexively sums up its own aesthetic qualities and ideals—and in ways that also bring me to the significance of the novel's title.

But first, animal life ultimately reconciles Velutha and Ammu to their own constitutive precarity, which is to say that nature and its tenuous rhythms provide a mirror to the human condition. On one level, this portrait of tenuous intertwining stages a rejoinder to liberal theories of politics, both highlighting the falsity of their enabling myths and indicating why they have often failed to offer satisfying frameworks for an environmental justice. Roy's narrative, that is, reproves liberalism's fictions of dignity for not only condoning human dominion over nature but also furnishing a skewed portrait of human co-belonging. It is in opposition to such fantasies of radical freedom and autonomy, then, that the novel valorizes an environmental consciousness as, apart from being independently salutary, essential to human rights. Much as Velutha's death vivifies the mutual suffering and beholdenness that ensnares all existence, so, too, do nature's symmetries map the contours of a counter-liberal matrix for reconceiving just interdependence—one disabused of the dualistic, human-centered privileging of intellection, reason, and speech. As we have seen, such a cosmology is unfolded within the novel's own aesthetic, which simulates the manifold incipiencies of nature and enmeshes the perceiving subject within their dynamism. In effect itself adumbrating the phenomenal field that incarnates consciousness, the narrative claims corporeal engagement as crucial to justice-ethics, illustrating how such an imaginative experiment might incrementally reverse the many miscarriages of justice that have come to define global modernity.

The God of Small Things

Even Roy's title announces the novel's fervent investment in the "small things"—a devotion that variously fuels its plot, animates its aesthetic, and influences its distinctive contributions to this book's theorization of the well-trodden terrain of debates surrounding human rights. Here again, it is within this attention to "smallness" that the novel's stylistic qualities and thematic concerns converge. In particular, the narrative reclaims the elementary units of lived experience as foundational to its ecological conception of justice, and from this vantage *The God of Small Things*'s nondualist ontology and its embodied politics of reading together elicit a type of phenomenological "return to the things themselves." Within that agenda, the novel espouses both its own subject matter and its imaginative project as avenues through which to disrupt global modernity's practiced, habituated modes of knowing; as Roy elsewhere describes such an exercise in disclosure, the narrative aims to reforge "the link" and "understanding" between human life and the rest of the fragile planet.[21] In addition to nature, these commitments emerge within the material properties of ordinary objects, the fugitive tributaries of memory, the inventive play of children, and, above all, the enigmatic energies of corporeal being. By conjoining those concerns based on their "small-ness," Roy suggests how their nontotalizable character might neutralize global modernity's regnant logic of economic efficiency, quantifying abstraction, empirical fact, human mastery, and egoistic self-interest.

The narrative's activity of renewal is thus an expansive one that quite explicitly bears on ontology. Within such an itinerary, moreover, Velutha is subtly identified as the novel's titular character—and hence the "god" of its recuperative enterprise. Such an overtly theological idiom should not be dismissed as incidental; rather, Roy marshals a vocabulary whose far-reaching implications I have already considered. For one, I addressed how such a gram-mar of divinity, faith, and enchantment gauges the limits of secularism as an ideology, pointing to how the secular thesis will fail to explain core facets of selfhood, co-belonging, and meaning alike. Differently, we encountered a rhetoric of "faith" as well as a figural God-concept within Merleau-Ponty's thought, wherein that idiom served to denote the paradoxical tenor of phe-nomenological awareness, with both its genesis in nonempirical knowledge and its fleeting, unpredictable emergence. Indeed, *The God of Small Things* enlists such a spiritualized idiom seemingly to fulfill both such functions. On one level, that language captures why the novel's own ideals flout the dominantly secular order of global modernity, with its emphasis on progress, linear and homogenous time, and scientific rationalism. In contrast to such ambitions, *The God of Small Things*'s lexicon of divinity commemorates those non-normative attachments, loyalties, and enchantments that inherently refuse codification and can only be deciphered vis-à-vis amorphous registers of faith and belief. On another level, *The God of Small Things*'s theological rhetoric avers the transitory nature of both the "small things" memorialized in its title and its own episodic glimpses of restorative insight. In this way, it implicitly lauds a posture of humility as necessary to grasp such unverifiable realities, while further extolling that mindset as ethically profitable.

Yet within this imaginative landscape, we must still ask what it means to interpret Velutha as a harbinger of such belief. If Velutha is the "god" of the narrative's linked creative and ethical sensibilities, what qualities does he embody; of what temperament is he an exemplar? In other words, what ideals does his character consecrate as fully ontological? And, more important, why must Velutha be sacrificed? Is he an inevitable casualty of the overarching designs of global modernity, and does he thus embody those countervailing orientations that civilization has had to expel and disavow? Does the ban on Velutha paradoxically acquire legibility for the values he stands in opposition to; does his interdiction somehow consolidate liberalism as an ethos and an ideology? If so, what alternatives might his perspective forebode? How might his outlook instead excavate the exclusions that underwrite liberalism's many enabling myths? In sum, if Velutha somehow represents the lowest of the low, the smallest of the small, whose death is erased from dominant versions of history as well as sanctioned by law, how might the competing vision of just fellowship that he augurs outline the contours of a surrogate topography of human rights—one arising, to quote Merleau-Ponty, "in a certain sense from below"?[22]

These are weighty questions, yet they convey the magnitude of what is at stake within *The God of Small Things*'s bold ontology—which is bold precisely in its insistence on modesty and smallness. What initially attracts Ammu to Velutha is his willingness to participate in certain kinds of imaginative and creative play. When invited into the children's games, Velutha simply concurs, without supervising, hastening, or unmasking their fantasies. This stance is acclaimed as quite exceptional, as the narrative comments:

> It is after all so easy to shatter a story. To break a chain of thought. To ruin a fragment of a dream being carried around carefully like a piece of porcelain.
>
> To let it be, to travel with it, as Velutha did, is much the harder thing to do. (181)

If Velutha is exemplary, that quality lies in his ability, as the novel explains, to "instinctively collud[e] in the conspiracy of their fiction" (181)—or, in other words, to safeguard the uninhibited faculties of the imagination. By giving himself over to the children's diversions, Velutha suspends his customary "adult" demeanor and the suspicious, self-interested motives that guide most of the novel's other characters. Indeed, Velutha's curiosity is much like the narrative's itself, raising the question of whether Velutha is, above all, a figure for a particular kind of literary imagination. Much as is required by the act of reading, Velutha's comportment bypasses the normalizing certitude of empirical fact, the neoliberal premium on rational self-interest, and the structures of oppression ingrained within much political discourse. By submitting himself to the etiquette of childhood play, he obeys a very different order of community that the one liberalism has ratified. It is in marked departure from the liberal onus to rationally self-determine that Velutha acquiesces to a confederacy forged through self-abandonment to the creative process, the unpredictable detours of experimental coparticipation, and the mysterious rhythms of insight and discovery. In order to inhabit the children's play, Velutha must open himself up to modes of truth rigidly foreclosed by the secularizing, disenchanted rules of global modernity. Precisely for these reasons Velutha epitomizes the sympathies of Roy's novel, representing an emissary of its particular species of "faith"—namely, a "faith" grounded in the small, fragile, minutia that compose the rudiments of lived experience.

Velutha's mindset is visibly contrasted with that of Comrade Pillai and the police inspector who authorize his death. As they surrender Velutha on the conservative altar of politics, they are instead described as

> men whom childhood had abandoned without a trace. Men without curiosity. Without doubt. Both in their own way truly, terrifyingly adult. They looked out at the world and never wondered how it worked, because they knew. *They* worked it. (248)

As foils to Velutha, they typify everything that *The God of Small Things* recoils from. They personify the self-aggrandizing, colonizing appetites of power. They are wholly entrapped in reasoned calculation, acknowledging things based solely on their instrumental use. They are certain of their own dominion, and that egoism procures illusions of sovereignty and grandeur. Lacking "doubt," they are further convinced of the authority of empiricism and are averse to the humble receptivity displayed by Velutha. "Look[ing] out at the world" rather than actively participating in it, they have retreated into the comfortable self-enclosure of the mind, marking the casualties of a prioritization of the intellect. In fact, the narrative invites the conclusion that it is precisely their dearth of imagination that permits them to decree Velutha's murder.

As such, Velutha's bearing is ultimately enshrined as an antidote to this practiced indifference of "adulthood," which Roy importantly construes as broadly symptomatic of Velutha's and our era. It is therefore not totally surprising that Velutha must meet with an inordinately tragic end, given that he symbolizes the very sensibilities that global modernity has outlawed and abolished. Indeed, the narrative's incantatory references to "The God of Small Things" are recurrently followed by the phrase "The God of Loss" (312), although not to oppose the "small things" to "loss" but rather to suggest their profound affinity. Much as it almost tenderly protracts Velutha's murder, so, too, is loss held up as formative of the fleshy immanence of corporeal being. Accordingly, while Roy may offer tribute to the kinds of imagination with which Velutha keeps company, *The God of Small Things* does not introduce his demeanor as a curative or panacea. Perhaps that is why his character is consigned to die—to accentuate the contingent, fleeting, ephemeral essence of phenomenological insight, creative expression, and social justice alike. As such, we might also read Velutha as a figure for a particular mode of paradox—one uniquely catalyzed within the reverberating incipiencies of embodiment, as well as the tumultuous rhythms that cohere the lifeworld in its entirety.

Conclusion

In sum, much of the force of Arundhati Roy's *The God of Small Things* is sustained by its layered metaphorics of touch and embodiment, along with the particular texture of aesthetic experience that those energies actuate. This symbolism of embodiment overwrites how the body politic is typically constructed, subverting the myth of the dignified, integrated, self-determining individual that supports dominant articulations of human rights. Within *The God of Small Things,* embodiment instead marks the porous, interwoven solidarities that regulate not only human sociality but also the cosmos as a whole. Such an explanatory prism figures embodiment as a site of creative intermingling, generativity, and play—even while that condition materializes a ubiquitously shared vulnerability and brokenness. In this latter sense, we can understand why the narrative's contemplation of horrific death is an imaginative exercise paradoxically necessary to re-endow the overly abstract, idealized liberal body with its essential vitality and fleshiness. For such reasons has *The God of Small Things* functioned as this book's concluding example of an embodied politics of reading, demonstrating how and why a phenomenology of embodiment necessarily collaborates with a particular species of aesthetic experience, as they together harness the body's affective faculties of responsiveness and engagement. It illustrates how and why literature might enable an imaginative remapping of human rights, in the process expanding their purview beyond the orbit of their narrowly liberal formulations.

Coda

Small Places, Close to Home

Our era is destined to judge itself not from on high, which is mean and bitter, but in a certain sense from below.

—Merleau-Ponty, *The World of Perception*

Where, after all, do human rights begin? In small places, close to home—so close and small that they cannot be seen on any maps of the world.... Such are the places where every man, woman, and child seeks equal justice, equal opportunity, equal dignity without discrimination. Unless these rights have meaning there, they have little meaning anywhere.

—Eleanor Roosevelt, delivered to the United Nations, March 27, 1958

An excerpt from Arundhati Roy's collection of essays fittingly titled *Field Notes on Democracy* (2009) sums up many of the inquiries that have been at the heart of this book. Roy meditates on what she perceives as the failure of democracy in contemporary India, yet her remarks also speak poignantly to the present-day predicament of human rights. As Roy asks:

The question here, really, is: what have we done to democracy? What have we turned it into? What happens once democracy has been used up? When it has been hollowed out and emptied of meaning? What happens when each of its institutions has metastasised into something dangerous? What happens now that democracy and the Free Market have fused into a single predatory organism with a thin, constricted imagination that revolves almost entirely around the idea of maximising profit? Is it possible to reverse this process? Can something that has mutated go back to being what it used to be?[1]

There is little doubt that the languages of human rights have fallen victim to the semantic as well as institutional misuse that Roy laments. Our era—while often victoriously deemed that of human rights—has also watched the rhetoric of human rights become ever more sullied by wrongdoing and self-interest. Even while appeals to human rights often resemble little more than opportunistic clichés, the politics of human rights renders their norms and ostensible safeguards casual bedfellows of global capital. Within such a climate, human rights provide the warrant for both the international policing of the global South and its mortgaging to northern economic centers, as well as to the many other instruments of neoimperial hegemony. This syndrome by no means portends the obsolescence or demise of human rights, as some foretell. However, it goes without saying that much of the emancipatory potential of human rights talk has been forfeited, directly eroding the hopes and dreams that spawned the contemporary human rights movement in the middle of the twentieth century.

This book has contended with precisely the sorts of linguistic and other types of atrophy that Roy decries. At the same time, I have ventured a tentative yes to Roy's two concluding queries—that is, a yes to the notion that it is possible to "reverse the process" of such stagnation and decay. I have looked in particular to both narrative literature and a phenomenology of embodiment in order to craft that answer, and those dual enterprises have together facilitated what I have termed an "embodied politics of reading." Such a model for explaining the varied commerce between aesthetics and politics implicitly marshals a defense of a specific kind of literary engagement, which I have lauded for its ability to interrupt the cycles of pollution and inertia that progressively compromise the vocabulary of human rights. As such, phenomenologically charged reading practices have allowed me to pursue essential clearings within the multiplying languages of human rights—clearings within which something irreplaceable about social justice re-emerges, paradoxical and transitory though it may be. Much as Roy bewails the enfeebled "imagination" that has come to regulate our current political and economic world order, I, too, have affirmed the irreplaceable work of imaginative experience. Namely, I have suggested how the literary medium might replenish and recuperate our increasingly depleted cultural and social imaginaries, counteracting the very patterns of which Roy despairs.

On the one hand, then, literature has provided a forum in which to interrogate the reigning assumptions about selfhood that sustain liberal articulations of human rights. This activity of critique has required that we mine the exceptions and foreclosures naturalized by dominant human rights discourses and norms. Each of this book's literary case studies has therefore indicted liberal topographies of the human for, to draw again on Roy's reflections, promulgating a "thin," "constricted" portrait of selfhood and community alike. This anemic account of the subject manifests itself within a collection of interrelated liberal tenets concerning freedom, individual autonomy, the sovereignty of reason, equality, the construct of the person, and the rule of law. But first and foremost, I have examined how the dual myths of bodily integrity and human dignity conspire to legislate many of the liberal democratic sphere's historical as well as contemporary exclusions. These twinned enabling fictions are, without question, "indispensable"—to also recall Coetzee's language, which opened this book—to the explanatory authority of human rights. They undoubtedly represent crucial measures within the broad architecture of human rights; however, as benchmarks, they also quarantine and negate other, equally indispensable facets of human experience. This, in turn, gives rise to the paradox that while the premium on bodily integrity may be vital to the legibility of human rights discourses and norms, it has also served to author a strangely truncated, bloodless, and decorporealized vision of the subject.

On the other hand, literature has simultaneously provided the vehicle for far more than critique. An embodied politics of reading has also opened up and thereby verified those corporeal dimensions of cognition and expression that liberal formulations of human rights tend to either nullify or police. Whereas the enabling fictions of dignity and corporeal integrity submerge and discredit the multiform rhythms and intensities of embodiment, literature has helped to excavate those very energies of selfhood. To such ends, I have argued that an imaginative remapping of human rights must necessarily begin with aesthetic experience—with its exemplary capacity to harness the body's many faculties of participation and belonging. All in all, such a literary-theoretical odyssey might thereby resuscitate distinctly embodied habits of cognition to illumine, in Merleau-Ponty's words, the "spark which means we share a common fate."[2]

My doubled agenda of critique and refurbishment has consequently established the profit of an ontology of the embodied subject for negotiating broad questions about social justice. Yet the questions might still remain: What sort of ethic, or wider fabric of commitments, can ultimately be extracted from such a politics of reading? What values and ideals are ancillary to a hermeneutic attention to embodiment, as well as the onus to theoretically comprehend the phenomenal field that actuates embodied cognition? Might such an account of aesthetics nourish a distinct cosmology, for instance, of the type at issue in *The God of Small Things*? And how might such a vision of social justice be located within the larger intellectual and political evolution of human rights? Can a model of social justice grounded in phenomenology claim cousins or antecedents in such a history? In conclusion, I'd like to suggest that the ecological conception of just coexistence that I have developed does in fact correspond with—and therefore demands that we revisit—such an earlier moment in the emergence of human rights.

Looking backward to a preceding phase in the globalization of human rights is by no means contrary to the spirit of phenomenology, which also founds philosophical inquiry on a kind of return. Within the problematics that have occupied this book, we might, then, conceive of that itinerary of return as fulfilling dual functions. First, viewing it as a type of homecoming can affirm and reinforce our sense of what human rights norms should both nurture and portend. Second, that effort might help to revitalize the discourses of human rights in the midst of their semantic colonization. In other words, if human rights have, to again cite Roy, "metastasized" into an often predatory, obstructionist idiom, such a return might both "downsize" human rights and restore what our contemporary era has squandered.[3]

Here, the widely cited words in the epigraph above—delivered by Eleanor Roosevelt at the United Nations in 1958, on the tenth anniversary of the UDHR—offer an appropriate point of departure for such a project of renewal and recovery. Roosevelt asks, "Where, after all, do human rights begin?"[4] And she answers that question by invoking an assortment of sentiments that tellingly echo those that this book has celebrated. Roosevelt, too, advances the notion that "small places, close to home" are necessary in fostering appreciation for human rights, and she furthermore describes their normative force as contingent on the production of "meaning." Of course, the fact that Roosevelt at once appeals to a rhetoric of equality and progress should give pause. Nevertheless, in the midst of that appeal, she heralds the sorts of commitments that both phenomenology and my literary examples have exhibited. It is in this respect that Roosevelt's language of "meaning" is significant. Whereas she might have cited the juridical bindingness or legal authority of human rights, she instead avers their "meaning." In doing so, she asserts that their force cannot derive strictly from the antiseptic realms of politics and law but instead must exceed those static, rule-bound frameworks. This construal of human rights importantly casts them as articles of faith and the property of a certain kind of imagination.

Of greatest importance, however, Roosevelt enlists the idea of "smallness" as a cipher for her distinctly modest approach to human rights. No doubt such a reduced purview stands in marked contrast with the totalizing scale and ambitions of global politics, and we might thus distill from it a number of rebukes. Whereas human rights discourses have inspired grand narratives of achievement and success, Roosevelt cautions against such bold aspirations, instead emphasizing what their epic proportions overlook. In this way, her words both forecast and forewarn against the infirmity that has only increasingly come to afflict human rights talk, with great detriment. However, Roosevelt explicitly countermands her own embrace of "smallness" to those cycles of misappropriation and inflation that have overtaken the languages of human rights. And in doing so, Roosevelt extols precisely those spaces that liberalism has conventionally expelled from its definitions of politics. For Roosevelt, human rights must originate within the local, domestic, routine, and familiar—as opposed to the public, all-encompassing domains that political theory typically valorizes. Moreover, she explains these sites of meaning as "so close and small that they cannot be seen on any maps of the world." By situating respect for human rights within such scenes eclipsed within politics, law, and history alike, she validates the worth of private, commonplace, unremarkable lives. And by no means last, while Roosevelt does not overtly chide her audience, that is in fact the thrust of her words. Indeed, they are excerpted from a speech titled "In Your Hands: A Guide to Community Action." In effect, her insistence that human rights must be forged "close to home" effectively endows us with primary responsibility for their precarious future.

Roosevelt, Roy, Merleau-Ponty: these thinkers each converge on shared ideas concerning social justice. Let me, then, look in conclusion to Merleau-Ponty's strikingly similar reflections in the wake of World War II, when power politics were again newly carving up the world. As Merleau-Ponty comments, "Our era is destined to judge itself not from on high, which is mean and bitter, but in a certain sense from below."[5] Merleau-Ponty here equally espouses an ethic that is local, ecological, and inflected with humility. In this way, his remonstrance, too, pertains to the contemporary discourses of human rights, as they increasingly disburse "mean and bitter" judgments from "on high." Merleau-Ponty, too, urges us to reorient talk of human rights closer to the ground, away from both the idealism and the platitudes in which politics often deals. He thereby makes a parallel appeal to retrieving what our era has lost sight of, defending the need to re-anchor our expectations for social justice in the real-world challenges presented by the singular, ordinary, and unexceptional. To therefore end on the same note that I began, the proliferation of human rights discourses and norms is often levied as a narrative of triumph—whether of law, of international diplomacy, or of a particular conception of the human. Yet precisely through a sustained attention to the "small things" and "small places" that make up the lived realities of human experience might we begin to recast human rights with reference to their appropriate provenance—auguring what we might call a globalization of human rights from below.

❧ Notes

Introduction

1. Cited in Ignatieff, *Human Rights as Politics and Idolatry,* 53. There is an ever more voluminous body of scholarship that weighs in on the intellectual history of human rights. See, for instance, Barnett, *Empire of Humanity;* Moyn, *The Last Utopia;* Beitz, *The Idea of Human Rights;* Normand and Zaidi, *Human Rights at the UN;* and Hunt, *Inventing Human Rights.*

2. Hannah Arendt's treatment of this paradox in *The Origins of Totalitarianism* remains perhaps the most widely cited.

3. Such a characterization of human rights is often partner to the charge of their cultural imperialism, although that basis for attacking human rights is increasingly seen as outmoded. Adamantia Pollis and Peter Schwab are usually credited with first launching that critique with *Human Rights* and *Toward a Human Rights Framework,* although they have since revised that position. See Pollis, "Cultural Relativism Revisited"; Pollis and Schwab, *Human Rights.* Yet for many scholars the cultural relativism critique still carries substantial force, for instance, as Makua Mutua deems the human rights movement "a civilizing crusade aimed primarily at the third world." See *Human Rights,* 19.

4. See Scott, *Only Paradoxes to Offer.* Among countless other sources that construe human rights in terms of paradox, see Douzinas, *The End of Human Rights;* Slaughter, *Human Rights, Inc.*, 11–13; Brown, "Suffering the Paradoxes of Rights"; Glendon, "Propter Honoris Respectum," 1171; Parekh, *Hannah Arendt and the Challenge of Modernity.*

5. *Giving Offense,* 14.

6. Article 1 of the UDHR unequivocally proclaims that "all human beings are born free and equal in dignity and rights." In law, the concept of dignity is central to the juridical processes and legal documents of a wide variety of nation-states, including, among many others, Finland, Brazil, Angola, Peru, Hungary, Canada, New Zealand, and Australia. See Bagaric and Allan, "The Vacuous Concept of Dignity," 261–63. Roberto Andorno similarly observes how international human rights instruments repeatedly invoke the concept of dignity. See "Human Dignity and Human Rights."

Discussions of dignity and human rights are voluminous, but for a historical and philosophical overview, see Kretzmer and Klein, *The Concept of Human Dignity in Human Rights Discourse.* For the normative force of the concept of dignity within human rights discourse, see Schachter, "Human Dignity as a Normative Concept." For the converse argument that dignity is a "vacuous concept" that "is used by academics, judges, and legislators when rational justifications have been exhausted," see

Bagaric and Allan, "The Vacuous Concept of Dignity," 260. See also Singer, *Applied Ethics,* 228. Jack Donnelly does not deny the shared nature of dignity; however, he disputes the notion that such an ideal is necessarily linked to the concept of rights. *Universal Human Rights in Theory and Practice.*

7. For instance, Mary Ann Glendon attributes such a function to dignity, which for her unifies the many disparate rights enumerated in the UDHR. See "Propter Honoris Respectum," 1175.

8. For such an argument, see Douzinas, *The End of Human Rights,* 217.

9. This terminology owes much to Ian Baucom, even though Baucom argues that what he calls "an Enlightenment theory of the human" supports human rights. See *Specters of the Atlantic,* 56. Likewise, for an analysis of "the liberal rights tradition," see Shapiro, *The Evolution of Rights in Legal Theory,* 11. See also Kahn, *Putting Liberalism in Its Place.*

10. For such language, see Cheah, *Inhuman Conditions.*

11. According to Benhabib, the international migration of human rights discourses has promoted a "creative jurisgenerative politics," wherein standardized, rote connotations undergo revival and amplification, especially when requisitioned by nondominant actors. *Another Cosmopolitanism,* 49.

12. See Ignatieff, *Human Rights as Politics and Idolatry,* 90. Upendra Baxi describes the reality wherein more and more issues and concerns fall under the purview of human rights as "overproduction," leading her to characterize the label *human rights* as a "floating signifier." *The Future of Human Rights,* 66, 40. For a discussion of the "open-endedness" and "exhortatory nature" of human rights instruments, see Cheah, *Inhuman Conditions,* 154.

13. As Wai Chee Dimock notes, "The language of rights is a language burdened by little awareness of conflicting, overlapping, or incommensurate claims. For that reason, it also has no ability to predict its own limits, no provision for any sort of self-qualifying responsiveness." "Rethinking Space, Rethinking Rights," 254–55. Ignatieff likewise characterizes the problem as a tendency to think of rights as "trumps" rather than as a "basis for deliberation." *Human Rights as Politics and Idolatry,* 95.

14. See *Modern Social Imaginaries.* See also Appadurai, *Modernity at Large,* 58.

15. See Kahn, *The Cultural Study of Law.* For a statement of the need to "tak[e] seriously the social character of human rights," see Dallmayr, "'Asian Values' and Global Human Rights," 177.

16. *The Alchemy of Race and Rights,* 149.

17. As such, this book resuscitates many of the Critical Legal Studies movement's allegations about rights talk within the American context. CLS scholars commonly critiqued rights for their encouragement of egoism, alliance with consumerism and capitalism, silencing of competing values, and absolutist rhetoric, among other complaints. See Glendon, *Rights Talk.* Other important CLS thinkers include Janet E. Halley, Richard W. Bauman, Duncan Kennedy, David W. Kennedy, Andrew Altman, John Finnis, and Roberto Unger. For the relevance of CLS critiques to human rights, see Kennedy, *The Dark Sides of Virtue.* See also Kelman, *A Guide to Critical Legal Studies.* Moreover, it was not foreign within the CLS movement to appeal to phenomenology as an exit from poststructuralism in staging a critique and recuperation of rights. While his scholarship does not extensively develop the implications of Merleau-Ponty's thought, this was Peter Gabel's approach in *The Bank Teller and Other Essays,* 43.

18. For examples of such scholarship, see Caruth, *Trauma;* Felman, *The Juridical Unconscious;* LaCapra, *History and Its Limits;* Scarry, *The Body in Pain;* Fassin and Rechtman, *The Empire of Trauma;* and Cubilié, *Women Witnessing Terror.*

19. See Keymer, "Sentimental Fiction," 578; Bell, *Sentimentalism, Ethics, and the Culture of Feeling,* 2; Hume, *A Treatise of Human Nature,* 371. See also Todd, *Sensibility,* 3. Julie Stone Peters broadly views the recent attention to human rights by literary critics as staging a return to eighteenth-century views about the "humanist union of literature and rights." "'Literature,' the 'Rights of Man,' and Narratives of Atrocity," 274.

20. Schaffer and Smith, *Human Rights and Narrated Lives.* See also Dawes, *That the World May Know;* Goldberg, *Beyond Terror.*

21. *Human Rights, Inc.,* 39. Barbara Harlow also explains of the UDHR, "Its thirty articles translated the standard literary paradigm of individual versus society and the narrative conventions of emplotment and closure by mapping an identification of the individual within a specifically international construction of rights and responsibilities. The Declaration, that is, can be read as recharting the trajectory and peripeties of the classic *Bildungsroman."* See *Barred,* 252–53. For the idea of an "ethics of subject formation," see also Ong, *Flexible Citizenship;* and Grewal, *Transnational America.*

22. *The World of Perception,* 81.

23. *Summertime,* 198–99, 231.

24. See "Editor's Column."

25. Texts commonly cited for offering overly enthusiastic models of globalization include Appadurai, *Modernity at Large;* Appiah, *Cosmopolitanism;* Bhabha, *The Location of Culture;* Hardt and Negri, *Empire.*

26. See Gikandi, "Globalization and the Claims of Postcoloniality," 639.

27. See Glendon, "Propter Honoris Respectum."

28. *On Cosmopolitanism and Forgiveness,* 31–32, 43.

29. See Derrida, *Rogues,* 38.

30. For a related argument, see Dillon, *Semiological Reductionism,* 10, 32.

31. For a critique of canon formation within postcolonial studies, see Lazarus, "The Politics of Postcolonial Modernism."

32. *Transnational America,* 122.

33. See Appadurai, *Fear of Small Numbers,* 65.

34. Indeed, it is tempting to link such a critical orientation to the elision of embodiment within much Foucauldian and Marxist thought. As critics have argued, Foucauldian treatments of the body have often tended to reduce it to its exteriority, regarding it as a mere surface or medium on which compulsory norms become inscribed. See *History of Sexuality,* 145–46.

35. Said, *Humanism and Democratic Criticism,* 66, 77.

36. Ibid., 630.

37. Appiah, "Is the 'Post-' in the 'Postcolonial' the 'Post-' in the 'Postmodern'?" For the inverse argument that postmodernism needed to "become postcolonial," see Quayson, *Postcolonialism,* 154.

38. *Humanism and Democratic Criticism,* 22.

39. Ibid., 11, 61.

40. No doubt my theoretical project might equally be construed as a revival of certain currents within postcolonial theory. For instance, Frantz Fanon's thought is characterized by highly visceral and affective imagery and language.

41. *Undoing Gender,* 179.

42. Coole and Frost, *New Materialisms.*

43. For different statements of such a project, whether self-consciously grounded in phenomenology or not, see Mbembe, *On the Postcolony,* 5–8; Ahmed, *Strange Encounters;* Gandhi, *Affective Communities;* Radhakrishnan, *Theory in an Uneven World,* 21–24; Schueller, *Locating Race.*

44. I thank Simon During for the phrase the "experiential turn" and the idea that it might offer an umbrella term for capturing these shifts. Among the works I refer to are Coole, *Merleau-Ponty and Modern Politics;* Bennett, *The Enchantment of Modern Life;* During, *Modern Enchantments;* Connolly, *Why I Am Not a Secularist;* Asad, *Formations of the Secular;* Mahmood, *Politics of Piety;* Hirschkind, *The Ethical Soundscape;* Berlant, *Cruel Optimism;* Lakoff and Johnson, *Philosophy in the Flesh;* Johnson, *The Meaning of the Body.*

1. Bodily Integrity and Its Exclusions

1. *The Origins of Totalitarianism,* 297. For related discussions of this tension, see, among many others, Balfour and Cadava, "The Claims of Human Rights," 280; Darian-Smith and Fitzpatrick, "Introduction," 6; Asad, *Formations of the Secular,* 129; Rancière, "Who Is the Subject of the Rights of Man?"; and Benhabib, *The Rights of Others,* 11.

2. Arjun Appadurai argues that pressure to use the rhetoric of human rights has only heightened the self-purifying tendencies of nationalism. *Fear of Small Numbers,* 65.

3. Grosz, *Volatile Bodies,* 5. See also Mensch, *Embodiments,* 4.

4. See Cheah, "The Body of the Law," 3. Cheah also discusses an embodied theory of social justice, although one that emphasizes the "structures of violence" that forge bodily identity (23–25).

5. *Friends of Interpretable Objects,* 108.

6. Ibid., 110. Likewise, Roberto Esposito argues that the development of the legal category of the "person" can be traced to account for the law's nullification of embodiment and ensuing sociopolitical exclusions. "The Dispositive of the Person."

7. *Imaginary Bodies,* 109.

8. These limits are also visible within human rights witnessing. For instance, Richard A. Wilson makes such an argument about the human rights report, which favors "realist and legalistic" renditions of truth decontextualized from key events. "Representing Human Rights Violations."

9. For related arguments, see Brooks, "Policing Stories," 32; Felman, *The Juridical Unconscious,* 5.

10. *Powers of Freedom,* 69, 87.

11. For a discussion of how bodily integrity precedes the attribution of human dignity, see Dean, *The Frail Social Body,* 1.

12. Scott, *Only Paradoxes to Offer,* 5–6. Scott's anxiety about the abstract logic of human rights has many historical precursors. Edmund Burke complained of the French *Déclaration des droits de l'Homme et du citoyen* that rights would lead people to become "intoxicated...with the powers of abstract thought." Quoted in Waldron, *"Nonsense upon Stilts,"* 88. See also Hesse and Post, "Introduction," 25.

13. Scott, *Only Paradoxes to Offer,* 7.

14. For studies that investigate the symbolic connection between the body politic and the body natural in the work of early modern political theorists such as Edward Forsett and Thomas Hobbes, see Kantorowicz, *The King's Two Bodies;* Hale, *The Body Politic;* and Rolls, *The Theory of the King's Two Bodies.* For scholarship that applies this historical link to theorize the contemporary nation-state and its connection to literature, see Aldama, *Violence and the Body;* Russell, *Reading Embodied Citizenship;* and Keown, *Postcolonial Pacific Writing.* See also Cohen, *A Body Worth Defending* and Santner, *The Royal Remains.* In *Spectral Nationality,* Pheng Cheah contemplates the function of what he calls the "organismic metaphor" within both postcolonial nationalisms and the genre of the Bildungsroman, the conventions of which many of my literary case studies display.

15. As Davis explains, it ironically also saw "in the perfectibility of the human body a Utopian hope for social improvement." "Constructing Normalcy," 8–9.

16. See Hubbard, "Abortion and Disability;" Bérubé, "Citizenship and Disability;" Turner, *Vulnerability and Human Rights.*

17. Connolly, *Why I Am Not a Secularist,* 26.

18. Warner, *Publics and Counterpublics,* 165–68.

19. Ibid., 165. See also Asad, *Formations of the Secular,* 184.

20. For such an argument, see Chakrabarty, *Habitations of Modernity,* 105. For the view that Enlightenment discourses of progress silence suffering, see also Baxi, *The Future of Human Rights,* 35.

21. Asad, *Formations of the Secular,* 84.

22. Grosz, *Volatile Bodies,* 22–23.

23. For the antipathy to wasteful pain within civilizing missions, see Asad, *Formations of the Secular,* 111.

24. *The Origins of Totalitarianism,* 295–96. Subsequent page numbers for this work appear in the text.

25. Ibid., 297. For a book-length study of Arendt's engagement with the many paradoxes presented by human rights, see Parekh, *Hannah Arendt and the Challenge of Modernity.*

26. One possible explanation would be that Arendt's focus on the category of citizenship and other technologies of law blinds her to an exit from those impasses, as well as to the distressing oversights within her own thought.

27. Hume, *A Treatise of Human Nature,* 371. See also Todd, *Sensibility,* 3. Many such eighteenth-century accounts of sentiment asserted its embodied character, although not in ways that rendered sentiment egalitarian or universally shared. See Brewer, "Sentiment and Sensibility," 24–28.

28. *Regarding the Pain of Others,* 39, 102.

29. Richard Rorty has maintained that the "sentiments" and "sentimental education" inspired by "sad and sentimental stories" should be segregated from the operations of reason. "Human Rights, Rationality, and Sentimentality," 122–25. In contrast, Martha Nussbaum configures emotion as merely one facet of reason that corresponds with a distinctly liberal vision of political life. See *Poetic Justice,* 121. As Nussbaum explains, the brand of feeling awakened by literature must be "developed in a specifically democratic way, as an essential part of thinking and judging well in a pluralistic democratic society." *Cultivating Humanity,* 95–96.

30. Along such lines, critics complain that trauma studies—with its emphasis on oral testimony and speech—is invested in Eurocentric assumptions about selfhood that write off other cultures' conventions surrounding mourning and memory. For a survey of such critiques, see Mallot, "Body Politics and the Body Politic"; Schaffer and Smith, *Human Rights and Narrated Lives,* 22–23.

31. Scarry, *The Body in Pain,* 4, 13, 29.

32. Ibid., 4.

33. For example, see Asad, *Formations of the Secular,* 80–81.

34. For related arguments about speech, see Slaughter, "A Question of Narration;" Slaughter, "Narration in International Human Rights Law"; and Lyotard, "The Other's Rights."

35. Notably, Slaughter carefully distinguishes this construct from other Enlightenment-based formulations of the human. Ibid., 19. Subsequent page numbers for this work appear in the text.

36. To decipher the contemporary permutations of human rights rhetoric is thus to revisit the tried and true tropes of Edward Said's *Orientalism* and other studies extending his enduring work. See also Spurr, *The Rhetoric of Empire.* For a critique of how humanitarian reportage "essentializes" its victims, see Fassin, "Humanitarianism as a Politics of Life," 512.

37. "Publics and Counterpublics," 72, 90.

38. Mortenson and Relin, *Three Cups of Tea.* Notably, the book led the *New York Times* bestseller list for twenty weeks during 2008 and is increasingly incorporated into American high school curricula.

39. For a related argument, see Dawes, *That the World May Know,* 34.

40. Betty Mahmoody's 1991 *Not Without My Daughter* here offers another example of a text that elides anxieties about Islam into a fascination with an infectious Third World.

41. For a discussion of *The Kite Runner,* as well as the former President George W. Bush's investment in the novel, see Slaughter, *Human Rights, Inc.,* 320–21.

42. "Savages, Victims, Saviors," 202–3. See also Mamdani, "The Politics of Naming." For the argument that "the story of an encounter with unfathomable evil is only intelligible through race," see Razack, *Dark Threats and White Knights,* 23.

43. Spurr, *The Rhetoric of Empire,* 76–108. At once, many such texts psychologize the wrongdoer, investigating the various environmental and developmental factors that can allow an individual to commit inhumane acts. Ishmael Beah's *A Long Way Gone* (2008) is particularly revealing in this respect. Beah's memoir follows first the massacre of his entire village and then his conscription into fighting Sierra Leone's civil war, documenting the consequences of a prolonged exposure to violence on childhood emotional well-being.

44. Even Mortenson is suggested in *Three Cups of Tea* to be especially well suited temperamentally to deal with Pakistani inefficiency because of his own "non-linear," less regimented relationship to modern time (4).

45. *The Postcolonial Exotic,* 33.

46. For the argument that the consumption of human rights narratives "reinvent(s) imagined securities" and "dispel[s] the fear of otherness by containing it[, which] becomes a means to the reader's own self-affirmation as an empowered agent," see Schaffer and Smith, *Human Rights and Narrated Lives,* 25.

47. See LaCapra, "Traumatropisms."

48. Indeed, *Kabul Beauty School*'s subtitle, displayed not on its cover but on the internal title page, additionally exploits the veil to read "An American Woman Goes behind the Veil."

49. *The Politics of Piety,* 165–66.

50. McClintock, *Imperial Leather,* 23. For a similar argument that "the eroticization of pain is merely one of the ways in which the modern self attempts to secure its elusive foundation," see Asad, *Formations of the Secular,* 119–20.

2. Embodying Human Rights

1. Moran, *Introduction to Phenomenology,* 398.

2. Ibid., 410.

3. Coole, *Merleau-Ponty and Modern Politics,* 7.

4. Moran, *Introduction to Phenomenology,* 395.

5. Dermot Moran's Routledge *Introduction to Phenomenology* bemoans that, were it not for Merleau-Ponty's early death, "there is no doubt that he would have been regarded as the most brilliant of contemporary French philosophers" (391). For the many rejoinders that Foucault, Lacan, and other poststructuralists made to Merleau-Ponty, see Carman and Hansen, introduction to *Cambridge Companion.* Carman and Hansen credit Gilles Deleuze as unique in acknowledging a debt to Merleau-Ponty. See also Coole, *Merleau-Ponty and Modern Politics,* 105; Dillon, *Semiological Reductionism,* 38.

6. See "Merleau-Ponty and the Touch of Malebranche," 181–205.

7. Young's essay is published in *On Female Bodily Experience.* See also Weiss, *Body Images.*

8. *An Ethics of Sexual Difference,* 151, 164, 174. Differently, Kaja Silverman argues that Merleau-Ponty lends "chronological priority [to] self-display over seeing." See *World Spectators,* 137. For an analysis of Merleau-Ponty that studies his metaphor of light, see Vasseleu, *Textures of Light.*

9. Elizabeth Grosz rebukes him for a wholesale "avoidance of the question of sexual difference and specificity." See *Volatile Bodies,* 103, 108. See also Stawarska, "From the Body Proper to Flesh," 91–106, 92.

10. For example, see Ahmed, *Queer Phenomenology.*

11. Richard Shusterman refers to Merleau-Ponty as "something like the patron saint of the body." See "The Silent, Limping Body of Philosophy," 151–80, 151.

12. See Coole, "The Intertia of Matter," 101.

13. Elizabeth Grosz refers to them as wholly "prediscursive," although their status is somewhat more complicated. *Volatile Bodies,* 96.

14. Coole, *Merleau-Ponty and Modern Politics,* 7.

15. *Sense and Non-sense,* 50.

16. See Levin, "Justice in the Flesh," 35–44, 37.

17. *The Phenomenology of Perception,* 173.

18. *Sense and Non-sense,* 97.

19. *The Phenomenology of Perception,* xv.

20. *The Visible and the Invisible,* 136.

21. "Eye and Mind," 123.

22. Coole describes this as "a dialectical approach that recognizes the reciprocity and entwining of material and symbolic forms." *Merleau-Ponty and Modern Politics*, 12.

23. *The Phenomenology of Perception*, xiii–ix. Elsewhere, Merleau-Ponty describes how an embodied consciousness subverts the insidious tendencies of scientific rationalism to disclose the mutual affinity of all life, or how "all the beings which objective thought placed at a distance draw singularly nearer to me." *Sense and Non-sense*, 94.

24. *The Visible and the Invisible*, 138.

25. For such a term, see Ahmed, *Strange Encounters*, 49.

26. *The Visible and the Invisible*, 143.

27. "Justice in the Flesh," 38, 35.

28. *Merleau-Ponty and Modern Politics*, 225. Jean-Philippe Deranty also defends Merleau-Ponty's critique of humanism, along with the ethics it purveys, over Agamben's thought in "Witnessing the Inhuman."

29. *Strange Encounters*, 47. Sara Ahmed additionally foregrounds the "encounter" as a way to avoid reading the body as privatized and isolated (an impulse that she indicts in much feminist theory), and instead oriented toward "inter-embodiment." Ibid.

30. *Merleau-Ponty's Ontology*, 166. See also Grosz, *Volatile Bodies*, 100.

31. *Sense and Non-sense*, 90; *The Visible and the Invisible*, 152.

32. Some philosophers argue that he instead introduces a "third term" between immanence and transcendence. See Wrathall, "Motives, Reasons, Causes."

33. For a classic discussion of the polarities inscribed within colonialist discourse, see Nandy, *The Intimate Enemy*. See also Fitzpatrick, *The Mythology of Modern Law*.

34. Debates about whether or not Merleau-Ponty's phenomenology results in another form of anthropomorphism abound. For the argument that his thought does yield such problematic consequences, see Radhakrishnan, *History, the Human, and the World Between*, 197. For the inverse argument that his thought actually produces a "decentering of human reflexivity," see Dillon, *Merleau-Ponty's Ontology* (xiii).

35. See Dillon, *Merleau-Ponty's Ontology*, xii, xvi.

36. For example, see Cheyfitz, "Balancing the Earth."

37. *Nature*, 85–86.

38. *The Phenomenology of Perception*, 79.

39. *The World of Perception*, 50–51.

40. *Sense and Non-sense*, 313.

41. For the argument that "the human rights violation is constructed in opposition to the 'common crime,'" see Wilson, "Representing Human Rights Violations," 141.

42. Some philosophers of social justice importantly challenge human rights norms precisely by thus advocating for their substitution with alternative measures of human flourishing and progress, which for instance is the rationale behind Martha Nussbaum and Amartya Sen's capabilities approach. Sen argues, "If we see development in terms of enhancement of human living and the freedom to live the kind of life that we have reason to value, then there is a strong case for focusing on 'functionings' and the 'capability' to function." "Conceptualizing and Measuring Poverty," 36. See also Nussbaum, "Capabilities and Human Rights."

43. *Humanism and Terror*, xxxviii.

44. *Nature*, 208.

45. *Sense and Non-sense,* 52; *The Phenomenology of Perception,* vii.

46. For such an argument, see also Alcoff, *Visible Identities,* 110–11.

47. Quotation from *Sense and Non-sense,* 87.

48. Quotation from *The Phenomenology of Perception,* 71.

49. *Sense and Non-sense,* 179.

50. *Nature,* 129.

51. *Why I Am Not a Secularist,* 3.

52. *Politics of Piety,* 121.

53. "Religious Reason and Secular Affect," 841–42.

54. *The World of Perception,* 40.

55. *The Visible and the Invisible,* 149.

56. *The World of Perception,* 75.

57. That said, some argue that Merleau-Ponty's "deep commentaries on the arts…generate no philosophy of art in themselves," a conclusion this analysis disagrees with. For such an argument, see Gilmore, "Between Art and Philosophy."

58. *Sense and Non-sense,* 28.

59. "Eye and Mind," 123.

60. *The Visible and the Invisible,* 143.

61. Quotation from *The World of Perception,* 41.

62. "Merleau-Ponty and the Touch of Malebranche," 193.

63. *The Visible and the Invisible,* 152.

3. Constituting the Liberal Subject of Rights

1. For such a discussion of the incident, see Chakravorty, "The Rushdie Incident as Law-and-Literature Parable."

2. The quoted phrase is from Frantz Fanon's *The Wretched of the Earth.* For the argument that Saleem is an allegory for the nation, see Hogan, "*Midnight's Children*"; Kortenaar, *Self, Nation, and Text.* Kane reads Saleem as a "metaphor of the body politic" in "The Migrant Intellectual and the Body of History," 95. See also Gorra, *After Empire,* 111; Rege, "Victim into Protagonist?"; Thompson, "Superman and Salman Rushdie." For the idea that the novel "reveals a profound discomfort with the very idea of postcolonial national identity," see Israel, *Outlandish,* 137. Likewise, for a critique of the ways the novel genders nationalism, see Natarajan, "Woman, Nation, and Narration." For the argument that Rushdie is "suspicious" of the nation-state for its fundamental inability to include women's perspectives, see Heffernan, "Apocalyptic Narratives," 472.

3. Moyn argues that decolonization should not be characterized as a human rights movement. "Why Anticolonialism Wasn't a Human Rights Movement."

4. For a treatment of the novel through the interpretive lens of "mourning, melancholy, and nostalgia," see Chiu, "Melancholy and Human Rights," 25. Timothy Brennan notably interprets "the disease of nationalism" as a question "above all of human rights." *Salman Rushdie and the Third World,* 98–99.

5. Various critics see Rushdie as putting forth the idea of a *secular* nationalism. See Singh, "Secularist Faith in Salman Rushdie's *Midnight's Children*"; Kortenaar, *Self, Nation, and Text.* But on the other hand, other critics decipher Rushdie's "target" as "secular rationalism." See Booker, "*Midnight's Children,* History, and Complexity,"

294. Indeed, Rushdie has been quite outspoken in his nonfictional writings about both the "secular ideal" in *Midnight's Children* and the need for secularism in India. See *Imaginary Homelands,* 16.

6. "Declarations of Independence," 9–10.

7. See Kane, "The Migrant Intellectual and the Body of History"; Su, "Epic of Failure," 546; and Singh, "Secularist Faith in Salman Rushdie's *Midnight's Children,*" 158.

8. See Heffernan, "Apocalyptic Narratives," 473; Reder, "Rewriting History and Identity," 237.

9. Critics have observed that the Midnight Children's Conference is an obvious corollary to the Congress. See Gorra, *After Empire* 113–14, 140.

10. As David Lipscomb notes, Rushdie had Stanley Wolpert's *A New History of India* next to him while writing the novel. Wolpert describes the Constitution as exhibiting "Nehru's personal ideals" and quotes from its preamble that its purposes were "to secure to all its citizens . . . JUSTICE social, economic, and political; LIBERTY of thought, expression, belief, faith and worship; EQUALITY of status and opportunity; and to promote among them all FRATERNITY assuring the dignity of the individual and the unity of the Nation." Wolpert, *A New History of India,* 359.

11. Austin, *The Indian Constitution,* 50. Many historians regard Nehru as the main proponent of the ideology of rights as it appears in the Indian Constitution. See Setalvad, *The Indian Constitution,* 214; Wolpert, *A New History,* 359.

12. Ghosh, *The Constitution of India,* 68.

13. Sripati, "Human Rights in India," 96.

14. See Ghosh, *The Constitution of India,* 69–70; Setalvad, *The Indian Constitution.* In 1988, Rushdie published a rather vehement editorial in support of the Charter 88 movement in Britain. In the essay, Rushdie cites the UDHR and human rights as constructs that are vague but nonetheless "we all know what we mean by." See *Imaginary Homelands,* 165. Subsequently, in October 2000, Rushdie celebrated the newly adopted Human Rights Act. See *Step across This Line,* 307–9.

15. See Austin, *The Indian Constitution;* Ghosh, *The Constitution of India,* 75. The right to property was also removed from the Constitution by amendment in 1978, see Sripati, "Human Rights in India," 96–97.

16. *The Jaguar Smile: A Nicaraguan Journey* is overtly preoccupied with the function of a national constitution, as well as with human rights. Rushdie frames the crisis in Nicaragua as being about both "human rights" and "self-determination" (17–19), and he devotes an entire chapter of the book to the Nicaraguan constitution. He begins the chapter in language strikingly pertinent to this discussion: "The most important task facing the National Assembly was the drafting of the new Nicaraguan constitution" (70). Rushdie next catalogs the various legal "rights" and thereafter proceeds to bemoan that fact that "as long as the state of emergency lasted, the constitution would be little more than a piece of paper; the President would retain most of the power, and a number of civil rights would be suspended" (74), which he then immediately relates to Gandhi's emergency.

17. Quoted in Nehru, *The Unity of India,* 139.

18. See Juraga, "'The Mirror of Us All,'" 169; Merivale, "Saleem Fathered by Oskar," 86; and Kortenaar, *Self, Nation, and Text,* 65–76.

19. Slaughter, *Human Rights, Inc.* Likewise, for a discussion of the postcolonial Bildungsroman and its connection to the organismic metaphor, see Cheah, chapter 5 of *Spectral Nationality.*

20. See Kortenaar, "Postcolonial Ekphrasis," 237, 243. For the argument that it is "an invitation to conquer foreign lands [that] mortifies Saleem," see Brennan, *Salman Rushdie and the Third World,* 82.

21. For the novel's gender politics, see Chakrabarty, *Habitations of Modernity,* 29–30; Hogan, *"Midnight's Children,"* 530.

22. The rule of law and a judiciary were historically promoted as "one of the first marks of progress along European lines" and mechanisms for imparting broad norms tied to "civility." Viswanathan, *Masks of Conquest,* 92. See also Gikandi, *Maps of Englishness;* Fitzpatrick, *The Mythology of Modern Law;* and Chakrabarty, "Postcoloniality and the Artifice of History," 5–6.

23. "'In the Name of Politics,'" 36.

24. For the idea that the term *riot* arose in the late nineteenth century as a strategy of colonial management, see Das, *Life and Words,* 205–6. For a discussion of "the fear of the mob within the modern form of democracy" in *Midnight's Children,* see Bahri, *Native Intelligence,* 167.

25. Merleau-Ponty, *The Phenomenology of Perception,* xv.

26. "Postcoloniality and the Artifice of History," 11–13.

27. Ghosh, *The Constitution of India,* 68.

28. Austin, *The Indian Constitution,* 317–18.

29. For the argument that the children's congress adjudicates the merits of secular nationalism and the Habermasian public sphere, see Strand, "Gandhian Communalism and the Midnight Children's Conference," 997.

30. *The Nation and Its Fragments,* 55.

31. In a single year of the emergency, estimates are that 8 million sterilizations were performed, with 1.7 million in September 1976 alone. Gwatkin, "Political Will and Family Planning," 29.

32. For the suspension of fundamental rights, see Setalvad, *The Indian Constitution,* 221; Austin, *The Indian Constitution,* 207–8. Wolpert's *A New History of India* has this to say about the attitude of the Indian populace to the emergency:

> Parliamentary government, democratic elections, freedom of speech and of the press, and the rule of law were, after all, part of the gloss of western modernization introduced in the last phase of British rule to a civilization that found them as strangely exotic and foreign as their Anglo-Saxon Liberal and Radical advocates; while the "emergency" powers assumed by Indira to save her Raj seemed destined to outlast those imported institutions and ideals that were enshrined in India's Constitution as fundamental rights. (404)

David Lipscomb, however, offers a salient critique of Wolpert's account. He complains that it "comes close to painting a portrait of wide-eyed natives scratching their heads at 'western' ideas like freedom of speech and the rule of law and then bowing their heads submissively, in that ancient way of theirs, to Gandhi's emergency rule." "Caught in a Strange Middle Ground," 174.

33. Klieman, "Indira's India," 247–48.

34. See Palmer, "India in 1975," 102.

35. For the debate on Gandhi's decrees, see Palmer, "India in 1975," 104.

36. See Klieman, "Indira's India," 244.

37. Quotation from Cheah, *Inhuman Conditions,* 166–67.

38. "Righting Wrongs," 524.

39. Notably, critics differ on whether Saleem actually dies at the end of his narrative.

40. "The Right to Have Rights," 353.

4. Women's Rights and the Lure of Self-Determination

1. For such a phrase, see Lionnet, *Postcolonial Representations*, 159.

2. Okin's *Is Multiculturalism Bad for Women?* represents perhaps the best-known statement of this debate.

3. Rao, "The Politics of Gender and Culture," 169. See also Nivedita Menon, "Between the Burqa and the Beauty Parlor?," 209; Afkhami, "Gender Apartheid, Cultural Relativism, and Women's Human Rights," 234.

4. *Is Multiculturalism Bad for Women?*, 16.

5. See "Report of the World Conference to Review and Appraise the Achievements of the United Nations Decade for Women: Equality, Development and Peace," Nairobi, July 15–26, 1985, http://www.earthsummit2002.org/toolkits/women/un-doku/un-conf/narirobi-2.html#IV.%20Areas%20of%20Special%20Concern.

6. *Woman at Point Zero*, viii.

7. Badran, "Competing Agenda," 220–21. See also Zabus, *Between Rites and Rights*, 97.

8. For a similar observation, see Harlow, *Resistance Literature*, 137. Salti argues that this tendency makes her fiction "difficult to classify as a specific type in Arabic literature." "Paradise, Heaven and Other Oppressive Spaces," 154.

9. Important academic treatments of El Saadawi include Hitchcock, *Dialogics of the Oppressed;* Lionnet, *Postcolonial Representations;* Malti-Douglas, *Men, Women, and God(s);* and Royer, *A Critical Study of the Works of Nawal El Saadawi.*

10. For an extensive survey of the different allegations levied by Arab and Anglophone critics alike, see Amireh, "Framing Nawal El Saadawi," 236.

11. As Malti-Douglas describes, "Her fiction has been castigated as mere propaganda, as tireless repetition of her radical message." *Men, Women, and God(s)*, 1.

12. Quoted in Al-Ali, *Gender Writing/Writing Gender*, 32.

13. George Tarabishi scathingly condemns her writing, although accordingly in militantly conservative terms, for instance, as he describes Firdaus as "challeng[ing] the biological laws of nature." *Woman against Her Sex*, 17.

14. Amireh and Majaj, introduction to *Going Global*, 7.

15. Amireh, "Framing Nawal El Saadawi," 215, 219, 224.

16. Of course, the fact that El Saadawi's novels are composed in Arabic might in part explain this neglect. Notably, El Saadawi's husband, Dr. Sherif Hetata, performs most of her translations, with El Saadawi's oversight. He maintains, "My problem with Nawal's books in translation is that I believe some of them can only be translated by me—especially the complex ones where she's playing with language." See El Saadawi's interview with Peter Hitchcock, "Living the Struggle." The English versions of most of her books are either prefaced or conclude with an addendum contextualizing the material for a specifically English-speaking and Western readership.

17. For a discussion of El Saadawi's novels in terms of their reception within postcolonial studies and the question of whether "political value [can] be squared with aesthetic value," see Felski, *Literature after Feminism*, 156.

18. As an example of criticism that does read El Saadawi through an established hermeneutic lens, Hitchcock applies Bakhtin's notion of dialogism to the novel. *Dialogics of the Oppressed,* xiv.

19. Samira Aghacy quotes El Saadawi as "insist[ing] that the struggle for human rights must be fought without hesitation." "Nawal El Saadawi," 2–4. Brinda Mehta describes her as "one of the most ... outspoken defenders of human rights from the Arab world." *Rituals of Memory,* 152–53.

20. *Memoirs from the Women's Prison,* 54.

21. See El Saadawi's statement at the Final Declaration of the Brussels Tribunal, April 17, 2004, http://www.nawalsaadawi.net/articlesnawal/tribunal.htm.

22. Both Hitchcock and Lionnet tangentially relate *Woman at Point Zero* to human rights. While Hitchcock does not explicitly evoke the term, he reads the novel as illumining central challenges for "humanism." Differently, Lionnet frames it explicitly with reference to human rights and follows her analysis with a chapter on the relationship between female genital excision and human rights.

23. Bunch, "Transforming Human Rights," 14.

24. Ibid.; Sullivan, "The Public/Private Distinction," 126. For the argument that "women are not seen as subjected by the state as such, so their condition is regarded as prelegal, social hence natural, so outside international human rights accountability," see MacKinnon, "Crimes of War, Crimes of Peace," 93.

25. Malti-Douglas explains that chicken is a luxury food in Egypt, an association that would not be familiar to many readers. *Men, Women, and God(s),* 63.

26. For such an argument, see Baucom, *Specters of the Atlantic,* 6–7.

27. For Marx's classic critique of human rights, see "On the Jewish Question," 42; Douzinas and Gearey, *Critical Jurisprudence,* 210–16.

According to Rey Chow, human rights "must also be seen as an inherent part— entirely brutal yet also entirely logical—of transnational corporatism, under which anything, including human beings or parts of human beings, can become exchangeable for its negotiated equivalent value." *The Protestant Ethnic,* 21. Julie Stone Peters argues that human rights "were born of the marketplace." "'Literature'," 265–66.

28. For the argument that human rights collaborate with transnational regimes of "development," see Grewal, *Transnational America.*

29. *The Hidden Face of Eve,* xiv. See also her statement that capitalism in particular works to "cut the clitoris of women psychologically." Interview in *Literature and Medicine,* 65.

30. This conjunction has been noted by El Saadawi in her critical writings, where she argues that economic equality for women within both society and the family is precursory to their acquisition of wider political entitlements. She comments on this disparity: "About 65% of all productive labour is carried out by women whereas they earn only 5% of world income. This often obliges women to live at the expense of the men in the family." See "Toward a Philosophy That Will Awaken the Conscience of the Human Race," http://www.nawalsaadawi.net/articlesby/awakenconscience.htm.

31. For a discussion of such a strategy, see Amireh and Majaj, introduction to *Going Global,* 9. For a provocative discussion of the ways Western idealizations of authenticity end up circularly colluding with "the image that fundamentalists transmit of Muslim women as emblematic of cultural revival, integrity and authenticity," see Moghissi, *Feminist and Islamic Fundamentalism.* Likewise, for the notion that Islam

itself signifies "the powerful popular appeal of authenticity," see Karam, "Women, Islamisms, and State."

32. Hitchcock further notes the novel's alliance with testimony (35). Lionnet also labels the novel "a lyrical testimony that exemplifies... the possibility of resistance to hegemonic pressure and to the cultural master narrative" (141).

33. Quotation from "Race, Gender, and the Politics of Reception," 131.

34. *Oxford English Dictionary.*

35. Felman and Laub, *Testimony,* 5–6.

36. Introduction to *Just Advocacy?,* 13.

37. See Grace, *The Woman in the Muslim Mask.*

38. *Resistance Literature,* 125.

39. For a discussion of El Saadawi's relationship to the medical profession, see Valassopolous, "'Words Written by a Pen Sharp as a Scalpel.'"

40. It is further significant that El Saadawi's reservations about medical discourse parallel her concerns about legal reasoning, for instance, as she has vocally condemned both Egyptian and Islamic law for denying women key protections.

41. *Nature,* 85–86.

42. *The World of Perception,* 50–51.

43. *The Visible and the Invisible,* 143.

44. See Levison and Levison, "Women's Health and Human Rights," 140, and also El Saadawi, "Imperialism and Sex in Africa," 22.

45. Levinson and Levinson, "Women's Health and Human Rights," 142.

46. See Lewis and Mills, introduction to *Feminist Postcolonial Theory.*

47. *Postcolonial Representations,* 159.

48. "Female Genital Mutilation," 226. For another overview of debates about terminology, see also Zabus, *Between Rites and Rights,* 2.

49. I retain both terms in tandem precisely to capture the tensions that inflect them.

50. "Aberrant 'Islams' and Errant Daughters."

51. Mayer, "Cultural Particularism," 177.

52. Land Center for Human Rights, "Egypt."

53. "Egypt Makes First Arrest over Female Circumcision," Alarabiya.net, August 13, 2009.

54. "Imperialism and Sex in Africa," 22.

55. *The Hidden Face of Eve,* xiv. See also "Imperialism and Sex in Africa," 25.

56. Introduction to *Feminist Postcolonial Theory,* 13. For discussions of Western engrossment with the process, see also Grewal, *Transnational America,* 179; Hancock, "Overcoming Willful Blindness," 250.

57. "Female Genital Mutilation," 225.

58. *Under Western Eyes,* 19.

5. J. M. Coetzee's *Disgrace*

1. See Mutua, *Human Rights,* 150, 126.

2. Postamble, South African Interim Constitution, 1993, http://www.polity.org.za/html/govdocs/legislation/1993/constit0.html?rebookmark=1.

3. For the South African TRC's relationship to other national contexts, see Posel, "History as Confession."

4. Villa-Vicencio and Verwoerd, "Constructing a Report," 281.

5. For an extended discussion of the coverage, see Rotberg, "Truth Commissions," 5; and Gallagher, *Truth and Reconciliation,* 121.

6. Gallagher, *Truth and Reconciliation,* 115. For the problematic effects of this practice, see Gutman and Thompson, "The Moral Foundations of Truth Commissions," 24.

7. "Passages to Freedom," 17–18.

8. Coetzee, *Doubling the Point.*

9. For an overview of these allegations and related debates, see Bethlehem, "Pliant/compliant," 20; Gready, *Writing as Resistance;* Peck, *A Morbid Fascination,* 6; Gallagher, *A Story of South Africa,* 12; and Head, *J. M. Coetzee,* 8–13.

10. *Giving Offense* and many essays in *Doubling the Point.*

11. For a discussion of such tensions, see Sanders, *Complicities,* 1, 11.

12. For Gordimer, this corresponds with a dehistoricizing tendency on Coetzee's part, a criticism she makes of *Life & Times of Michael K,* wherein "Coetzee's heroes are those who ignore history." "The Idea of Gardening," 6.

13. *Stranger Shores,* 192.

14. *Doubling the Point,* 339–40.

15. For a discussion of the extent to which *Disgrace* has dominated criticism, see Gagiano, "Adapting the National Imaginary," 814. For the critical argument that Coetzee intended the novel as a direct commentary on South Africa, see Glenn, "Gone for Good."

16. See McDonald, "Disgrace Effects." For the April 5, 2000, ANC news briefing, "White Media Portray African Leaders as Barbaric," see http://www.anc.org.za/anc/newbrief/2000/news0406.txt. The ANC and the Democratic Alliance continued to bicker over this statement after Coetzee won the Nobel. See http://iafrica.com/news/sa/275456.htm.

17. Attwell, "Race in *Disgrace."*

18. For other criticism that reads the novel as allegorizing the TRC, see Poyner, "Truth and Reconciliation"; Sanders, *Ambiguities of Witnessing;* Rose, "Apathy and Accountability"; and Saunders, "*Disgrace* in the Time of a Truth Commission."

19. See Minow, *Between Vengeance and Forgiveness,* 22, 63.

20. Gutman and Thompson describe this policy as "the most problematic practice in that, while only a relatively small number of applicants were granted amnesty, they were often the "most egregious perpetrators." "The Moral Foundations of Truth Commissions," 24.

21. For a discussion of the TRC's reliance on a confessional mode, see Posel, "History as Confession." For a discussion of confession within *Disgrace,* see Kossew, "The Politics of Shame and Redemption" and Sanders, "Disgrace," 370.

22. For an extended discussion of the influence of religion on confessional literatures in South Africa as well as the TRC, see Gallagher, *Truth and Reconciliation,* 118–20. See also Rotberg, "Truth Commissions," 7; Rigby, *Justice and Reconciliation,* 134; Du Toit, "Human Rights Programs," 20; and Mamdani, "Amnesty or Impunity?"

23. A full one-third of all prisoners detained without trail during apartheid came from this province, and it is also the second-poorest of the nine South African provinces. Krog, *Country of My Skull,* 47.

24. Rape, including "pack rape," has become increasingly prevalent in South Africa. Altman, *Global Sex,* 8. South Africa has one of the highest rape rates in the

world; close to half of these assaults are child rapes. For one such report, see http://www.worldnetdaily.com/news/printer-friendly.asp?ARTICLE_ID=25806.

25. See Krog, *Country of My Soul*, 239.

26. Various critics have read her refusal in light of the historical deployments of rape narratives. See Graham, "Reading the Unspeakable," 435.

27. Lucy's abnegation of legal recourse has received much critical attention. For the argument that it represents a "refusal to be raped," see Spivak, "Ethics and Politics," 21. For its being a "refusal to resist," see Farred, "Back to the Borderlines."

28. See the South African Human Rights Commission website, at http://www.sahrc.org.za/ and, for example, Kistner, "The Elided Performative."

29. Rigby, *Justice and Reconciliation*, 131.

30. See Minow, *Between Vengeance and Forgiveness*, 10.

31. For a discussion of such risks, see Gallagher, *Truth and Reconciliation*, 115.

32. Soraya is referred to as "honey-brown" (1) and "Muslim" and Melanie as "the dark one." And, indeed, even Bev Shaw's ethnicity is arguably preserved as potentially ambiguous, for instance, when Lurie's fixates on her hair, which he describes as "a mass of little curls" that "must grow that way" (81).

33. Rape and other forms of violence against women were not widely acknowledged as human rights abuses until the 1980s, and Amnesty International did not issue its first report on rape until 1992. See Altman, *Global Sex*, 123.

34. "Crimes of War, Crimes of Peace."

35. For the viewpoint that Coetzee sought to "dissolve clear boundaries" between the two attacks, see Graham, "Reading the Unspeakable," 443. Alternately, for the argument that they should be read as distinct in light of the degree of their narration, see Cornwell, "Realism, Rape, and J. M. Coetzee's *Disgrace*."

36. *Doubling the Point*, 97. Mark Sanders describes apartheid in terms of an interdiction of desire and reads the TRC's project as "to restore the conditions of possibility for desire." "Remembering Apartheid," 65.

37. The criteria stipulated in the act define a publication as "undesirable" if

(a) it is "indecent or obscene or offensive or harmful to public morals";
(b) it is "blasphemous or offensive to the religious convictions or feelings" of a "section";
(c) it "brings any section…into ridicule or contempt";
(d) it is harmful to inter-section relations;
(e) it prejudices security, welfare, peace and good order;
(f) it discloses part of a judicial proceeding in which offensive material is quoted. See Van Rooyen, *Censorship in South Africa*.

38. In an interview from *Doubling the Point*, Coetzee elaborates that when "certain topics are forbidden [it] creates an unnatural concentration on them" (300).

39. Merleau-Ponty, *Sense and Non-sense*, 97.

40. For the argument that preserving thick versions of identity is particularly important to processes of political transition, see Hesse and Post, *Human Rights in Political Transitions*, 29–31.

41. *Sense and Non-sense*, 57.

42. *The Phenomenology of Perception*, vii.

43. See "Two Concepts of Self-Determination," 26.

44. See Spivak, "Righting Wrongs," 534. Jeremy Bentham voiced an early statement of such an objection to rights, despairing of how they obscure the "sacrifices" required for coexistence, whereas Bentham cautioned that "all men, on the contrary, are born in subjection, and the most absolute subjection." Bentham and Bowring, *The Works of Jeremy Bentham,* 498. The allegation that rights talk silences considerations of responsibility is also a common CLS complaint. See Glendon, *Rights Talk,* 76. From a different vantage point, Achille Mbembe and Deborah Posel posit that democracy should entail more than "simply the idea of rights" and undertake matters of "obligation." See "Editorial," 284. For a critique of such communitarian objections to rights, see also Perry, *The Idea of Human Rights.* Likewise, Paul Gordon Lauren historicizes rights to argue that they more accurately emerged through "discussions of duty." See *The Evolution of International Human Rights,* 5. Of course, not all theorists argue that the individualism fostered by rights is an inherently egoistic one. See Waldron, "*Nonsense upon Stilts,*" 192.

45. Minow, *Between Vengeance and Forgiveness,* 52.

46. *No Future without Forgiveness,* 34–35.

47. Cited at http://www.servat.unibe.ch/icl/sf10000.html.

48. Minow, *Between Vengeance and Forgiveness,* 52.

49. *Complicities,* 121–27. Moreover, Sanders argues that the notion of *ubuntu* in particular guided the TRC's approach to testimony. See *Ambiguities of Witnessing,* 9. For multiple references to and meditations on the status of *ubuntu,* see also Krog, *Country of My Skull,* 143, 213.

50. *Oxford English Dictionary.*

51. For one overview of these debates, see Sunstein and Nussbaum, *Animal Rights.*

52. For a discussion of animal rights, embodiment, and phenomenology in *Elizabeth Costello,* see Anker, "*Elizabeth Costello.*"

53. For a critique of the "'like-us' model of sameness" for evaluating animal rights, see MacKinnon, "Of Mice and Men."

54. Such a language is also present in a number of Coetzee's other recent writings, in particular in *Elizabeth Costello.* See Anker, "*Elizabeth Costello.*"

55. Merleau-Ponty, *Nature,* 129.

56. See the epigraph to this book's introduction.

57. In her response to *The Lives of Animals,* Marjorie Garber describes Coetzee's approach as staging "a debate between poetry and philosophy." See "Reflections," 79. For one theoretical example among countless, see Derrida, "The Animal That Therefore I Am." Derrida suggests that the entire philosophical tradition has disavowed the possibility of representing the reality of the animal.

58. For a philosophical argument grounded in cognitive science that music, as well as aesthetic experience broadly speaking, can uniquely animate embodied registers of perception, see Johnson, *The Meaning of the Body.*

6. Arundhati Roy's "Return to the Things Themselves"

1. For Roy's reception, see Boehmer, "East Is East and South Is South."

2. For how Roy has become the most prominent antiglobalization voice in India, see Mullaney, "'Globalizing Dissent'?" Other critics argue that Roy refuses "to

be positioned within any large political agenda." See Alexandru, "Towards a Politics of the Small Things," 165.

3. Graham Huggan calls her ecological writing "the most eye-catching eco-critical intervention to date by a recognized postcolonial writer." "'Greening' Post-colonialism," 705.

4. *The Algebra of Infinite Justice,* 122.

5. For a discussion of how Rushdie's acclaim legitimized Roy as a "canonical" postcolonial author, see Alexandru, "Towards a Politics of the Small Things," 163–64.

6. That said, some critics have nevertheless interpreted *The God of Small Things* as gratifying the codes of postmodernism. See Tickell, *"The God of Small Things."*

7. Rushdie, *Midnight's Children,* 523.

8. For such parallels, see also Siddiqi, *Anxieties of Empire and the Fiction of Intrigue;* Tickell, *"The God of Small Things."*

9. For instance, *The God of Small Things* also references "mercurochrome" (59) and a "fisherman" painting (14) similar to the one hanging over Saleem's bed.

10. Some critics have dismissed these tactics as little more than self-exoticizing ploys; however, that assessment absorbs Roy into the market-driven literary production against which she vehemently reacts. See Huggan, *The Postcolonial Exotic,* 77.

11. Žižek, *The Sublime Object of Ideology,* 165.

12. *The Algebra of Infinite Justice,* 133.

13. Ibid., 47, 135.

14. Ibid., 280.

15. *The Phenomenology of Perception,* 71. Not coincidentally, Merleau-Ponty devotes substantial attention to theorizing childhood consciousness. See "The Child's Relations with Others."

16. For such a distinction, see Johnson, *The Meaning of the Body,* 87.

17. *On the Postcolony,* 8.

18. *On the Postcolony,* 173–74. For the argument that modernity's eclipse of embodiment renders death an especially acute existential crisis, see Shilling, *The Body and Social Theory,* 177.

19. For critics who emphasize such an encounter with "Otherness," see Alexandru, "Towards a Politics of the Small Things"; Thormann, "The Ethical Subject of *The God of Small Things,*" 305.

20. *Strange Encounters,* 49.

21. *The Algebra of Infinite Justice,* 122–23.

22. *The World of Perception,* 68.

Coda

1. Roy, "Democracy's Failing Light."

2. *The World of Perception,* 67.

3. For the notion of "downsizing" human rights, see Mignolo, "Citizenship, Knowledge, and the Limits of Humanity," 314.

4. Remarks at the United Nations, March 27, 1953, quoted in Lash, *Eleanor,* 81. Also cited and discussed in Glendon, *A World Made New,* 239–40.

5. *The World of Perception,* 68.

❧ WORKS CITED

Afkhami, Mahnaz. "Gender Apartheid, Cultural Relativism, and Women's Human Rights in Muslim Societies." In *Women, Gender, and Human Rights: A Global Perspective,* edited by Marjorie Agosín, 234–45. New Brunswick, N.J.: Rutgers University Press, 2001.

Aghacy, Samira. "Nawal El Saadawi: Better to Pay and Be Free Than to Pay and Be Oppressed." *Al-Raida* 93–94. (Spring/Summer 2001): 2–4.

Ahmed, Sara. *Queer Phenomenology: Orientations, Objects, Desires.* Durham, N.C.: Duke University Press, 2006.

———. *Strange Encounters: Embodied Others in Post-coloniality.* New York: Routledge, 2000.

Al-Ali, Nadje Sadig. *Gender Writing/Writing Gender: The Representation of Women in a Selection of Modern Egyptian Literature.* Cairo: American University Press, 1994.

Alcoff, Linda. *Visible Identities: Race, Gender, and the Self.* Oxford: Oxford University Press, 2006.

Aldama, Arturo J. *Violence and the Body: Race, Gender, and the State.* Bloomington: Indiana University Press, 2003.

Alexandru, Maria-Sabina. "Towards a Politics of the Small Things: Arundhati Roy and the Decentralization of Authorship." In *Authorship in Context: From the Theoretical to the Political,* edited by Kyriaki Hadjiafxendi and Polina Mackay, 163–81. New York: Palgrave Macmillan, 2007.

Altman, Dennis. *Global Sex.* Chicago: University of Chicago Press, 2001.

Amireh, Amal. "Framing Nawal El Saadawi: Arab Feminism in a Transnational World." *Signs* 26.1 (2000): 215–49.

Amireh, Amal, and Lisa Suhair Majaj. "Introduction." In *Going Global: The Transnational Reception of Third World Women Writers,* edited by Amal Amireh and Lisa Suhair Majaj, 1–26. New York: Garland, 2000.

Andorno, Roberto. "Human Dignity and Human Rights as a Common Ground for a Global Bioethics." *Journal of Medicine and Philosophy* 34.3 (2009): 223–40.

Anker, Elizabeth S. "*Elizabeth Costello,* Embodiment, and the Limits of Rights." *New Literary History* 42.1 (2011): 169–92.

Appadurai, Arjun. *Fear of Small Numbers.* Durham, N.C.: Duke University Press, 2006.

———. *Modernity at Large: Cultural Dimensions of Globalization.* Minneapolis: University of Minnesota Press, 1996.

Appiah, Kwame Anthony. *Cosmopolitanism: Ethics in a World of Strangers.* New York: Norton, 2006.

———. "Is the 'Post-' in the 'Postcolonial' the 'Post-' in the 'Postmodern'?" In *Dangerous Liaisons: Gender, Nation, and Postcolonial Perspectives,* edited by Anne

McClintock, Aamir Mufti, and Ella Shohat. Minneapolis: University of Minnesota Press, 1997.

Arendt, Hannah. *The Origins of Totalitarianism.* New York: Harcourt, 1966.

Asad, Talal. *Formations of the Secular: Christianity, Islam, Modernity.* Stanford, Calif.: Stanford University Press, 2003.

Attwell, David. "Race in *Disgrace.*" *Interventions* 4.3 (2002): 331–41.

Austin, Granville. *The Indian Constitution: Cornerstone of a Nation.* New Delhi: Oxford University Press, 1966.

Badran, Margot. "Competing Agenda: Feminists, Islam, and the State in Nineteenth- and Twentieth-Century Egypt." In *Women, Islam, and the State,* edited by Deniz Kandiyoti, 201–36. London: Macmillan, 1991.

Bagaric, Mirko, and James Allan. "The Vacuous Concept of Dignity." *Journal of Human Rights* 5.2 (2006): 257–70.

Bahri, Deepika. *Native Intelligence: Aesthetics, Politics, and Postcolonial Literature.* Minneapolis: University of Minnesota Press, 2003.

Balfour, Ian, and Eduardo Cadava. "The Claims of Human Rights: An Introduction." *South Atlantic Quarterly* 103.2/3 (2004): 277–96.

Baucom, Ian. *Specters of the Atlantic: Finance Capital, Slavery, and the Philosophy of History.* Durham N.C.: Duke University Press, 2005.

Baxi, Upendra. *The Future of Human Rights.* New York: Oxford University Press, 2002.

——. *Human Rights in a Posthuman World: Critical Essays.* Oxford: Oxford University Press, 2007.

Beah, Ishmael. *A Long Way Gone: Memoirs of a Boy Soldier.* New York: Farrar, Straus and Giroux, 2007.

Beitz, Charles R. *The Idea of Human Rights.* New York: Oxford University Press, 2009.

Bell, Michael. *Sentimentalism, Ethics, and the Culture of Feeling.* New York: Palgrave Macmillan, 2000.

Benhabib, Seyla. *Another Cosmopolitanism.* New York: Oxford University Press, 2008.

——. *The Rights of Others: Aliens, Residents, Citizens.* Cambridge, U.K.: Cambridge University Press, 2005.

Bennett, Jane. *The Enchantment of Modern Life: Attachments, Crossings, Aesthetics.* Princeton, N.J.: Princeton University Press, 2001.

Bentham, Jeremy, and John Bowring. *The Works of Jeremy Bentham.* Vol. 2, pt. 2. Edinburgh: W. Tait, 1839.

Berlant, Lauren. *Cruel Optimism.* Durham, N.C.: Duke University Press, 2011.

Bérubé, Michael. "Citizenship and Disability." *Dissent* (Spring 2003): 52–57.

Bethlehem, Louise. "Pliant/compliant; grace/*Disgrace;* plaint/complaint." *scrutiny2* 7.1 (2002): 20–24.

Bhabha, Homi K. *The Location of Culture.* New York: Routledge, 1994.

Boehmer, Elleke. "East Is East and South Is South: The Cases of Sarojini Naidu and Arundhati Roy." *Women: A Cultural Review* 11.1–2 (2000): 61–70.

Booker, M. Keith. "*Midnight's Children,* History, and Complexity: Reading Rushdie after the Cold War." In *Critical Essays on Salman Rushdie,* edited by M. Keith Booker, 283–313. New York: G. K. Hall, 1999.

Brennan, Timothy. *Salman Rushdie and the Third World: Myths of the Nation.* New York: St. Martin's Press, 1989.

Brewer, John. "Sentiment and Sensibility." In *The Cambridge History of English Romantic Literature,* edited by James Chandler, 21–43. New York: Cambridge University Press, 2009.

Brooks, Peter. "Policing Stories." In *Law's Madness,* edited by Austin Sarat and Martha Merrill Unphrey. Ann Arbor: University of Michigan Press, 2003.

Brown, Wendy. "Suffering the Paradoxes of Rights." In *Left Legalism/Left Critique,* edited by Wendy Brown and Janet Halley, 420–34. Durham, N.C.: Duke University Press, 2002.

Bueno, Eva Paulino. "Race, Gender, and the Politics of Reception." In *Going Global: The Transnational Reception of Third World Women Writers,* edited by Amal Amireh and Lisa Suhair Majaj, 115–47. New York: Garland, 2000.

Bunch, Charlotte. "Transforming Human Rights from a Feminist Perspective." In *Women's Rights, Human Rights: International Feminist Perspectives,* edited by Julie Peters and Andrea Wolper, 11–17. New York: Routledge, 1995.

Butler, Judith. "Merleau-Ponty and the Touch of Malebranche." In *The Cambridge Companion to Merleau-Ponty,* edited by Taylor Carman and Mark B. Hansen, 181–205. Cambridge, U.K.: Cambridge University Press, 2005.

———. *Undoing Gender.* New York: Routledge, 2004.

Carman, Taylor, and Mark B. N. Hansen. Introduction to *The Cambridge Companion to Merleau-Ponty,* edited by Taylor Carman and Mark B. N. Hansen, 181–205. Cambridge, U.K.: Cambridge University Press, 2005.

Caruth, Cathy, ed. *Trauma: Explorations in Memory.* Baltimore: Johns Hopkins University Press, 2003.

Chakrabarty, Dipesh. *Habitations of Modernity: Essays in the Wake of Subaltern Studies.* Chicago: University of Chicago Press, 2002.

———. "'In the Name of Politics': Democracy and the Power of the Multitude in India." *Public Culture* 19.1 (2007): 35–57.

———. "Postcoloniality and the Artifice of History." *Representations* 37 (Winter 1992): 1–26.

Chakravorty, Pinaki. "The Rushdie Incident as Law-and-Literature Parable." *Yale Law Journal* 104.8 (1995): 2213–47.

Chatterjee, Partha. *The Nation and Its Fragments: Colonial and Postcolonial Histories.* Princeton, N.J.: Princeton University Press, 1993.

Cheah, Pheng, and Elizabeth Grosz. "The Body of the Law: Note toward a Theory of Corporeal Justice." In *Thinking through the Body of the Law,* edited by Pheng Cheah, David Fraser, and Judith Grbich, 3–25. New York: New York University Press, 1996.

———. *Inhuman Conditions: On Cosmopolitanism and Human Rights.* Cambridge, Mass.: Harvard University Press, 2006.

———. *Spectral Nationality: Passages of Freedom from Kant to Postcolonial Literatures of Liberation.* New York: Columbia University Press, 2003.

Cheyfitz, Eric. "Balancing the Earth: Native American Philosophies and the Environmental Crisis." *Arizona Quarterly* 65.3 (2009): 139–62.

Chiu, Jeannie. "Melancholy and Human Rights in *A Nostalgist's Map of America* and *Midnight's Children.*" *Literature Interpretation Theory* 16 (2005): 25–39.

Chow, Rey. *The Protestant Ethnic and the Spirit of Capitalism.* New York: Columbia University Press, 2002.

Coetzee, J. M. *Age of Iron*. New York: Penguin, 1990.

———. *Disgrace*. New York: Viking, 1999.

———. *Doubling the Point: Essays and Interviews*. Cambridge, U.K.: Harvard University Press, 1992.

———. *Giving Offense: Essays on Censorship*. Chicago: University of Chicago Press, 1996.

———. *Life and Times of Michael K*. New York: Penguin, 1983.

———. *Stranger Shores: Literary Essays, 1986–1999*. New York: Penguin, 2001.

———. *Summertime*. New York: Viking, 2009.

———. *Waiting for the Barbarians*. New York: Penguin, 1980.

Coetzee, J. M., and Amy Gutmann. *The Lives of Animals*. Princeton, N.J.: Princeton University Press, 1999.

Cohen, Ed. *A Body Worth Defending: Immunity, Biopolitics, and the Apotheosis of the Modern Body*. Durham, N.C.: Duke University Press, 2009.

Connolly, William E. *Why I Am Not a Secularist*. Minneapolis: University of Minnesota Press, 1999.

Coole, Diana. "The Inertia of Matter and the Generativity of Flesh." In Coole and Frost, 92–115.

———. *Merleau-Ponty and Modern Politics after Anti-humanism*. New York: Rowman and Littlefield, 2007.

Coole, Diana, and Samantha Frost, eds. *New Materialisms: Ontology, Agency, and Politics*. Durham, N.C.: Duke University Press, 2010.

Cornwell, Gareth. "Realism, Rape, and J. M. Coetzee's *Disgrace*." *Critique* 43.4 (2002): 307–22.

Cubilié, Anne. *Women Witnessing Terror: Testimony and the Cultural Politics of Human Rights*. New York: Fordham University Press, 2005.

Dallmayr, Fred. "'Asian Values' and Global Human Rights." *Philosophy East and West* 52.2 (2002): 173–89.

Darian-Smith, Eve, and Peter Fitzpatrick. "Introduction." In *Laws of the Postcolonial*, edited by Eve Darian-Smith and Peter Fitzpatrick. Ann Arbor: University of Michigan Press, 1999.

Das, Veena. *Life and Words: Violence and the Descent into the Ordinary*. Berkeley: University of California Press, 2007.

Davis, Lennard J. "Constructing Normalcy." In *The Disability Studies Reader*. 2nd ed., edited by Lennard J. Davis, 3–16. New York: Routledge, 2006.

Dawes, James. *That the World May Know*. Cambridge, Mass.: Harvard University Press, 2007.

Dean, Carolyn J. *The Frail Social Body: Pornography, Homosexuality, and Other Fantasies in Interwar France*. Berkeley: University of California Press, 2000.

Deranty, Jean-Philippe. "Witnessing the Inhuman: Agamben or Merleau-Ponty." *South Atlantic Quarterly* 107.1 (2008): 165–86.

Derrida, Jacques. "The Animal That Therefore I Am (More to Follow)." Translated by David Wills. *Critical Inquiry* 28 (2002): 369–418.

———. "Declarations of Independence." *New Political Science* 15 (1986): 7–15.

———. *On Cosmopolitanism and Forgiveness (On Thinking and Action)*. London: Routledge, 2001.

———. *Rogues: Two Essays on Reason*. Stanford, Calif.: Stanford University Press, 2005.

Dillon, M. C. *Merleau-Ponty's Ontology*. 2nd ed. Evanston, Ill.: Northwestern University Press, 1997.

——. *Semiological Reductionism: A Critique of the Deconstructionist Movement in Postmodern Thought.* Albany: State University of New York Press, 1995.

Dimock, Wai Chee. "Rethinking Space, Rethinking Rights: Literature, Law, and Science." In *Materializing Democracy: Toward a Revitalized Cultural Politics,* edited by Russ Castronovo and Dana D. Nelson, 248–66. Durham: Duke University Press, 2002.

Donnelly, Jack. *Universal Human Rights in Theory and Practice.* Ithaca, N.Y.: Cornell University Press, 1989.

Douzinas, Costas. *The End of Human Rights.* Oxford: Hart, 2000.

Douzinas, Costas, and Adam Gearey. *Critical Jurisprudence: The Political Philosophy of Justice.* Portland, Ore.: Hart, 2005.

During, Simon. *Modern Enchantments: The Cultural Power of Secular Magic.* Cambridge, Mass.: Harvard University Press, 2002.

Du Toit, André. "Human Rights Programs." In *Truth Commissions: A Comparative Assessment.* Cambridge, Mass.: Harvard Law School Human Rights Program and World Peace Foundation, 1997.

"Editor's Column: The End of Postcolonial Theory?" *PMLA* 122.3 (2007).

El Saadawi, Nawal. *The Hidden Face of Eve: Women in the Arab World.* New York: Zed, 1980.

——. "Imperialism and Sex in Africa." In *Female Circumcision and the Politics of Knowledge,* edited by Obioma Nnaemeka, 21–26. Westport, Conn.: Praeger, 2005.

——. "Interview." *Literature and Medicine* 14.1 (1995).

——. "Living the Struggle." Interview with Peter Hitchcock. *Transition* 61 (1993): 170–79.

——. *Memoirs from the Women's Prison.* Translated by Marilyn Booth. Berkeley: University of California Press, 1986.

——. *Woman at Point Zero.* Translated by Sharif Hetata. New York: Zed, 1983.

Esposito, Roberto. "The Dispositive of the Person." Lecture, Cornell University School of Criticism and Theory, Ithaca, N.Y., June 28, 2011.

Fanon, Frantz. *The Wretched of the Earth.* Translated by Richard Philcox. New York: Grove, 1963.

Farred, Grant. "Back to the Borderlines: Thinking Race Disgracefully." *scrutiny2* 7.1 (2002): 16–24.

Fassin, Didier. "Humanitarianism as a Politics of Life." *Public Culture* 19.3 (2007): 499–520.

Fassin, Didier, and Richard Rechtman. *The Empire of Trauma: An Inquiry into the Condition of Victimhood.* Princeton, N.J.: Princeton University Press, 2009.

Felman, Shoshana. *The Juridical Unconscious: Trials and Traumas in the Twentieth Century.* Cambridge, Mass.: Harvard University Press, 2002.

Felman, Shoshana, and Dori Laub. *Testimony: Crises of Witnessing in Literature, Psychoanalysis, and History.* New York: Routledge, 1992.

Felski, Rita. *Literature after Feminism.* Chicago: University of Chicago Press, 2003.

Fitzpatrick, Peter. *The Mythology of Modern Law.* New York: Routledge, 1992.

Foucault, Michel. *The History of Sexuality.* Vol. 1. New York: Random House, 1978.

Gabel, Peter. *The Bank Teller and Other Essays on the Politics of Meaning.* San Francisco: Acada, 2000.

Gagiano, Anne. "Adapting the National Imaginary: Shifting Identities in Three Post-1994 South African Novels." *Journal of Southern African Studies* 30.4 (2004): 811–24.

Gallagher, Susan Vanzanten. *A Story of South Africa: J. M. Coetzee's Fiction in Context.* Cambridge, Mass.: Harvard University Press, 1991.

Gandhi, Leela. *Affective Communities: Anticolonial Thought, Fin-de-Siècle Radicalism, and the Politics of Friendship.* Durham, N.C.: Duke University Press, 2005.

Garber, Marjorie. "Reflections." In *The Lives of Animals,* 73–84. Princeton, N.J.: Princeton University Press, 1999.

Gatens, Moira. *Imaginary Bodies: Ethics, Power, and Corporeality.* New York: Routledge, 1995.

Ghosh, Pratap Kumar. *The Constitution of India: How It Has Been Framed.* Calcutta: World Press Private, 1966.

Gikandi, Simon. "Globalization and the Claims of Postcoloniality." *South Atlantic Quarterly* 100.3 (2001): 627–58.

———. *Maps of Englishness.* New York: Columbia University Press, 1996.

Gilmore, Jonathan. "Between Art and Philosophy." In *The Cambridge Companion to Merleau-Ponty,* edited by Taylor Carman and Mark B. N. Hansen, 291–317. Cambridge, U.K.: Cambridge University Press, 2005.

Glendon, Mary Ann. "Propter Honoris Respectum: Knowing the Universal Declaration of Human Rights." *Notre Dame Law Review* 73 (1997): 1153–76.

———. *Rights Talk: The Impoverishment of Political Discourse.* New York: Free Press, 1991.

———. *A World Made New: Eleanor Roosevelt and the Universal Declaration of Human Rights.* New York: Random House, 2001.

Glenn, Ian. "Gone for Good: Coetzee's *Disgrace.*" *English in Africa* 36.2 (2009): 79–98.

Goldberg, Elizabeth Swanson. *Beyond Terror: Gender, Narrative, Human Rights.* New Brunswick, N.J.: Rutgers University Press, 2007.

Gordimer, Nadine. "The Idea of Gardening." *New York Review of Books,* February 2, 1984, 3, 6. Reprinted in *Critical Essays on J. M. Coetzee,* edited by Sue Kossew, 139–44. New York: G. K. Hall, 1998.

Gorra, Michael. *After Empire: Scott, Naipaul, Rushdie.* Chicago: University of Chicago Press, 1997.

Grace, Daphne. *The Woman in the Muslim Mask: Veiling and Identity in Postcolonial Literature.* Sterling, Va.: Pluto, 2004.

Graham, Lucy Valerie. "Reading the Unspeakable: Rape in J. M. Coetzee's *Disgrace.*" *Journal of Southern African Studies* 29.2 (2003): 433–44.

Gready, Paul. "The Politics of Human Rights." *Third World Quarterly* 24.4 (2003): 745–54.

———. *Writing as Resistance.* Lanham, Md.: Lexington, 2003.

Grewal, Inderpal. *Transnational America: Feminisms, Diasporas, Neoliberalisms.* Durham, N.C.: Duke University Press, 2005.

Grosz, Elizabeth. *Volatile Bodies: Toward a Corporeal Feminism.* Bloomington: Indiana University Press, 1994.

Gutman, Amy, and Dennis Thompson. "The Moral Foundations of Truth Commissions." In Rotberg and Thompson, 22–44.

Gwatkin, Davidson R. "Political Will and Family Planning: The Implications of India's Emergency Experience." *Population and Development Review* 5.1 (1979): 29–59.

Hale, David G. *The Body Politic: A Political Metaphor in Renaissance English Literature.* The Hague: Mouton Press, 1971.

Hamacher, Werner. "The Right to Have Rights (Four-and-a-Half Remarks)." *South Atlantic Quarterly* 103.2–3 (2004): 343–56.

Hancock, Ange-Marie. "Overcoming Willful Blindness: Building Egalitarian Multicultural Women's Coalitions." In *Female Circumcision and the Politics of Knowledge,* edited by Obioma Nnaemeka, 245–74. Westport, Conn.: Praeger, 2005.

Hardt, Michael, and Antonio Negri. *Empire.* Cambridge, Mass.: Harvard University Press, 2000.

Harlow, Barbara. *Barred: Women, Writing, and Political Detention.* Hanover, N.H.: Wesleyan University Press, 1992.

———. *Resistance Literature.* New York: Methuen, 1987.

Head, Dominic. *J. M. Coetzee.* Cambridge, Mass.: Cambridge University Press, 1997.

Heffernan, Teresa. "Apocalyptic Narratives: The Nation in Salman Rushdie's *Midnight's Children.*" *Twentieth Century Literature* 46.4 (2000): 470–91.

Hesford, Wendy S., and Wendy Kozol. "Introduction." In *Just Advocacy? Women's Human Rights, Transnational Feminisms, and the Politics of Representation.* New Brunswick, N.J.: Rutgers University Press, 2005.

Hesse, Carla, and Robert Post. "Introduction." In *Human Rights in Political Transitions: Gettysburg to Bosnia,* edited by Carla Hesse and Robert Post, 13–36. New York: Zone, 1999.

Hirschkind, Charles. *The Ethical Soundscape: Cassette Sermons and Islamic Counterpublics.* New York: Columbia University Press, 2006.

Hirsi Ali, Ayaan. *Infidel.* New York: Free Press, 2007.

Hitchcock, Peter. *Dialogics of the Oppressed.* Minneapolis: University of Minnesota Press, 1993.

Hogan, Patrick Colm. "*Midnight's Children:* Kashmir and the Politics of Identity." *Twentieth Century Literature* 27.4 (2001): 510–44.

Hosseini, Khaled. *The Kite Runner.* New York: Riverhead, 2003.

———. *A Thousand Splendid Suns.* New York: Riverhead, 2008.

Hubbard, Ruth. "Abortion and Disability." In *The Disability Studies Reader,* edited by Lennard J. David, 93–103. 2nd ed. New York: Routledge, 2006.

Huggan, Graham. "'Greening' Postcolonialism: Ecocritical Perspectives." *Modern Fiction Studies* 50.3 (2004): 701–33.

———. *The Postcolonial Exotic: Marketing the Margins.* New York: Routledge, 2001.

Hume, David. *A Treatise of Human Nature.* Mineola, N.Y.: Dover, 2003.

Hunt, Lynn. *Inventing Human Rights: A History.* New York: Norton, 2007.

Ignatieff, Michael. *Human Rights as Politics and Idolatry.* Princeton, N.J.: Princeton University Press, 2001.

Irigary, Luce. *An Ethics of Sexual Difference.* Translated by Carolyn Burke and Gillian C. Gill. Ithaca, N.Y.: Cornell University Press, 1993.

Israel, Nico. *Outlandish: Writing between Exile and Diaspora.* Stanford, Calif.: Stanford University Press, 2000.

Johnson, Mark. *The Meaning of the Body: Aesthetics of Human Understanding.* Chicago: University of Chicago Press, 2007.

Juraga, Dubravka. "'The Mirror of Us All': *Midnight's Children* and the Twentieth-Century Bildungsroman." In *Critical Essays on Salman Rushdie,* edited by M. Keith Booker, 160–87. New York: G. K. Hall, 1999.

Kahn, Paul. *The Cultural Study of Law: Reconstructing Legal Scholarship.* Chicago: University of Chicago Press, 1997.

———. *Putting Liberalism in Its Place.* Princeton, N.J.: Princeton University Press, 2005.

Kane, Jean M. "The Migrant Intellectual and the Body of History: Salman Rushdie's *Midnight's Children.*" *Contemporary Literature* 37.1 (1996): 94–118.

Kantorowicz, Ernst. *The King's Two Bodies: A Study in Medieval Political Theology.* Princeton, N.J.: Princeton University Press, 1957.

Karam, Azza M. "Women, Islamisms, and State." In *Muslim Women and the Politics of Participation,* edited by Mahnaz Afkhami and Erika Friedl. Syracuse, N.Y.: Syracuse University Press, 1997.

Kelman, Mark. *A Guide to Critical Legal Studies.* Cambridge, Mass.: Harvard University Press, 1987.

Kennedy, David. *The Dark Sides of Virtue: Reassessing International Humanitarianism.* Princeton, N.J.: Princeton University Press, 2004.

Keown, Michelle. *Postcolonial Pacific Writing: Representations of the Body.* London: Routledge, 2005.

Keymer, Thomas. "Sentimental Fiction: Ethics, Social Critique, and Philanthropy." In *The Cambridge History of English Literature, 1660–1780,* edited by John Richetti, vol. 1, 572–601. New York: Cambridge University Press, 2005.

Kistner, Ulrike. "The Elided Performative: The Human Rights Commission's Inquiry into Racism in the Media." *Pretexts: Literary and Cultural Studies* 10.2 (2001): 195–217.

Klieman, Aaron S. "Indira's India: Democracy and Crisis Government." *Political Science Quarterly* 96.2 (1981), 241–59.

Kortenaar, Neil Ten. "Postcolonial Ekphrasis: Salman Rushdie Gives the Finger Back to Empire." *Contemporary Literature* 38.2 (1997): 232–59.

———. *Self, Nation, and Text in Salman Rushdie's "Midnight's Children."* Montreal: McGill-Queen's University Press, 2004.

Kossew, Sue. "The Politics of Shame and Redemption in J. M. Coetzee's *Disgrace.*" *Research in African Literatures* 34.2 (2003): 155–62.

Kretzmer, David, and Eckart Klein. *The Concept of Human Dignity in Human Rights Discourse.* The Hague: Kluwer Law International, 2002.

Krog, Antjie. *Country of My Skull.* New York: Riverhead, 2000.

LaCapra, Dominick. *History and Its Limits.* Ithaca, N.Y.: Cornell University Press, 2009.

———. *Writing History, Writing Trauma.* Baltimore: Johns Hopkins University Press, 2000.

Lakoff, George, and Mark Johnson. *Philosophy in the Flesh: The Embodied Mind and Its Challenge to Western Thought.* New York: Basic, 1999.

Land Center for Human Rights. "Egypt: The Problem of Female Circumcision." *Pambazuka New: Pan-African Voices for Freedom and Justice* 489 (July 8, 2010).

Lash, Joseph P. *Eleanor: The Years Alone.* New York: Norton, 1972.

Lauren, Paul Gordon. *The Evolution of International Human Rights: Visions Seen.* Philadelphia: University of Pennsylvania Press, 1998.

Lazarus, Neil. "The Politics of Postcolonial Modernism." In *Postcolonial Studies and Beyond,* edited by Ania Loomba, Survir Kaul, Matti Bunzl, Antoinette Burton, and Jed Esty, 423–37. Durham, N.C.: Duke University Press, 2005.

Lemmon, Gayle Tzemach. *The Dressmaker of Khair Khana*. New York: HarperCollins, 2011.

Levin, David Michael. "Justice in the Flesh." In *Ontology and Alterity in Merleau-Ponty*, edited by Galen A. Johnson and Michael B. Smith, 35–44. Evanston, Ill.: Northwestern University Press, 1990.

Levison, Julie H., and Sandra P. Levison. "Women's Health and Human Rights." In *Women, Gender, and Human Rights: A Global Perspective*, edited by Marjorie Agosín, 125–51. New Brunswick, N. J.: Rutgers University Press, 2001.

Lewis, Reina, and Sara Mills. "Introduction." In *Feminist Postcolonial Theory: A Reader*, edited by Reina Lewis and Sara Mills, 1–23. Edinburgh: Edinburgh University Press, 2003.

Lionnet, Françoise. *Postcolonial Representations: Women, Literature, Identity*. Ithaca, N. Y.: Cornell University Press, 1995.

Lipscomb, David. "Caught in a Strange Middle Ground: Contesting History in Salman Rushdie's *Midnight's Children*." *Diaspora* 1.2 (1991): 163–85.

Lyotard, Jean-Francois. "The Other's Rights." In *On Human Rights: The Oxford Amnesty Lectures*, edited by Stephen Shute and Susan Hurley, 135–74. New York: Basic Books, 1993.

MacKinnon, Catherine. "Crimes of War, Crimes of Peace." In *On Human Rights: The Oxford Amnesty Lectures*, edited by Stephen Shute and Susan Hurley, 83–110. New York: Basic Books, 1993.

———. "Of Mice and Men: A Feminist Fragment on Animal Rights." In Sunstein and Nussbaum, 263–76.

———. *Women's Lives, Men's Laws*. Cambridge, Mass.: Harvard University Press, 2005.

Mahmood, Saba. *Politics of Piety: The Islamic Revival and the Feminist Subject*. Princeton, N. J.: Princeton University Press, 2005.

———. "Religious Reason and Secular Affect: An Incommensurable Divide?" *Critical Inquiry* 35 (Summer 2005): 836–62.

Mahmoody, Betty. *Not Without My Daughter*. With William Hoffer. New York: St. Martin's, 1991.

Mallot, J. Edward. "Body Politics and the Body Politic: Memory as Human Inscription in *What the Body Remembers*." *Interventions* 8.2 (2006): 165–77.

Malti-Douglas, Fedwa. *Men, Women, and God(s): Nawal El Saadawi and Arab Feminist Poetics*. Berkeley: University of California Press, 1995.

Mamdani, Mahmood. "Amnesty or Impunity? A Preliminary Critique of the Report of the Truth and Reconciliation Commission of South Africa." *Diacritics* 32.3–4 (2002): 33–59.

———. "The Politics of Naming: Genocide, Civil War, Insurgency." *London Review of Books* 8 (March 2007): 5–8.

Marx, Karl. "On the Jewish Question." In *The Marx-Engels Reader*, edited by Robert C. Tucker, 26–52. New York: Norton, 1978.

Mayer, Ann Elizabeth. "Aberrant 'Islams' and Errant Daughters." In *Muslim Women and the Politics of Participation*, edited by Mahnaz Afkhami and Erika Friedl. Syracuse, N. Y.: Syracuse University Press, 1997.

———. "Cultural Particularism as a Bar to Women's Rights: Reflections on the Middle Eastern Experience." In *Women's Rights, Human Rights: International Feminist Perspectives*, edited by Julie Peters and Andrea Wolper. New York: Routledge, 1995.

Mbembe, Achille. *On the Postcolony.* Berkeley: University of California Press, 2001.

——. "Passages to Freedom: The Politics of Racial Reconciliation in South Africa." *Public Culture* 20.1 (2008): 5–18.

Mbembe, Achille, and Deborah Posel. "Editorial: A Critical Humanism." *Interventions* 7.3 (2005): 382–86.

McClintock, Anne. *Imperial Leather: Race, Gender, and Sexuality in the Colonial Contest.* New York: Routledge, 1995.

McDonald, Peter D. "Disgrace Effects." *Interventions* 4.3 (2002).

Mehta, Brinda. *Rituals of Memory in Contemporary Arab Women's Writing.* Syracuse, N.Y.: Syracuse University Press, 2007.

Menon, Nivedita. "Between the Burqa and the Beauty Parlor? Globalization, Cultural Nationalism, and Feminist Politics." In *Postcolonial Studies and Beyond,* edited by Ania Loomba, Survir Kaul, Matti Bunzl, Antoinette Burton, and Jed Esty, 206–32. Durham, N.C.: Duke University Press, 2005.

Mensch, James R. *Embodiments: From the Body to the Body Politic.* Evanston, Ill.: Northwestern University Press, 2009.

Merivale, Patricia. "Saleem Fathered by Oskar: Intertextual Strategies in *Midnight's Children* and *The Tin Drum.*" In *Reading Rushdie: Perspectives on the Fiction of Salman Rushie,* edited by D. M. Fletcher, 83–96. Amsterdam: Rodopi, 1994.

Merleau-Ponty, Maurice. "Eye and Mind." In *The Merleau-Ponty Aesthetics Reader: Philosophy and Painting,* edited by Galen A. Johnson. Evanston, Ill.: Northwestern University Press, 1993.

——. *Humanism and Terror.* Translated by John O'Neill. Boston: Beacon, 1969.

——. *Nature: Course Notes from the College de France.* Translated by Robert Vallier. Evanston, Ill.: Northwestern University Press, 2003.

——. *The Phenomenology of Perception.* Translated by Colin Smith. New York: Routledge Classics, 2002.

——. *The Primacy of Perception and Other Essays on Phenomenological Psychology, Philosophy of Art, History, and Politics.* Translated by William Cobb. Evanston, Ill.: Northwestern University Press, 1964.

——. *Sense and Non-sense.* Translated by Hubert L. Dreyfus and Patricia Allen Dreyfus. Evanston, Ill.: Northwestern University Press, 1964.

——. *The Visible and the Invisible.* Translated by Alphonso Lingis. Evanston, Ill.: Northwestern University Press, 1968.

——. *The World of Perception.* Translated by Oliver Davis. New York: Routledge Classics, 2008.

Mignolo, Walter D. "Citizenship, Knowledge, and the Limits of Humanity." *American Literary History* 18.2 (2006): 312–31.

Minow, Martha. *Between Vengeance and Forgiveness.* Boston: Beacon, 1998.

Moghissi, Haideh. *Feminist and Islamic Fundamentalism.* New York: Zed, 1999.

Mohanty, Chandra Talpade. *Feminism without Borders: Decolonizing Theory, Practicing Solidarity.* Durham, N.C.: Duke University Press, 2001.

Moran, Dermot. *Introduction to Phenomenology.* New York: Routledge, 2000.

Mortenson, Greg, and David O. Relin. *Three Cups of Tea.* New York: Dial Books for Young Readers, 2009.

Moyn, Samuel. "Why Anticolonialism Wasn't a Human Rights Movement." In *The Last Utopia: Human Rights in History,* 84–119. Cambridge, Mass.: The Belknap Press of Harvard University Press, 2010.

Mullaney, Julie. "'Globalizing Dissent'? Arundhati Roy, Postcolonial and Local Feminism in the Transnational Economy." *Journal of Postcolonial Writing* 40.1 (2002–3): 56–70.

Mutua, Makau. *Human Rights: A Political and Cultural Critique.* Philadelphia: University of Pennsylvania Press, 2002.

Nafisi, Azar. *Reading Lolita in Tehran: A Memoir in Books.* New York: Random House, 2003.

Nandy, Ashis. *The Intimate Enemy: Loss and Recovery of Self under Colonialism.* London: Oxford University Press, 1983.

Natarajan, Nalini. "Woman, Nation, and Narration in *Midnight's Children.*" In *Scattered Hegemonies,* edited by Inderpal Grewal and Caren Kaplan, 76–89. Minneapolis: University of Minnesota Press, 1994.

Nehru, Jawaharlal. *The Unity of India: Collected Writings, 1937–40.* London: Billing and Sons, 1942.

Normand, Roger, and Sarah Zaidi. *Human Rights at the UN: The Political History of Universal Justice.* Bloomington: Indiana University Press, 2007.

Nussbaum, Martha. "Capabilities and Human Rights." In *Global Justice and Transnational Politics: Essays on the Moral and Political Challenges of Globalization,* edited by Pablo De Greiff and Ciaran Cronin, 117–50. Cambridge, Mass.: MIT Press, 2002.

——. *Cultivating Humanity: A Classical Defense of Reform in Liberal Education.* Cambridge, Mass.: Harvard University Press, 1997.

——. *Poetic Justice.* Boston: Beacon, 1995.

Okin, Susan Moller. *Is Multiculturalism Bad for Women?* Edited by Joshua Cohen, Matthew Howard, and Martha C. Nussbaum. Princeton, N.J.: Princeton University Press, 1999.

Ong, Aihwa. *Flexible Citizenship: The Cultural Logics of Transnationality.* Durham, N.C.: Duke University Press, 1999.

Palmer, Norman D. "India in 1975: Democracy in Eclipse." *Asian Survey* 16.2 (1976): 95–110.

Parekh, Serena. *Hannah Arendt and the Challenge of Modernity: A Phenomenology of Human Rights.* New York: Routledge, 2008.

Peck, Richard. *A Morbid Fascination: White Prose and Politics in Apartheid South Africa.* Westport, Conn.: Greenwood, 1997.

Perry, Michael J. *The Idea of Human Rights: Four Inquiries.* New York: Oxford University Press, 1998.

Peters, Julie Stone. "'Literature,' the 'Rights of Man,' and Narratives of Atrocity: Historical Backgrounds to the Culture of Testimony." *Yale Journal of Law and the Humanities* 17 (Summer 2005): 253–83.

Pollis, Adamantia. "Cultural Relativism Revisited: Through a State Prism." *Human Rights Quarterly* 18 (1996): 316–44.

Pollis, Adamantia, and Peter Schwab, eds. *Human Rights: New Perspectives, New Realities.* Boulder, Colo.: Lynne Rienner, 2000.

——. *Toward a Human Rights Framework.* New York: Praeger, 1982.

Posel, Deborah. "History as Confession: The Case of the South African Truth and Reconciliation Commission." *Public Culture* 20.1 (2008): 119–41.

Poyner, Jane. "Truth and Reconciliation in JM Coetzee's *Disgrace.*" *scrutiny2* 5.2 (2000): 67–77.

Quayson, Ato. *Postcolonialism: Theory, Practice, or Process?* Malden, Mass.: Polity, 2000.

Radhakrishnan, R. *History, the Human, and the World Between.* Durham, N.C.: Duke University Press, 2008.

——. *Theory in an Uneven World.* Malden, Mass.: Blackwell, 2003.

Rancière, Jacques. "Who Is the Subject of the Rights of Man?" *South Atlantic Quarterly* 103.2/3 (2004): 311–22.

Rao, Arati. "The Politics of Gender and Culture in International Human Rights Discourse." In *Women's Rights, Human Rights: International Feminist Perspectives,* edited by Julie Peters and Andrea Wolper, 167–75. New York: Routledge, 1995.

Razack, Sherene H. *Dark Threats and White Knights: The Somalia Affair, Peacekeeping, and the New Imperialism.* Toronto: Toronto University Press, 2004.

Reder, Michael. "Rewriting History and Identity: The Reinvention of Myth, Epic, and Allegory in Salman Rushdie's *Midnight's Children.*" In *Critical Essays on Salman Rushdie,* edited by M. Keith Booker, 225–49. New York: G. K. Hall, 1999.

Rege, Josna E. "Victim into Protagonist? *Midnight's Children* and the Post-Rushdie National Narratives of the Eighties." *Studies in the Novel* 29.3 (1997): 342–75.

Rigby, Andrew. *Justice and Reconciliation: After the Violence.* Boulder, Colo.: Lynne Rienner, 2001.

Rodriguez, Deborah. *Kabul Beauty School: An American Woman Goes behind the Veil.* With Kristin Ohlson. New York: Random House, 2007.

Rolls, Albert. *The Theory of the King's Two Bodies in the Age of Shakespeare.* Lewiston, N.Y.: Edwin Mellen Press, 2000.

Rorty, Richard. "Human Rights, Rationality, and Sentimentality." In *On Human Rights: The Oxford Amnesty Lectures,* edited by Stephen Shute and Susan Hurley, 111–34. New York: Basic Books, 1993.

Rose, Jacqueline. "Apathy and Accountability: South Africa's Truth and Reconciliation Commission." *Raritan* 21.4 (2002): 175–95.

Rose, Nikolas. *Powers of Freedom: Reframing Political Thought.* Cambridge, U.K.: Cambridge University Press, 1999.

Rotberg, Robert I. "Truth Commissions and the Provision of Truth, Justice, and Reconciliation." In *Truth v. Justice: The Morality of Truth Commissions,* edited by Rotberg and Dennis Thompson, 3–21. Princeton, N.J.: Princeton University Press, 2000.

Roy, Arundhati. *The Algebra of Infinite Justice.* New York: HarperCollins, 2002.

——. *Field Notes on Democracy: Listening to Grasshoppers.* Chicago, Ill.: Haymarket Books, 2009.

——. *The God of Small Things.* New York: HarperCollins, 1997.

Royer, Diana. *A Critical Study of the Works of Nawal El Saadawi, Egyptian Writer and Activist.* Lewiston, N.Y.: Edwin Mellen Press, 2001.

Rushdie, Salman. *Imaginary Homelands.* New York: Penguin, 1982.

——. *The Jaguar Smile: A Nicaraguan Journey.* New York: Picador, 1987.

———. *Midnight's Children.* New York: Penguin, 1981.

———. *Step across This Line: Collected Nonfiction, 1992–2002.* New York: Modern Library, 2003.

Russell, Emily. *Reading Embodied Citizenship: Disability, Narrative, and the Body Politic.* New Brunswick, N.J.: Rutgers University Press, 2011.

Said, Edward. *Humanism and Democratic Criticism.* New York: Columbia University Press, 2004.

———. *Orientalism.* New York: Random House, 1979.

Salti, Ramzi. "Paradise, Heaven, and Other Oppressive Spaces: A Critical Examination of the Life and Work of Nawal el-Saadawi." *Journal of Arabic Literature* 15.2 (1994).

Sanders, Mark. *Ambiguities of Witnessing: Law and Literature in the Time of a Truth Commission.* Stanford, Calif.: Stanford University Press, 2007.

———. *Complicities: The Intellectual and Apartheid.* Durham, N.C.: Duke University Press, 2002.

———. "Disgrace." *Interventions* 4.3 (2002): 363–73.

———. "Remembering Apartheid." *Diacritics* 32.3–4 (2002): 60–80.

Santner, Eric L. *The Royal Remains: The People's Two Bodies and the Endgames of Sovereignty.* Chicago: University of Chicago Press, 2011.

Sarat, Austin, and Thomas Kearns, eds. *Human Rights: Concepts, Contests, Contingencies.* Ann Arbor: University of Michigan Press, 2001.

Saunders, Rebecca. "*Disgrace* in the Time of a Truth Commission." *Parallax* 11.3 (2005): 99–106.

Scarry, Elaine. *The Body in Pain: The Making and Unmaking of the World.* New York: Oxford University Press, 1985.

Schachter, Oscar. "Human Dignity as a Normative Concept." *American Journal of International Law* 77.4: 848–71.

Schaffer, Kay, and Sidonie Smith. *Human Rights and Narrated Lives: The Ethics of Recognition.* New York: Palgrave, 2004.

Schueller, Malini Johar. *Locating Race: Global Sites of Post-Colonial Citizenship.* Albany: State University of New York Press, 2009.

Scott, Joan Wallach. *Only Paradoxes to Offer: French Feminists and the Rights of Man.* Cambridge, Mass.: Harvard University Press, 1997.

Sen, Amartya. "Conceptualizing and Measuring Poverty." In *Poverty and Inequality,* edited by David B. Grusky, S. M. Ravi Kabur, and Amartya Kuma Sen, 30–46. Stanford, Calif.: Stanford University Press, 2006.

Setalvad, M. C. *The Indian Constitution: 1050–65.* Bombay: Bombay University Press, 1967.

Shapiro, Ian. *The Evolution of Rights in Legal Theory.* New York: Cambridge University Press, 1986.

Shilling, Chris. *The Body and Social Theory.* London: Sage, 1993.

Shusterman, Richard. "The Silent, Limping Body of Philosophy." In *The Cambridge Companion to Merleau-Ponty,* edited by Taylor Carman and Mark B. Hansen, 151–80. Cambridge, U.K.: Cambridge University Press, 2005.

Siddiqi, Yumna. *Anxieties of Empire and the Fiction of Intrigue.* New York: Columbia University Press, 2008.

Silverman, Kaja. *World Spectators.* Stanford, Calif.: Stanford University Press, 2000.

Singer, Peter. *Applied Ethics.* Oxford: Oxford University Press, 1986.

Singh, Sujala. "Secularist Faith in Salman Rushdie's *Midnight's Children.*" *New Formations* 41 (Autumn 2000): 158–92.

Slaughter, Joseph. *Human Rights, Inc.: The World Novel, Narrative Form, and International Law.* New York: Fordham University Press, 2007.

——. "Narration in International Human Rights Law." *Comparative Literature and Culture* 9.1 (2007).

——. "A Question of Narration: The Voice in International Human Rights Law." *Human Rights Quarterly* 19.2 (1997): 406–30.

Sontag, Susan. *Regarding the Pain of Others.* New York: Farrar, Straus and Giroux, 2003.

Spivak, Gayatri Chakravorty. "Ethics and Politics in Tagore, Coetzee, and Certain Scenes of Teaching." *Diacritics* 32.3–4 (2002): 17–31.

——. "Righting Wrongs." *South Atlantic Quarterly* 103.2/3 (2004): 523–81.

Spurr, David. *The Rhetoric of Empire: Colonial Discourse in Journalism, Travel Writing, and Imperial Administration.* Durham, N.C.: Duke University Press, 1993.

Sripati, Vijayashri. "Human Rights in India: Fifty Years after Independence." *Denver Journal of International Law and Policy* 26 (Fall 1997): 93–136.

Stawarska, Beata. "From the Body Proper to Flesh: Merleau-Ponty on Intersubjectivity." In *Feminist Interpretations of Maurice Merleau-Ponty,* edited by Dorothea Olkowski and Gail Weiss, 91–106. University Park: Pennsylvania State University Press, 2006.

Strand, Eric. "Gandhian Communalism and the Midnight Children's Conference." *ELH: English Literary History* 12 (2005): 975–1016.

Su, John. "Epic of Failure: Disappointment as Utopian Fantasy in Salman Rushdie's *Midnight's Children.*" *Twentieth-Century Literature* 47.4 (2001): 545–68.

Sullivan, Donna. "The Public/Private Distinction in International Human Rights Law." In *Women's Rights, Human Rights: International Feminist Perspectives,* edited by Julie Peters and Andrea Wolper, 126–34. New York: Routledge, 1995.

Sunstein, Cass R., and Martha C. Nussbaum, eds. *Animal Rights: Current Debates and New Directions.* New York: Oxford University Press, 2004.

Tamen, Miguel. *Friends of Interpretable Objects.* Cambridge, Mass.: Harvard University Press, 2001.

Tarabishi, George. *Woman against Her Sex.* Atlantic Highlands, N.J.: Saqi, 1988.

Taylor, Charles. *Modern Social Imaginaries.* Durham, N.C.: Duke University Press, 2004.

Thompson, Jon. "Superman and Salman Rushdie: *Midnight's Children* and the Disillusionment of History." *Journal of Commonwealth and Postcolonial Studies* 3.1 (1995): 1–23.

Thormann, Janet. "The Ethical Subject of *The God of Small Things.*" *JCSP: Journal for the Psychoanalysis of Culture and Society* 8.2 (Fall 2003): 299–307.

Tickell, Alex. *Arundhati Roy's "The God of Small Things."* New York: Routledge, 2007.

——. "*The God of Small Things:* Arundhati Roy's Postcolonial Cosmopolitanism." *Journal of Commonwealth Literature* 38.1 (2003): 73–89.

Todd, Janet M. *Sensibility: An Introduction.* London: Methuen, 1986.

Toubia, Nahid. "Female Genital Mutilation." In *Women's Rights, Human Rights: International Feminist Perspectives,* edited by Julie Peters and Andrea Wolper, 224–37. New York: Routledge, 1995.

Turner, Bryan S. *Vulnerability and Human Rights.* University Park: Pennsylvania State University Press, 2006.

Tutu, Desmond. *No Future without Forgiveness.* London: Rider, 1999.

Valassopolous, Anastasi. "'Words Written by a Pen Sharp as a Scalpel': Gender and Medical Practice in the Early Fiction of Nawal El Saadawi and Fatmata Conteth." *Research in African Literatures* 35.1 (2004): 87–107.

Van Rooyen, J. C. W. *Censorship in South Africa.* Cape Town: Juta, 1987.

Vasseleu, Cathryn. *Textures of Light: Vision and Touch in Irigaray, Levinas, and Merleau-Ponty.* New York: Routledge, 1998.

Villa-Vicencio, Charles, and Wilhelm Verwoerd. "Constructing a Report: Writing Up the 'Truth.'" In Rotberg and Thompson, 279–92.

Viswanathan, Gauri. *Masks of Conquest: Literary Study and British Rule in India.* New York: Columbia University Press, 1989.

Waldron, Jeremy. *"Nonsense upon Stilts": Bentham, Burke, and Marx on the Rights of Man.* London: Methuen, 1987.

Warner, Michael. *Publics and Counterpublics.* Brooklyn, N.Y.: Zone, 2002.

Weiss, Gail. *Body Images: Embodiment as Intercorporeality.* New York: Routledge, 1999.

Williams, Patricia J. *The Alchemy of Race and Rights.* Cambridge, Mass.: Harvard University Press, 1991.

Wilson, Richard A., ed. *Human Rights, Culture, and Context: Anthropological Perspectives.* Chicago: Pluto, 1997.

———. "Representing Human Rights Violations: Social Contexts and Subjectivities." In Wilson, 134–60.

Wolpert, Stanley. *A New History of India.* 7th ed. New York: Oxford University Press, 2004. First edition published 1977.

Wrathall, Mark A. "Motives, Reasons, Causes." In *The Cambridge Companion to Merleau-Ponty,* edited by Taylor Carman and Mark B. Hansen, 111–28. Cambridge, U.K.: Cambridge University Press, 2005.

Young, Iris Marion. *On Female Bodily Experience.* New York: Oxford University Press, 2005.

———. "Two Concepts of Self-Determination." In Sarat and Kearns, 25–44.

Zabus, Chantal. *Between Rites and Rights: Excision in Women's Experiential Texts and Human Contexts.* Stanford, Calif.: Stanford University Press, 2007.

Žižek, Slavoj. *The Sublime Object of Ideology.* New York: Verso, 1989.

✿ INDEX

aesthetics, 9, 14, 173–74; as embodied, 3, 9, 14, 49, 65, 76, 118, 130–36, 147, 169, 182–84, 186–88, 199–205, 208, 213–14, 217, 219, 221–22; realism, 154. *See also* Merleau-Ponty, Maurice

Ali, Ayan Hirsi, 38

animal being, 18, 22, 60, 64, 151, 166–67, 169, 176–84, 214–15

animal rights, 18, 177

Arendt, Hannah, 16, 26–28, 58, 65, 225n2

art. *See* aesthetics

Asad, Talal, 143–44, 229n23, 231n50

autonomy: of art, 75; economic, 125–26, 153; as liberal standard, 18, 26, 29, 34, 40, 129, 145–46, 165, 186, 221; women's, 10, 123. *See also* self-determination

Beah, Ishmael, 42, 45, 230n43

Benhabib, Seyla, 6

Biko, Steve, 153

Bildungsroman, 32–33, 88, 227n21, 234n19

biopolitics, 27

bodily integrity: contradictions of, 4, 19, 33, 47, 135, 138; as enabling myth, 2, 16, 26, 78, 104; link to body politic, 4, 16, 19–21, 34, 41, 59, 81, 104, 108, 139, 191; relationship to dignity and human rights, 28, 42–43, 92, 123, 139–40, 181, 222; as standard, 4, 25, 118, 123, 143

body politic, 48, 87, 229n14; exclusions within, 35, 39, 41, 44, 46, 93, 207; as metaphor, 10, 19–21, 34, 61, 106, 219; and nationalism, 86, 100, 111. *See also* bodily integrity

Booker Prize, 79, 120, 189, 191

Born Into Brothels, 45

Butler, Judith, 14, 51, 77

capabilities approach, 232n42

capitalism: and class, 90; as commodification, 39, 125, 136–37, 145–46; finance, 5; as neoliberalism, 5; and patriarchy, 146; relationship to human rights,

6, 12–13, 43, 120, 124–27, 187, 221, 237n27

Cartesianism. *See* dualism

censorship. *See* freedom: of expression

Chakrabarty, Dipesh, 92–93

Chatterjee, Partha, 102

Cheah, Pheng, 109, 226n12, 228n4, 229n14

citizenship, 2, 16, 27, 31, 58

Coetzee, J. M., 1, 2, 3–4, 14, 120, 222; *Doubling the Point*, 169; *Elizabeth Costello*, 177; *Giving Offense*, 168; 1987 Jerusalem Prize acceptance speech, 165; *Summertime*, 9–10; *Waiting for the Barbarians*, 153. See also *Disgrace*

colonial discourse, 35–46. *See also* exoticism

communitarianism, 139, 151, 174–76

Connolly, William, 23, 73

Constituent Assembly (India), 84, 95

constitutionalism, 83–84, 94–98, 190

Convention on the Elimination of Discrimination Against Women, 116

cosmopolitanism, 12, 45

Critical Legal Studies, 7, 226n17

cultural rights, 116

Dean, Carolyn J., 15, 34–35, 228n11

Derrida, Jacques, 12, 13, 53, 82–83

Descartes, Rene, 17

desire, 151, 211–12; and censorship, 153, 168; imperial, 39, 42–43, 164–65, 182; rights of, 164–69. *See also* sexuality

dignity 14, 26, 123, 138, 143, 151; as enabling myth, 2, 181, 215; relevance to human rights, 3, 16, 28, 45–47, 222, 225–26n6 and 7. *See also* bodily integrity

disability, 21, 22, 25, 59

Disgrace (Coetzee), 10, 147, 149–85, 194, 196

divinity. *See* faith

Douzinas, Costas, 7

dualism, 51; of human rights, 4, 26, 31, 47, 83; and oppression, 17, 48, 54–55, 62–63,